To Stephen,

Many thanks for your years of hard work at Apogeaflow

Best wishes for Oliver and John

Christmas 2023

Britain's Industrial Revolution in 100 OBJECTS

To Dawn, who hears so much of the past through my research. To Rosa, Sophia and David, who may learn something of the lives their forebears led in these pages.

Other books by John Broom

Cricket in the First World War: Play up! Play the Game
(Pen & Sword History, 2022)

Cricket in the Second World War: The Grim Test
(Pen & Sword History, 2021)

Reported Missing in the Great War: 100 Years of Searching for the Truth
(Pen & Sword Military, 2020)

Faithful in Adversity: The Royal Army Medical Corps in the Second World War
(Pen & Sword Military, 2019)

Opposition to the Second World War: Conscience, Resistance & Service in Britain 1933–45
(Pen & Sword Military, 2018)

A History of Cigarette and Trade Cards: The Magic Inside the Packet
(Pen & Sword History, 2018)

Fight the Good Fight: Voices of Faith from the Second World War
(Pen & Sword Military, 2016)

Fight the Good Fight: Voices of Faith from the First World War
(Pen & Sword Military, 2015)

Britain's Industrial Revolution in 100 OBJECTS

John Broom

Pen & Sword
HISTORY

First published in Great Britain in 2023 by
Pen & Sword History
An imprint of
Pen & Sword Books Ltd
Yorkshire – Philadelphia

Copyright © John Broom 2023

ISBN 978 1 39900 393 3

The right of John Broom to be identified as Author of this work has been asserted by him in accordance with the Copyright, Designs and Patents Act 1988.

A CIP catalogue record for this book is
available from the British Library.

All rights reserved. No part of this book may be reproduced or transmitted in any form or by any means, electronic or mechanical including photocopying, recording or by any information storage and retrieval system, without permission from the Publisher in writing.

Typeset by Mac Style
Printed in the UK by CPI Group (UK) Ltd, Croydon, CR0 4YY.

Pen & Sword Books Limited incorporates the imprints of Atlas, Archaeology, Aviation, Discovery, Family History, Fiction, History, Maritime, Military, Military Classics, Politics, Select, Transport, True Crime, Air World, Frontline Publishing, Leo Cooper, Remember When, Seaforth Publishing, The Praetorian Press, Wharncliffe Local History, Wharncliffe Transport, Wharncliffe True Crime, White Owl and After the Battle.

For a complete list of Pen & Sword titles please contact

PEN & SWORD BOOKS LIMITED
47 Church Street, Barnsley, South Yorkshire, S70 2AS, England
E-mail: enquiries@pen-and-sword.co.uk
Website: www.pen-and-sword.co.uk

Or

PEN AND SWORD BOOKS
1950 Lawrence Rd, Havertown, PA 19083, USA
E-mail: Uspen-and-sword@casematepublishers.com
Website: www.penandswordbooks.com

Contents

Acknowledgements — vii
Introduction — viii

SECTION ONE – MAKING, WORKING AND GROWING — 1

1. The Coke-Powered Blast Furnace — 2
2. Benjamin Huntsman Clock — 5
3. Bessemer Converter — 8
4. Sheffield Cutlery Bowie Knife — 10
5. Newcomen Beam Engine — 13
6. James Watt's Rotary Steam Engine — 16
7. The Laxey Wheel — 19
8. Richard Arkwright's First Mill at Cromford — 22
9. The Flying Shuttle — 25
10. The Spinning Jenny — 27
11. Robert Owen's Silent Monitor — 29
12. Coal Mine Ventilation Door — 32
13. Miners' Safety Lamp — 36
14. Pit Pony Inkwell — 38
15. Chimney Sweep's Brush — 42
16. Truck Token — 45
17. Slate Tiles — 47
18. Josiah Wedgwood Receipt — 50
19. Brixham Trawler — 53
20. The Turnip — 55
21. Leicester Longwool Sheep — 57
22. Jethro Tull's Seed Drill — 59
23. Threshing Machine — 62

SECTION TWO – TRAVELLING, TRANSPORTING AND TRADING — 65

24. Turnpike Toll Board — 66
25. Canal Lock — 69
26. Narrowboat — 72
27. Navvy's Pick and Shovel — 75
28. Barton Aqueduct Arch — 78
29. The Euston Arch — 81
30. Bradshaw's Railway Guide — 84
31. Broad Gauge Turntable — 87
32. Third Class Rail Carriage — 89
33. SS *Great Eastern* Chains — 92
34. Dock Warehouses — 95
35. Tram Lines — 98
36. The Red Flag — 102
37. Penny-farthing Bicycle — 104
38. 1884 Metropolitan Line Map — 107
39. *The Wealth of Nations* by Adam Smith — 110
40. Diagram of the *Brookes* Slave Ship — 113
41. Tobacco Tin — 116
42. Raw Cotton Bale — 119
43. *Glad Tidings* Ship — 122
44. Victorian Tea Set — 125
45. Opium Pipe — 128
46. David Livingstone Lithograph — 131

SECTION THREE – PROTESTING AND REFORMING — 135

47. Luddite Hammer — 136
48. Peterloo Handkerchief — 139
49. *Old Sarum* Painting — 143
50. Swing Riots Lithograph — 146
51. Tolpuddle Martyrs Tree — 148
52. Richard Oastler Medal — 151
53. Anti-Corn Law League Membership Cards — 153
54. The People's Charter — 157
55. Co-operative Wholesale Society Cigarette Card — 160
56. A Sheffield Saw — *163*
57. The Communist Manifesto — 166
58. Trade Union Banner — 168
59. Bryant & May Matchbox — 171
60. Keir Hardie Election Poster — 174

SECTION FOUR – LIVING AND LEARNING — 177

61. A Piece of Old Rope — 178
62. Carbolic Steam Spray Device — 181

63. Everlasting Pill	184	83. Methodist Hymn Book	244
64. Prison Treadmill	187	84. Pawnbroker Sign	247
65. Convict Ship	190	85. Public House Sign	250
66. *Punch* Cartoon: *A Court for King Cholera*	194	86. Shop Doorbell	253
		87. Colman's Mustard Poster	256
67. Broad Street Pump	197	88. Vimto Monument	259
68. The *War Cry*, 6 August 1887	200	89. Penny Black Stamp	262
		90. The Pillar Box	265
69. Victorian Tinplate Bath	203	91. Metropolitan Police Helmet	268
70. William Morris Wallpaper	206	92. 1861 Census Return	271
71. Great Exhibition Telescopic View	209	93. Michael Faraday's Electrical Generator	273
72. Board School Slate	212	94. Public Lavatory	276
73. Ragged School Door	215	95. Swimming Bath Tile	279
74. Metamorphic Library Steps	218	96. Postcard of West Park, Hull	282
75. Mechanics' Institute Poster	221	97. King George III's Bathing Machine	285
76. Friendly Society Banner	224		
77. *Self-Help* by Samuel Smiles	227	98. John Hulley's Wenlock Olympian Society Silver Medal	289
78. *Punch* Magazine Cover	230		
79. *The Illustrated London News*, 14 May 1842	232	99. FA Cup Final Programme, 1882	292
		100. W.G. Grace Bats and Balls	295
80. Charles Dickens's Writing Desk	235		
81. Saltaire Congregational Church	238	*Index*	298
82. Music Hall Pass	241		

Acknowledgements

I would like to thank Alex Simon and Dan Holdsworth for their comments, feedback, insights and queries on this period of history. Also, Linne Matthews, for her ever-assiduous editing and encouragement. Jon Wilkinson has produced yet another outstanding book cover and Laura Hirst has overseen the production process with her usual efficiency. Thanks also to Matthew Blurton for his very skilful design of the pages.

Introduction

Britain's Industrial Revolution emerged during the eighteenth century and lasted through to the outbreak of the First World War in 1914. It was a great age of steam, canals, railways and factories, which drastically changed Britain's economy, landscape and culture.

Work that had once been carried out in small workshops and people's homes was substantially transferred into large factories, mines and mills. The harnessing of steam power enabled continuous motion, which changed the rhythms and demands of work. New inventions in iron and steel manufacturing allowed for the production of stronger and more durable metals. These, in turn, would be used to build a new Britain. Developments in textile manufacturing made Britain the 'workshop of the world'. Newcomen and Watt engines provided the power for Britain's Industrial Revolution.

Industrialisation also involved a loss of freedom. The pre-industrial artisan laid great stress on their independence, but the industrial system that required discipline and control destroyed much of this. Employees now had to work to the timetables laid down by merchant capitalists. Factory discipline or the perils of the coalmine became the lot of many.

New techniques and technologies in agriculture paved the way for change. Food production increased due to improvements in crop rotation, selective breeding and farm machinery.

The growing demand for coal and manufactured goods from 1750 onwards revealed serious problems with Britain's transport system. Because of the essential necessity of coal, many mine owners and industrial speculators began financing new networks of canals in order to link their mines more effectively with the growing centres of population and industry. A selection of objects relating to the expansion of Britain's canal network feature in this book.

Most roads were in a terrible state – many poorly maintained and even major routes flooded during the winter. Stagecoach journeys were long and uncomfortable. Faced with these difficulties, local authorities applied for 'Turnpike Acts' that allowed for new roads to be constructed, paid for out of tolls placed on passing traffic. The improvements achieved by eighteenth-century road builders were breathtaking. By the 1830s, the stagecoach journey from London to Edinburgh took just two days, compared to nearly two weeks only half a century before.

A railway boom in the 1840s created a national network that changed everything. Once railways came along, people lived differently, worked differently, ate differently, had holidays differently, did almost everything differently. The creation of suburbs came about because people no longer needed to live on top of their work. Fresh fish and vegetables could be transported hundreds of miles. People were brought together and life was opened up.

Britain was able to use new forms of sea transportation to exploit the resources of its vast empire. The trade in tea, tobacco and cotton enriched a few, provided a functional standard of living for many, but impoverished those in other lands.

Revolutionary change brought with it political and social unrest. Many workers, understandably unconvinced that material change would arrive via piecemeal and reluctant political reform, took direct action in destroying the machines that had robbed them of their livelihoods. Others combined in trade unions, campaigns such as Chartism and, eventually, a coherent political party of Labour.

The amelioration of the worst effects of economic and social dislocation achieved

INTRODUCTION

varying degrees of success, in workhouses, prisons, hospitals, hostels and schools. Some argued against the abuse of alcohol whilst others sought to house the homeless. Opportunities for a better standard of living opened up for those of steady working-class and middle-class backgrounds. Trips to the seaside, weekends in local parks and the enjoyment of organised sport became popular. Many travelled to London for the first time to see the Great Exhibition of 1851. Literacy rates increased and the British public lapped up information and entertainment from newspapers, periodicals and novels.

The churches of the period endeavoured to encourage worker discipline and the individual striving for betterment. Industry, prudence and thrift were values propagated in chapels, mechanics' institutes and public libraries. These values found their own bible in Samuel Smiles's *Self-Help* book. Shops provided an ever-expanding variety of goods, many with brand names that are familiar to this day. The names, ages and occupations of Britons living through the Industrial Revolution were collected, tracked and analysed each decade in a vast census. They were able to communicate swiftly and effectively with each other through an efficient network of postboxes and prepaid stamps.

Today, the legacy of Britain's Industrial Revolution is all around us. Artefacts can remind us of, and transport us back to, a period of unprecedented dynamism, innovation and drive. They can link us to our forebears. They can provoke amazement, enquiry and nostalgia. The 100 objects featured in this book encompass a wide range of fascinating topics, and the keen reader can develop their knowledge and interests further by investigating the recommended books and visits associated with each one.

Section One

Making, Working and Growing

1: The Coke-Powered Blast Furnace

In 1709, at Coalbrookdale in Shropshire, Abraham Darby the Elder began to fuel a blast furnace with coke instead of charcoal. How did he come to this revolutionary development, which many historians argue ushered in the modern industrial world?

The son of a yeoman farmer and locksmith, one family legend has it that Abraham's great-great-uncle, Dud Dudley, had attempted during the English Civil War to smelt iron using coke, but the iron produced was not of sufficient quality to satisfy the charcoal ironmasters. Apprenticed to a manufacturer of brass mills for grinding malt for brewing, the young Abraham noted the use of coke – coal with the sulphur content burned off – to fuel malting ovens, thus avoiding the sulphur contaminating the beer. This method also had the advantage of avoiding the use of expensive charcoal.

In September 1708, Abraham leased a furnace at Coalbrookdale, near the river Severn, and began blasting iron using Shropshire 'clod coal' – a material very low in sulphur content. Coke's initial advantage was its lower cost, mainly because making coke required much less labour than cutting trees and making charcoal, but using coke also overcame localised shortages of wood, especially in Britain and on the Continent. Metallurgical grade coke will bear heavier weight than charcoal, allowing for larger furnaces.

Coke iron was initially only used for foundry work, making pots and other cast-iron goods, but Darby's eldest son, Abraham Darby II, built a new furnace at nearby Horsehay and began to supply the owners of finery forges with coke pig iron for the production of bar iron. Coke pig iron was by this time cheaper to produce than

Abraham Darby's original blast furnace, now part of Coalbrookdale Museum of Iron. (*Wikimedia Commons/Michael Garlick*)

1: THE COKE-POWERED BLAST FURNACE

charcoal pig iron. The use of a coal-derived fuel in the iron industry was a key factor in the British Industrial Revolution. The Coalbrookdale venture was partly funded by a loan from the Goldney family, who had made their wealth in the transatlantic slave trade.

Darby the Elder died in 1717 at the relatively young age of 39 at his home in Madeley, Shropshire. He had built himself a house at Coalbrookdale with his wealth but did not live long enough to move in. His son and eventual successor, Abraham Darby II, was only 6 years old at the time and the business endured a period of uncertainty as its various shareholders either mortgaged their shares or took out letters of administration in an attempt to sell off the works. Joshua Sergeant, Abraham's brother-in-law, bought back some shares on behalf of his nieces and nephews. This allowed the younger Abraham to take up a management position at Coalbrookdale.

In 1715, Coalbrookdale Company had already cast the first cylinders for a Thomas Newcomen steam engine in iron, rather than the expensive brass. Under Darby the Elder's successors, the company went from strength to strength. In 1763, it cast a massive cylinder of 74 inches diameter for the Walker Colliery on Tyneside. The company laid an iron railway at its own works in 1767, having made the first iron wheels to run on rails in 1729. Richard Trevithick commissioned the company in 1802 to make him the world's first railway locomotive.

Perhaps the most iconic reminder of the might of the Coalbrookdale Company can be seen today in the small, picturesque town of Ironbridge. In September 1775, a group of subscribers came together to form a company for the building of a bridge across the river Severn between Benthall and Madeley near the Coalbrookdale Works. At first, it was intended that the bridge be built of stone, brick or timber but eventually the committee of shareholders, which included Abraham Darby III (son of Abraham Darby II), accepted a tender from the Coalbrookdale Company to construct a bridge in cast iron, the first such bridge to be built anywhere. To finance the building of the bridge, the company issued sixty-four shares, with entitlement to income from the tolls. One of the first share certificates, signed by Abraham Darby III and other significant businessmen, features in the Elton Gallery at the Ironbridge Gorge Museum.

The casting of members for the bridge occupied 1777 and 1778, and involved the rebuilding and enlarging of the Coalbrookdale furnace. The main rib castings each weighed over 5 tons and were 70 feet long. The bridge opened to all traffic on New Year's Day 1781.

The world-famous cast-iron bridge across the river Severn at Ironbridge, Shropshire. (*Wikimedia Commons/Tk420*)

Smelting iron with coke revolutionised the iron industry, liberating it from the limitation imposed by costs of charcoal burning. It also shifted the fuel used for making steel from renewable wood to a fossil fuel, and so helped preserve native woodland. As the quality of the iron produced by coke smelting improved, it could be used to manufacture steam engines, bridges, and many other inventions of the era. Appreciation of the enormous contribution made by Abraham Darby I and his successors is key to understanding the Industrial Revolution.

Places to visit

Today, Darby's original 1709 blast furnace forms part of the Coalbrookdale Museum of Iron, itself one of the extensive attractions of Ironbridge Gorge Museums, which includes the rather splendid Blists Hill Victorian Town, the Iron Bridge and the Coalport China Museum.

Further reading

Barrie Trinder, *The Most Extraordinary District in the World: Ironbridge and Coalbrookdale* (2005).
Arthur Raistrick, *Dynasty of Ironfounders: The Darbys of Coalbrookdale* (1953).

2: Benjamin Huntsman Clock

This elegant clock, housed in the Kelham Island Museum in Sheffield, includes the first known use of a revolutionary steelmaking process developed by Benjamin Huntsman. It marks the beginning of industry in the 'Steel City' – a name that has been affectionately applied to Sheffield for a century or more.

Benjamin Huntsman, whose work revolutionised the manufacture of steel during Britain's Industrial Revolution, hailed from the Lincolnshire market town of Epworth. His parents were farmers and devout Quakers, eschewing the more lascivious pleasures of life. As a boy, he showed an aptitude for mechanical work and was apprenticed aged 14 to a clockmaker. Having completed his seven-year training, he set up as a clock, lock and toolmaker in Doncaster, where he was appointed to look after the town's clock. He was also able to practise surgery and served as an oculist, refusing to take money from the poor for these services.

He was dissatisfied with the quality of the metal available for the production of clock and pendulum springs so he started to experiment on how to improve it. The steel used at that time was 'cementation' steel, which came from Germany, although small quantities had been produced in Yorkshire from about 1642. Forged from a number of bars bound together, the quality of the steel varied and it had many imperfections.

Huntsman moved to Handsworth, near Sheffield, in 1740. He had spent several years trying to obtain a suitable product before discovering a way of melting his steel in the clay crucibles that glassmakers used for melting glass. Molten steel could thus be made for the first time, so constituent parts could be mixed together to make a superior product. Each melting crucible was able to hold about 34 pounds of blistered steel. A flux was added and the crucibles were then covered, and heated by coke for about three hours. The molten steel was then poured into moulds and the crucibles reused. The resulting metal was hard but flexible and was ideal for a wide range of domestic and commercial products, including razors and cutlery.

Huntsman first used his crucible-cast steel in his longcase clock. The timepiece contains a large rectangular slab of steel, accompanied by a description: 'This clock made by Benjamin Huntsman contains the first successful results of his invention of crucible cast steel 1740.' However, in the city that was to become synonymous with the manufacture of knives, forks and spoons, Sheffield cutlers refused to buy Huntsman's steel, preferring instead the softer metal they imported from Germany. In response, the enterprising Huntsman exported his wares to France.

(John Broom)

Crucible clay pots used for producing steel at the Abbeydale Industrial Hamlet, Sheffield. (*John Broom*)

Gradually, imported French cutlery, made from Huntsman steel, started to threaten the livelihoods of the Sheffield cutlers. At first, they tried to persuade the government to ban the export of steel to France, although they had to concede defeat and began to use the locally produced metal in their own workshops. Sheffield's steel industry continued to develop. Huntsman moved his business to the district of Attercliffe in 1751, winding down on the clockmaking side of his work to concentrate full-time on steel manufacturing.

Despite his undoubted innovative business abilities, Huntsman had not patented his crucible process, believing the practice to run counter to his Quaker principles. His method was copied by a Sheffield ironfounder named Walker. A probably apocryphal story has it that Walker entered the Huntsman works dressed as a starving beggar, asking to spend the night by a warm fire, in order to study the process.

By 1763, Huntsman's trademark was well known. Offered a Fellowship of the Royal

Robin Bell's *Teeming* statue depicting crucible steelmaking, Meadowhall Shopping Centre, Sheffield. (*John Broom*)

Society, he declined, as he believed it was against his Quaker principles to be so honoured. He also refused to have his portrait painted as he felt this was not what a Quaker should do.

In 1770, Huntsman moved his premises to Worksop Road, Attercliffe, where he continued to prosper until his death in 1776. Benjamin Huntsman's remains lie in the Nonconformist Hill Top Cemetery, Attercliffe Common. For two centuries, he lay in close proximity to Sheffield's huge iron and steelworks. Today, the area is more associated with the Sheffield Arena and Meadowhall Retail Park. When the Meadowhall Shopping Centre opened in 1991, sculptor Robin Bell created *Teeming*, depicting three steelworkers using Huntsman's crucible process. The plaque next to the bronze artwork begins:

> BENJAMIN HUNTSMAN (1704–1776) WAS A CLOCK & WATCHMAKER FROM DONCASTER WHO CAME TO SHEFFIELD IN SEARCH OF QUALITY STEEL FOR CLOCK SPRINGS. THE TECHNIQUE OF STEEL MAKING WHICH HE DEVELOPED USING CLAY CRUCIBLE POTS REVOLUTIONISED QUALITY CONTROL & ENABLED SHEFFIELD STEEL TO BECOME PRE-EMINENT IN THE PRODUCTION OF STEEL.

Elsewhere in the city, he is remembered in the naming of a building in his honour at the Northern General Hospital, and the world-famous Crucible Theatre commemorates his innovation. Ironically, for such a devout Quaker, his name adorns a Wetherspoon public house in the city centre.

Places to visit

- Abbeydale Industrial Hamlet is a working museum in the south of the City of Sheffield. They manufacture steel using techniques that originated with Benjamin Huntsman's invention of the crucible steel process.
- The Kelham Island Industrial Museum in Sheffield has that seminal Huntsman clock on display, as well as several hugely impressive objects from the city's metal industry history.
- Benjamin Huntsman's grave, Hilltop Chapel, Attercliffe Common.

Further reading

Kenneth C. Barraclough, *Benjamin Huntsman* (1976).

3: Bessemer Converter

One of the most iconic and sublime artefacts from Britain's Industrial Revolution takes pride of place outside the Kelham Island Industrial Museum in the steel city of Sheffield. The egg-shaped piece of machinery, known as a Bessemer converter, enabled Sheffield to continue its trajectory as the iron and steelmaking centre of the Empire, and was responsible for much of the metallic infrastructure of Britain's railway system that is still in use today.

The Bessemer converter enabled the cheap mass-production of steel from molten pig iron. It worked on the principle of removing impurities from the iron by an oxidation process, by blowing air through the molten iron. This process also raised the temperature of the iron to ensure it remained molten.

Its inventor, Henry Bessemer, took out a patent on the process in 1856. His converter tilted down to pour the molten pig iron in through the top, and then it swung back to a vertical position. A blast of air was then blown through the base of the converter, causing spectacular but dangerous flames and fountains to shoot out of the top. The converter was tilted again and the newly made steel was teemed or poured out. Bessemer's initial converters could make 7 tons of steel in half an hour.

As with many technological breakthroughs in history, war was the mother of invention. Bessemer was of French Huguenot ancestry, his father forced to flee the country because of the 1789 revolution. Henry had previously made money from inventing a steam-powered machine for making bronze powder. He had also patented a method of making a continuous ribbon of plate glass.

Henry Bessemer later claimed that his steel converter was inspired by a conversation he had with Napoleon III of France in 1854 about the demand for high-quality steel for better artillery. He wrote that it 'was the spark which kindled one of the greatest revolutions that the present century had to record, for during my solitary ride in a cab that night from Vincennes to Paris, I made up my mind to try what I could to improve the quality of iron in the manufacture of guns'. The result was a transformation in steel production, from the making of high-end small items like cutlery and tools to great military weapons such as cannon.

Bessemer unveiled his process at a meeting of the British Association in Cheltenham in a lecture on 24 August 1856, titled 'The Manufacture of Malleable Iron and Steel without Fuel', which was transcribed in *The Times* newspaper. In 1858, he moved to Sheffield, licensing his method to two Sheffield ironmasters – John Brown and George Cammell – for £27,000. Their production rate soared within two years and by the late 1870s,

(John Broom)

3: BESSEMER CONVERTER

Bessemer's invention marked the beginning of mass steel production, as huge amounts could be produced in a relatively short time compared to using Benjamin Huntsman's crucible process (*see* chapter 2). Whilst Bessemer's original sights had been set on meeting the ever-increasing demand for war machinery, the availability of mass-produced steel enabled many industries to replace the less-reliable cast iron. The dangers of using cast iron for major engineering works was tragically and dramatically brought home when the Tay Bridge collapsed in 1879, killing an estimated seventy-five people.

The new steel was most widely used for railway infrastructure such as bridges and tracks that were extending across the British Empire and elsewhere. Bessemer died a hugely wealthy man. Unlike several other inventors and entrepreneurs of Britain's Industrial Revolution, he had managed to display the business acumen to outwit his competitors and effectively protect his intellectual property. Between 1838 and 1883, he took out 129 patents for a huge range of inventions, including a method of avoiding seasickness by means of a hydraulically controlled ship's cabin.

On 26 June 1879, Bessemer received a knighthood for his contribution to science and was made a fellow of the Royal Society. He died in March 1898 and is buried at West Norwood Cemetery, London.

Henry Bessemer, from *Vanity Fair*, 1880.

10,000 tons of Bessemer steel was being produced in the town every week – almost a quarter of Britain's output.

Places to visit

- Kelham Island Museum in Sheffield contains the last-ever Bessemer converter in industrial use. It was used by British Steel until its decommissioning in 1974.
- The Science Museum in London has on display an original 1865 Bessemer converter previously used at the Barrow Haematite Steel Company Limited.

Further reading

Henry Bessemer, *Sir Henry Bessemer, F.R.S.: an autobiography* (1905).
Kathleen Tracey, *Henry Bessemer: Making Steel from Iron* (2005).

4: Sheffield Cutlery Bowie Knife

This mid-nineteenth-century Bowie knife, with a 6⅜-inch spear-point blade, was made by the Sheffield cutlery firm Edward Barnes & Son, active from 1833 to 1888. Made for the American export market, it was one of several million steel items produced in the 'Steel City' during Britain's Industrial Revolution.

Cutlery is a specific term given to any tool with an edge that cuts, for example knives, razors, scalpels, scissors and scythes. Although commonly referred to as cutlery, items without a sharp edge, such as spoons, forks and serving implements, are known in the trade as flatware.

Sheffield's cutlery industry can trace its recorded history back to the reign of Edward I, when, in 1297, a Robertus le Coteler – Robert the Cutler – was listed in hearth tax records. Chaucer mentioned a Sheffield whittle in *The Canterbury Tales*, and in the mid-sixteenth century, the Earls of Shrewsbury set up Cutlers' Juries to control the trade, which included the registration of cutlers' marks, and the controlling of the apprenticeship system and working practices.

In 1624, Parliament passed an Act of Incorporation, establishing the Company of Cutlers in Hallamshire. This organisation assumed control over apprenticeships, admitting freemen and registering cutlers' marks, and regulating the quality of cutlery produced. However, as working dynamics changed during Britain's Industrial Revolution, these powers reduced in 1814 to the registration of cutlers' marks.

Sheffield had become an important metalworking centre due to the availability of nearby raw materials such as iron ore, coal, charcoal, and stone for grinding wheels. Although now a major city, before the Industrial Revolution the area was little more than a scattered collection of villages and hamlets. With many hills and valleys in the topography, several fast-flowing rivers drove the waterwheels that were used to power heavy drop hammers, tilt hammers and grinding wheels. By 1660, over thirty sites on Sheffield's river system had been dammed for driving grinding wheels.

Demand for high-quality cutlery and other metal goods saw the number of Sheffield waterwheels increase from thirty-six in 1700 to ninety-seven in 1800. The invention of Old Sheffield Plate by Thomas Boulsover in 1743 caused a further increase in demand for Sheffield metallurgy. By fusing silver to sheets of copper, silver items became more affordable. In 1773, the Sheffield Assay Office was founded so that sterling silver items could be hallmarked close to their place of manufacture rather than having to be taken to London, risking the attentions of highwaymen.

Experiments by Benjamin Huntsman in the 1740s resulted in the crucible steel process (*see* chapter 2). Blister steel was melted in a crucible with a purifying agent, which allowed the slag and impurities to be skimmed off and the carbon to be evenly distributed in the molten metal. The finished product could also be poured into moulds, to make any shape. This allowed for the large-scale production of steel and resulted in a stronger and harder final product. Consequently, Sheffield was able to push ahead of other competitors, supplying the growing worldwide demand for cutlery.

Despite the possibilities brought about by the development of steam engines from the 1780s onwards to power cutlery-making machinery, much of Sheffield's cutlery output remained in the hands of the Little Mesters – highly skilled craftsmen who took on a handful of employees and apprentices based in a small riverside workshop or their own homes. Each mester would be a specialist in one part of the process such as forging, grinding or hafting (the fitting of a handle). One item of cutlery would pass through many varied skilled hands before making it to market. This system continued right through to the Second World War, but a handful of Little Mester workshops still survive in Sheffield.

Remarkably, the most renowned cutlery production in the world broadly happened within a square mile of Sheffield's centre, as the specialisation of processes meant that the mesters needed to work within close proximity to each other. The town's main export market was America, with an estimated third of Sheffield's working population of 18,000 in 1812 working

Cutlers' Hall, Sheffield – the third such building on the city centre site, the first one having been built in 1638. (*Chemical Engineer/Creative Commons*)

in cutlery. The Sheffield-produced Bowie knife became an icon of American expansionist culture. Several had patriotic adornments on the blade and handle. This booming trade lasted until 1861, when trade tariffs caused a contraction. Knives and machetes used on slave plantations in America and the Caribbean were also made in Sheffield. Competition started to emerge from German and American cutlery makers who embraced mechanisation and mass production techniques.

Electroplating techniques developed in Birmingham gradually replaced the traditional Sheffield method of plating. A thin layer of pure silver could be added to a base metal such as nickel using electrolysis. Over time, items produced using the Old Sheffield plate method became highly collectable. Today, stainless steel cutlery made in Sheffield still carries the reputation of high quality, underpinned with centuries of tradition from its manufacture in Britain's Steel City.

Places to visit

- Cutlers' Hall in Orchard Square, Sheffield, contains a selection of old Hallamshire knives, some of which date back to the reign of Elizabeth I. The building hosts the annual Cutlers' Feast, a tradition stretching back nearly 400 years.
- Kelham Island Museum in Sheffield contains a range of objects used by Sheffield's Little Mesters. The Little Mesters Street in the museum includes the remaining mesters who work in the tradition of their cutlery-making forebears.
- Shepherd Wheel Workshop, in the picturesque Porter Brook river valley, was one of the many small water-powered grinding workshops that were scattered along Sheffield's rivers. Now restored, the workshop hosts regular demonstrations of knife grinding.

Further reading

Joan Unwin & Ken Hawley, *Sheffield's Industries: Cutlery, Silver and Edge Tools* (2008).
Clyde Binfield & David Hey (eds.), *Mesters to Masters: A History of the Company of Cutlers in Hallamshire* (1997).

5: Newcomen Beam Engine

The only Newcomen beam engine in the world still in its original site can be found at Elsecar, near Barnsley. Built in 1795 to extract water from Elsecar New Colliery, its working life lasted until 1923, drawing up to 600 gallons per minute at its peak. Today, site tours include a demonstration of the restored engine in action. Good fortune accompanies its continued existence on the site, the then owners having refused a blank cheque offered by Henry Ford to have the machine dismantled and taken to America.

The problem of mines flooding with groundwater was one that had vexed generations

(John Broom)

The beam of the Newcomen Engine at Dartmouth. (*Chris Allen/ Dartmouth Newcomen engine/CC BY-SA 2.0*)

of miners the world over. During the 1600s, countries across Europe switched from wood to coal as their main source of fuel. Thus, mines were deepened and, as a result, often became flooded after penetrating underground water sources.

Credited with being the first person to solve the problem of flooded mines is Spaniard Jerónimo de Ayanz. In 1606, he registered the earliest patent for a machine that used steam power to propel water from mines. The Spanish inventor used his steam engine to remove water from silver mines in Guadalcanal, Seville.

In 1698, Thomas Savery, a Devonshire engineer and inventor, took out a patent on an engine that could draw water from flooded mines using steam pressure. Savery's machine employed a cylinder and piston driven by two steam boilers to perform this feat. This allowed for the near-continuous pumping of water from mines, albeit only from shallow depths. As the demand for coal grew in Britain, so did the imperative of finding a solution to the problem of mine flooding.

In 1712, Thomas Newcomen, a Devonian ironmonger and Baptist lay preacher, invented an 'atmospheric' engine that eliminated the need for accumulated steam pressure, which had led to several explosions of Savery's engine. This was the breakthrough that the mining industry needed – the first commercially successful machine that operated a water pump via a steam engine. Newcomen and his partner John Calley built the first successful engine of this type at the Coneygree Coalworks near Dudley in the West Midlands. The nearby Black Country Living Museum has a working replica of this engine.

Newcomen's engine still required a continuous flow of cold water to cool the steam cylinder and a constant energy source to reheat the cylinder. However, it was the benchmark of the steam engine for the following half-century, utilised to drain wetlands, supply water to towns and provide the power to pump water to power factories and mills via a waterwheel.

The machine uses a piston working within an open-topped cylinder. Chains connect the piston to a rocking beam, and at the other end, a rod connects the beam to the pumps in the mine. On the outboard stroke, the cylinder fills with steam from the boiler and then cold water injects into the cylinder to change the steam back to water and create a vacuum. The vacuum then pulls the piston down and, via the rocking beam, raises the plunger in the water pump.

Newcomen constructed an engine for Griff Colliery, near Nuneaton, in 1714, 'to draw water by the impellent force of fire'. The first engine, which was working by 1715, was capable of pumping 16,700 litres of water per hour from the mine, with a maximum depth of 140 feet.

Despite the Newcomen engine having a poorer fuel efficiency than Watt's engine (*see chapter 6*), it continued to be ordered by many mine owners well into the nineteenth century as the cost was a one-off payment, rather than an annual licence fee as demanded by the Boulton & Watt Company.

Despite his importance in British and indeed world technological history, comparatively little

5: NEWCOMEN BEAM ENGINE

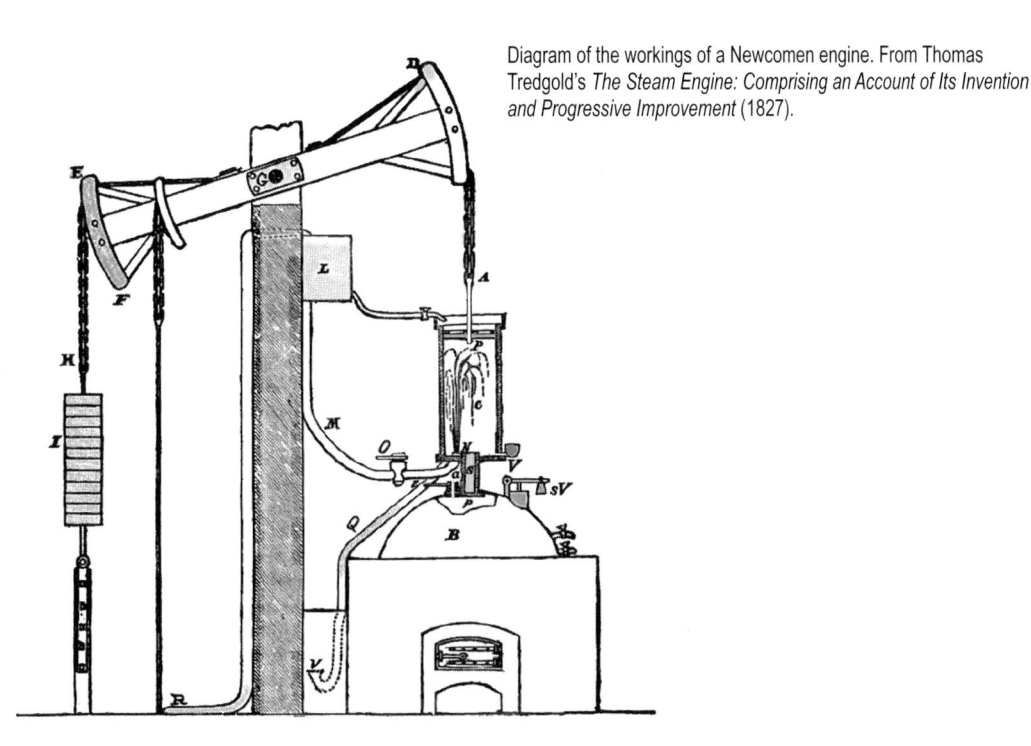

Diagram of the workings of a Newcomen engine. From Thomas Tredgold's *The Steam Engine: Comprising an Account of Its Invention and Progressive Improvement* (1827).

is known about Newcomen's later life. After 1715, his engines were commissioned and sold through the Proprietors of the Invention for Raising Water by Fire company. Newcomen died at the London house of fellow Baptist and business associate Edward Wallin in 1729. He was buried in the Nonconformist Bunhill Fields on London's outskirts, but the exact site of his grave is unknown. Four years after his death, about 125 Newcomen engines were in use across the coal, tin and lead mining districts of Britain and on the European continent.

Places to visit

- National Museum of Scotland, Edinburgh, contains a Newcomen engine made in Falkirk in 1811. Standing at over 30 feet high, it was made by the Carron Company and operated at the Caprington Colliery, Ayrshire. Working demonstrations take place throughout the day.
- The Elsecar Heritage Centre near Barnsley has a Newcomen engine that was restored to full working condition in 2015.
- The Newcomen Memorial Engine at Dartmouth is the oldest surviving steam engine, having been erected in 1725.

Further reading

Eric Preston, *Thomas Newcomen of Dartmouth and the Engine that Changed the World* (2012).
Thomas Crump, *A Brief History of the Age of Steam* (2007).
L.T.C. Rolt & J.S. Allen, *Steam Engine of Thomas Newcomen* (1977).

6: James Watt's Rotary Steam Engine

James Watt's development of rotary steam power would drive the Industrial Revolution. Whether it be powering the wheels of factories or driving railway locomotives and steamships that made the world a seemingly smaller place, Watt's engines were relentless and reliable. Unlike water power, they ran in all seasons and weathers. Unlike wind, they provided continuous force.

Watt was a Scottish instrument maker who was working at the University of Glasgow. In 1765, he was put to work repairing a small model of a Newcomen engine (*see* chapter 5). He considered ways in which to reduce the large amount of steam consumed by Newcomen's model, removing the need to constantly cool then reheat the steam cylinder. Watt came up with the idea of a separate condenser to allow the steam cylinder to maintain a constant temperature, thus improving efficiency.

Watt went into partnership with industrialist John Roebuck and patented his design in 1769. Roebuck went bankrupt in 1773 but introduced Watt to Birmingham entrepreneur Matthew Boulton. They formed arguably the most successful partnership of the Industrial Revolution in 1775. Boulton had the vision to realise that Watt's engine could extend far beyond the pumping of water from mines. He also possessed the financial clout to enable Watt to develop a single, then double-acting rotary steam engine that doubled the power of his separate steam cylinder.

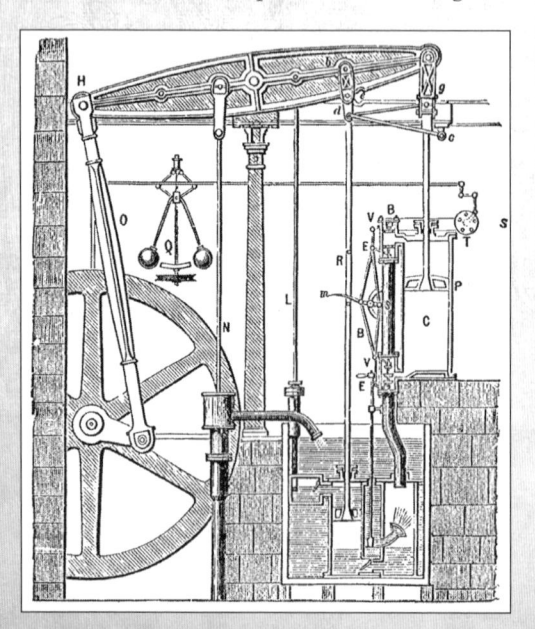

Boulton owned the Soho Works near Birmingham. He acquired the patent rights to Watt's design. Watt's association with Boulton gave him access to some of the best ironworkers in the world. Renowned iron master John Wilkinson had developed precision boring techniques for cannon, which were then used to make reliable boilers for Watt's engines. In 1796, Boulton and Watt established the Soho Foundry in order to make their own parts for

James Watt, by Carl Frederik von Breda, 1792.

Sketch of a steam engine designed by Boulton & Watt, 1784.

steam engines. By 1800, the firm was making over forty engines per year.

The Boulton & Watt engine allowed the machine operator to control the speed of the engine with a centrifugal governor. It also possessed a new gear system designed by William Murdoch, called 'sun and planet' gearing, which converted linear motion into rotary motion, thus allowing for the future use of steam power in driving factory wheels. The combination of Watt's and Murdoch's technical brilliance and Boulton's vision and financial acumen saw the steam engine rise to power a wide range of manufacturing operations and, eventually, domestic and international travel.

The Boulton & Watt engine was initially bought by Cornish mine owners, but soon it was in use in paper, flour, cotton and iron mills as well as distilleries, canals and waterworks. Both Watt and Boulton were elected fellows of the Royal Society in 1785.

James Watt was born in Greenock on 18 January 1736. His father was a prosperous shipwright and the family were Presbyterians. Despite his religious background, Watt became a deist, rejecting revelation as a source of

Statue of James Watt inside St Paul's Cathedral. The inscription on the plaque reads:

NOT TO PERPETUATE A NAME, WHICH MUST ENDURE WHILE THE PEACEFUL ARTS FLOURISH, BUT TO SHOW THAT MANKIND HAVE LEARNED TO HONOUR THOSE WHO BEST DESERVE THEIR GRATITUDE, THE KING, HIS MINISTERS, AND MANY OF THE NOBLES AND COMMONERS OF THE REALM RAISED THIS MONUMENT TO JAMES WATT WHO DIRECTING THE FORCE OF AN ORIGINAL GENIUS EARLY EXERCISED IN PHILOSOPHIC RESEARCH TO THE IMPROVEMENT OF THE STEAM-ENGINE ENLARGED THE RESOURCES OF HIS COUNTRY INCREASED THE POWER OF MAN AND ROSE TO AN EMINENT PLACE AMONG THE MOST ILLUSTRIOUS FOLLOWERS OF SCIENCE AND THE REAL BENEFACTORS OF THE WORLD.

BORN AT GREENOCK MDCCXXXVI

DIED AT HEATHFIELD IN STAFFORDSHIRE MDCCCXIX

divine knowledge, but believing that empirical reason and observation of the natural world are exclusively logical, reliable, and sufficient to determine the existence of a Supreme Being as the creator of the universe.

Watt was educated at home, then Greenock Grammar School. He went on to work in his father's workshops, showing skill in creating engineering models. Following problems at the family business, Watt moved to Glasgow to find work as a mathematical instrument maker. He successfully restored to full working order a collection of astronomical instruments that had been brought to the city from Jamaica. He was able to set up a workshop at the university and became friends with Adam Smith (*see* chapter 39). Watt's workshop made parts for telescopes and barometers, and made and repaired quadrants, parallel rulers and scales.

In 1759, Watt formed a partnership with architect and businessman John Craig to manufacture and sell musical instruments and toys. This partnership lasted for the next six years, and employed up to sixteen workers. Watt married twice, in 1764 to Peggy Miller, who died in childbirth in 1772, and in 1777 to Ann MacGregor. Watt and his family lived in Birmingham between this date and 1790.

Somewhat of a polymath, Watt also designed a letter and drawing copying machine, used in offices into the twentieth century. In addition, by 1794, he was manufacturing apparatuses to produce, clean and store gases for the new Pneumatic Institution at Hotwells in Bristol. In 1816, he took a trip on the paddle steamer *Comet*, a product of his inventions, to revisit his home town of Greenock. He died in 1819 and was buried in the parish church at Handsworth, Birmingham. To this day, his name is in everyday use as a unit of mechanical and electrical power.

Places to visit

- The National Museum of Scotland houses a Boulton and Watt steam engine, one of the oldest surviving in the world. It was built in 1786 to pump water for the Barclay & Perkins Brewery in Southwark, London. Made double-acting in 1796, it was then capable of grinding barley and pumping water. At that time, no one else could supply a steam engine that performed both these actions at once. It remained in service at the brewery until 1884.
- Kinneil House, Bo'ness, contains the ruin of a cottage in which Watt worked at perfecting his steam engine. At the time, he was in partnership with John Roebuck, who lived in the main house.
- The Energy Hall in London's Science Museum contains the attic workshop of James Watt, preserved as it was when he died in 1819. This time capsule contains original furniture, windows, doors, fireplace and over 8,000 objects with which Watt worked.

Further reading

Ben Russell, *James Watt: Making the World Anew* (2014).
Caroline Archer-Parré & Malcolm Dick, *James Watt (1736–1819): Culture, Innovation and Enlightenment* (2020).
David Miller, *The Life and Legend of James Watt: Collaboration, Natural Philosophy and the Improvement of the Steam Engine* (2019).

7: The Laxey Wheel

10,197. - I.O.M. LAXEY WHEEL

(Library of Congress)

The Laxey Wheel in the Isle of Man is known as *Lady Isabella* after the wife of the Lieutenant Governor, Charles Hope, who opened the wheel in 1854. It was used to pump water from the Great Laxey Mines. It is the largest working waterwheel in the world, with a diameter of 72 feet 6 inches.

Before the widespread use of the steam engine, the vertical waterwheel powered the early stages of Britain's Industrial Revolution. As industry demanded ever-increasing amounts of power, rivers became saturated with waterwheels, thus, experimentation and innovation were required to make existing wheel sites operate with greater efficiency.

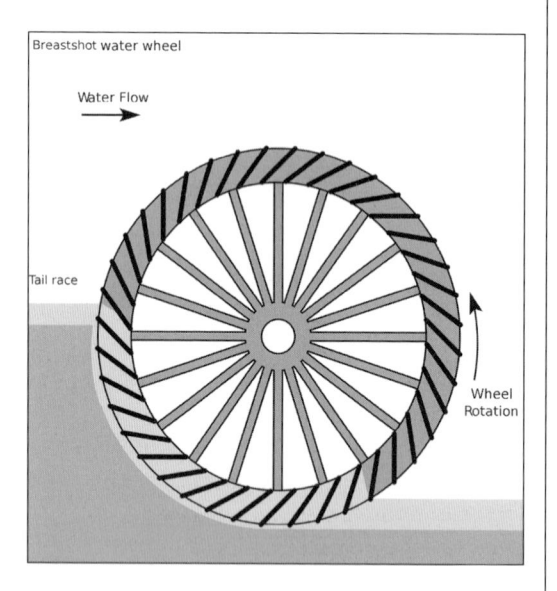

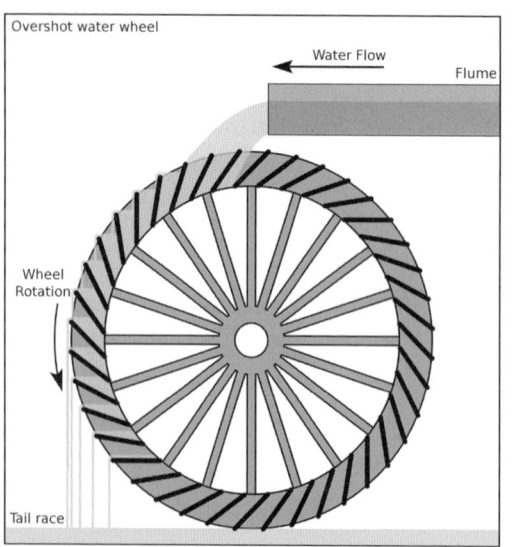

Waterwheels had been in use in various industries since classical antiquity. In Britain, they had been used for grinding corn and making weapons for centuries. Greater use of machinery and the need for more power in the Industrial Revolution meant that water and steam power supplanted human and animal power.

Before 1700, industry was driven predominantly by human, wind and animal power. Domestic system workers used primitive spinning wheels and looms that were hand-powered. In the fields, farmers used the power of horses and oxen to drive ploughs. Wind-powered mills ground corn. Some workshops and mills used water power, in the form of an undershot waterwheel.

As the demand for water power grew, in lowland Britain the breastshot wheel became the most favoured design. The leading force in breastshot wheel improvements was John Smeaton. Born in Castleford, Yorkshire, he moved to London aged 18 and became apprenticed to a philosophical instrument maker. He started to attend meetings of the Royal Society and submitted papers for members' perusal. At the age of 27, the Royal

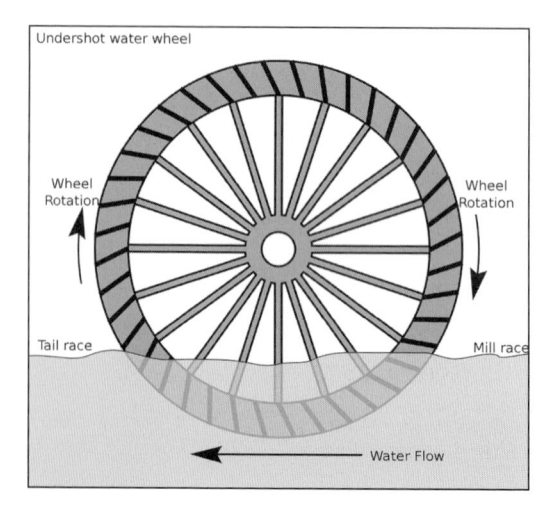

Society awarded him the Copely gold medal, for experiments with different types of waterwheel.

Smeaton concluded that gravity wheels, where water entered in line with or above the axial plane – overshot or breastshot wheels – had almost three times the efficiency of undershot wheels, where the wheel turned by the momentum of natural water flow velocity. Thus, many undershot wheels were converted to breastshot.

Appointed engineering manager at the Carron Ironworks in Falkirk, Smeaton improved the quality of iron, enabling the production of the first iron waterwheel axle in 1769. Unlike wooden ones, iron waterwheels did not expand and contract and were easier to shape into curves. Thus, larger, more powerful wheels could be built to provide for the needs of the expanding textile and other industries.

William Fairbairn, a Scottish engineer, widened the breastshot wheel in the early to mid-1800s, going on to win two Royal Society gold medals for his efforts. This meant that waterwheels continued in regular use right through to the twentieth century.

Richard Arkwright's water frame was one of the first factory machines to be powered by water. Used for spinning cotton into yarn – a laborious, time-consuming process when done by hand – the water frame dramatically increased the efficiency of cotton spinning and set the stage for the production of textiles on an unprecedented scale. From being modest in size and scope, from the late eighteenth century waterwheels could now power a whole succession of factory machines. Arkwright's mill, opened in 1771, was one of several built next to fast-flowing rivers in order to harness the natural power of nature. Water-powered reciprocating devices were also used to drive trip hammers and blast furnace bellows.

Such was the advantage that British industry gained from water-powered spinning technology that successive governments sought to retain a near monopoly on the process. Laws were passed to restrict the export of the machinery and even the emigration of people with thorough knowledge of the improved technology. This protectionist policy proved futile. In 1790, a young spinner named Samuel Slater emigrated to America, taking with him a wealth of knowledge about spinning technology. He became a partner in a Rhode Island textile mill the following year as New England became the heartland of American textile manufacturing.

John Smeaton and then William Fairbairn had taken a millennia-old technology and elevated it to address the burgeoning needs of Britain's Industrial Revolution.

Places to visit

- The Laxey Wheel, Isle of Man.
- The most powerful waterwheel built in the United Kingdom is the 100hp Quarry Bank Mill waterwheel at Styal, Cheshire. A high breastshot design, it was retired in 1904 and replaced with several turbines. Now restored, it is one of many points of interest to the student of Britain's Industrial Revolution.
- Located within the Dinorwic workshops of the National Slate Museum in Llanberis, North Wales, is the biggest working waterwheel in mainland Britain. Built by De Winton of Caernarfon, it has a diameter of 51 feet.

Further reading

Jonathan Brown, *Water Power and Watermills: An Historical Guide* (2011).
Martin Watts, *Watermills* (2006).

8: Richard Arkwright's First Mill at Cromford

The factory system of manufacturing that began in the eighteenth century was based on the concentration of industry into large specialised establishments. Prior to the growth of large-scale factories, most manufacturing in Britain had taken place via the domestic system. Here, individual workers and their families would use hand tools or simple machinery to manufacture goods in their own homes, or workshops attached to their homes. Work could be completed at a pace and rhythm that suited each individual, and was often combined with the pursuit of subsistence agriculture under the open-field system.

The development of water-powered and then steam-powered machines for clothmaking necessitated the building of large buildings to house the machines, and large waterwheels and engine houses from which to generate the factory's power.

Richard Arkwright's Cromford Mill in Derbyshire is generally regarded as the first factory to have been built in Britain, or indeed the world. Arkwright, a former wigmaker, needed a location that had a fast-flowing river to provide power. Such areas tended to be away from major centres of population so he had to establish a whole town, complete with housing, shops, a pub and other services, to attract a workforce.

In response to the series of ongoing wars against France, the principle of the

Richard Arkwright's original mill at Cromford. (*Alethe/Creative Commons*)

Robert Owen's school at New Lanark Mills. (*M.J. Richardson/Creative Commons*)

interchangeability of parts in the manufacture of muskets meant that production could be centred in one location and mass-produced, rather than each component passed from one individual craftsman to another. Whilst providing a massive impetus to industrial expansion, for many workers the effect on their work-life balance was catastrophic. Formerly, workers had been independent artisans who owned their own tools and designated their own working hours, often working with their families.

The factory system meant that the employer owned the tools and raw materials and was able to set the hours and other conditions under which the workers laboured. For the first time, hundreds of thousands of people had to leave their houses to undertake work, under the supervision of a foreman or overseer. Workers became increasingly concentrated in towns and cities, within walking distance of their workplaces. Consequently, builders of substandard housing and landlords of shabby accommodation could exploit them. Poor sanitation was often a hallmark of factory workers' housing, although this was by no means universal (*see* chapter 81). In addition, as women or children could operate many of the machines, wages were driven down. Conditions were often unsafe and accidents a common occurrence. Several employers took on as workhouse apprentices orphaned children or those whose families could no longer afford to keep them and offered a subsistence existence in return for long hours of grinding labour.

Not all factory owners sought merely to extract the maximum of output from their workforce for the minimum reward. Robert

Quarry Bank Mill, Cheshire. (*John Broom*)

Owen, who assumed ownership of New Lanark Mills, by the banks of the river Clyde, believed he had a moral duty to provide for the comfort and betterment of his workers. He outlawed the employment of children under the age of 10 and established a school to teach them the skills to enable a better future life. He established an on-site co-operative shop and replaced the physical chastisement of errant workers with a system of colour-coded signals, indicating the current performance level of each employee.

Places to visit

- New Lanark Mills, Scotland. Most of Robert Owen's factory still remains, and is a most fascinating place to visit, having been awarded the status of a UNSECO world heritage site.
- Quarry Bank Mill, at Styal in Cheshire, is a fine example of a late eighteenth-century mill, complete with operational machinery on the factory floor. One particularly evocative part of the mill complex is the Apprentice House, which formerly housed several dozen children at once and in which some harrowing tales can be heard.
- Cromford Mill near Matlock affords a pleasant excursion. The old factory buildings contain artisan outlets, an antiques shop, a bookshop and a range of eateries. There are few reminders of the grim lives its establishment presaged.

Further reading

Ian Donnachie, *Robert Owen: Social Visionary* (2005).
David Hanson, *Children of the Mill: True Stories from Quarry Bank* (2015).

9: The Flying Shuttle

John Kay's flying shuttle greatly accelerated the weaving process, allowing the shuttle carrying the weft threads to be passed through the warp threads faster and over a greater width of cloth. It meant only one operator per loom was needed, rather than a second to catch the shuttle. The invention was patented in 1733 as a 'New Engine or Machine for Opening and Dressing Wool'. Kay himself called the device a 'wheeled shuttle' for the handloom, but others coined the term 'flying shuttle' due to its continuous speed.

Kay had been born into a yeoman farmer's family in 1704, but his father died before his birth. The 14-year-old John was apprenticed to a handloom weaver, and quickly displayed his ingenuity by designing a metal substitute for a natural reed used in the weaving process. He left his apprenticeship and travelled the country selling the wire reeds, before returning home to Bury, Lancashire, to marry.

In 1730, Kay patented a cording and twisting machine for worsted. Having patented his shuttle in 1733, he formed a partnership in Colchester to begin their manufacture. However, in an early indication of the unrest that was to hamper the technological advances of Britain's Industrial Revolution, Colchester's weavers, anxious about its effects on their livelihoods, got up a petition to King George II to have the device prohibited. The shuttle also caused an imbalance in cloth production, as those engaging in spinning the yarn could not keep up with demand caused by the improvement in weaving efficiency.

Kay also had problems convincing woollen manufacturers in his native Bury that his shuttle was sufficiently robust. He worked on improvements to his 1733 design, although this was later to dog him as they were at variance with his original patent. Kay moved to Leeds in 1738, experiencing problems with collecting the annual fifteen-shilling licence fee royalty for each shuttle in use.

Numerous near-copies of the flying shuttle caused Kay to launch patent infringement lawsuits. However, even when successful in court, he found that the compensation was less than his legal costs. The cloth manufacturers formed a Shuttle Club, syndicating the costs of any of their members brought to court by Kay. This combination of patent piracy and mutual protection nearly brought him to bankruptcy.

In 1745, Kay and Joseph Stell patented a cloth ribbon weaving machine but could not invest in product development due to the former's legal

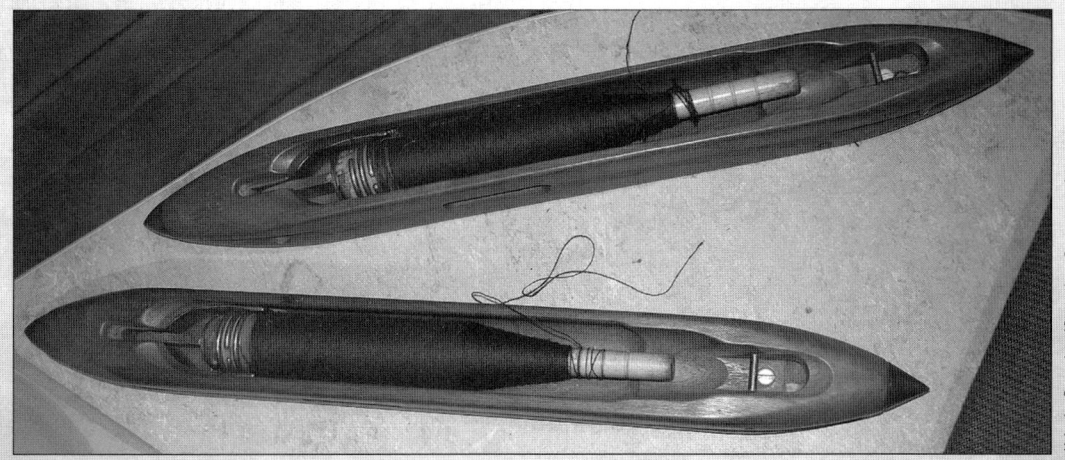

(Linda Spashet/Creative Commons)

The impressive monument to John Kay in Bury, Lancashire. (Repton1x/Creative Commons)

costs. Kay left Leeds and returned to Bury, where he worked on improvements to the spinning process, courting further unpopularity from local spinners.

Disillusioned with the reception in England to his technological innovations, Kay moved to France in 1747. Here he negotiated with the French government the sale of his patent in return for 3,000 livres plus an annual pension of 2,500 livres, the equivalent of just over £32,000 in today's money. Copies of the flying shuttle helped to begin the mechanisation of the French textile industry and once again, Kay found himself trying unsuccessfully to enforce his monopoly. He briefly returned to England before settling across the Channel. He spent his final years developing and building machines for cotton manufacturers in Sens and Troyes. With his pension withdrawn by the French government, he died in penury, on an unknown date estimated to be in 1779.

Although unappreciated in his lifetime and dying a forgotten man, the town of Bury still pays tribute to John Kay; there are pubs named after him, as are the Kay Gardens. In 1903, the *Bury Times* argued that the town 'owed John Kay's memory an atonement' and that people should contribute to a memorial to 'that wonderfully ingenious and martyred man'.

Places to visit

- Bury, Lancashire, has a memorial to John Kay, erected in 1908 and paid for by Henry Whitehead, a wealthy local mill owner. Standing at over 30 feet high, its inscription reads:

  TO PERPETUATE THE NAME AND FAME OF JOHN KAY OF BURY. WHOSE INVENTION IN THE YEAR 1733 OF THE FLY SHUTTLE QUADRUPLED HUMAN POWER IN WEAVING & PLACED ENGLAND IN THE FRONT RANK AS THE BEST MARKET IN THE WORLD FOR TEXTILE MANUFACTURES. HE WAS BORN IN BURY IN 1704, AND DIED IN EXILE AND POVERTY IN FRANCE, WHERE HE LIES IN AN UNKNOWN GRAVE.

- Manchester Town Hall houses a mural by Ford Madox Brown that depicts John Kay and his flying shuttle.

Further reading

John Lord, *Memoir of John Kay of Bury: Inventor of the Fly-Shuttle ... with a Review of the Textile Trade and Manufacture from Earliest Times* (1923).

10: The Spinning Jenny

The spinning jenny was one of the most important pieces of technology invented during Britain's Industrial Revolution. The jenny reduced the amount of work needed to produce cloth, with one worker able to work eight spools. Eventually, the spools grew to 120. The spinning jenny was another machine to come out of Lancashire, its inventor being James Hargreaves of Oswaldtwistle. Hargreaves was illiterate and began work as a handloom weaver. According to baptismal records, he fathered thirteen children.

The town of Oswaldtwistle lies 3 miles east of Blackburn, from where 'Blackburn greys' were produced in the early eighteenth century. This cloth was made from linen warp and cotton weft imported from India (*see* chapter 42) before being sent to London to be printed. Following the widespread use of John Kay's flying shuttle (*see* chapter 9), cotton production was struggling to keep up with the market's demand as weaving productivity doubled.

Hargreaves' invention comprised a metal frame with eight wooden spindles at one end. A set of eight rovings was attached to a beam on the frame. The rovings, when extended, passed through two horizontal bars of wood that could be clasped together. These bars could be drawn along the top of the frame by the spinner's left hand, thus extending the thread. The spinner used his right hand to rapidly turn a wheel that caused all the spindles to revolve and the thread to be spun. When the bars were returned, the thread wound onto the spindle. A pressing wire, or faller, guided the threads onto the right place on the spindle.

Mindful of the opposition and attacks that John Kay had faced, Hargreaves gradually rolled out his new invention, selling jennies to a few trusted neighbours. Initially, the Blackburn spinners were happy with the efficiency gains but the medium-term effect was to lower the price of yarn due to an increase in supply. A group of Blackburn spinners broke into Hargreaves' house and smashed his machines. He fled to Nottingham in 1768, making jennies for a Mr Shipley. He set up a textile business in

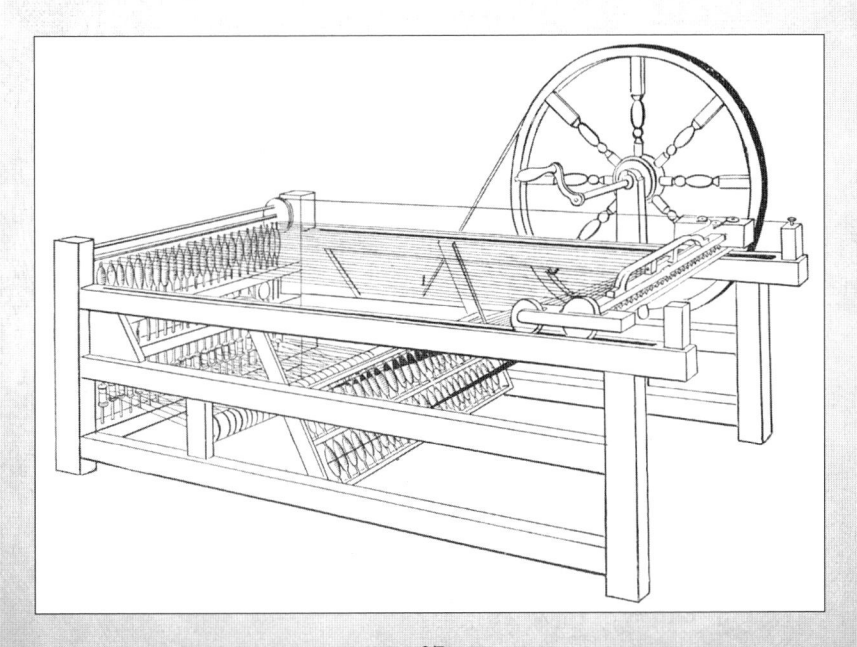

An early spinning jenny on display at the Helmshore Mills Textile Museum, Lancashire. (*Clem Rutter/ Creative Commons*)

Hockley with Thomas James and in 1770 took out a patent on the spinning jenny, 'a machine for spinning, drawing and twisting cotton'.

Like John Kay, Hargreaves found that people were copying his innovation. He sent notice to a number of spinners in Lancashire that he was to begin legal action against them. After negotiations, his case fell apart when it was learned he had sold several in the past. The spinning jenny continued in common use in the cotton industry until about 1810, when the spinning mule superseded it.

Myth surrounds the origin of the etymology of the spinning jenny. One popular account is that a female family member of the Hargreaves family called Jenny accidentally knocked over a spinning wheel. Although on the floor, the wheel remained working as normal even though the spindle stood upright. Hargreaves then realised that the spinning process could be done with vertical as well as horizontal spindles. However, the more probable and prosaic reason for the name was that 'jenny' was a common contemporary abbreviation for engine.

Hargreaves continued to work at the mill he had established with Thomas James until his death in 1778. James gave Hargreaves' widow £400 to buy out his half of the business. Hargreaves was buried in the churchyard of St Mary's, Nottingham. When Samuel Crompton invented the spinning mule in about 1779, he stated he had learned to spin in 1769 on a jenny that Hargreaves had built.

Places to visit

- Quarry Bank Mill in Cheshire contains a working model of a spinning jenny.

Further reading

Edward Baines, *History of the Cotton Manufacture in Great Britain* (1835).
Geoffrey Timmins, *Four Centuries of Lancashire Cotton* (1994).

11: Robert Owen's Silent Monitor

This small, four-sided wooden block, known as a 'silent monitor', was used by Robert Owen as a means of imposing discipline at his New Lanark Mills. The device was introduced by Owen after he and his partners took over the mills in 1800.

Robert Owen was strongly opposed to the use of corporal punishment so, in order to keep discipline at the mills, he devised the 'silent monitor'. It was hung next to each worker, with each side displaying a different colour. 'Bad' behaviour was represented by the colour black; 'indifferent' by blue; 'good' by yellow; and 'excellent' by white. The superintendent was responsible for turning the monitors every day, according to how the worker had behaved. A daily note was then made of the conduct of the workers in the 'books of character', which were provided for each department in the mills.

Before the Industrial Revolution in Britain most workers controlled their own pace, timing and conduct at work. Factory discipline radically changed this. Employers now dictated how, when and in what manner work was done. The era brought a huge shift in the way people's working lives were organised. We have already seen how employers collected workers into workshops or 'manufactories' that they owned. Initially, these workers controlled their own hours, workplace and conduct. They took breaks at will and were free to socialise. However, a later change was to have unpleasant consequences. Factory discipline was imposed and employers now dictated the hours and patterns of work and conduct on the job. Workers were rewarded not just for their output but also for their behaviour. Likewise, they could be penalised for even minor infractions.

The poster overleaf, which is displayed at Helmshore Mills in Lancashire, details the various fines in place for undesirable behaviours. Other factories expected even higher standards, with a list of fines including:

- Any worker found dirty at his work – 1 shilling
- Washing himself – 1 shilling – for wasting time
- Leaving his oil can out of its place – 6 shillings – inefficient
- Spinning with gas light too long – 2 shillings – for wasting valuable gas
- Heard whistling – 1 shilling
- Being five minutes late – 2 shillings
- Being sick and not finding a replacement – 6 shillings – this penalty pays for the cost of wasted steam that went unused because of the worker's absence

Children working long hours in textile mills were often a target for punishment. The extent of the working day made them extremely tired and they often found it difficult to maintain the speed required by the overlookers. Sometimes, children were hit with a strap to make them work faster. One former factory boy, Jonathan Downe, told an 1822 parliamentary committee chaired by Michael Sadler:

> When I was seven years old I went to work at Mr. Marshalls factory at Shrewsbury. If a child was drowsy, the overlooker touches the child on the shoulder and says, 'Come here'. In a corner of the room there is an iron cistern filled with water. He takes the boy by the legs and dips him in the cistern and sends him back to work.

Children were punished for arriving late for work and for talking to the other children. Some accounts mark out some factory owners as verging on the sadistic. After Sarah Carpenter's father died when she was 8, the family had to enter the Bristol Workhouse. Her elder brother was sent away to work at the notorious Cressbrook Mill in Derbyshire and Sarah followed a couple of years later. In 1849, she was interviewed about her childhood experiences, revealing:

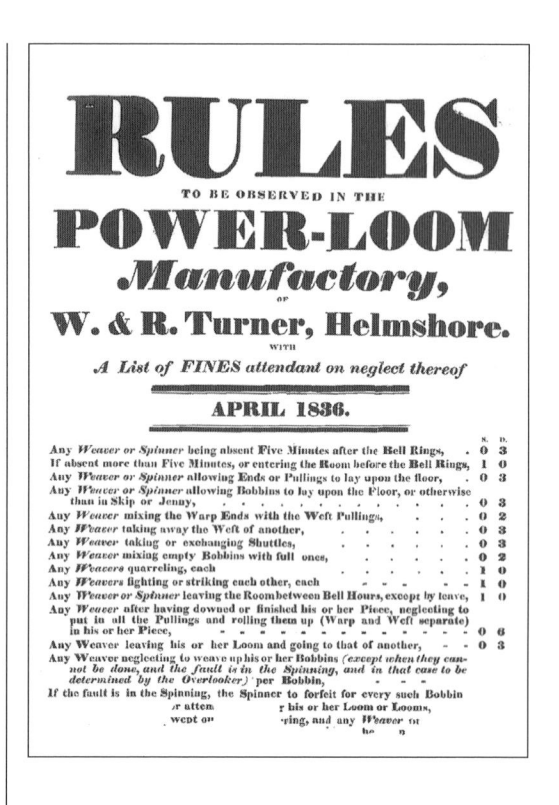

> There was an overlooker called William Hughes ... He came up to me and asked me what my drawing frame was stopped for. I said I did not know because it was not me who had stopped it. A little boy that was on the other side had stopped it, but he was too frightened to say it was him. Hughes started beating me with a stick, and when he had done I told him I would let my mother know. He then went out and fetched the master in to me. The master started beating me with a stick over the head till it was full of lumps and bled. My head was so bad that I could not sleep for a long time, and I never been a sound sleeper since.

Parish apprentices who might seek to escape from the horrors of their employment would usually be caught and returned to face a beating. Persistent runaways might be sent to prison. On return to the factory, they might be placed in irons. Robert Blincoe, who had worked in a stocking-weaving mill in Nottinghamshire from the age of 7, recalled:

> The blacksmith had the task of riveting irons upon any of the apprentices whom the master ordered. These irons were very much like the irons usually put upon felons. Even young women, if they suspected of intending to run away, had irons riveted on their ankles, and reaching by long links and rings up to the hips, and in these they were compelled to walk to and fro from the mill to work and to sleep.

In contrast to these sadistic punishments, Robert Owen's silent monitor seems relatively benign.

Places to visit

- New Lanark Mills by the river Clyde includes a tour around a recreated floor of Robert Owen's factory, featuring the silent monitor.
- The Apprentice House at Quarry Bank Mill at Styal in Cheshire highlights the severe conditions that many child factory workers experienced.

Further reading

John Brown, *A Memoir of Robert Blincoe, an Orphan Boy* (2019).
Ian Donnachie, *Robert Owen: Social Visionary* (2011).
Sue Wilkes, *The Children History Forgot: Young Workers of the Industrial Age* (2011).

12: Coal Mine Ventilation Door

This drawing, from a parliamentary enquiry into working conditions in coal mines, shows a boy 'trapper' whose job it was to manually open and shut the adjoining ventilation door to allow for a freer flow of air through the mine.

Coal mines were cramped, poorly ventilated and highly dangerous. They employed large numbers of children to perform vital tasks underground. The youngest member of the family was often employed as a trapper. Trappers would usually sit in total darkness for up to twelve hours at a time, waiting to let the coal tub through the door. Their working lives were tedious and very dangerous. If they fell asleep, it could affect the safety of the whole workings.

Older children and women were employed as hurriers, also known as drammers, pulling and pushing tubs full of coal along roadways from the coalface to the pit bottom. The younger children worked in pairs, one as a hurrier, the other as a thruster, but the older children and women worked alone. Hurriers would be harnessed to the tub, and thrusters would help hurriers by pushing the tubs of coal from behind with their hands and the tops of their heads. Full tubs could weigh over 12cwt and would have to be moved through roadways that were often only 2 to 4 feet high.

Getters were the oldest and strongest members of the family – almost always grown men or strong youths. Their job was to cut the coal from the seam with a pickaxe. Getters were the only members of the family who would work continually with a candle or safety lamp, as they needed the light to see the coalface.

It was dangerous work, with children frequently injured or killed by explosions, roof falls or being run over by carts. Hurriers were often harnessed to their heavy carts, which had to be dragged a distance of about 50 yards at a height of about 3 feet.

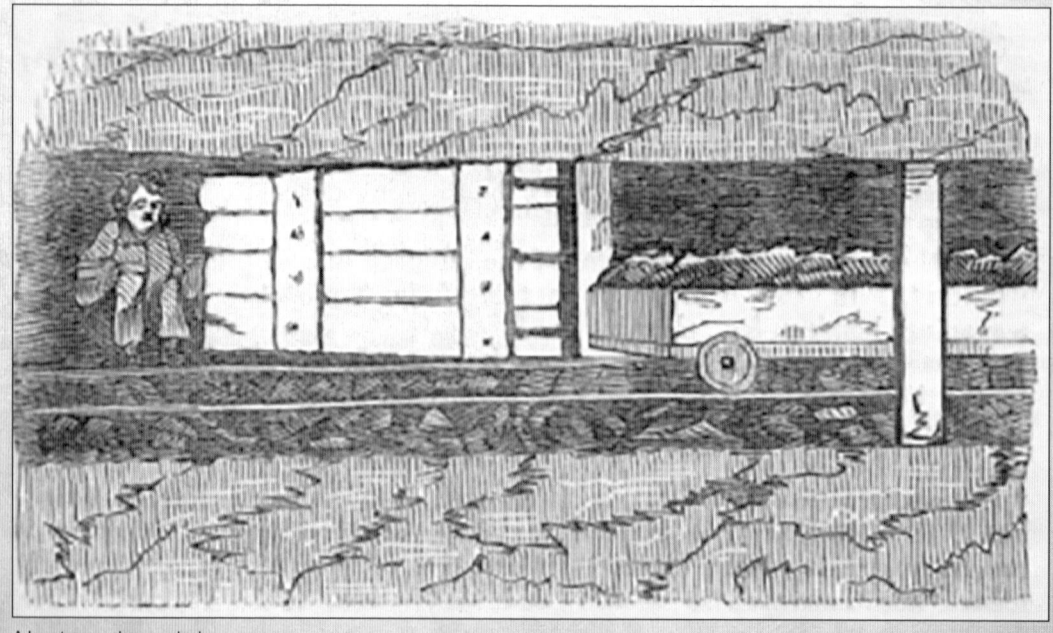

A boy trapper in a coal mine.

12: COAL MINE VENTILATION DOOR

One of the worst mining disasters involving children occurred at Huskar Pit, Silkstone, near Barnsley. Wednesday, 4 July 1838 had been humid, sunny and warm above ground. Three hundred feet below the surface, about fifty children and thirty-three coal getters were cutting and moving coal. Amongst the small boys was 7-year-old Joseph Burkinshaw, earning sixpence per day as a trapper for twelve hours' work powered by candlelight. At 2 pm, a vicious summer thunderstorm began and streams began to overflow. The flooding water extinguished the fire in the engine that powered the winding gear. Workers were instructed to stay underground and wait to be rescued. Forty of the children, wrongly interpreting the sound of thunder as a firedamp explosion, ignored the instruction and began making their way to an opening. Tragically, water burst through and poured down the slope, trapping and drowning twenty-six of the children.

The bodies were recovered and transported to their homes by cart. A verdict of accidental death by drowning was reached. The owners of the mine, the Clarke family, provided a memorial to the children, erected in Silkstone churchyard in 1841. Part of the inscription reads:

Huskar Pit memorial, Silkstone churchyard. (*John Broom*)

Take ye heed, watch and pray; for ye know not when the time is. [Mark 13:33]

THIS MONUMENT
Was erected to perpetuate the remembrance of an awful visitation of the Almighty which took place in this Parish on the 4th day of July 1838.

On that eventful day the Lord sent forth His Thunder, Lightning, Hail and Rain, carrying devastation before them, and by a sudden irruption of Water into the Coalpits of R.C. Clarke Esqr. Twenty-six human beings whose names are recorded here were suddenly summon'd to appear before their Maker.

READER REMEMBER!
Every neglected call of God will appear against Thee at the Day of Judgement. Let this solemn Warning then sink deep into thy heart and so prepare thee that the Lord when he cometh may find thee WATCHING.

Huskar Pit memorial, in woodland near Silkstone Common. (*John Broom*)

Fuelled by horror and indignation at the loss of twenty-six children, public clamour and the dedication of Anthony Ashley-Cooper led to the establishment of a Commission of Enquiry into the State of Children in Employment, which ran from 1840 to 1842. Some of the evidence gathered was heartbreaking. Mary Davis, described as a 'pretty little girl' of 6 years old, was found fast asleep against a large stone underground in the Plymouth Mines, Merthyr. After being wakened, she said, 'I went to sleep because my lamp had gone out for want of oil. I was frightened for someone had stolen my bread and cheese. I think it was the rats.'

Publication of the report and the ensuing public outcry forced Robert Peel's government into passing the Coal Mines Regulation Act in August 1842. From 1 March 1843, it became illegal for women, or any child under the age of 10, to work underground in Britain. However, like the 1833 Factory Act, inspection arrangements were inadequate, with only one inspector to cover the whole of Britain. Furthermore, he had to give notice before visiting a mine. Even so, many families with a large female contingent were still forced to move to mill towns in search of work.

To this day, the children of Silkstone Primary School remember the Huskar Pit disaster every day, as the memorial to their tragic forebears forms part of their school uniform logo.

Places to visit

- All Saints Church, Silkstone, stands in the middle of the village, with the mining disaster memorial in a prominent position by the roadside. Its florid apocalyptic inscription is worth contemplating.
- The Big Pit Museum and Blaenafon is part of the National Museum of Wales. The free-to-enter attraction contains many fascinating displays, including one on children working in the pits.
- The National Coal Mining Museum near Wakefield, Yorkshire, includes features on children and women working down the mines.

Further reading

Robert McIntosh, *Boys in the Pits: Child Labour in Coal Mines* (2001).
Ceri Thompson, *From the Cradle to the Coalmine: The Story of Children in Welsh Mines* (2014).

13: Miners' Safety Lamp

Miners over several generations had good cause to thank Sir Humphry Davy for the invention of his 1815 safety lamp, designed for use in mines where flammable gasses such as methane lurked.

This memorial, located in Hednesford, Staffordshire, commemorates over 3,500 miners from the Cannock Chase coalfields who lost their lives at work. The idea of enclosing the flame was not unique to Davy. William Clanny had successfully tested a safety lamp at Herrington Mill near Sunderland in 1813, winning medals from the Royal Society of Arts. Engine wright George Stephenson also devised a lamp that allowed the air to keep the flame alive to enter through tiny perforations. The flame could not pass back through the holes to ignite the gasses, known colloquially as firedamp. He demonstrated the efficacy of his lamp at Killingworth Colliery, near Newcastle upon Tyne, a month before Davy presented his lamp design to the Royal Society.

Davy's lamp, with its innovative wire gauze sieve, was first trialled at Hebburn Colliery, near Jarrow, on 9 January 1816. News of its invention had been made public at a meeting in Newcastle the previous November at the Royal Society, when Davy presented a paper describing the lamp, for which he was awarded the society's Rumford Medal. Davy's paper recognised the existence of Stephenson's lamp as an alternative but considered his solution superior.

Davy lamp memorial, Hednesford. (Elliott Brown/Creative Commons)

Davy's lamp consisted of a wick with the flame enclosed inside a mesh screen which acted as a flame arrestor. Air, including any firedamp, could pass through the mesh freely enough to support combustion, but the holes were too fine to allow a flame to propagate through them and ignite any firedamp outside the mesh. It originally burned a heavy vegetable oil.

The public immediately recognised the significance of Davy's invention, due to the publicity his Royal Society paper had received. Conversely, the self-educated Stephenson was accused of stealing Davy's idea for what was dubbed his 'Geordie lamp' as his formal demonstration had followed Davy's. It was felt that all versions previous to Davy's were unsafe.

The proud north-eastern industrial community was not prepared to let this slight drop; they formed a local committee of enquiry, which exonerated Stephenson from the accusations. Evidence showed that he had been working contemporaneously to Davy to develop the Geordie lamp, and a local subscription raised £1,000 in his honour. However, Davy and his supporters refused to accept the committee's findings, claiming an uneducated man such as Stephenson could not come up with

Humphrey Davy.

the solution he had. Stephenson himself admitted that he had arrived at a practical solution on the basis of an erroneous theory. Practical, experience-based knowledge could not sit comfortably against theoretical-inspired findings. After a decade and a half of ill will, in 1833 a House of Commons committee found that Stephenson had equal claim to having invented the safety lamp. Davy, who died in 1829, had never let go of his claim that Stephenson had stolen his idea.

The Stephenson lamp was used almost exclusively in north-eastern England, whereas the Davy lamp was used everywhere else. Davy's safety lamp also served as an indicator of choking gases, including carbon dioxide. Miners could place the lamp close to the ground to detect such gases, which are denser than air and so could collect in depressions in the mine. If the air was oxygen-poor, the lamp flame would be extinguished, giving an early indication of an unhealthy atmosphere and allowing miners to escape before they died of asphyxiation.

Acclamation for Davy's invention was swift. *The Cumberland Pacquet* reported:

> The Lamp offers absolute security to the miner ... With the excellent ventilation of the Whitehaven Collieries and the application of Sir HUMPHRY's valuable instrument, the accidents from the explosion of [carburetted] hydrogene ... will by this happy invention be avoided.

Sadly, mine explosions were not a thing of the past. Paradoxically, the Select Committee on Accidents in Mines reported in 1835 that the introduction of the Davy lamp had led to an increase in mine accidents. Mine owners had grown confident in sinking ever deeper and more extensive shafts and seams than before, eager to provide the fuel for Britain's expanding industries. Thus, areas previously closed for safety reasons were reopened. In addition, most miners had to provide their own lamps, and many preferred the superior lighting and lesser cost of the naked light of a candle. Furthermore, the gauze covering on the Davy lamp was easily damaged and the wire prone to rusting or breaking.

The deeper and wider the mines were dug, the less adequate the ventilation and the humble lamp proved no match against insufficient air supply in such mines. An overreliance on the Davy lamp to herald the presence of gases had meant that more effective safety measures were neglected.

Places to visit

- The National Coal Mining Museum, near Wakefield, has a collection of over fifty mining safety lamps. It is an excellent day out, with a trip down a mineshaft and on to an old Yorkshire coal seam a particular highlight.

Further reading

Raymond Lamont Brown, *Humphry Davy: Life Beyond the Lamp* (2004).
Hunter Davies, *George Stephenson: The Remarkable Life of the Founder of the Railways* (2004).
David Ross, *George and Robert Stephenson: A Passion for Success* (2018).

14: Pit Pony Inkwell

This striking inkwell was formed from the hoof of a pit pony called Kruger. The pony met his end in the Senghenydd Colliery Disaster of 14 October 1913. The event was the worst mining accident in British history, in which 439 men died. Following an enquiry about breaches of regulations, the mine owners and manager were fined £24. A local paper concluded: 'miners' lives at 1s 11/4d each'. The circumstances in which the hoof was made into an inkwell are not known, but it acts as a reminder of the important role played by pit ponies during Britain's Industrial Revolution.

'Pit pony' was a generic term used to describe any horse, pony or mule that was used in underground mine working in Britain from the mid-eighteenth until the late twentieth century.

It is thought that ponies were first used underground in the Durham coalfield in 1750. The Silkstone Colliery disaster of 1838 (*see* chapter 12) led to the Mines and Collieries Act of 1842, which banned the employment of women, girls and boys under 10 underground. Thus, the use of horses and ponies for hauling tubs of coal along the mining seams became much more widespread.

Usually stabled underground in shaft mines, ponies rarely saw the light of day. They were fed on a diet high in chopped hay and maize. They might only come to the surface during the colliery's annual holiday. An eight-hour shift would be typical, with 30 tons of coal hauled during that time. Like the children they replaced, pit ponies had to work in areas with insufficient height, causing back injuries.

One former miner working in 1905 recalled:

For protection they wore a skullcap and bridle made of leather. A pony had to be three years old before it was allowed down the pit. They learned to walk with their heads down and could open [air doors] in the roadway. It knew which door needed pulling and which doors it could push. They used to be ridden, though we weren't supposed to ride ... Females were released into the meadows to give birth and returned to the pit after recuperation. Offspring were contracted to the pit when aged three.

An 1879 engraving of a pit pony being lowered underground.

In 1887, the Coal Mines Regulation Act provided some protection for horses working underground. A Pit Ponies' Protection Society – later the National Equine Defence League – was founded by Francis Cox in 1908. The Scottish Society to Promote Kindness to Pit Ponies was established in 1911 and a Royal Commission report was published which led to further protections.

The plight of ponies was highlighted in 1904 when John William Bell, a young collier, was awarded the Fitzwilliam Medal for Kindness due to his actions when working at the Elsecar Collieries near Barnsley. Bell stayed behind with his pony while his workmates escaped from a collapsing coal seam. This facilitated the eventual rescue of both Bell and the pony. So impressed was Countess Maud Fitzwilliam, a member of the family that owned the extensive coal mining estates across Wentworth, that she awarded Bell the prize as well as using the story as a means of further promoting the rights of pit ponies. Sadly, Bell died down a mine in 1910, hit by a falling rock as he tried to come to the aid of a stricken colleague.

The famous music hall singer and comedian Harry Lauder became an advocate for the rights of pit ponies, pleading their case to Winston Churchill when the two met in the House of Commons in 1911. Lauder said about Churchill that he:

> could talk for hours about my wee four-footed friends of the mine. But I think I convinced him that the time has now arrived when something should be done by the law of the land to improve the lot and working conditions of the patient, equine slaves who assist so materially in carrying on the great mining industry of this country.

The British Coal Mines Act of the same year stipulated that ponies had to be 4 years old, checked by a vet and their feet shod before going underground. They commonly worked past the age of 20.

The use of pit ponies hit a peak in 1913, when 70,000 animals were reportedly working underground in Britain's mines. Over time, they were replaced by mechanical haulage systems. By 1984, the National Coal Board employed fifty-five ponies. They were gradually retired, with

Galloway Pony sculpture by Stephen Charnock on the river Irwell trail between Bacup and Salford. Located in the exact location of the old winding engine, it shows how horses were used to winch coal from the area's first deep mine.

Sultan the Pit Pony sculpture at Penallta Parc. (*Phil Matthews/ Penallta pit pony/CC BY-SA 2.0*))

two going to work at the National Coal Mining Museum at the former Caphouse Colliery near Wakefield. Robbie – believed to be the last colliery horse to work underground in Britain – was retired from the Pant y Gasseg colliery near Pontypool in May 1999.

In many mines, ponies were favoured over horses due to the narrow seams in which they had to work. A height of 12 hands – 48 inches – was the limit. The most common breed was Shetland, but Welsh, Russian, Dartmoor and Cornish were also widely used in Britain.

Places to visit

- Parc Penallta, near Caerphilly, contains the massive sculpture *Sultan the Pit Pony*. Best viewed from the air, *Sultan* was sculpted from the remaining slag heap from Penallta Colliery by Welsh artist Mick Petts between 1996 and 1999; 60,000 tons of coal shale, dirt and stone were used to construct the 656-foot long artwork. The name *Sultan* was chosen by local residents in honour of the final pit pony to work at the colliery. Park trails criss-cross the sculpture.
- The Fforest Uchaf Farm, near Pontypridd, is known as the Pit Pony Sanctuary. Here the visitor can learn about the history of pit ponies and meet the few remaining Welsh ex-pit ponies.

Further reading

John Bright, *Pit Ponies* (1986).
Mike Kirkup, *Pit Pones* (2008).
Derek Hollows, *Voices in the Dark: Pony Talk & Mining Tales* (2011).

15: Chimney Sweep's Brush

This careworn chimney sweep, John Colfer of Wexford, Ireland, carries the brush with which he would have dislodged soot from Victorian-era chimneys. However, several chimney sweeps had a more human and direct method of cleaning chimneys – the child chimney sweep.

Children were widely used as chimney sweeps in Britain for about 200 years. Following the gutting of the City of London during the Great Fire of September 1666, new regulations stipulated that fireplaces had to be built with narrower chimneys. Thus, the chimneys needed to be frequently cleaned to avoid blockages. As the number of houses with chimneys increased apace with the growth of towns and cities, so the demand for chimney sweeps was greater. Small boys had to crawl through chimneys that were only about 18 inches wide.

Chimney tops were grouped together and the routes of flues often involved two or more right angles and combined horizontal and vertical sections. One flue in Buckingham Palace had fifteen angles, with its narrowest section being 9 inches. The master sweep was unable to climb into such small spaces himself and employed climbing boys to go up the chimneys to dislodge the soot. These boys might be orphaned workhouse paupers, or from families who could not afford to keep their child. The ideal starting age was around 6, but sometimes children as young as 4 were used.

The author's 8-year-old great-great-great-grandfather, the nominatively determined Stephen Broom, was indentured as an apprentice sweep from St Andrew's Workhouse in Norwich in 1795. His master was Thomas Holmstead, a master sweep of East Dereham, Norfolk. The workhouse guardians also provided Mr Holmstead with forty shillings and a set of clothes for young Stephen. Unlike the case for many apprentice sweeps, this arrangement had a productive outcome as Stephen Broom himself rose to become a master sweep and lived to the age of 75.

An apprentice agreed to obey his master for a period of seven years. Once the apprenticeship was completed, he would become a journeyman sweep and would continue to work for a master sweep of his choice. The master would then take on other apprentices.

A child sweep would pull his cap down over his face and hold a large flat brush over his head. Using his back, elbows and knees, he would shimmy up the flue in the manner of a caterpillar. The practice of climbing up chimneys in the nude was termed 'buffing it', which could result in knees and elbows being scraped raw.

The Affectionate Parent's Gift, an 1828 engraving of a child sweep.

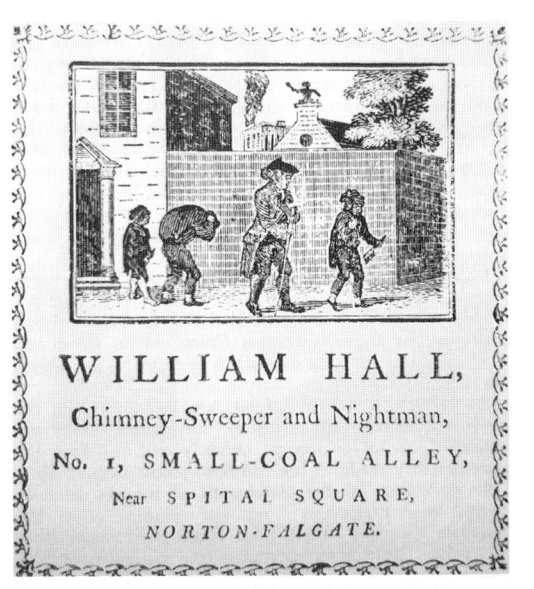

A late eighteenth-century sweep's handbill, showing his three chimney boys.

On reaching the top of the flue, the child would slide down at speed to ground level with the brush dislodging the soot, which would fall over him. He then collected the soot for his master, who could sell it to farmers and gardeners to enrich their soil. Often, child sweeps went up hot chimneys, and sometimes up those that were alight in order to extinguish the fire. In extreme situations, boys would get stuck and die in the chimneys.

Health effects were devastating. Bathing opportunities were rare, with intervals ranging from once per week to three times per year. Children suffered from stunted growth and disfigurement. Especially badly affected were knees and ankle joints. Lung infections and other respiratory diseases were common and eyelids became sore and inflamed. The first recorded form of industrial cancer was unique to chimney sweeps. The boys would often develop 'chimney sweep cancer' – which affected the scrotum, usually striking boys in their adolescence, and was painful and fatal.

The passing of legislation to improve the lot of chimney sweep apprentices was slow. The 1788 Act for the Better Regulation of Chimney Sweepers and their Apprentices limited a master to six apprentices but was not properly enforced. An 1817 report to Parliament highlighted the appalling conditions in which some apprentice sweeps worked. A Friendly Society for the Protection and Education of Chimney-Sweepers' Boys had been established in 1800. The Chimney Sweepers Act of 1834 banned the apprenticing of boys under the age of 14. Apprentices were not allowed to climb flues to extinguish fires. Again, this was widely disregarded, as people believed it was safer for them to have the flues cleaned by a climbing boy rather than a brush on an extended pole.

The Chimney Sweepers and Chimneys Regulation Act 1840 made it illegal for anyone under the age of 21 to sweep chimneys. Yet again, this was generally ignored. A further enquiry gathered information across 1852 and 1853, but no action was taken. The Chimney

Sweepers Regulation Act 1864 authorised fines and imprisonment for master sweeps who ignored the law. In 1863, the Reverend Charles Kingsley wrote *The Water Babies, A Fairy Tale for a Land Baby*. The story of a boy chimney sweep who escaped his cruel life and went on a fantasy adventure, it raised public awareness of the awful conditions under which chimney sweeps worked.

In February 1875, 12-year-old chimney sweep George Brewster, having been sent up a chimney at Fulbourn Hospital by his master, William Wyer, became stuck. A desperate attempt was made to reach him, including pulling down a wall, but he was found fatally impaired. Wyer was found guilty of manslaughter and Brewster's death instigated a campaign for reform. In September 1875, The Chimney Sweepers Act passed through Parliament, ending the practice of using children as human chimney sweeps.

Places to visit

- The National Trust Museum of Childhood at Sudbury Hall, Derbyshire, has a display on child chimney sweeps and an immersive experience of a dark chimney climb for children.

Further reading

Benita Cullingford, *Chimneys and Chimney Sweeps* (2003).
K.H. Strange, *The Climbing Boys: A Study of Sweeps' Apprentices, 1773–1875* (1972).

16: Truck Token

As if long working days and poor health and safety measures were not enough misery for the British industrial worker of the eighteenth and nineteenth centuries, many mine and factory owners sought to further exploit their workforce by the truck system, sometimes known as the tommy system.

In lieu of wages paid in cash, employers would issue tokens to their workforce that were redeemable only in a shop owned by the employer or his family.

William Cobbett, the political agitator and journalist, described the system in his *Rural Rides*, published in 1830, having seen it in operation in Wolverhampton and Shrewsbury:

A truck token from Blantyre Colliery, Scotland.

The manner of carrying on the tommy system is this: suppose there to be a master who employs a hundred men. That hundred men, let us suppose, to earn a pound a week each. This is not the case in the iron-works; but no matter, we can illustrate our meaning by one sum as well as by another. These men lay out weekly the whole of the hundred pounds in victuals, drink, clothing, bedding, fuel, and house-rent. Now, the master finding the profits of his trade fall off very much, and being at the same time in want of money to pay the hundred pounds weekly, and perceiving that these hundred pounds are carried away at once, and given to shopkeepers of various descriptions; to butchers, bakers, drapers, hatters, shoemakers, and the rest; and knowing that, on an average, these shopkeepers must all have a profit of thirty per cent., or more, he determines to keep this thirty per cent. to himself; and this is thirty pounds a week gained as a shop-keeper, which amounts to £1,560l. a year. He, therefore, sets up a tommy shop: a long place containing every commodity that the workman can want, liquor and house-room excepted.

One Manchester cotton worker sought a prosecution against his employer in 1827, on the basis that he had received only two shillings in wages in nine months, stating the rest 'he was obliged to take [in goods] from the manufacturer's daughter, who was also the cashier'.

In November 1830, the truck system, alongside the Corn Laws, became a focus of demonstrations in Merthyr Tydfil. These demonstrations, allied to calls for political reform, eventually escalated into the Merthyr Rising of 1831. Bloody riots lasted for several days and claimed the lives of many Welsh miners, not to mention those of several of the soldiers dispatched to quell them.

Initially it could be argued that tommy or truck shops met a need for many mining communities as there were often no other shops in the vicinity of the newly sunk pits at which the miners could buy essential supplies. However, it increasingly became common practice for the goods to be of poor quality and prices to become excessive. Some shops also encouraged workers to buy on credit, leading to them becoming permanently indebted to their employers and unable ever to contemplate changing jobs.

An Act of Parliament of 1831 declared the truck system illegal. However, in the South Wales coal and iron ore fields, several ironmasters and mine owners continued to use truck tokens until the passing of the Truck Amendment Act of 1887.

Today, truck tokens are items cherished by collectors. However, they speak of an era of exploitation for those who originally held them nearly 200 years ago.

Places to visit

- The Cyfartha Museum and Art Gallery near Merthyr Tydfil includes a display relating to the Merthyr Rising of 1831.

Further reading

William Cobbett, *Rural Rides* (1830).
Chris Aspin, *The First Industrial Society: Lancashire 1750–1850* (1995).

17: Slate Tiles

These reclaimed Penrhyn slate tiles are very popular today in house renovations and for ornamental use in gardens. However, their subtle markings and natural beauty belie the hard lives of the men who quarried and mined the product in North Wales during Britain's Industrial Revolution.

Slate quarrying in North Wales has a history stretching back over 1,800 years. Slates were used to build parts of the Roman fort in Segontium in Caernarfon, and in Edward I's castle at Conwy. When Britain's Industrial Revolution arrived in the eighteenth century, the slate industry rapidly expanded.

As small settlements such as Manchester exploded into large towns and then cities with the coming of mills and factories, there was an enormous demand for slates to roof the long terraces of houses built as homes for the workers – as well as the foundries and factories themselves. Produced as thicker slab, slate had a wider variety of uses including flooring, worktops and headstones.

In 1787, the 'Great New Quarry' of Dinorwig opened on the slopes between the present village of Dinorwig and Llyn Peris lake. By the 1870s, it employed over 3,000 men. The most important slate-producing areas were in north-west Wales, and included the Penrhyn Quarry near Bethesda, the Nantlle Valley quarries, and Blaenau Ffestiniog, where the slate was mined rather than quarried. Penrhyn and Dinorwig were the two largest slate quarries in the world, and the Oakeley mine at Blaenau Ffestiniog was the world's largest slate mine. Slate had become one of Wales's most important industries.

Prior to Britain's Industrial Revolution, slate had been extracted on a small scale by groups of quarrymen who paid a royalty to the landlord, carted slate to the ports, and then shipped it around north-western Europe. Towards the

Reclaimed Penrhyn slate. (*Anne-Lise Heinrichs/Creative Commons*)

close of the eighteenth century, the landowners began to operate the quarries themselves on a larger scale.

The first steam engine to be used in the slate industry was for a pump installed at the Hafodlas Quarry in the Nantlle Valley in 1807, but most quarries relied on water power to drive machinery. One important milestone in the development of the industry came in 1831, when the government abolished slate duty. The coming of the railways also aided rapid industrial expansion, with special narrow-gauge lines laid to transport slate from quarries and mines to the ports and thence to other parts of Britain, the European continent and the USA.

The world-famous Ffestiniog line, constructed between 1833 and 1836, transported slate from Blaenau Ffestiniog to the coastal town of Porthmadog, where it was loaded onto ships. The railway was graded so that loaded slate wagons

Loading slates into slate wagons, Penrhyn Quarry, *c*.1913. Picture featured in The Penrhyn Quarry, 1913. (*Rhion Pritchard/Creative Commons*)

could be run by gravity downhill all the way from Blaenau Ffestiniog to the port. The empty wagons were hauled back up by horses, which travelled down in 'dandy' wagons.

The gradual introduction of mechanisation made most aspects of the industry more efficient. In 1859, John Whitehead Greaves invented the Greaves sawing table to produce blocks for the splitter, then, in 1856, introduced a rotary machine to dress the split slate. The splitting of the blocks to produce roofing slates proved resistant to mechanisation and production with a mallet and chisel continued. From the 1860s, further uses were found for the thicker slab pieces of slate, including flooring, tombstones and billiard tables.

Wales produced over four fifths of all British slates in this period, with Caernarfonshire the biggest producer among all Welsh counties. In 1898, the slate trade in Wales as a whole reached its peak, with 17,000 men producing 485,000 tons of slate. Quarrymen would work the slate in gangs of between three and eight members. A gang of four would typically consist of two rockmen who would blast the rock to produce blocks, a splitter, who would split the blocks with hammer and chisel, and a dresser. Other roles were the bad rockmen, who usually worked in crews of three, removing unworkable rock from the face, and the rubbish men, who cleared waste rock from the galleries and built the tips of waste that surrounded the quarry.

Like many industries of the later period of Britain's Industrial Revolution, egregious working conditions led to industrial disputes. The North Wales Quarrymen's Union (NWQMU) was formed in 1874, and the same year there were disputes at Dinorwig and then at Penrhyn, both ending in victory for the workers. One of the founders of the union, Morgan Richards, described in 1876 the conditions when he started work in the quarries forty years before:

I well remember the time when I was myself a child of bondage; when my father and neighbours, as well as myself, had to rise early, to walk five miles before six in the morning, and the same distance home after six in the evening; to work hard from six to six; to dine on cold coffee, or a cup of buttermilk, and a slice of bread and butter; and to support (as some of them had to do) a family of perhaps five, eight or ten children on wages averaging from 12*s* to 16*s* a week.

The Anglesey Barracks, Dinorwig Quarry, Gwynedd. Quarry workers would sleep there during the week before walking home to their families on a Sunday. (*Rhion Pritchard/Creative Commons*)

Cultural differences between management and workers made the situation worse. The owners and top managers at most of the quarries were English-speaking, Anglican and Tory, while the quarrymen were Welsh-speaking and mainly Nonconformist and Liberal.

One such period of strife, at the Penrhyn Quarry between 1900 and 1903, marked the beginning of the industry's decline. A three-year strike began on 22 November 1900. The union's funds for strike pay were inadequate, and there was a great deal of hardship among the 2,800 workers. Lord Penrhyn reopened the quarry in June 1901, and about 500 men returned to work, causing ill feeling in the working community. Eventually, the workers were forced to return to work in November 1903 on terms laid down by Lord Penrhyn. A number of the men considered to have been prominent in the union were not re-employed, and many of those who had left the area to seek work elsewhere did not return. The dispute left a lasting legacy of bitterness in the Bethesda area. The importation of slate from abroad marked the beginning of the end for this iconic Welsh industry.

Places to visit

- The National Slate Museum resides in some of the buildings of the old Dinorwig Quarry near Llanberis. The museum's displays include Victorian slate-workers' cottages that once stood at Tanygrisiau near Blaenau Ffestiniog.
- In Blaenau Ffestiniog, the Llechwedd Slate Caverns have been converted into a visitor attraction. Visitors can travel on the Miners' Tramway or descend into the Deep Mine, via a funicular railway.
- In July 2021, UNESCO inscribed the slate landscape of north-western Wales as a World Heritage Site. A drive or walk through the area reveals some sublime landscapes.

Further reading

David Gwyn, *Welsh Slate: Archaeology and History of an Industry* (2015).
John Idris Jones, *Slate, Sail and Steam: A History of the Industries of Porthmadog* (2016).
Ivor Wynne Jones, *Victorian Slate Mining* (2003).

18: Josiah Wedgwood Receipt

This receipt, issued on 30 June 1770, records several items of pottery bought from Josiah Wedgwood by the Right Honourable Lady Winterton.

Amongst the goods purchased were: '4 oval baskets and stands, 1 round ditto, 2 round… sugar bowls, 2 oblong composites, 4 oval ditto, 2 dozen plates. Returned a pair pebble gilt candlestick vases'.

Wedgwood had opened his Etruria Works the previous year. The factory was built on land that he knew lay on the proposed route of the Trent and Mersey Canal, which opened in 1777. Indeed, Wedgwood was a major investor in the canal, which was crucial for the importation of raw materials such as clay and stone, and the export of finished wares. The site was close to local collieries, which supplied the huge quantities of coal needed to fire and power the steam engines. The name of the factory was inspired by the Italian district of Etruria, where there were ongoing excavations of porcelain dating back to the time of the Etruscans. Behind the façade lay several courtyards with ovens and kilns. Wedgwood also built a village for his workers for their mutual benefit.

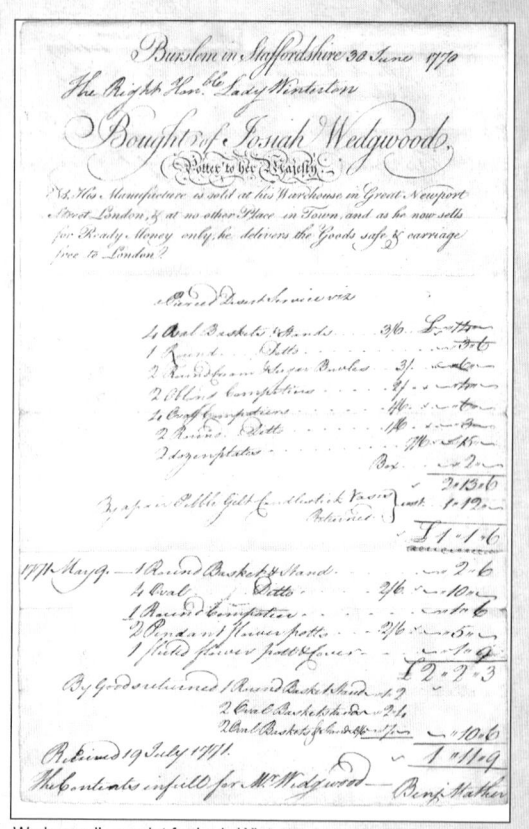

Wedgwood's receipt for Lady Winterton.

> His manufacture is sold at his warehouse in Great Newport Street London & at no other place in town, as he now sells for ready money only he delivers the good safe of carriage free to London.

Born at Burslem, Stoke-on-Trent, in 1730, Wedgwood was the eleventh and final child of a potter. His maternal grandfather was a Nonconformist Unitarian minister and Josiah would continue to follow this interpretation of the Christian faith for the remainder of his life. With a pottering lineage stretching back over four previous generations, he had founded his company in 1759, having served an apprenticeship under his eldest brother, Thomas. A bout of childhood smallpox left Josiah with a permanently weak knee. (In 1768, he had to have his right leg amputated because of ongoing complications from his childhood illness.) Unable to operate a potter's wheel, he turned his focus to design, leaving others to do the manufacturing. At the time, the family's pottery business produced cheap and low-quality products.

Josiah Wedgwood by Joshua Reynolds.

Wedgwood leased the Ivy Works in Burslem and, in partnership with Thomas Bentley, utilised the new science of chemistry to improve the use of fire, clay and glazing. Blessed with an injection of capital from a favourable marriage, he was able to transform the works into the first pottery factory. Chiming in with the renewed interest in classical Greek and Roman civilisation in the late 1760s and early 1770s, Wedgwood's expensive goods were in great demand from the upper classes. His customers included Queen Charlotte, who allowed him to name the line she purchased 'Queen's Ware'. He also produced cheaper goods that were within affordable reach of most ordinary people. He used transfer printing, which gave similar effects to hand painting for a fraction of the cost. His unique glazes exceeded the quality of anything else on the market. He began to export his pottery in 1764.

Wedgwood was adept at marketing his wares, opening showrooms in London to give the public the chance to see his complete range of earthenware and stoneware, which were considerably cheaper than their porcelain equivalents. Firstly situated in Great Newport Street and then in St James's Square, the showrooms became one of the most fashionable meeting places in London and Wedgwood quickly established similar venues in Bath, Liverpool and Dublin in addition to the one he already had at Etruria. He realised the marketing potential of gradually releasing his new goods onto the market, so each item in turn was given the time to be the star attraction.

In 1773, he published the first Ornamental Catalogue, to increase awareness of, and demand for, his goods. The same year, Catherine the Great of Russia ordered a 952-piece hand-painted green Frog Service from the company. The canny entrepreneur ensured that the set was on public display before it was shipped to Russia, with crowds thronging to catch a glimpse of it. The £2,700 that the empress paid for it did not represent good business in isolation for Wedgwood's but the publicity it brought was invaluable.

By 1784, the Etruria Works was exporting 80 per cent of its produce. Wedgwood employed clerks fluent in French, German, Italian and Dutch so customers from those countries would

Plate from La Grenouillière (Frog Marsh) service for Catherine II of Russia – Wedgwood, 1774, creamware.

have their letters answered in their native tongue. He is credited as a pioneer of modern marketing, using direct mail, money-back guarantees, travelling salesmen carrying pattern boxes for display, self-service, free delivery, buy one get one free, and illustrated catalogues. In doing so, he met the demands of the consumer revolution and growth in wealth of the middle classes that helped drive the Industrial Revolution in Britain. He was feted by William Gladstone as 'the greatest man who ever, in any age or country, applied himself to the important work of uniting art with industry'. He was a member of the Lunar Society, which met at the house of his close friend Erasmus Darwin, in Birmingham. A keen slavery abolitionist, Wedgwood also produced several *Am I Not a Man and a Brother* anti-slavery medallions, which was a design copied onto a range of campaigning souvenirs, including clay pipes (*see* chapter 40).

Wedgwood died at home in 1795. He was buried at the entrance of St Peter ad Vincula Church, Stoke-on-Trent, as he was not a member of the Church of England. His company maintained production at Etruria until the 1940s. Sadly, the original factory buildings were demolished in the 1960s, with only one structure, a roundhouse, remaining. Historians are unsure as to whether it was used as a storeroom, a counting house or stables, or for grinding raw materials.

Places to visit

- The Victoria and Albert Museum Wedgwood Collection is on permanent display at the Wedgwood Museum and Visitor Centre at Barlaston, Stoke-on-Trent. It comprises over 165,000 works of art, ceramics, manuscripts and photographs charting the factory's history, design and ceramic production.
- A blue plaque, attached to 12 Greek Street, London, site of the old Wedgwood Mews showrooms, is in the distinctive Wedgwood blue pottery style.
- Wedgwood's grave is now within the grounds of Stoke Minster.

Further reading

Anthony Burton, *Josiah Wedgwood: A New Biography* (2020).
Brian Dolan, *Josiah Wedgwood: Entrepreneur to the Enlightenment* (2004).
Robin Reilly, *Josiah Wedgwood 1730–1795* (1992).

19: Brixham Trawler

This painting, by renowned maritime artist William Adolphus Knell, shows a Brixham trawler, one of 400 such vessels that worked out of the eponymous South Devon port. By the early decades of the nineteenth century, the town's fishermen needed to expand their range further than the overfished waters of South Devon. The solution was the Brixham trawler. Of sleek build, its tall gaff rig gave the boat sufficient speed to make long-distance trips out into the Atlantic Ocean. The trawler was robust enough to tow large trawls of fish in deep water and gave Brixham the title of 'Mother of Deep-Sea Fisheries'.

The Brixham trawler made large-scale trawl fishing in the oceans and seas around Britain possible for the first time. A mass migration of fishermen and their families took place from the south of England to east coast fishing ports such as Scarborough, Hull, Grimsby, Harwich and Yarmouth. The song *Scarborough Fair* relates to the herring catch that took place each August as huge shoals of the fish swam along the east coast.

The Lincolnshire village of Grimsby grew to become the largest fishing port in the world by the mid-nineteenth century. A 1796 Act of Parliament had authorised the dredging of the haven and construction of new quays, but it was only in 1846, with the formation of the Grimsby Dock Company and the advent of the Brixham trawler, that the port's expansion developed apace. It fell to Prince Albert, ever the supporter of innovation, to lay the foundation stone of Grimsby's Royal Dock in 1849, which was opened by his wife, Queen Victoria, five years later.

The dock gates and cranes operated by hydraulic power, a contemporary innovation. Grimsby's fishing dock complex grew, as did that of Kingston upon Hull, across the Humber estuary in the East Riding of Yorkshire. A direct rail line was built between Grimsby and the Billingsgate Fish Market in London, creating a national market for fresh Grimsby fish.

One consequence of the Industrial Revolution was that fishermen became much more effective

A Brixham Trawler, by William Adolphus Knell.

Hull trawler *Socrates*, early 1900s. (clydeships.co.uk/Fog Horn)

The earliest steam-powered fishing boats first appeared in the 1870s using the trawl system of fishing as well as lines and drift nets. They were large boats, up to 90 feet in length with a beam of about 20 feet and could travel up to 11 knots.

Steam fishing boats had many advantages. They were usually about 20 feet longer (6.1m) than the sailing vessels so they could carry more nets and catch more fish. They could travel faster and further and with greater freedom from weather, wind and tide. As less time was spent travelling to and returning from the fishing grounds, more time could be spent catching fish. The steamboats also gained the highest prices for their fish, as they could return quickly to harbour with their fresh catch. Steam trawlers were introduced at Grimsby and Hull in the 1880s, and by 1890, an estimated 20,000 men were fishing the North Sea.

Hull fishermen trawled in the Silver Pits area, about 30 miles east of Spurn Point. Between 1854 and 1887, over 1,000 fishing smacks were registered in the Yorkshire town, as it saw an influx of fishermen from around the country. The development of the fishing industry in the late nineteenth century both revolutionised the leading towns from which the trawlers sailed and offered the choice of healthy, fresh sea fish to the diets of those who could afford to taste what the sea brought forth.

and efficient. Nowhere was this change in situation more evident than in the North Sea, which the British trawler fleet came to dominate during the latter part of the nineteenth century. Much of modern fisheries policy can be traced back to this period and this area. By the end of the nineteenth century there were over 3,000 fishing trawlers working British waters – nearly 1,000 of them registered in Grimsby.

Despite the dominance of the Brixham trawler, other types of vessel also fished the waters around Britain. The Lancashire nobby worked the north-western coast of England as a shrimp trawler from 1840 onwards. The Manx nobby trawled around the Isle of Man as a herring drifter. The fifie was also used as a herring drifter along the east coast of Scotland from the 1850s. The bawley and the smack were used in the Thames Estuary and off East Anglia.

Places to visit

- The Scarborough Maritime Heritage Centre has many artefacts telling the tale of the town's fishing history.
- The Hull Maritime Museum contains a range of ship models and maritime art. Located in the town's impressive Victorian Dock Offices, the author spent many happy childhood hours immersing himself in his adopted city's past.
- The Grimsby Fishing Heritage Centre tells the story of the town's prominent fishing industry.

Further reading

Arthur Credland, *Fishing from the Humber: Images of England* (2002).
Edgar B. March, *Sailing Trawlers* (1970).
Mike Smylie, *The Fishing Boats Story* (2017).

20: The Turnip

From the Middle Ages, the farming of land in English villages involved a system of three-year strip rotation of crops. Peasants would work the land, often across three fields, split into separate strips. Those who had the right to be allocated strips would meet annually to divide the land up for the following year.

Of the three fields, typically a different crop would be grown in two of them on a rotation system – wheat or rye in one and oats, barley or peas in the other. Each year, one field was left fallow in order for the soil to regain the nutrients used up by two consecutive years of cultivation. In these days before artificial fertilisers, without crop rotation the nutrient level in each field would decline, decreasing crop yields over time. An area of common land would also be set aside where peasants could graze their animals.

In the centuries before the great Agricultural Revolution, increasing amounts of land were being enclosed, meaning that a fence or hedge surrounded a field. Enclosed fields usually had one owner rather than being communally farmed, and were not subdivided into strips. The increase in profits from the wool trade during the Late Middle Ages resulted in the enclosing of more land for grazing sheep.

Charles, 2nd Viscount Townshend, succeeded to his title in 1687, also inheriting estates at Raynham in Norfolk. Townshend was a skilled politician who rose to the position of Secretary of State in the reign of George I. After retiring from politics, he turned his attention to his land. He practised a type of crop rotation in use in Holland that involved a four-year cycle and the use of turnips and clover as two of the rotated crops. Turnips had been grown in East Anglia since the 1660s for winter cattle feed. Townshend sought to expand their use in this form of four-course crop rotation.

The humble but revolutionary turnip. Eighteenth-century etching by M. Bouchard. (*Wellcome Collection*)

Wheat would be grown in one field, clover or ryegrass in the second, oats and barley in the third, and turnips or swedes in the fourth. Clover added nitrogen compounds to the soil through its root nodules. More nutritious than grass, clover was ideal for grazing livestock. In turn, the livestock produced manure, which was ploughed back into the soil.

Townshend's popularisation of turnips, as well as earning him the soubriquet 'Turnip Townshend', also meant the end of the fallow field and an increase in winter fodder crops for the sustenance of animals. His efforts revolutionised animal husbandry and he was often keen to

Viscount Townshend. (*National Portrait Gallery/Wikimedia Commons/Public domain*)

extol the virtues of his investigations. The poet Alexander Pope said rather drily of him: 'he was particularly fond of that kind of rural improvement which arises from Turnips; it was the favourite subject of his conversation.'

His development of new methods of agriculture made large, enclosed farms even more profitable. Wheat exports increased from 11.5 million quarters in 1705 to 95 million quarters by 1765. No longer was it necessary to slaughter livestock before the onset of winter, thus it became possible to breed in greater numbers, and the quality of meat and other products yielded improved.

Between 1700 and 1845, enclosure swept England, with 600,000 acres taken out of collective ownership and divided into private holdings. Furthermore, the common land was enclosed, removing communal grazing rights. This forced many peasants off the land as they were unable to provide documents proving their right to hold any property. Others were allocated smallholdings that were too small to make a living from. Many quickly sold up to larger landowners. Homelessness, poverty and begging to survive increased.

Places to visit

- Laxton in Nottinghamshire is the only remaining village in England that still uses the old three-course open-field system. The three open fields, divided into strips farmed by tenants of the Laxton estate, are still managed today by a jury reporting to the manorial Court Leet. A village visitor and heritage centre can be found in the grounds of The Dovecote public house. It has displays showing the history of the open-field system, aerial shots of the village, a description of how the system operates and suggestions as to why it still exists in Laxton.
- Raynham Hall in Norfolk, where Viscount Townshend finessed his agricultural innovations, hosts a variety of cultural events. It also contains glamping pods in the grounds that are available for hire.

Further reading

Susanna Wade Martins, *'Turnip' Townshend: Statesman and Farmer* (1990).
Mark Overton, *Agricultural Revolution in England: The Transformation of the Agrarian Economy 1500–1850* (1996).

21: Leicester Longwool Sheep

This Leicester Longwool sheep, quietly contemplating life in the shade of a tree, can be traced back in lineage over 250 years to the animals selectively bred by British agriculturalist Robert Bakewell in the eighteenth century.

Bakewell introduced stockbreeding methods that transformed the quality of Britain's cattle, horses and sheep. He was born at Dishley Grange near Loughborough in Leicestershire in 1725 into a family of tenant farmers. As a young man, Bakewell travelled extensively throughout Britain and Europe, learning about other farming methods. On his return home, having served his apprenticeship under his father, he assumed control of the farm in 1760 on his father's death.

One quarter of the farm was given over to arable farming, with the rest set aside for grass. Bakewell pioneered grassland irrigation, diverting rivers and building canals to flood the fields, and establishing experimental plots to test different manure and flooding methods. However, his great innovation, one that meant he appeared in generations of school textbooks covering the period of Britain's Industrial Revolution, was to begin breeding 'in-and-in'.

Previously, livestock of both sexes were kept together in the fields, breeding randomly. The result was several hybrid breeds with their own unique, but random, characteristics. Bakewell separated males from females, allowing mating only deliberately and specifically between selected livestock. By inbreeding his livestock, he was able to accentuate traits he thought were desirable, such as the quality and thickness of the fleece, and the amount of meat the animal produced. His New Leicester sheep were noted for their size, fine bones and long, lustrous wool.

(Glenn Brunette/Creative Commons)

They were bred by selectively using the Lincoln Longwool breed, a hornless sheep with a square, meaty body and straight top lines, and the best of locally available Leicestershire sheep. They possessed fatty forequarters, in keeping with the popular contemporary taste for fatty shoulder mutton.

Bakewell was also an innovator in the breeding of cattle primarily for beef. He crossed long-horned heifers and a Westmorland bull, eventually creating the Dishley Longhorn. Several farmers followed his lead and between 1700 and 1786, the average weight of a bull sold for slaughter more than doubled, from 370 pounds to 840 pounds.

Bakewell hired out his rams to farmers in surrounding counties. He started in 1760, hiring at 17*s* 6*d* per ram; by 1786, he let twenty rams for 1,000 guineas, and this rose to 1,200 guineas for just three rams in 1789, the equivalent of £90,000 today.

In 1783, Bakewell formed The Dishley Society, to protect the integrity of his breeds, which were by now being used by contemporary agriculturalists such as Thomas Coke, 1st Earl of Leicester. Dishley Society members were bound by a set of rules designed to maintain the purity of the breed. On Bakewell's death in 1795, twelve of his neighbours formed themselves into the Bakewell Club and bought up his sheep with the intention of maintaining them.

Bakewell's New Leicester sheep were exported widely, including to Australia and North America, and succeeding generations of farmers have used their bloodline to develop new breeds to keep pace with changing market preferences for meat and textiles. In the UK, the bloodlines of Bakewell's sheep survive in the English Leicester, or Leicester Longwool, breed. His methods were copied by farmers rearing cattle and horses. Charles Darwin, in his *On the Origin of Species* (1859), cited Bakewell's work as evidence of how evolutionary processes worked. Two distinct varieties of sheep, kept by two different farmers who had practised selective breeding, had been bred from the same Bakewell sheep ancestors over a fifty-year period.

Registered flocks of sheep whose direct lineage can be traced back to Bakewell's sheep are now found in all parts of the British Isles, as well as countries as diverse as Australia, New Zealand, South Africa, France, Spain, Portugal, Canada, USA, Colombia, British Guiana, India, Japan, Iran, Hungary, Russia, China, Turkey and Switzerland. However, fewer than 500 registered breeding Leicester Longwool ewes remain in the United Kingdom.

Places to visit

- Melton Mowbray Livestock Auctions. In late 2019, the New Dishley Society presented an engraved plaque representing the work of Robert Bakewell. The plaque sits near the café area and there are storyboards detailing his achievements.

Further reading

Pat Stanley, *Robert Bakewell and the Longhorn Breed of Cattle* (2015).

22: Jethro Tull's Seed Drill

This wheeled wooden frame, constructed of elm wood, was a key invention which enabled the more efficient planting of crops, and thus for an increase in food production that was needed to feed the growing British population. The seed drill allowed for a semi-automated and controlled distribution and plantation of wheat seed.

It was designed by agricultural improver Jethro Tull in 1701 and became the progenitor of many other mechanised planters and ploughs, the principles of which are still used in several of today's agricultural tools and vehicles. This scale model was made from information recorded in one of Tull's later publications.

This horse-drawn seed drill worked by carving three channels into the soil then dropping seeds held in containers at regular intervals. A harrow, or trailing bar, then gathered soil and evenly spread it back over the channels. The drill included a hopper to store the seed, a cylinder to move it and a funnel to direct it. At the front, a plough created the row. The drill represented a major step towards the mechanisation of crop cultivation. The principle of operation depended upon a toothed portion of the wheel shaft, which rotated against a spring-held tongue, releasing the seed at regular intervals as the drill moved forward. The seeds were then directed by guides

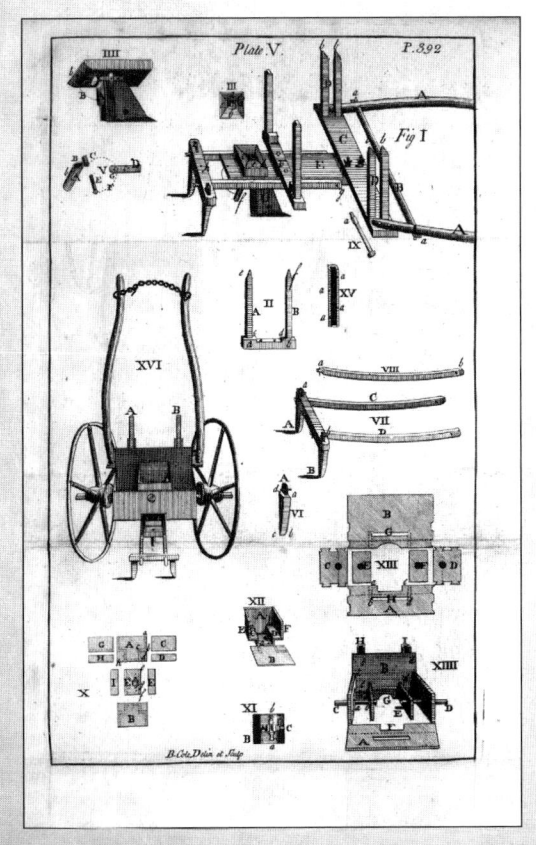

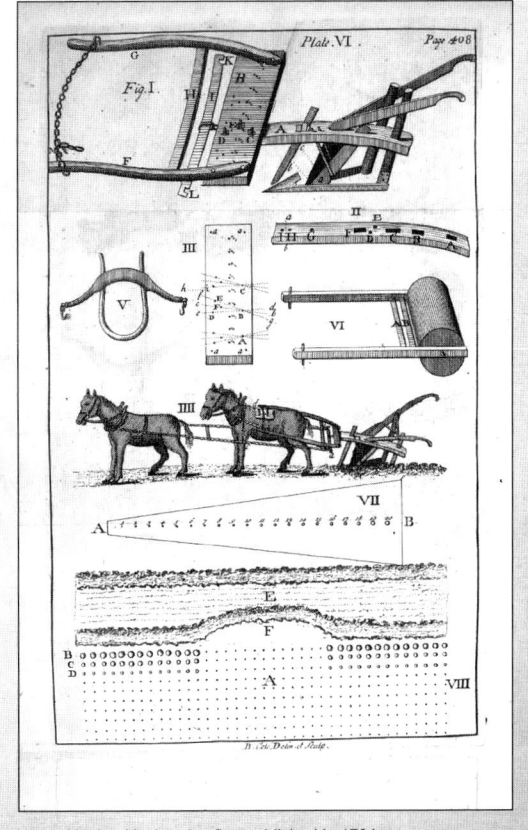

Diagram and scale model of a seed drill, taken from an edition of Tull's *Horse-Hoeing Husbandry*, first published in 1731.

attached to the shares, which cut channels in the soil. The spacing of the seeds was controlled by the number of teeth around the wheel shaft.

Jethro Tull had been born in 1674 into a comfortable life. His parents held an estate in Berkshire. Having gained a place at St John's College, Oxford, he withdrew from the university to move to London, where he studied the pipe organ before becoming a law student at Gray's Inn. He qualified as a barrister in 1699 before embarking on a tour of Europe to find a cure for a pulmonary disorder from which he was suffering. During his time on the Continent, he studied agrarian practices, including pulverising soil before planting and ensuring seeds were evenly spaced.

Returning to England, Tull turned his back on the legal profession and settled down to work on his family's Berkshire estate. At the time, seeds were thrown into furrows by hand (broadcasting), or were planted individually. Tull had noted these inefficiencies and instructed his staff to drill at very precise, low densities. His desire for greater efficiency was stimulated by intellectual curiosity and the fact that the cost of seeds had recently more than doubled. Frustrated by his staff's lack of co-operation, he developed the seed drill, which limited the wastage of seeding and made the crop easier to weed.

Tull's invention was the first agricultural machine with moving parts. Early iterations were driven by one person before the three-row machine was developed. Wheels were added along with the facility to have it pulled by horsepower. Initially, Tull met with limited success. In 1709, he moved to Prosperous Farm in Hungerford, and two years later decided to return to Europe, once again to improve his health as well as for further study on alternative agricultural techniques.

Returning to Berkshire in 1714, Tull made adaptations to both his system and machinery. He pulverised the earth between the rows,

Jethro Tull.

believing that the released nutrients would act as a substitute for manure. What this did enable was the removal of weeds, allowing for wheat to be grown in the same field for thirteen successive years without a fallow period or the application of manure.

Jethro Tull went on to make more groundbreaking inventions. His horse-drawn hoe dug up the soil, loosening it for planting while also pulling up unwanted weed and grass roots. Prosperous Farm thrived, with less seed waste, better plant aeration and less weed growth all serving to increase his yields.

Flushed with success with his own farming ventures, Tull sought to publicise his innovations in his book *The New Horse-Hoeing Husbandry: Or, an Essay on the Principles of Tillage and Vegetation*, published in 1731, in which he argued for the application of scientific method to farming, although mistakenly asserting that manure did not help plants to grow. The book caused great controversy, and arguments continued for another century before his eventual vindication. Tull's complete arable farming system was a major influence on the agricultural revolution and its impact influences farming techniques to this day.

Places to visit

- Prosperous Farm, near Hungerford, still exists. By sticking to public footpaths close to the farm, you can look across the landscape on which Tull's innovations were practised.
- The Science Museum in South Kensington contains a replica model of Tull's original seed drill and a 1955 painting by Alfred Thomson of Tull demonstrating it. Check before visiting that the items are currently on display.

Further reading

George F. Tull & Maisie Robson, *Jethro Tull: A Berkshire Life* (2012).
G.E. Fussell, *Jethro Tull: His Influence on Mechanized Agriculture* (1973).

23: Threshing Machine

Invented at the end of the eighteenth century, the threshing machine played a central role in changing agricultural practices and reshaping landowner and labourer relationships during the nineteenth century. Threshing machines separate grain from stalks and husks, thus improving the mechanisation of agriculture. They drastically reduced the amount of human labour needed to harvest and process grain yield.

Previously, grain was threshed with a flail – a wooden staff with a shorter swinging stick attached. The flail needed intensive labour and was time-consuming. It also incurred wastage as some of the grain and chaff became damaged. Although hugely efficient and profitable for those who owned them, the threshing machine became a hated object as it symbolised a lost way of life, and indeed, lost livelihoods (*see* chapter 50 on the Swing Riots).

The creation of the threshing machine is largely attributed to Andrew Meikle in 1786. Born in Saltoun, Haddingtonshire in 1719, Meikle was a country millwright. His machine used fluted rollers to feed sheaves of corn to a rotating drum, which beat the corn against a curved concave casing. The ears of corn and the chaff fell through a grate while the straw continued horizontally out of the drum casing. Meikle's father, James, also a millwright, had invented a mechanical fan that separated the ears from the chaff.

Horsepower and water power drove the first threshers, but later models were steam-powered. In 1797, William Spicer Dix, a brewer and landowner, urged farmers to adopt the threshing

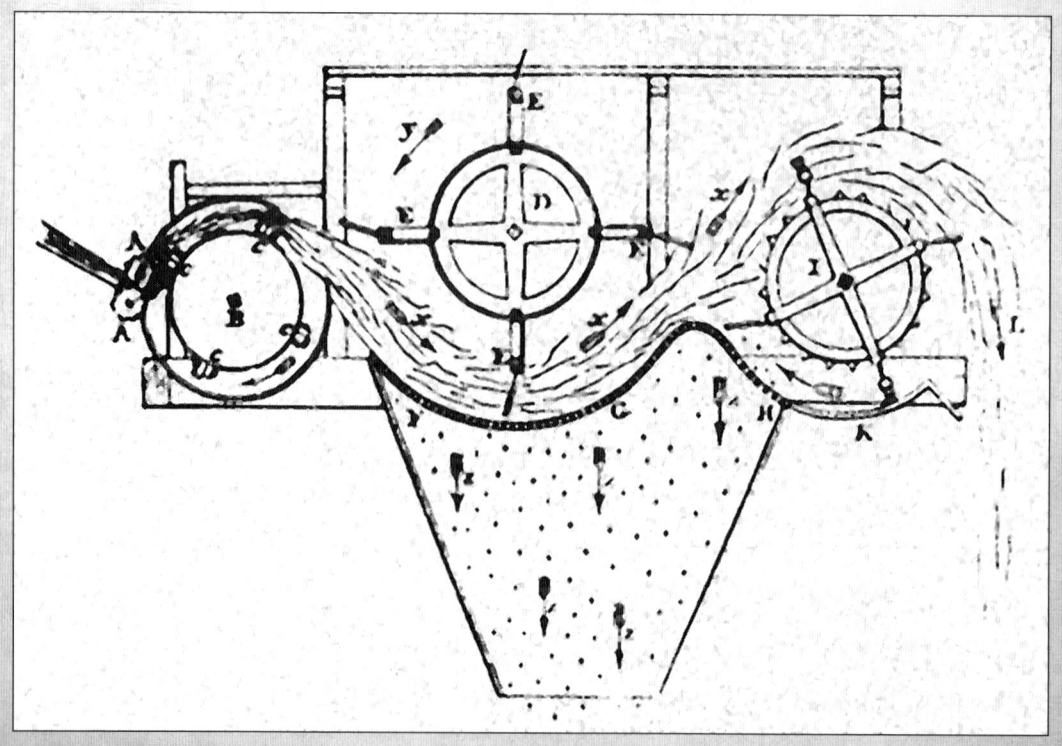

Diagram of the inner workings of Meikle's threshing machine.

23: THRESHING MACHINE

machine: 'By this Machine one man, or a woman, can clear as much grain in one day, as can be done with the flail in ten days, without bruising, injuring, or leaving any ears.'

Dix reckoned that by investing in this new technology, farmers could expect a tenfold increase in productivity, declaring:

> I trust it will be allowed that clearing corn from the ears by friction, ... clearing ten times more in a day than any man can thresh with the flail, of preserving the reed unhurt, is not only the most effectual method, but it is also the most advantageous to the farmers, since by this using this machine ... they will be able to carry to market nearly every grain grown on their farms.

He also claimed that the threshing machine would help feed many more people. At the time, Thomas Malthus, in *An Essay on the Principle of Population* (1798), was arguing that population growth was about to outpace the country's ability to meet the resource needs of the people. Dix maintained that widespread use of the threshing machine would eliminate the catastrophic cyclical famines and diseases that Malthus prophesised would come from rapid population growth.

> If, by introducing this Machine to the world, and recommended the methods here laid down to be practiced by the farmers, to enable them annually such an immense quantity of corn, I should be fortunate as to see it universally adopted, I shall think myself happy in having been of home service to my country.

By 1789, Meikle was offering his threshing machines for sale and, over ensuing years, other inventions made improvements to its effectiveness.

Use of the threshing machine quickly spread. Labour shortages caused by the Napoleonic Wars were overcome and by 1830, it is estimated there were over a thousand threshing machines in use in central and southern England. By 1880, steam had become the predominant source of power in farming, although only the wealthiest of farmers and landowners could afford to own a steam-

Andrew Meikle.

driven thresher. Smaller landowners would hire a machine from a firm, which would also send along a specialist technician to operate it.

Andrew Meikle died in 1811 at the grand age of 92. Today, every combine harvester incorporates a threshing machine that has its origins in his 1786 prototype. In 2011, Meikle was one of seven inaugural inductees into the Scottish Engineering Hall of Fame.

Places to visit

- The National Museum of Rural Life in East Kilbride contains examples of early threshing machines.
- The Museum of Rural Life based at the University of Reading provides a broad and detailed overview of technological and social changes during the Agricultural Revolution.

Further reading

Gordon E. Mingay, *Agricultural Revolution: Changes in Agriculture, 1650–1880* (1977).
Mark Overton, *Agricultural Revolution in England: The Transformation of the Agrarian Economy 1500–1850* (1996).

Section Two

Travelling, Transporting and Trading

24: Turnpike Toll Board

This toll board, which currently stands on the road between New Mill and Honley in West Yorkshire, gives the cost of being allowed to pass through the turnpike gate that once stood on the Smithy Place junction. Different tolls were charged for carriages, carts, horses and other animals and were listed in detail on the board, which was originally erected by the New Mill District Turnpike Trust.

From 1663 to 1836, the collection of tolls from travellers facilitated the improvement of many British roads. Tollhouses were built beside barriers across the road, known as turnpikes, at which travellers had to pause to pay a toll, the amount charged depending on the nature of his or her traffic. The term 'turnpike' derives from a defensive frame of pikes that could be turned to allow passage of horses. By the time of Britain's Industrial Revolution, it had come to mean a gate set across the road to stop carts until a toll was paid.

By 1780, a comprehensive network of reliable major roads linked major centres of population across Britain. This marked an advance from the days when each parish would be responsible for the maintenance of the roads within its boundaries. Now, the priority was long-distance commercial traffic, with one sixth of English roads being turnpiked. The creation of a system of well-maintained roads was one of the major achievements of the early phase of Britain's Industrial Revolution. These highways allowed the rapid and efficient transportation of goods and passengers throughout the land, reducing travelling costs.

Turnpike roads had to be approved by a Private Act of Parliament. A body of local trustees, having been granted an Act of Parliament to build a new turnpike road, had the power to levy tolls on the users of a specified stretch of road, generally around 20 miles in length. Some of this revenue would then be used to maintain and improve that stretch of road, with further profit going to investors and shareholders. Although the powers under an Act were limited to a period of twenty-one years, in practice, Acts for continuation of the trusts meant that they remained responsible for most English trunk roads until the 1870s.

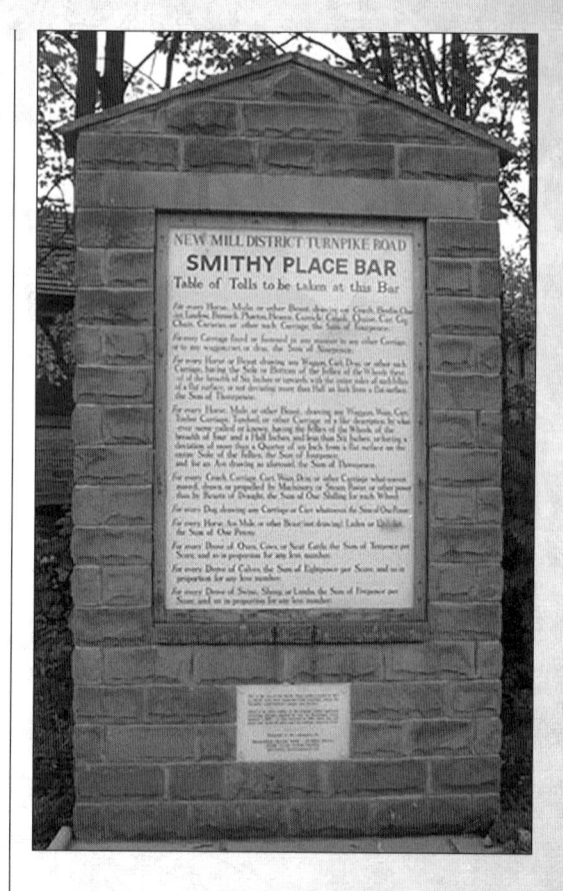

Amongst the improvements that the turnpike tolls invested in were drainage, gradients, width and running surface of existing highways as well as investment in new lengths of road to bypass poor sections, and the construction of embankments, cuttings and bridges.

Tollhouses were often built at points where it was least likely that vehicle or horse users could evade payment, for example at a bridge or

Penparcau tollhouse, St Fagans National History Museum, Cardiff. (*Dave Snowden/Creative Commons*)

crossroads. By the nineteenth century, a particular style was evolving of a single-storey cottage with a polygonal bay window so the tollkeeper could keep a watch of traffic approaching in either direction. Next to the tollhouse would be a stout and substantial gate, built to bar free passage along the road.

Better roads led to better vehicles, which horses pulled more efficiently and at much faster speeds. Although heavy goods were still conveyed more efficiently by water, road transport became the best means of carrying goods and people rapidly and safely between the booming towns of late eighteenth and early nineteenth-century England.

Not everyone viewed the turnpike roads and their tolls favourably. Between 1839 and 1844, a group of Welsh men and women who self-styled themselves Merched Beca ('Daughters of Rebecca') attacked and destroyed about 250 tollhouses and tollgates with axes. The rioters blackened their faces and wore women's clothes to avoid being recognised. The army was sent to stop the protesters, and several were arrested and jailed or transported to Australia.

At their peak in the 1830s, over 1,000 turnpike trusts administered about 30,000 miles of turnpike road in England and Wales, taking tolls at almost 8,000 toll gates. Such routes were profitable in the stagecoach era, but toll revenue declined sharply with the coming of the railways. Many of these tollhouses can still be seen on Britain's roads, frequently carrying names such as tollbar, toll cottage, roundhouse or paygate. Almost no gates still exist, but some examples of toll boards remain. Most turnpike trusts remained responsible for the maintenance of England's trunk roads until the 1870s. The trusts were dissolved in the subsequent two decades, when tollhouses were sold, gates torn down and responsibility for the main roads passed to Highway Boards. The 1888 Local Government Act assigned the entire maintenance of main roads to county councils.

Grange Road Bridge and Turnpike Gate, London, c.1820.

Places to visit

- The National Museum of Wales at St Fagans contains a tollhouse and gate built in 1771 that formerly stood near Aberystwyth. The building has just one room with a single fireplace.
- The crossing of the river Avon at Bathampton has a range of tolls needed to cross the Bathampton Toll Bridge. Built in 1872, towards the end of the turnpike era, the charges range from 50p for a motorcycle to £2 for a bus or coach.
- The Tolson Museum in Huddersfield has several items relating to the history of the turnpike era.

Further reading

Geoffrey Wright, *Turnpike Roads* (2008).
William Albert, *The Turnpike Road System in England: 1663–1840* (2007).

25: Canal Lock

This awe-inspiring run of sixteen locks – part of a total of twenty-nine locks on the Kennet and Avon Canal approaching Devizes – have a rise of 237 feet in 2 miles and take over five hours to traverse in a narrowboat. Designed by John Rennie, they form one of the Seven Wonders of the Canal System and are a testament to the engineering genius that helped build the transport infrastructure of Britain's Industrial Revolution.

The development of a vast network of canals across Britain during the eighteenth century meant that engineers faced the challenge of ensuring their man-made waterways could keep moving despite the undulations and contours of the natural landscape. The lock, which had been in use in Europe since the fourteenth century, was central to their work, making it possible for boats to climb the highest hills and mountains.

The inland waterways of Britain's Industrial Revolution were home to many different types of lock, many of which still exist. Single locks consist of one lock gate and are the most straightforward to use. Not only is it the quickest and simplest way to move the boat from one height to another but it is also the most economical use of water. Broad locks are double the width of a single or narrow lock, allowing one wide boat or two narrowboats to go through together. Double locks were designed to increase speed and avoid delays. Lock flights were often doubled by building them side by side. This type of lock saves water as more than one boat can go through at a time.

(Arpingstone/Creative Commons)

Bingley Five Rise Locks. (*Boerkevitz/Creative Commons*)

In Britain, the very first lock flight was built on the Sankey Canal in 1757, but the earliest of significant size was the ten-rise flight at Runcorn, which brought the Duke of Bridgewater's Canal down to the river Mersey and was constructed in 1773. The most awe-inspiring lock flight in Britain is the sixteen continuous locks at Caen Hill. Engineered by John Rennie, they solved the problem of climbing the final section of the 87-mile long Kennet and Avon Canal into Devizes.

Locks were the conduits that allowed the extensive canal network to flow during Britain's Industrial Revolution. Originally, stop locks controlled the flow between different canal companies' water. The move to ever-deeper coal mining and the expanding manufacture of heavy goods of iron and steel to delicate items such as pottery meant these commodities had to be transported across the country. The existing road network could not handle such cargo and the vehicles needed to move this produce did not exist. Canals were the answer to moving heavy and delicate objects over long distances.

Barges could transport nearly 40 tons of goods, far exceeding the capacity of packhorses or a horse and cart. However, not all parts of the country were served with navigable river systems. As the heartland of Britain's Industrial Revolution grew in the north and Midlands, canals became the preferred solution. The first purpose-built Industrial Revolution canal, the Sankey Canal, carried coal from St Helens to the river Mersey and the expanding port of Liverpool. Two years after it opened, in 1759 work started on the Bridgewater Canal. The canal's patron, the Duke of Bridgewater, sought a way to transport coal from his mines at Worsley into the centre of Manchester. Borrowing £25,000 to fund the project, he employed James Brindley to design the waterway, which included a series of tunnels as well as the remarkable Barton Aqueduct (*see* chapter 28).

The Duke's shrewd investment paid off and he was able to sell his coal in Manchester for half the previous price. This ushered in the era of Canal Mania, in which vast sums of money poured into canal construction. By 1774, over thirty-three government Acts had been passed providing for canals, all in the Midlands, where there were no comparative or realistic alternative means of water transport.

With the end of the American War of Independence in 1783, and a long run of good harvests, disposable income increased and with it came a rise in the number of people looking to invest their capital in businesses with which they had little personal association. The number of canal Acts of Parliament passed rose from one in 1790 to twenty in 1793. The amount of capital sunk into digging out channels and building up embankments rose from £90,000 to £2,824,700 (over £300 million at 2023 value). Many of these investments proved profitable, but some canals in more rural areas, such as the Herefordshire and Gloucestershire Canal, never paid a dividend. Others, such as the Grand Western Canal, planned to run through Somerset and

25: CANAL LOCK

Devon, were never completed. Nevertheless, by 1840, Britain's canal network extended to nearly 4,500 miles.

Canals opened up new markets for goods and allowed seaports to connect to inland trade. Canals allowed for the greater exploitation of coal reserves. Industries could now relocate to coalfields or move to towns, and the materials and products moved either way. Of over 150 canal Acts from 1760 to 1800, ninety were primarily for coal transportation. Canals also stimulated new ways of raising capital, as the majority were built as joint stock companies, with each having to apply for an Act of Parliament. The creation of canals created a new workforce, the navvies (*see* chapter 27), increasing spending power at a time when industry needed new markets and each canal needed people to load and unload.

Paradoxically, the canals' great success proved their undoing. The engineering expertise that developed to build embankments, cuttings and tunnels was subsequently utilised to construct Britain's railways. Unlike canals, railways could transport fresh produce before it had a chance to rot, were not liable to freezing in winter and running dry in summer, or subject to leakage.

Statue of James Brindley at Coventry Canal Basin. (Elliott Brown/Creative Commons)

Places to visit

- The Caen Hill Flight on the Kennet and Avon Canal in Wiltshire contains an impressive run of sixteen locks.
- Bingley Five Rise Locks is the steepest staircase of locks on the longest canal in the country – the Leeds and Liverpool Canal.
- The London Canal Museum, near King's Cross, has displays on canal construction, narrowboats, cargo and narrowboat families.

Further reading

John Sergeant & David Bartley, *Barging Round Britain: Exploring the History of our Nation's Canals and Waterways* (2016).
Stan Yorke & Trevor Yorke, *English Canals Explained: An Illustrated Guide to Waterways & How They Work* (2003).
Anthony Burton & Derek Pratt, *Britain's Canals: Exploring their Architectural and Engineering Wonders* (2020).

26: Narrowboat

Narrowboats were working boats that travelled the inland waterways that served as the arteries of Britain's Industrial Revolution. Until the second half of the eighteenth century, there was no standardisation of inland waterway craft, and, like the early railways with their different track gauges, boat size varied on the different river navigations around the country. Narrowboats were chiefly designed for carrying cargo, though some packet boats carried passengers, luggage, mail and parcels.

The first canals to feature locks in the now standard size were those designed by James Brindley and approved by Parliament in 1766, including the Staffordshire and Worcestershire Canal and the Trent and Mersey Canal. Although construction took many years, the lock size became standard for many canal-building projects.

It was the great canal engineer James Brindley who first proposed what is now the standard narrowboat size of 7 feet wide by about 70 feet long. When building the Trent and Mersey Canal he reached agreement with the proprietors to build locks that could accommodate boats of that size. The narrowness of the dimensions was partly influenced by the fact that costs needed to be kept down in the building of the Harecastle Tunnel between Kidsgrove and Tunstall – at 1.6 miles, then the longest in the country. The first canals to feature standard size locks that could hold a narrowboat were approved by Parliament in 1766. The Staffordshire and Worcestershire Canal also included such locks.

During the height of the canal boom, from the mid-eighteenth to the mid-nineteenth century, there were hundreds of companies operating narrowboats, transporting goods around the waterway system. Some traversed the country whilst others offered local services. The first examples were horse-drawn. They were made of

Horse-drawn cruising on the Montgomery Canal. (*Mike Fascione/CC BY-SA. 2.0*)

wood and most have now sadly rotted away or been broken up.

The long-distance boats were typically crewed by a man steering the boat and a boy leading the horse. The man would spend long periods on the boat whilst his family would live on land. However, as competition from the railways began to bite, it became economically unfeasible to keep a house. Therefore, whole families would often live on the boat, working as unpaid crew. This had the positive side effect of keeping families together.

The rear portion of the boat became the cabin. Crammed into the tiny space would be a warm stove and a steaming kettle as well as gleaming brass, fancy lace, painted housewares and decorated plates. The itinerant lifestyle of a boatman's family made it impossible for children to attend school. Most boat people were effectively illiterate and ostracised by those living on the bank. Some companies, including the Grand Junction Canal Company, were not keen on this practice and banned families from boarding boats on their waterways.

By the end of the nineteenth century, it was common to paint roses and castles on narrowboats and their fixtures and fittings. Ornate lettering would display the boat's name and owner. Boats often worked in pairs, known as butties, giving twice the living accommodation and twice the cargo-carrying capacity.

Towards the end of the nineteenth century, some companies began to introduce boats powered by steam engines. Fellows Morton & Clayton Ltd (FMC), who operated a large fleet of horse-drawn boats, used steam-powered boats from 1886, some of which converted from horse boats. Steamboats were used mostly on long-distance runs between London, Birmingham, Leicester and Nottingham. Like the railways, they worked 'fly' – non-stop day and night to a strict timetable.

Whilst the steamers could run relentlessly, unlike horse-drawn boats, they did have their

A narrowboat family in the early twentieth century.

disadvantages – the engine, boiler and coal to power the boat took up a large amount of the cargo space. More crew were needed to keep the engine firing; a pair would require seven men – four on the steamer and three on the butty. From 1906, FMC experimented with various gas engines and in 1912 fitted their first Bolinder (a Swedish engine) to narrowboat *Linda*.

Canals fell into decline after the First World War and many sections were filled in. However, today there is a thriving trade in narrowboat holidays. Groups of narrowboat enthusiasts ensure that inland waterway traditions are maintained as they ply their way up and down the canals and river navigations that made Britain's Industrial Revolution possible.

Places to visit

- The National Waterways Museum, Ellesmere Port, Cheshire. Sited at the northern end of the Shropshire Union Canal, the museum's collections include canal boats, traditional clothing, painted canal decorative ware and tools.
- The Canal Museum at Stoke Bruerne, Northamptonshire, occupies two floors of an historic corn mill. The country's first canal museum, it offers a fascinating insight into the rich waterway heritage of Stoke Bruerne and the Grand Union Canal and the people who lived and worked on them. Attractions include trips on a narrowboat.
- The Kennet & Avon Canal Museum in Devizes, Wiltshire, has a range of exhibits about the conception, design, usage and eventual commercial decline of the Kennet and Avon Canal, as well as its subsequent restoration.

Further reading

Tom Chaplin, *Narrow Boats* (2017).
L.T.C. Rolt, *Narrow Boat* (2014).
Julian Dutton, *Water Gypsies: A History of Life on Britain's Rivers and Canals* (2021).

27: Navvy's Pick and Shovel

This proud *Unknown Navvy*, commemorated in bronze and unveiled at Gerrards Cross Station in the early 1990s, carries on his back the tools of his trade – the pick and shovel. All around us, we can see the results of the labour undertaken by those modest tools. Every railway and canal embankment and cutting is testament to the backbreaking and dangerous work these men did to shape the landscape of Britain's Industrial Revolution.

The term 'navvy' is a shortened form of 'navigators', those who dug the first navigation canals in the eighteenth century. Railway navvies soon came to form a distinct group of their own, set apart by the special nature of their work. They were recruited from across Britain – especially Ireland, where the famine of the early 1840s created a massive incentive to seek a better life westwards in the USA or eastwards on the British mainland. Recent research suggests that about 30 per cent of nineteenth-century navvies in Britain were Irish immigrants.

The building of Britain's inland waterways and railways was very labour-intensive. It has been estimated that at the height of railway mania, one in every 100 people employed in Britain was a navvy – an army of 250,000 workers, a body of men larger than the British Army and Royal Navy combined. By 1850, they had already laid 3,000 miles of track.

The construction of Britain's railways was mainly undertaken by hand; tens of thousands of miles of tracks were landscaped and laid by men using picks, shovels and wheelbarrows. The work was physically taxing – a strong navvy could move 20 tons of earth per day – requiring a diet high in calories. Meal caravans would accompany gangs of navvies but the food was often of poor quality.

Due to the itinerant nature of their work, navvies usually lived in makeshift shanty towns. Huts made of rough turf and timber and situated close to the tunnel, embankment or cutting under construction, would typically accommodate twenty men, who paid 1½*d* per night for their bed. A place on the floor could be had for less – 1*d* for five nights. Shanty towns were usually insanitary and prone to outbreaks of typhus, cholera and dysentery. An episode of the Channel 4 archaeology programme *Time Team*, titled 'Blood, Sweat and Beers', excavated a shanty town that housed navvies who had built the Settle to Carlisle line, which demonstrated the relentless and dangerous existence they faced.

Navvies travelled from job to job. Many were single men but some had families who would move with them. Sometimes work would be suspended as navvies and their families left for better-paid seasonal work bringing in the later summer harvest. A navvy would often change his name when moving between jobs, especially if he

Unknown Navvy statue, Gerrards Cross Station, Buckinghamshire. (*Harry Mitchell/Creative Commons*)

Otley Navvy Memorial. (*John Broom*)

had left his previous employment under a cloud. This created a problem in case of injury or death, as his next of kin would be almost impossible to trace. In 1887, a campaign called for navvies to keep their real names and addresses on a piece of paper about their person, but few did so, being distrustful of the authorities.

Employers would frequently look for ways of decreasing a navvy's pay, issuing fines for drunkenness, laziness or belligerence. Pay was good compared to many of their contemporaries employed in factories – five shillings per day was not unusual. However, like the strategy employed by factory and mine owners who paid their workers in tokens only redeemable at a shop owned by them, the railway companies would run a tavern where navvies would receive their pay. Much of this reward for gruelling and thirst-inducing work would disappear quickly over the other side of the bar.

'Going for a randy' was navvy slang for going on a drinking binge that could last several days. Navvies evolved a lifestyle and culture of their own, gaining a reputation for fighting, hard living and hard drinking. Their language included many rhyming slang words, similar to that developed by cockneys, so that outsiders would find it difficult to follow their conversation. For example, 'boots' were 'daisy roots', 'trowel' was 'bark and growl', and 'shovel' was 'Lord Lovel'.

'Respectable' Victorians viewed them as degenerate and a threat to social order, but much of the criticism was unjustified. Navvies' work hard/play hard attitude reflected a desire to live for the moment. Serious and fatal accidents were all too common. Tunnels would often collapse when under construction. The sooner the railway was built, the sooner the shareholders' profits would come rolling in, so health and safety procedures were minimal. A dead navvy's widow might receive £5 in compensation for her husband's death, but often it would be far less.

One of the most impressive, and deadly, feats of engineering achieved by the navvies was the building of the 3-mile long Woodhead Tunnels, which drove the Sheffield to Manchester line through the Pennines. The death rate between 1839 and 1852 was higher than that of the soldiers who had fought at the Battle of Waterloo. The tunnels earned the grim epithet 'the railwayman's graveyard'. During the excavation of the first tunnel, thirty-two navvies were killed, with another 250 seriously injured. There was a Parliamentary Enquiry but its findings were not acted upon for years. Even by the 1880s and

The infamous Woodhead Tunnels, Dunford Bridge. (*John Broom*)

1890s, work-related incidents were still killing navvies at the rate of 500 per year.

Due to their reputation of getting the job done, British navvies were in high demand. Several were recruited to work on the European mainland, where they would often be paid up to twice as much as the local workforce. Navvies also drew the admiration of Victorian moralist Samuel Smiles (*see* chapter 77) for their hard work, initiative and self-reliance. In 1861, he wrote: 'In most cases they had to make for themselves a way; for there was none to point out the road, which until then had not been travelled.'

Places to visit

- St James's Church at Woodhead, Derbyshire, just off the A628 between Penistone and Hadfield, contains the unmarked graves of many navvies who were killed in the construction of the Woodhead Tunnels. From a car park at Dunford Bridge, a few miles away, a walk up onto the moors with an Ordnance Survey map will bring you across the ventilation shafts sunk during the tunnels' construction.
- All Saints Church in Otley, West Yorkshire, contains an impressive memorial to the twenty-four navvies killed during the construction of the nearby Bramhope Tunnel.
- The Standedge Tunnel and Visitor Centre near Marsden, West Yorkshire, contains displays on the early navvies who built the tunnel.

Further reading

David Brooke, *The Railway Navvy: 'That Despicable Race of Men'* (1983).
Terry Coleman, *The Railway Navvies: A History of the Men who Made the Railways* (2015).
Ultan Cowley, *The Men who Built Britain: A History of the Irish Navvy* (2001).

28: Barton Aqueduct Arch

This unprepossessing bricked-up archway, situated on Barton Road in Manchester, once formed part of one of the most impressive engineering achievements of Britain's Industrial Revolution. It was moved 15 yards from its original location in the late nineteenth century to allow for road widening. The Barton Aqueduct, of which the arch formed a part, opened on 17 July 1761 to carry the Bridgewater Canal over the river Irwell at Barton upon Irwell. Designed by James Brindley, it was Britain's first navigable aqueduct.

Brindley was one of those characters to whom Britain's Industrial Revolution gifted a chance of eminence without the then privilege of a formal education. When called before a parliamentary committee in 1759 to give evidence on the safety and efficacy of his designs, he brought with him not a set of intricate drawings, but some clay that he moulded into a trough to show how it could form a watertight seal. When asked to produce a drawing of the aqueduct he proposed to build, Brindley replied that he had no paper representation of it but would demonstrate his intention by use of a model. He then went out and bought a large round of Cheshire cheese, which he divided into two equal halves. He used each half to represent the semi-circular arches, laying a long rectangular object over the top to show the course of the canal.

Contemporary engineers were sceptical of the Duke of Bridgewater's plan to have Brindley build him the aqueduct as part of the scheme to transport coal from his estate at Worsley into Manchester, Liverpool and beyond. At 200 yards long, 12 yards wide and

The remains of the Barton Aqueduct, preserved today in Manchester.

28: BARTON AQUEDUCT ARCH

A 1793 pen and ink by G.F. Yates showing horses pulling narrowboats across the Barton Aqueduct.

sitting 39 feet above the river, the Barton Aqueduct was a significant undertaking. Like the Darby iron bridge that was to come, it was a contemporary marvel. Writers wondered at the sight and crowds came to admire the spectacle of horses and men hauling a narrowboat 40 feet above the ground.

The Barton Aqueduct was to remain in use for over a century, and was the forerunner of future great water-carrying constructions built by Thomas Telford and John Rennie and the railway viaducts of George Stephenson and Isambard Kingdom Brunel. During Britain's Industrial Revolution, navigable aqueducts allowed vessels to cross at high and low levels while conserving water that would be lost in the operation of locks. They also served as markers of the new technological confidence spreading through the nation, which are still inspiring awe today.

Perhaps the most iconic aqueduct from Britain's Industrial Revolution is the Pontcysyllte Aqueduct on the Llangollen Canal, formerly known as the Ellesmere Canal. As part of the aqueduct's design, ox blood was added to the lime mortar to bind the masonry together. Allegedly, this was following an ancient superstition that the blood of a strong animal would strengthen a structure.

The Pontcysyllte Aqueduct is Britain's longest and highest, built between 1796 and 1805 as part of an abortive project to create a canal from Ruabon and Shropshire to the Mersey. Its name derives from 'pont', meaning bridge, and the Welsh verb 'cysylltu', to connect. It consists of a trough of cast iron sitting on tall stone piers. At 1,007 feet long and standing over 100 feet above the river Dee, the water flows southwards. A footpath ran along one side for the horses that towed the canal boats, with the other side being a sheer drop separated only by the wall of the iron trough.

Thomas Telford commonly receives the accolade for the design and erection of the

Engraving of the Pontcysyllte Aqueduct, 1806, by Francis Jukes.

Pontcysyllte Aqueduct, although previously, William Jessop, the Ellesmere Canal's chief engineer, was credited. It would be fair to say that both had a hand in it. William Hazledine cast the ironwork at the nearby Plas Kynaston estate, whose owner was one of the originators of the canal scheme. The original intent was to run the canal northwards from the Trevor basin but the challenge of the Welsh hills, along with the eclipse of canals by the railways, put paid to the scheme.

The Edstone Aqueduct, on the Stratford-upon-Avon Canal in Warwickshire, is the longest cast-iron aqueduct in England at 479 feet. Unusually, the towpath is at the base of the canal, not at water level. Work on the canal began in 1793 and eventually reached the 25 miles to Stratford-upon-Avon in 1816, with access to the Grand Union Canal at the Kingswood Junction. Funded by local land agent William James, the scheme was engineered by William Whitmore. The aqueduct itself was prefabricated, formed from thirty-five separate cast-iron sections bolted together. It carried the waterway across three railway tracks, a road, a stream and a field. Thirteen brick piers, making fourteen spans, hold up the aqueduct.

Places to visit

- The Trevor Basin Visitor Centre, at the end of the Pontcysyllte Aqueduct on the Llangollen Canal, contains models, videos and displays about the famous waterway. Eleven miles of the canal is designated a UNESCO World Heritage Site.
- The Edstone Aqueduct can be traversed by narrowboat.
- The remains of the Barton Aqueduct can be seen on Barton Road, Manchester.

Further reading

Victoria Owens, *James Brindley and the Duke of Bridgewater: Canal Visionaries* (2015).
Julian Glover, *Man of Iron: Thomas Telford and the Building of Britain* (2015).

29: The Euston Arch

Passengers arriving at Euston station to travel northwards would pass through the Propylaeum, complete with Greek Doric columns around 40 feet in height. It was as if they were entering a temple complex. Sadly, this grand façade was destroyed in the iconoclastic 1960s, when the railways were subjected to acts of carnage in the name of modernisation and reform. However, during Britain's Industrial Revolution, railway stations became more than merely places to board and leave trains, but locations of admiration and beauty as homage was paid to one of the wonders of the age – the steam train.

The world's first recorded railway station was The Mount on the Oystermouth Railway in Swansea, in south-western Wales. Passenger services began in 1807 in carriages drawn by horses. The opening of the Liverpool to Manchester Railway (L&MR) in 1830 saw the construction of the Crown Street station in Liverpool, which incorporated an engine shed. Crown Street was demolished in 1836 and the Liverpool terminus of the line moved to Lime Street. Meanwhile, the Manchester terminus was sited on Liverpool Road.

These early stations had few amenities. They were sometimes built with both passenger and goods facilities. If a line was dual-purpose, there would often be a goods depot apart from the passenger station. Many railway stations that date from the time of Britain's Industrial Revolution are redolent of the Gothic architectural style popular during the Victorian era. The grander the station, the higher the prestige reflected on the town or railway company.

Euston station in London, built by the London and Birmingham Railway (L&BR), was the first of these edifices. The coming of the railway had halved the travelling time

The famous Euston Arch, print from 1851.

The original Manchester terminus of the Liverpool and Manchester Railway. Passengers entered from the street and ascended to the platforms at first floor level.

between the two cities from twelve hours to six – an achievement that warranted architectural celebration. The train sheds were designed by Robert Stephenson and chief engineer Charles Fox. Passengers would step from the trains straight into waiting carriages, which would then pass through the iconic Euston Arch. The interior of the station was in neoclassical style, designed by Philip Hardwick, a founder member of the Royal Institute of British Architects.

Huddersfield station has, according to former poet laureate Sir John Betjeman, 'the most splendid façade in England'. Built on land then owned by the Ramsden family, large benefactors of the West Riding town, the station entrance boasts a central pavilion, colonnaded wings and corner pavilions. It has Grade I listed building status.

York station was the work of the 'Railway King', George Hudson. A local draper who inherited a minor fortune from a relative, he founded the York and North Midland (Y&NMR) company in the first railway boom in the 1830s, and became a dominant figure in the Railway Mania era of the 1840s. He was quoted as having the ambition to 'mak all t'railways cum t'York'. In 1841, Hudson began work on the ancient city's terminus and was granted permission to break through the old Roman wall so his station and hotel could sit within the limits of the medieval city. However, this proved inadequate for a station of York's strategic importance on the railway network, and the building we see today, situated just outside the city, was begun in 1873. The station roof is a masterpiece of Victorian engineering, supported by classical columns topped with Corinthian capitals. The white rose of Yorkshire and the North Eastern Railway's coat of arms embellish the structure.

Apart from the great classical constructions that adorn Britain's major towns and cities, the Victorian railway builders erected picturesque stations in less prominent settlements. Ribblehead, in the North Riding of Yorkshire, saw the railway arrive in 1876. Its station, on a remote Pennine plateau, is ornamental style. The Settle–Carlisle line, upon which the Ribblehead station sits, was built by the labour of 6,000 navvies, about 100 of whom died in the process of making the famous Ribblehead Viaduct (*see* chapter 27).

Ribblehead Station, Yorkshire. (*Alan Southworth/Ribblehead Station/CC BY-SA 2.0*)

The construction of railway stations formed part of the £3 billion spent on Britain's railway network between 1845 and 1900. The 423 million passengers travelling on trains in 1870 entered and exited through stations both grand and picturesque. Holiday, business, migration and sightseeing trips began at these iconic buildings. Stepping across their thresholds today takes the thoughtful traveller back to those prosaic and pleasurable passages of life.

Places to visit

- Liverpool Lime Street station's frontage resembles a château and is the world's oldest railway terminus in use.
- Manchester's Liverpool Road terminus now forms part of the Museum of Science and Industry.
- The National Railway Museum in York houses the gates of the old Euston station.
- Ribblehead station in North Yorkshire has a small museum in the booking office, with stained-glass company roundels in the windows.

Further reading

Simon Jenkins, *Britain's Best 100 Railway Stations* (2017).
Tim Bryan, *Railway Stations* (2017).
Jeffery Grayer, *101 Railway Stations: A Journey of Variety* (2018).

30: Bradshaw's Railway Guide

In October 1839, George Bradshaw produced his first railway timetable. By the time of his death in 1853, and beyond, the series continued to expand into a range of timetables and guides to Britain, the European continent, India, the USA, Canada, Australia, New Zealand and parts of the Middle East.

Bradshaw was born at Windsor Bridge in Pendleton, Lancashire, in 1801. On leaving school, he became apprenticed to a Manchester engraver. In 1820, he set up his own engraving business in Belfast, returning to Manchester in 1822 as an engraver and printer, principally of maps. Before his first railway guide came out, he had already published *Bradshaw's Maps of Inland Navigation*, detailing the canals of the industrial north of England. His 1839 book, which was bound in cloth and cost 6*d*, was titled *Bradshaw's Railway Time Tables and Assistant to Railway Travelling*. In 1840, the title was changed to the snappier *Bradshaw's Railway Companion*, and the price doubled to 1*s*. Bradshaw's books coincided with the introduction of standardised Railway Time by the Great Western Railway in November 1840.

Before the introduction of the railways, the time in any particular place in Britain was calculated according to the position of the sun. Thus, almost every town observed its own local time. Bristol Mean Time was ten minutes behind Greenwich Mean Time, and Cardiff Mean Time was thirteen minutes behind GMT. The expansion of the railway network and the publication of timetable guides such as *Bradshaw's* meant that a standard way of measuring time was needed. If a passenger saw that a train left Cardiff bound for London at 10 am, did that mean 10 am local Cardiff time, or 10 am London time?

The British railway companies agreed on a single standard Railway Time based on GMT in December 1847. By the mid-1850s, most public clocks in Britain were set to GMT and it finally became Britain's legal standard time in 1880.

From December 1841, new volumes were published regularly at the cost of 6*d* under the title *Bradshaw's Monthly Railway Guide* and their accompanying maps showed all lines in operation and 'in progress' across England and Wales during the great railway boom of the 1840s and 1850s. In June 1847, Bradshaw brought out *Bradshaw's Continental Railway Guide*, giving the timetables of European railways.

Bradshaw was not the first to use the railway network as a basis for a guidebook. James Scott Walker had produced a guide to the Liverpool and Manchester Railway back in 1830, giving a

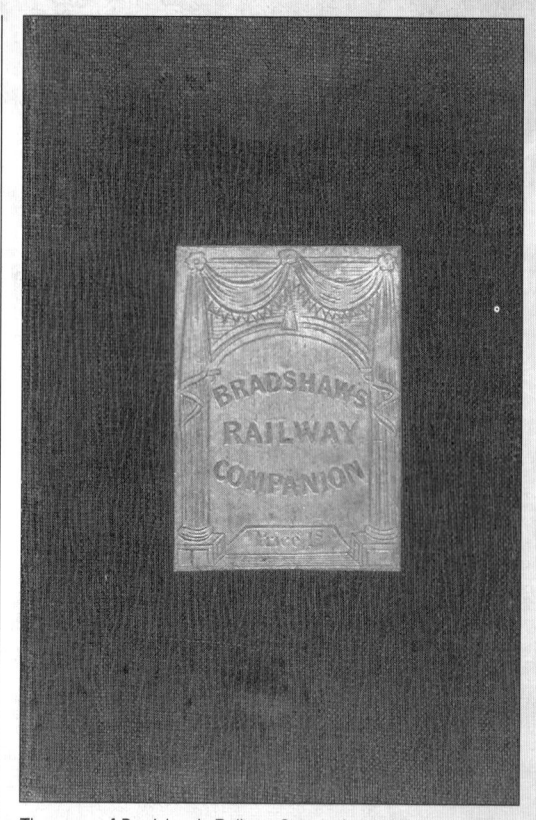

The cover of *Bradshaw's Railway Companion*, published in 1839.

George Bradshaw.

textual description of features accessible along the newly opened line. As the railway boom continued, directors of the railway companies were keen to encourage ways to promote their new lines, and an increasing number of tourist guides were produced as new railways opened across the country. These began to include attractive engravings and maps.

George Measom was commissioned to produce a series of official guides to most major railway companies. These were lavishly illustrated and covered not only the usual tourist sights, but also many descriptions and illustrations of industrial and commercial enterprises. Beginning in the 1880s, Cassell & Co. published a further series of official railway company guides, including photographs and fold-out maps.

Some railway companies were unhappy with Bradshaw's published timetables as they rivalled their own publications, but Bradshaw became a shareholder in several of the railway companies and stated his case at annual general meetings. His name became synonymous with the generic railway timetable, whether or not they were his own issues.

As the railway network grew, so did the size of *Bradshaw's* – from eight pages in 1841 to thirty-

A timetable from the 1850 railway guide.

two in 1845, and 946 by 1898. Maps, illustrations and descriptions were added of the main points of interest in each town served by the railways.

A prominent Quaker, Bradshaw was a noted philanthropist. While on tour in Norway in 1853, he contracted cholera and died, and was interred in the cemetery adjoining Oslo Cathedral. By the time of his death, *Bradshaw's* guides had become an institution. They were praised in acerbic style in *Punch* in 1865: 'Seldom has the gigantic intellect of man been employed upon a work of greater utility.' Over the decades, the price rose to two shillings in 1918 and half a crown in 1937, all the while updating all changes to train times and routes.

Between the two world wars, the verb 'to Bradshaw' was a derogatory term used in the Royal Air Force to refer to pilots who could not navigate well, having to use the course of railway lines as flight routes.

Phileas Fogg carries a *Bradshaw* in *Around the World in 80 Days*. The guide was also referenced by Sir Arthur Conan Doyle in his Sherlock Holmes stories, and Bram Stoker, who had Count Dracula consulting railway timetables when planning his voyage to England. Novelists Agatha Christie, G.K. Chesterton and Daphne du Maurier also wrote mention of *Bradshaw's* into their works.

Bradshaw's guides experienced a revival in popularity when Michael Portillo used an 1860 *Bradshaw's Handbook for Tourists in Great Britain & Ireland* as the basis of his *Great British Railway Journeys* BBC television series.

Places to visit

- The National Railway Museum at York houses several examples of *Bradshaw's* guides covering more than a century.

Further reading

George Bradshaw, *Bradshaw's Continental Railway Guide: 1853 Railway Handbook of Europe* (2016).
G. Royde Smith, *The History of Bradshaw: A Centenary Review of the Origin and Growth of the Most Famous Guide in the World* (1939).
John Christopher & Campbell McCutcheon, *Bradshaw's Guide: Bradshaw at the Seaside: Britain's Victorian Resorts* (2015).

31: Broad Gauge Turntable

This broad gauge turntable, housed at the Didcot Railway Centre in Oxfordshire, was originally laid in the Devonport Dockyard and is believed to date from the late 1860s. It serves as a reminder of the decades, from the 1830s through to the 1890s, when railways in Britain ran on two different track widths, or gauges. These competing systems brought railway companies into conflict.

The Gauge Wars is the term used to describe the intense competition between different railway companies and their backers as to what should be the standard width of track on Britain's railway network. Winning the Gauge Wars would mean control over the most lucrative routes for a railway company, as any subsequent lines built by other companies would need to conform to their existing track width.

The great engineer Isambard Kingdom Brunel had devised a broad gauge of 7 feet and a quarter inch in 1835 on his Great Western Railway (GWR). This was considerably in excess of the standard gauge 4 feet 8½ inches used by many other companies, including the London and South Western Railway (LSWR). Brunel believed broad gauge rail would mean faster and smoother journeys, whilst the narrower standard gauge had been pioneered by George Stephenson, who had been seeking to extend the original pre-steam railways that had been based on the width of a cart pulled by a horse. By the mid-1830s, the Great Northern Railway (GNR) and LSWR were in competition to run lines between London and Bath and Bristol. An Act of Parliament was awarded to the GNR.

Nine years later, the effects of the Gauge Wars were felt by passengers passing through Gloucester station, where the broad gauge Bristol and Gloucester Railway met the standard gauge Birmingham and Gloucester Railway (B&GR). Anyone travelling between the major cities of Birmingham and Bristol had to alight at Gloucester and change trains. Additionally, much time was wasted as goods had to be unloaded and reloaded.

The government, realising that what was becoming a national rail network could not be left to the rivalries of competing private companies, established a Gauge Commission to address the Gloucester problem and the general issues around the widespread use of two different gauges. In 1846, the Regulating of the Gauge of Railways Act was passed, coming down on the side of the standard gauge. All new railways had to use the 4 feet 8½ inch gauge unless they were directly connected to the GWR network. It was envisaged that there would eventually be seamless travel across a national rail network.

Undeterred, Brunel set about expanding the GWR broad gauge network. Mixed gauge lines were built southwards from the GWR so goods trains from northern industrial towns and cities could elide seamlessly between broad and standard tracks. Railways began to strip away at the monopoly that canal-based traffic had enjoyed in the Black Country. Brunel proposed a line from Birmingham to Wolverhampton to have a broad gauge as it linked into existing GWR lines. An Act of Parliament was agreed with the caveats that

The broad gauge turntable, Didcot Railway Centre. (*Rosser1963/Creative Commons*)

GWR broad gauge loco 4-2-2 Rover Class *Inkermann* passing under Moor Lane Bridge at Worle Junction on the Bristol to Taunton line. One of a collection of photographs of broad gauge locomotives taken by the Reverand A.H. Malan and presented by his son to the Great Western Railway in 1935. (The National Archives UK/Creative Commons)

the line would start from the mixed gauge Oxford and Rugby Railway (O&RR) and end at the standard gauge Grand Junction Railway (GJR) at Bushbury, near Wolverhampton.

As goods would have to be transhipped at Bushbury, an argument ensued between the existing GJR and the London and Birmingham Railway (L&BR) over their proposed merger with the Manchester and Birmingham Railway (M&BR). Construction costs shot up as the railway was rerouted to avoid the clash of gauges. In some instances, fights broke out between rival workmen.

Brunel died in 1859, and with his passing so ended the battles between the gauges. By 1861, mixed gauge lines to Paddington and other GWR routes allowed the company to gradually phase out the broad gauge lines during the 1870s. By 1875, the only remaining broad gauge line was one stretching beyond Bristol. A further branch was built in 1877 to form a link to St Ives. The final broad gauge train left Paddington on 20 May 1892, bound for Penzance. After that, everything was standard gauge only. Over the following weekend, railway labourers ripped up the last stretch of Isambard Kingdom Brunel's broad gauge track, converting 213 track miles to the standard gauge.

Despite losing the Gauge Wars, the GWR still saw a massive period of expansion, with new routes built and existing routes rationalised. It continued to be one of the leading railway companies, becoming one of the 'Big Four' after the rationalisation of the 1920s before finally being swallowed up in railway nationalisation by the Attlee government in 1948.

The Gauge Wars were arguably the earliest format conflict between two similar but incompatible technologies. More recent examples include VHS and Betamax video cassettes and Microsoft and Apple personal computers. Broad Gauge Way in Wolverhampton serves as an enduring physical reminder of the long-defunct type of track that Brunel had hoped would dominate the British rail network.

Places to visit

- The Didcot Railway Centre in Oxfordshire contains a section of broad gauge railway recreated using materials from a disused railway near Burlescombe in Devon, along with the original Didcot Transfer Shed Brunel broad gauge turntable.
- Old broad gauge tracks were used as fence posts on the Severn Valley Railway, and can still be seen near the Trimpley Reservoir in Worcestershire.

Further reading

Colin Maggs, *Isambard Kingdom Brunel: The Life of an Engineering Genius* (2017).
John McIlwain, *Isambard Kingdom Brunel: Remarkable Lives* (2019).
Andrew Roden, *Great Western Railway: A History* (2012).

32: Third Class Rail Carriage

The third class rail carriage, depicted here on a Churchman's cigarette card, was a feature of early railway travel. Often uncomfortable and exposed to the elements, the practice of using such open goods wagons to accommodate less wealthy patrons had earned the nickname 'Stanhope', a corruption of 'stand-ups', comparing the facilities unfavourably with the light horse-drawn gigs used by the wealthy at the time. Several third class carriages even lacked somewhere to sit, unlike the example shown in the picture.

Rail passengers taking a journey during Britain's Industrial Revolution could choose from three classes of ticket – first, second and third. Initially, the railways had implemented a two-class system for tickets. Like on the steamships and stagecoaches, first class travel was enclosed, whereas second class was open to the elements. The two-class system quickly transferred to other early railways.

However, by the late 1830s, the three-class system had become the norm for all new and existing railway companies. The three classes of travel would continue undisturbed until the 1870s, when the Midland Railway took the lead in phasing out second class carriages. First class passengers always had the best accommodation, their compartments containing soft furnishings and window glazing. Initially, second class carriages had roofs and padded seats, but were usually still open on either side, although this latter feature became less common up to the 1860s. Lastly, third class passengers travelled in little more than open trucks with wooden seats.

The Railway Regulation Act 1844 required all operators to provide a third class service. This was to ensure accessibility for poorer people to enable them to travel to find work. William Gladstone, the President of the Board of Trade, asked a select committee to produce six reports on the railways, resulting in *An Act to attach certain Conditions to the construction of future Railways authorised by any Act of the present or succeeding sessions of Parliament; and for other Purposes in relation to Railways* – commonly referred to as the 'Gladstone's Act' or the 'Railway Regulation Act'. Gladstone's original bill, a century ahead

SECOND & THIRD CLASS TRAVEL. 1840

(Author's collection)

William Gladstone, President of the Board of Trade.

of its time, had proposed state ownership of the railways, but this had been removed.

The Act stipulated that third class rail travel should cost 1*d* per mile, with an average speed of not less than 12mph. There should be one train with provision for third class passengers run on every line, every weekday, in both directions, stopping at every station. These became known as 'Parliamentary trains'. Third class carriages should be protected from the elements and include seating. In return for these obligations, railway companies were exempted from paying duty on revenue raised from third class travel. Although the price was still expensive for working people, they were allowed to carry 56lb of luggage for free, thus helping those migrating in search of work.

Many rail companies grudgingly accepted the new obligations, but often ran the Parliamentary trains in the early morning or late at night. They were fearful that second class passengers would switch to cheaper third class tickets now that the latter carriages had become tolerable. However, the Midland Railway improved its standards for passengers, including glazed windows and an oil lamp on the carriage roof. In 1875, the company removed second class travel and upgraded third class by relabelling their coaches. This caused some outrage, as it was thought that the lower orders would get to mix shoulder to shoulder with their 'betters'. Sir James Allport, general manager of the Midland Railway, offered the

George Augusts Sala cartoon – *Twice round the clock; or, The hours of the day and night in London* (1859) – showing the interior of a third class carriage.

PARLIAMENTARY TRAIN: INTERIOR OF A THIRD CLASS CARRIAGE.

robust response: 'If there is one part of my public life on which I look back with more satisfaction, it is with reference to the boon we conferred on third class travellers.' Other companies followed suit and for several decades, trains ran with the anomaly of first and third class travel, but no second, to comply with the terms of Gladstone's Act.

Parliamentary trains became the target of satire. Their basic comfort and slow progress due to the obligation to stop at every station was mocked in Gilbert and Sullivan's *Mikado*:

> The idiot who, in railway carriages,
> Scribbles on window-panes
> Will only suffer
> To ride on a buffer
> In Parliamentary trains.

The requirement for Parliamentary trains to stop at every station on a route, even though no passenger ever alighted there, proved cumbersome for railway companies. They formed the Passenger Duty Repeal Association in 1874 to campaign against the need to collect duties on all fares of through trains. In 1877, the Travelling Tax Abolition Committee was formed with the same aim.

At the same time, Britain's Industrial Revolution was producing cities teeming with people. The resultant overcrowding was becoming a major political issue, with one possible solution being to encourage people to live further away from their workplaces and to commute in daily. New housing and cheaper transport links, at less than $1d$ per mile, would be needed.

The principle of cheap transport for working people was reinforced by the passing of the Cheap Trains Act 1883, by a government led by William Gladstone, who had steered the previous Act through Parliament four decades earlier. It removed the passenger duty on any train charging less than $1d$ per mile and obliged the railway companies to operate a larger number of cheap trains. The number of cheap suburban services increased greatly and helped to mitigate overcrowding for many workers during Britain's Industrial Revolution.

Places to visit

- The London Transport Museum houses a collection of railway tickets and season passes, including many used for third class travel during Britain's Industrial Revolution.
- The Science Museum in London houses an open-topped third class carriage built for the Bodmin and Wadebridge Railway in 1834.

Further reading

D.N. Smith, *The Railway and its Passengers: A Social History* (1988).
Hamilton Ellis, *Railway Carriages in the British Isles from 1830 to 1914* (1965).
P.J.G. Ransom, *The Victorian Railway and How It Evolved* (1990).

33: SS Great Eastern Chains

This photograph of the chains of the SS *Great Eastern*, in front of which stands their designer, Isambard Kingdom Brunel, is one of the iconic images of Britain's Industrial Revolution. The chains were made at the Brown Lenox works at Pontypridd, and this picture was taken at Scott Russell's shipyard and ironworks on the Isle of Dogs.

The photograph projects all the confidence and ambition of the Victorian era. Although a short man at just 5 feet, Brunel stands in his 'stovepipe' hat and stacked-heel boots to give him height and presence. His formal clothes are dishevelled and muddied from the site, indicating his direct hand in the building process. The backdrop is dominated by the chains of the stern checking drum. This controlled the slow slide of the ship down to the water's edge, where it was launched by being lifted on the tide. SS

The *Charlotte Dundas*, drawn by J.C. Bourne and printed by C.F. Cheffins, 1803.

Great Eastern was an iron sail-powered, paddle wheel and screw-propelled steamship designed by Brunel. She was by far the largest ship ever built at the time of her 1858 launch, and had the capacity to carry 4,000 passengers from England to Australia without refuelling.

Smaller steam-powered boats had been invented in the first half of the eighteenth century. In 1783, the French steamboat *Pyroscaphe*, designed by Marquis de Jouffroy d'Abbans, was launched, carrying passengers along the river Seine. The paddle wheel was the main motive source on early steam-powered vessels. However, these were often unreliable; if the ship was subjected to excessive added weight, the submerged paddle wheel declined in performance. Early steamboats operated on inland lakes, rivers and canals.

In 1802, Scottish engineer William Symington successfully employed steam to the small riverboat *Charlotte Dundas*, used as a tugboat on the Forth–Clyde Canal. Another Scot, Henry Bell, designed a small steamship called the *Comet*, which he ran on the river Clyde in 1812.

Whilst neither the *Charlotte Dundas* nor the *Comet* were earth-shattering in their impact on British industry, they showed that steam power was possible on water and stimulated further developments. In 1820, a 141-foot-long steamship called the *James Watt* was launched. It was the biggest steamship of the time, powered by two Boulton & Watt engines, each driving a paddle wheel.

The first steamboat put to sea was Richard Wright's *Experiment*, which sailed from Leeds to Yarmouth in July 1813. The first steamship manufactured from iron was the 116-ton eponymous *Aaron Manby*, built by that ironmaster at his Horseley Ironworks in Staffordshire. The vessel crossed the English Channel in 1822, arriving in Paris on 22 June. The average speed for the voyage was 8 knots (9mph).

It is contested which was the first steamship to cross the Atlantic Ocean. The American SS *Savannah* sailed from New York to Liverpool in June 1819, although much of the voyage was made under sail. The British-built *Curaçao*, manufactured in Dover, crossed from the Netherlands to Surinam in 1827, whilst others claim the Canadian ship SS *Royal William* was the first to make the transatlantic trip entirely under steam.

In 1838, *Sirius*, owned by the British and American Steam Navigation Co., left Ireland with forty paying passengers for a historic voyage to New York. It took eighteen days. The vessel ran out of coal so the crew had to burn the cabin furniture and even a mast to maintain the steam engine. In doing so, they were able to lay claim to the first transatlantic passenger journey undertaken entirely by steam power.

As the *Sirius* was crossing the Atlantic, the rival Great Western Steamship Co.'s *Great Western* left Bristol. Despite leaving four days after the *Sirius*, the *Great Western* arrived in New York Harbour a mere four hours behind, still with 200 tons of coal in her bunkers. Soon two other major companies – the Peninsular Steam Navigation Co. and the Cunard Line – joined the fray. Over ensuing decades, the rival lines

An 1882 engraving of SS *Great Western*.

would seek to compete for the record fastest time across the Atlantic in what would become known as the Blue Riband.

Brunel's SS *Great Western* was the first purpose-built transatlantic steamship powered by a sidewheel paddle. It ushered in the era of the transatlantic ocean liner. A year later, Francis Pettit Smith built the SS *Archimedes*, the world's first screw propeller-driven steamship designed for the open seas.

In 1854, yet another Scottish engineer, John Elder, invented the compound steam engine. This used steam twice in each engine cycle, which meant that 1 ton of coal was now doing as much work as 3 tons had done in 1845. In 1868, British-Canadian shipping magnate Samuel Cunard launched the *Parthia* and the *Bactavia*, which could carry ten times the number of passengers as the first steamships. As the lighter steel replaced iron, ships grew larger still. The first superliner, the *Lusitania*, launched in 1907, although it would meet a tragic end courtesy of a German torpedo in 1915.

The development of seagoing steamships in the eighteenth and nineteenth centuries supported the rapid expansion of the British Industrial Revolution. Products manufactured in Britain – the self-styled 'workshop of the world' – were carried all over the Empire. Within fifty years, the cost of carrying goods by ship had fallen by over 70 per cent.

The opening of the Suez Canal in 1869 dramatically cut sailing times to far-flung parts of the Empire. By shortening the journey to the East, the number of refuelling stops and the quantity of fuel to be carried were reduced. Steam power became even more economically efficient. Imports of Indian raw cotton (*see* chapter 42) became even cheaper. Fast and reliable ships were also increasingly in demand for emigration and the military and administrative grip on Britain's empire. High-pressure boilers and engines developed in the 1870s secured the steamship's ascendancy and provided a boost for British shipbuilding: by the end of the century, 90 per cent of the large steamships in operation around the world were British built. Ships powered by steam engines allowed new trade routes, less dependent on wind patterns, to open up. They acted as a major driver of the first wave of trade globalisation between 1870 and 1914.

Places to visit

- The SS *Great Britain*, once the longest steamship in the world, attracts around 200,000 visitors per year at its home in a dry dock in the centre of Bristol.
- The *Charlotte Dundas* Heritage Trail at Falkirk celebrates the vessel and her creator, William Symington. Tarmacked and fully accessible, the route is a little under a mile.

Further reading

Douglas Burgess, *Engines of Empire: Steamships and the Victorian Imagination* (2016).
Stephen Fox, *The Ocean Railway: Isambard Kingdom Brunel, Samuel Cunard and the Revolutionary World of the Great Atlantic Steamships* (2003).
Helen Doe, *The First Atlantic Liner: Brunel's Great Western Steamship* (2017).

34: Dock Warehouses

This fine collection of warehouses is part of the West India Docks complex between Limehouse and Blackwall in London. The docks were designed in 1799 by civil engineer Ralph Walker as 'the Merchants' Place' and were opened in 1802. They covered 295 acres, including the ¾-mile-long canal, which ships entered through the lock in Blackwall Reach, thus being able to bypass the Isle of Dogs. All over the great ports of Britain, such warehouses stored the rum, tobacco, sugar, cotton, tea and other goods that rolled in from the nation's vast empire.

As the potential wealth that could be generated by importing raw materials and exporting manufactured goods grew throughout the period of Britain's Industrial Revolution, so the demand for adequate facilities for ships to berth and to load and unload their cargoes increased. During the eighteenth century, the improvement or construction of docks, harbours, quays and wharfage not only changed the physical landscape of coastal towns and ports, but also brought economic improvement and population increase to those areas.

These large feats of civil engineering usually required authorisation by an Act of Parliament. A whole series of Acts was passed in the eighteenth century that enabled a number of British ports to expand and acquire global prominence. Liverpool was a small fishing port in the 1700s but established itself as a key destination in the transatlantic West Indies trade, which included the shipment of slaves (*see* chapter 40). The first phase of Liverpool's dock-building was completed in 1715 following an Act of 1709. A series of later Acts authorised further phases of expansion. Particularly important was an

Looking south across the East India Dock, Blackwall, London, 1808. The smaller dock adjacent to the river Thames was originally the Brunswick Dock.

Act passed in 1762 that transferred control over Liverpool's dock to the town corporation, enabling it to undertake further rapid expansion through financial loans secured on the local rates. By 1824, the entire dock area extended to some 50 acres, and continued to grow.

Glasgow's port achieved success in the colonial tobacco trade (*see* chapter 41). An Act was passed in 1770 to extend the port based on plans devised partly by James Watt. Kingston upon Hull was an important centre in the whaling and fishing industries. The town's first inland dock, prosaically named 'The Dock', was the largest in the United Kingdom when it opened in 1778. A further ten major docks were built alongside the river Humber during Britain's Industrial Revolution, making Hull one of the pre-eminent ports of the Empire.

Before the construction of the docklands, shipping entering London had to queue on a stretch of the Thames between London Bridge and the Tower of London so they could land at quays for the collection of custom duties. It could take several weeks for a ship to berth. The West India Dock Company, whose investors were heavily involved in the slave trade, was granted an Act of Parliament in 1799 to create new docks where custom duties could be paid. Around 500 ships per year would bring in mainly sugar and rum, and 200 full-time labourers were employed to store the cargo in tall dockside warehouses.

A further dock system, known as the London Docks, was developed after an area of twenty-four streets, thirty-three courtyards and part of a churchyard was demolished to make way. Some privileged individuals with the right connections would bring parties of guests into the warehouses to be escorted around by a cooper to take a glass of each of different kind of wine and sherry from the many barrels stored there. Management, workers and seamen would also visit the vaults for a drink known as a 'waxer'.

The East India Company (*see* chapter 45) had previously created docks in London for the shelter and repair of ships, but in the early nineteenth century, it developed vast areas for the loading and unloading of cargo. The East India Docks opened at Blackwall in August 1806. By the end of the first decade of the nineteenth century, the Port of London had expanded significantly, with three dock systems on the north bank of the Thames downriver of London and several individual docks at Rotherhithe. Not only was the congestion on the river greatly

An 1880 bird's-eye view of Kingston upon Hull, showing the docks encircling the old town and stretching out along the river Humber.

eased, but London had become a storage port through which cargoes were able to pass on their journey from one part of the world to another.

These ports, as well as others such as Bristol and Newport in Gwent, became the nodes of empire, setting Britain at the heart of a global trading network and generating much wealth for the nation. Without them, Britain's Industrial Revolution would have been a far less impressive phenomenon.

Places to visit

- The Hull Maritime Museum is housed in the city's former Dock Offices, which were built in 1871. It was at the heart of the dock system, with ships regularly sailing past its windows. The author spent many fascinating boyhood hours there learning about the history of Hull's fishing and whaling industries.
- The Museum of London Docklands opened in 2003 and is part of the Museum of London. Located at Canary Wharf, it tells the story of the port of London and the related dockland communities from around 1600 to the present day. The museum is in an original warehouse at the West India Docks, built in 1802.
- The Merseyside Maritime Museum is located in Liverpool's Albert Dock complex. It tells the nautical history of this iconic seafaring city.

Further reading

Peter Stone, *The History of the Port of London: A Vast Emporium of Nations* (2017).
Michael Thompson, *Hull Docklands: An Illustrated History of the port of Hull* (1990).
Ian Collard, *Liverpool Docks Through Time* (2012).

35: Tram Lines

Between Rye and Camber in the county of Sussex lie the lines of the former tramway, opened in July 1895. It ran from a station near the Monk Bretton Bridge for about 2 miles, terminating beside the newly opened Rye Golf Club, and was later extended by about half a mile to Camber Sands. The lines serve as a reminder of the period between *c.*1870 and 1914, when trams were a regular feature in Britain's towns and cities, enabling the workers of Britain's Industrial Revolution to go about their business and pleasure seekers at coastal resorts to enjoy sightseeing trips.

Horse-drawn wagonways had been in use in Britain since before the Industrial Revolution. The first recorded surface-running horse-drawn wagonway was the 2-mile Wollaton Wagonway, built in 1603–4 to carry coal from mines at Strelley down to the river Trent at Wollaton, near Nottingham. In 1803, a Surrey Iron Railway was built between Mitcham and Croydon. The present-day South London Tramlink follows the same route.

The word 'tram' derives from a Scandinavian word for a beam or baulk of wood. When these beams were utilised as guides for wagons used in mining or other industrial activities, the tracks laid were referred to as 'tram ways'. The world's first passenger tram was the Oystermouth Line, running between Swansea and the Mumbles.

Remains of the track of the Rye and Camber Tramway. (*Author's collection*)

35: TRAM LINES

Early photograph of the Swansea and Mumbles horse-drawn tram.

The Mumbles Railway Act was passed by the British Parliament in 1804, and this first horse-drawn passenger tramway started operating in 1807. It was worked by steam from 1877.

Birkenhead on the Wirral Peninsula can lay claim to being the first town in Europe to operate a street tramway. Started by American entrepreneur George Francis Train, the track ran from Woodside Ferry to the main entrance of Birkenhead Park and was a horse-drawn car service of about 1½ miles. Train was also involved in the construction of a short-lived horse tramway in Cork, Ireland. Although his trams were popular with passengers, his designs had rails that stood above the road surface and obstructed other traffic. In 1861, Train was arrested and tried for 'breaking and injuring' Uxbridge Road in London. Undeterred, he opened the Darlington Street Railroad Company in 1862, but it too was short-lived, closing in 1865.

Horse-drawn trams had a range of structural problems that would soon be addressed by the application of various innovations. Firstly, an animal could only work so many hours on a given day. It had to be housed, groomed, fed and cared for on a daily basis. The manure produced by the horses had to be collected and stored by the company.

Gas trams operated in Lytham St Annes in Lancashire, Neath in West Glamorgan, and Trafford Park, Manchester, during the latter years of Britain's Industrial Revolution. Steam trams, with a small steam locomotive or tram engine at the head of a line of carriages, were also deployed in some areas. The Locomotives on Highways Act had previously stopped heavy steam-powered vehicles from churning up the roads. When steam trams were first considered, they too were deemed to be covered by these Acts. In 1873, the first steam tram was trialled in London, although the power it produced was barely enough to move itself, let alone haul a passenger carriage.

The first successful steam-powered tram of fare-paying passengers in Britain ran between Handsworth and West Bromwich in the Midlands from 1876. New legislation, in the form of the Use of Mechanical Power on Tramways Act of 1879, opened up the possibility of steam tramways in urban areas, but they were still subject to strict provisions, which included a speed limit of 10mph. All working parts had to be enclosed to within 4 inches of the roadway and no visible smoke or steam was to be emitted. The largest trailer cars produced were for the Wolverton and Stony Stratford line in Buckinghamshire in 1888, and seated 100 passengers. Although forty-five steam tramways opened in the 1880s, advances made in electric traction made the steam trams obsolete from the 1890s onwards.

Cable-powered trams became increasingly popular. The tram was pulled along a fixed track by a moving steel cable, with the power to move the cable provided at a powerhouse site a distance away from the vehicle. The London and Blackwall Railway, which opened for passengers in 1840, used such a system.

The Tramways Act was passed in August 1870 and provided protection for those local authorities through whom the tram routes were suggested. Local authority participation was encouraged in the operation of tramways, with each authority having the right to veto a new proposed tramway on their streets. In addition, they had the right of compulsory purchase for any tramway after twenty-one years of operation. Tramway companies had to pave and repair roadways damaged during the installation of the lines and pay rates on the land occupied by the rails. In London, the City Corporation used the veto to prevent tramway construction in the heart of the city, effectively preventing cross-city tram links.

Operators with double track systems were required to pave practically the entire road, whilst rates were levied on the extra 18 inches on either side of the track that were required to be paved. Despite all these obstacles, the tramway began to prosper and by the turn of the century, the tram had become a common sight in many towns and cities.

In Britain, the first electric tramway was Volk's Electric Railway, which opened in 1883 in Brighton. Previously, Robert Davidson built

Horse-drawn tram in Briggate, Leeds.

an electric locomotive that was demonstrated on the Edinburgh and Glasgow Railway in 1842, but, because all the early electric vehicles were propelled by battery power that had limited capabilities, interest in electric power as a motive source had waned. However, soon after the Volk's Railway opened, further electric tram services began in Northern Ireland with the Giant's Causeway Tramway and the Bessbrook and Newry Tramway. Blackpool introduced the conduit system in 1885, although problems with salt and sand led to a conversion to the overhead system in 1899, and the Ryde Pier Tramway appeared on the Isle of Wight in 1886.

In 1890, an electric line was constructed in the grounds of Craiglockhart as part of the Edinburgh International Exhibition. This differed from other lines as it featured an overhead wire to distribute the circuit. Although this line closed in November 1890 at the end of the Edinburgh International Exhibition, having carried in excess of 15,000 people, the principle of an overhead electric tramway had been established. When the Roundhay Park tramway in Leeds opened, it operated on this principle and demonstrated the simplicity and efficiency of this system. This design became the common mode of operation for most electric tramway systems, although not all local authorities appreciated the unsightly overhead and support equipment necessary.

The rate at which new tramways were constructed fell dramatically in the early 1900s. By 1910, there were over 300 tramway operators, but in the period from 1910 onwards, only five more opened. Saturation had been reached. After the war, the motorbus, with its greater flexibility of route, superseded the tram.

Places to visit

- Douglas on the Isle of Man still operates a horse-drawn tram service for visitors.
- The Great Orme Tramway at Llandudno, opened in 1902, is Britain's only funicular, or cable-hauled, tramway that travels on public roads. It climbs nearly a mile in the original, restored tramcars.
- Crich Tramway Village in the Derbyshire Peak District serves as Britain's National Tramway Museum. Here you can ride on vintage trams and enjoy a recreated street scene from the period when trams were a popular form of transport.
- The Beamish Open Air Museum in County Durham transports visitors between the various exhibits on a period tram.

Further reading

David Gladwin, *Horse and Steam Trams of Britain* (2014).
Peter Waller, *Britain's Preserved Trams: An Historic Overview* (2021).
Dennis Gill, *Trams: An Illustrated Anthology* (2011).

36: The Red Flag

This photograph shows Charles Rolls, later co-founder of Rolls-Royce, driving an 1896 Peugeot, preceded by man with a red warning flag walking in front. What caused the depiction of such a seemingly bizarre scene?

In 1865, Lord Palmerston's government passed the Locomotive Act, popularly known as the Red Flag Act. It stipulated that any self-propelled – i.e. non-horse or hand-powered – vehicle had to be preceded by a person carrying a red flag walking 60 yards in front.

At the time, such vehicles, which were cumbersome traction engines, could not travel at the speed of the fastest horse-drawn coach, so why the alarm? Horse-drawn carriage operators and the railway industry had both lobbied for the legislation, fearful of the potential impact that independently powered road vehicles might have on their businesses. A road speed limit for self-propelled vehicles was set at 4mph in the country and half that in towns. A hefty £10 fine was imposed for exceeding these. Each car needed to have a crew of at least three people – a driver, a stoker and the flagbearer.

Cars had started to appear in Europe in the second half of the nineteenth century. Originally steam-powered, they later ran on liquid fuels such as gasoline. Stagecoach and railway companies argued that motor cars should only be able to undertake short journeys – essentially as a taxi service between stagecoach inns and railway stations as a support for their existing infrastructures. The three-decade long restrictions placed on car use meant that the British automobile industry lost a competitive edge against its European, particularly its German, rivals. Thus, Britain's Industrial Revolution, having originally encouraged innovation and adaptation, had recoiled into favouring protection of the status quo. British car manufacturers never quite caught up.

Over the next thirty years, several improvements took place in the development of the motor car that increasingly made the terms of the Locomotive Act look absurd. On 14 November 1896, the Locomotives on Highways Act superseded the 1865 Act and the speed limit was raised to a breezy 14mph.

In celebration, motor car enthusiasts, led by Henry Lawson, organised an 'Emancipation Run', a rally from the Metropole Hotel in London to the hotel of the same name in Brighton. Breakfast was taken at Charing Cross Hotel, and Lord Winchelsea, a Conservative politician and noted advocate of motor transport, symbolically tore a red flag in half. Motorists were warned: 'Owners and drivers should remember that motor cars are on trial in England and that any rashness or carelessness might injure the industry in this country.' Fifty-eight vehicles had listed to start the run, but only thirty-three showed up on the day. Either thirteen or fourteen reached Brighton.

Lawson was a colourful character, turning his hand variously to bicycle design and racing, and was a pioneer of the motor car industry. He co-floated the Daimler Motor Company Limited in London in 1896, beginning manufacture in Coventry. Lawson had moved to Brighton in 1873, aged 21, thence to Coventry in the early 1880s. Alongside Frederick Simms, he founded the Motor Car Club of Britain in 1895.

Lawson then sought to monopolise the British car industry through buying up the rights to foreign patents. He variously formed the British Motor Syndicate, which collapsed in 1897, and the British Motor Company, British Motor Traction Company, The Great Horseless Carriage Company, Motor Manufacturing Company, and the Anglo-American Rapid Vehicle Company. All failed, with his one success coming with The Daimler Motor Company Limited.

In 1904, Lawson was found guilty of fraudulently obtaining money and was sentenced to one year's hard labour. A decade later, he was once again in hot water having committed fraud in his association with the Blériot Manufacturing Aircraft Company Ltd. He survived colder waters, being rescued following the torpedoing of the ferry *Sussex* in March 1916 while crossing the English Channel. Associates attributed his troubles to naivety and over-generosity rather than any particular greed or scheming.

One legacy of Lawson's that did survive was the annual commemoration of 'Emancipation Day'. On 14 November 1897, forty-four cars were driven by Motor Car Club members from Whitehall Place to Richmond Park, a distance of about 8 miles. The Brighton journey was undertaken the following year, with 135 club members taking part. A celebratory concert was held at Sheen House, with a five-course lunch washed down with fine wines. In 1899, a repeat of the drive to Brighton took place, and in 1900, the journey took the Motor Car Club, along with the newly formed Automobile Club, now the RAC, down to Southsea. Oxford was the chosen destination for 1902, with 'Non-Stop Certificates' having been introduced the previous year to acknowledge the most reliable motors.

The anniversary run still takes place, with an eligibility criterion stipulating that a participating car must have been built before 1 January 1905. At the start of each run, a red flag is symbolically torn asunder to mark the removal of the egregious restrictions that held back British motoring for three crucial decades at the end of the nineteenth century.

Places to visit

- The British Motor Museum at Gaydon, Warwickshire, tells the fascinating story of the nation's motor industry and houses the world's largest collection of historic British cars.
- The National Motor Museum at Beaulieu, near Brockenhurst in the New Forest, houses 250 road vehicles manufactured since the late nineteenth century. It has a collection of motoring books, journals, photographs, films and automobilia.

Further reading

James J. Fink, *The Automobile Age* (1988).
John Wood, *The British Motor Industry* (2010).

37: Penny-farthing Bicycle

James Starley, known as the father of the bicycle industry, invented the penny-farthing, or high-bicycle, in 1871. The bike was nicknamed so because it looked like a large English penny and smaller farthing side by side. The large front wheel enabled faster speeds but was very unsafe for the rider so high up in the air. It is an iconic object of cycling history and a reminder of the increasing personal mobility and freedom that many enjoyed as a result of Britain's Industrial Revolution.

The first practically used bicycle, the draisine, was invented by German Baron Karl von Drais in 1817. The draisine had no pedals so riders would propel it by pushing along the ground with their feet as in regular walking or running. The machine flourished briefly across Europe but cyclists came into conflict with pedestrians and soon found their boots wearing down due to the friction. Scottish blacksmith Kirkpatrick Macmillan is credited with inventing the mechanically propelled bicycle in 1839. Movement was transmitted to cranks in the rear wheel by connecting rods. Although a great improvement on self-propelled bikes, the machinery was heavy and required great physical effort to ride. In 1863, Frenchman Pierre Michaux developed the Michaux Velocipede, popularly known as the 'boneshaker', due to the roughness of the ride. A metal frame made it lighter than Macmillan's contraption.

The first tricycle had been invented in seventeenth-century Germany. From 1876 to 1884, James Starley's Coventry Rotary, the main bicycle production company in England, produced a wide variety of tricycles and multi-wheel cycles. At first, tricycles were used especially by those who could not ride high wheelers, such as women who were confined in the long dresses of the day, and short or non-athletic men. Between 1881 and 1886 in Great Britain, more tricycles were built than bicycles.

James Starley's nephew, John Kemp Starley, began production of his revolutionary road safety bicycle in 1885. The son of a gardener, Starley junior hailed from Walthamstow, Essex. Aged 17, he moved to Coventry to work with his inventor uncle and his partner building cycles. In 1877, Starley started a new business – Starley & Sutton Co. – with William Sutton, a local cycling enthusiast. Their aim was to develop bicycles that were safer and easier to use than the prevailing penny-farthings. They started by manufacturing tricycles, and by 1883, becoming part of the commercial branding fashion, advertised their products as 'Rover'.

Starley's Rover was a rear-wheel-drive, chain-driven cycle with two similar-sized

A vintage penny-farthing on the road at the Beamish Museum, County Durham. (*Darren Wilkinson/Creative Commons*)

John Starley on his Rover safety bicycle.

Coventry was the largest producer of bicycles in the world during the latter period of Britain's Industrial Revolution, with more than 450 different cycle manufacturers based in the city over a 100-year period. The Coventry Machinists Company was the first in Britain to mass-produce cycles, and steadily, more and more companies, such as Singer and Triumph, established in the city. Soon Coventry became internationally recognised as a place where only the very best machines were made, and the name 'Coventry' itself became a stamp of quality engineering and fine craftsmanship.

The latter decades of Britain's Industrial Revolution saw the wide take-up of bicycles among middle-class workers, who used them as their transportation. Members of the upper classes preferred the more expensive and less accessible tricycle as a mark of social distinction. In 1882, wealthy members of London society formed the Tricycle Union. This union sought to ban bicycles from park pathways and other public areas; cycling had become political.

The National Clarion Cycling Club was founded in 1894, an arm of the labour movement, with one of its stated aims being 'support for the principles of socialism'. The first branch opened in Birmingham as the Socialists' Cycling

wheels, making it more stable than the previous high-wheeler designs. It also had a saddle and handlebar grips. *Cycling* magazine praised the Rover, stating it had 'set the pattern to the world'. The bicycle then became popular across all classes in the late Victorian and Edwardian ages as both a leisure activity and means of transportation, and the phrase was used in their advertising for many years. In 1889, the company became J.K. Starley & Co. Ltd and, in the late 1890s, was renamed the Rover Cycle Company Ltd. After Starley's death in 1901, the Rover Company branched out into building motorcycles and cars.

A further addition to the bicycles we know today came in 1887, when John Boyd Dunlop, a Scottish veterinarian living in Belfast, sought to make his son's tricycle a more comfortable ride. Rather than the solid rubber tyres then in use, Dunlop invented the first pneumatic tyre, moving on from his son's trike to the larger wheels of racing bikes. Comfort levels for riders, and thus the popularity of the bicycle, increased further.

A group of women enjoying a cycle outing in County Down, 1895.

Club but soon renamed itself after *The Clarion* newspaper, a socialist organ.

Britain was experiencing a cycling boom at the time, as Starley's new safety bicycle, with its diamond-framed design, became popular. By the end of 1894, sister Clarion Clubs had sprung up in Liverpool, Bradford, Barnsley and the Potteries. In 1895, the five clubs met up at Ashbourne in Derbyshire for their first annual meeting, forming the National Clarion Cycling Club, self-styled as 'the association of the various Clarion Cycling Clubs for the purpose of Socialist propaganda and for promoting inter-club runs between the clubs of different towns'.

A corps of Clarion Scouts was established, with cycling trips being used to circulate socialist leaflets and copies of *The Clarion*. In March 1895, a new socialist magazine, *The Scout*, was launched for Scouts to read and circulate. It was subtitled *A Monthly Journal for Socialists* and its first edition included a set of 'Instructions for Scouts' written by *The Clarion*'s editor, Robert Blatchford. At the time, British socialists were divided between the Social Democratic Federation and the Independent Labour Party. Clarion Scouts were encouraged to support candidates of whichever groups were standing for election in their area in order to seek unity. By the end of 1895, there were thirty Clarion Clubs and by early 1897, membership of the national organisation stood at seventy clubs. Clarion Clubs reached their peak and extent of influence by 1914.

The development of the safety bicycle in the nineteenth century also gave women unprecedented mobility. As bicycles became safer and cheaper, more women had access to the personal freedom they embodied. The bicycle came to symbolise the 'New Woman' of the late nineteenth century, who might be active in social and political circles. Female cyclists gained a new sense of freedom of movement and thus broadened horizons. As the long-flowing, multi-layered dress and corset was the biggest obstacle for riding, more comfortable and less restrictive garments became the norm for the New Woman. The bicycle became known as the 'Freedom Machine' for many women.

Cycling's influence had reached the military, with fourteen Cyclist Corps having been formed by 1914. The bicycle was to be invaluable for reconnaissance and communications work, being lighter, quieter, and logistically much easier to support than horses. The author's grandfather, William George Broom, would serve in the 8th (Cyclist) Battalion of the Essex Regiment during the war.

Places to visit

- The National Cycle Museum in Llandrindod Wells, Powys, is home to over 260 vintage bicycles dating back to 1818. They promote all aspects of cycling history.
- Walton Hall and Gardens near Warrington, Cheshire, is home to a cycle museum, which includes a Hobby Horse, boneshaker, several penny-farthings and Rover safety bikes.
- The History of Coventry Transport Museum contains many vintage cycles, alongside collections of motor cars and motorbikes manufactured in the famous manufacturing city.

Further reading

Tom Ambrose, *The History of Cycling in Fifty Bikes* (2014).
Nick Clayton, *The Birth of the Bicycle* (2016).
James Witherell, *Bicycle History: A Chronological Cycling History of People, Races, and Technology* (2016).
Damien Kimberley, *Coventry's Bicycle Heritage* (2015).

38. 1884 Metropolitan Line Map

This map, issued by the Metropolitan Railway in 1884, shows the geographical features of the central London area with the route of the Metropolitan Line overlaid in red. Stations are marked with squares. Visitors to the Health Exhibition at South Kensington were provided with a copy of the map to enable them to undertake a smooth journey and perhaps explore further afield in London using the recently expanded underground rail network. The reverse of the map included 'places of amusement and interest in the vicinity of the Metropolitan Railway Co.'s Railway Stations'.

At the time of Queen Victoria's coronation in 1837, the population of England's capital city stood at 1.7 million. The Railway Mania period of the 1840s and 1850s brought even more people into the centre of the Empire, as easier access was facilitated. The congestion of everyday traffic was reaching saturation point as horses, people, carts, cabs and trams jostled for space. It could take ninety minutes to travel the 5 miles from Paddington to Bank by horse-drawn omnibus. An 1846 Royal Commission ruled that new railway lines and stations should be barred from the City and West End areas.

Various schemes were designed to address this problem. In 1855, William Moseley proposed a 'Crystal Way', an underground line from Cheapside to Oxford Circus enclosed by a glass arcade. Trains would run on the lowest level, with living space on the next two levels, then a street level of shops and an ornate glazed roof above a final level.

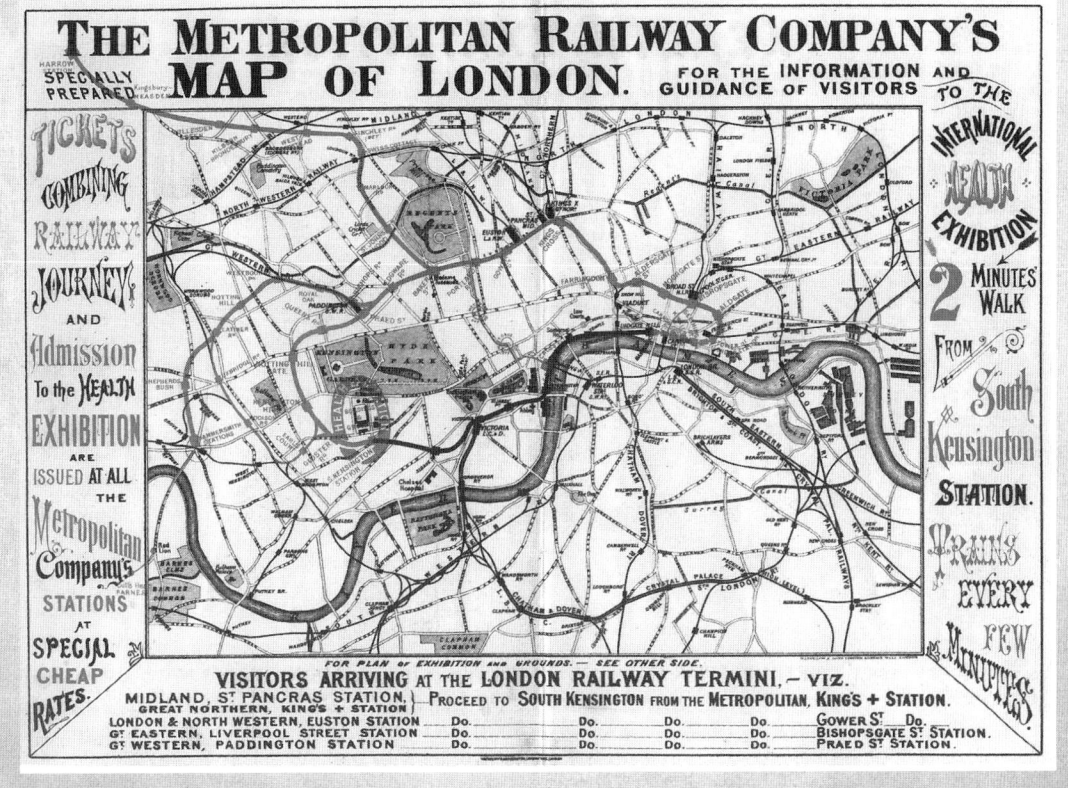

Charles Pearson, Solicitor to the City of London, saw social and economic advantages in a scheme that would build a railway to link together the mainline termini of the various railway companies pouring people in and out of London from north, east, south and west. In the process, the slums of the Fleet Valley could also be cleared, the slum dwellers being relocated to new suburbs. Cheap travel should then be provided to enable them to commute back into the city on a daily basis. Pearson's 1850s plans proved to be several decades ahead of their time and were rejected by Parliament.

However, a group of entrepreneurs formed the Metropolitan Railway Company in August 1854. This body planned to construct a new underground railway that would run for 3 miles from the Great Western Railway terminus at Paddington to the edge of the City of London at Farringdon Street, taking in the Great Northern Railway terminus at King's Cross. The undertaking was not without its critics. Objectors worried that the tunnels would collapse from the overhead weight of traffic, undermining the foundations of adjoining buildings. Furthermore, passengers would choke on the locomotives' sulphurous emissions. £1 million capital for the project was raised over five years.

The route mainly ran below existing roads to reduce the number of buildings that would need to be demolished. This 'cut and cover' method involved digging a trench 10 yards wide and 6 yards deep. Brick walls were then built and the cutting roofed over with a brick arch or iron girders. A further 2-yard deep layer of topsoil was deposited on top of the arch before the road was relaid.

Services were ready to begin in January 1863, using traditional locomotives fitted with water tanks in which to condense the steam. Despite this, smoke and fumes remained a problem. Open sections between some stations

Metropolitan Railway under construction in February 1861. A partially completed cut and cover tunnel close to King's Cross station, depicted in *The Illustrated London News*.

improved ventilation, but the convenience and rapidity of the new service far outweighed any minor discomfort for most passengers. Network expansion came soon afterwards, when Parliament approved a new line to form an 'inner circle' to join the Metropolitan Line to link the major railway termini. The Metropolitan District Railway company was chosen from around 250 different schemes and the first section of the District Line opened in 1868. After years of legal wrangling between rival underground companies, the Circle Line was eventually completed in 1884.

Part of the delay in expansion was caused by the competing visions of the directors of the two existing underground railway companies. Sir Edward Watkin saw the possibilities of the Metropolitan Line as a mainline railway linking to France via a Channel tunnel, whilst James Forbes favoured shorter extensions in partnership with companies like the London and South Western Railway.

By the 1880s, the underground lines had reached out into the suburbs and formed a circuit around central London. However, they did not cross the city, as the cut and cover method would have caused too much disruption to London's commercial life. Lines would therefore need to be driven deeper underground. It was electric motors that made the world's first deep-level railway, the City & South London Railway, possible.

The line, billed as the 'First Electric Railway in England', was opened by the Prince of Wales in November 1890. Two 3-yard-diameter tunnels ran between King William Street in the City and Stockwell. Hydraulic lifts installed at the stations transferred passengers between street and platform. Each train had three carriages hauled by electric locomotives. The carriages were narrow and furnished with tiny windows just below the roof because it was thought that passengers would not need to see out. Guards at the end of each carriage called out the names of stations, and opened and closed the gates for passengers.

Two further 'tube' railways, the Waterloo and City Railway and the Central London Railway, had opened by 1900 to serve a city that now boasted a population of 6 million. Travel across England's capital would never be the same again. The crowds flocking to Queen Victoria's funeral in 1901, marking the symbolic end of an era, would make good use of the new underground network.

Places to visit

- The London Transport Museum, in Covent Garden, tells the story of the city's transport network from 1800 onwards.
- A walking tour of London's disused railway stations, including Aldwych, is a fascinating journey into the capital's hidden past.

Further reading

Oliver Green, *London Underground: The Story of the Tube* (2019).
Christian Wolmar, *The Subterranean Railway: How the London Underground was Built and How it Changed the City Forever* (2020).

39: The Wealth of Nations by Adam Smith

Adam Smith's *The Wealth of Nations* is arguably the most important document published in 1776, superseding The American Declaration of Independence in terms of its global impact. This title page from the original printing gives the book's full title – *An Inquiry into the Nature and Causes of the Wealth of Nations*. In the book, Smith challenged the Mercantilist view that wealth was fixed and finite and thus that hoarding gold and imposing tariffs on foreign goods was the only way for a country to prosper. His economic theories proposed in *The Wealth of Nations* remain influential today, and he is often referred to as the father of capitalism.

Adam Smith was a Scottish economist and moral philosopher who was a key figure in that country's Enlightenment. His father had died before Smith's birth but he was able to enter the University of Glasgow aged 14 in 1737. He steadily rose through the ranks of academia before earning a professorship aged 28. He travelled on the Continent, seeing how the unproductive French economy, along with the policies of Louis XIV, had exhausted the nation's wealth.

One of *The Wealth of Nations*' key arguments was that individuals acting to fulfil their own needs and self-interest results in wider societal benefit by what Smith called the 'invisible hand'. People should be free to produce and exchange goods as they please so that they can unwittingly contribute to the greater good.

> He (or she) generally, indeed, neither intends to promote the public interest nor knows how much he is promoting it. By preferring the support of domestic to that of foreign industry, he intends only his own security and by directing that industry in such a manner as its produce may be of the greatest value, he intends only his own gain and he is in this, as in many other cases, led by an invisible hand to promote an end which was no part of his intention.

The division of labour within an economy results in a web of mutual independence and thus the free market promotes stability and prosperity.

Like Samuel Smiles eight decades later (*see* chapter 77), Smith wanted people to practise thrift, hard work, and enlightened self-interest. He believed the practice of enlightened self-interest was natural for the majority of people. Smith provided an example – a butcher does not supply meat based on good-hearted intentions, but because he profits by selling meat. If the meat he sells is poor, he will not have repeat customers and, thus, no profit. Therefore, it is in the butcher's interest to sell good meat at a price that customers are willing to pay, so that both parties benefit in every transaction. Smith believed the ability to think long-term would prevent most businesses from negatively exploiting customers. When that wasn't enough, he looked to the government to enforce laws.

Smith saw thrift and savings as important virtues, especially when savings were used to invest. Through investment, the industry would have the capital to buy more efficient machinery and encourage innovation. This technological leap forward would increase returns on invested capital and raise the overall standard of living. He regarded the responsibilities of the government as being limited to defence of a nation's borders, universal education, the building of infrastructure such as roads and bridges, the enforcement of legal rights and the punishment of crime. He cautioned invasively large government, writing, 'There is no art which one government sooner learns of another, than that of draining money from the pockets of the people.'

Smith proposed each country having a solid currency backed with hard metals such as gold. He hoped to curtail the government's ability to depreciate currency by circulating more of it to pay for wars or other wasteful expenditures. With hard currency acting as a check on spending, Smith hoped governments would be forced to keep taxes low and allow free trade across borders by eliminating tariffs. He argued that tariffs and other taxes only succeeded in making life more expensive for the people while also stifling industry and trade abroad.

Adam Smith.

To elucidate his opposition to tariffs, Smith used the example of making wine in Scotland. He pointed out that good grapes could be grown in Scotland in hothouses, but the extra costs of heating would make Scottish wine thirty times more expensive than French wines. Far better, he reasoned, would be to trade something Scotland had an abundance of such as wool, in return for French wine. Because France had a natural competitive advantage in producing wine, tariffs that aimed to create and protect a domestic wine industry would just waste resources and cost the public money.

The Wealth of Nations marked the birth of modern capitalism and economics. Ironically, Smith himself, the champion of the free market, spent the last years of his life as the Commissioner of Customs, responsible for tariffs enforcement. He took the work to heart and burned many of his clothes when he discovered they had been smuggled into shops from abroad.

Smith's theories remain popular with right-wing economists to this day. His profile appeared on the £20 bank note in 2007. The Adam Smith Institute, founded in the late 1970s, reckons itself one of the world's leading think tanks. It works to promote a free market, neoliberal ideas through research, publishing, media outreach and education, and has had a significant influence on British government policy over the past four decades, giving theoretical ballast to the various privatisations and deregulations that have transformed British society. Whether that is for the better or not is for you, the reader, to decide.

Places to visit

- A 10-foot high bronze statue of Adam Smith, unveiled in 2008, stands on Edinburgh's Royal Mile.
- Panmure House was Smith's Edinburgh home from 1788 to 1790. It was restored to house a centre for economic and social debate, formally opened in July 2018 by former Prime Minister Gordon Brown.

Further reading

Nicholas Phillipson, *Adam Smith: An Enlightened Life* (2011).
Ian Simpson Ross, *The Life of Adam Smith* (2010).

40: Diagram of the *Brookes* Slave Ship

This diagram of the *Brookes* slave ship was a powerful image used by those who campaigned for the cessation of Britain's involvement in the slave trade in the late eighteenth and early nineteenth centuries. Created in 1787, the image illustrates how enslaved Africans were transported to the Americas and depicts a slave ship fully loaded to its 454-person capacity. The *Brookes* was part of the triangular trade between Britain, the west coast of Africa and the Caribbean.

Thomas Clarkson, a leading abolitionist, wrote that the 'print seemed to make an instantaneous impression of horror upon all who saw it, and was therefore instrumental, in consequence of the wide circulation given it, in serving the cause of the injured Africans'. It was published in newspapers, pamphlets and books, and appeared on posters fixed to the walls of coffee houses and taverns.

The slave trade lay at the heart of Britain's wealth. Since the early sixteenth century, European vessels had traded African people as commodities in order to provide a captive workforce to exploit the economic potential of the Americas. Domestic demand for luxury goods such as tea and coffee, sugar, tobacco and cotton clothing grew, and these materials were produced by enslaved labour in the plantations of the Americas. Slaves were transported by vessels such as the *Brookes* from Africa to the West Indies. Having deposited its miserable human cargo, the ship would then load up on raw materials, take them back to Britain and then reload with manufactured items such as guns, cloth, iron and beer to be traded in Africa in return for further slaves.

It is estimated that British ships carried about 2.6 of the 12 million Africans transported across the Atlantic. Of this total, about 2 million died on the journey known as the Middle Passage.

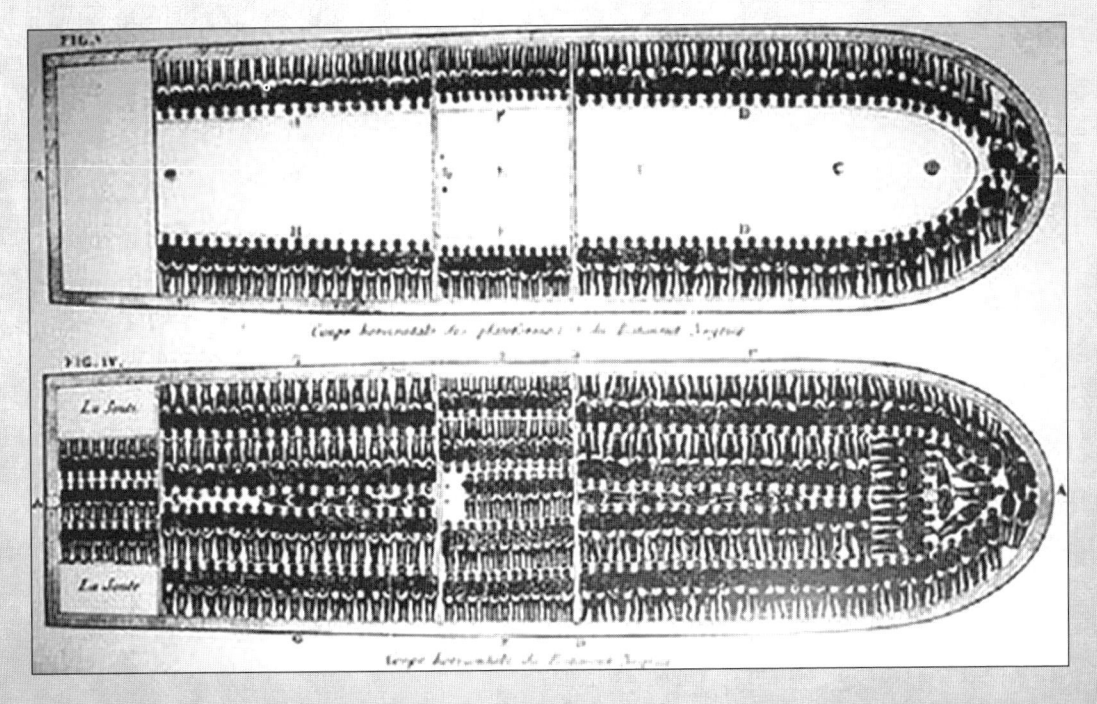

The voyage could last several months. Slaves were tightly packed into cramped spaces below deck, with each person being chained to the next. Sanitary conditions were wretched, and diseases such as smallpox, scurvy and measles common. In the West Indies, slaves were sold at auction and then became the property of their new owners. Brutal punishments to keep slaves in order were commonplace and any attempt to escape could be met with a lashing, or amputation of the toes. Despite this, in Jamaica, groups of runaway slaves formed 'Maroon' communities that fought against British soldiers.

The slave trade funded the Industrial Revolution as factory-made goods were exchanged for enslaved people. Profits made from the trade were often invested in burgeoning industries. For example, Abraham Darby had, in 1713, benefitted from a loan from a Bristol merchant who had profited from a slave trading expedition.

In 1787, the Committee for the Abolition of the Slave Trade was established, comprising Quakers, MPs and other abolitionists who were morally opposed to the trade. William Wilberforce represented the committee in Parliament. They used a range of campaigning

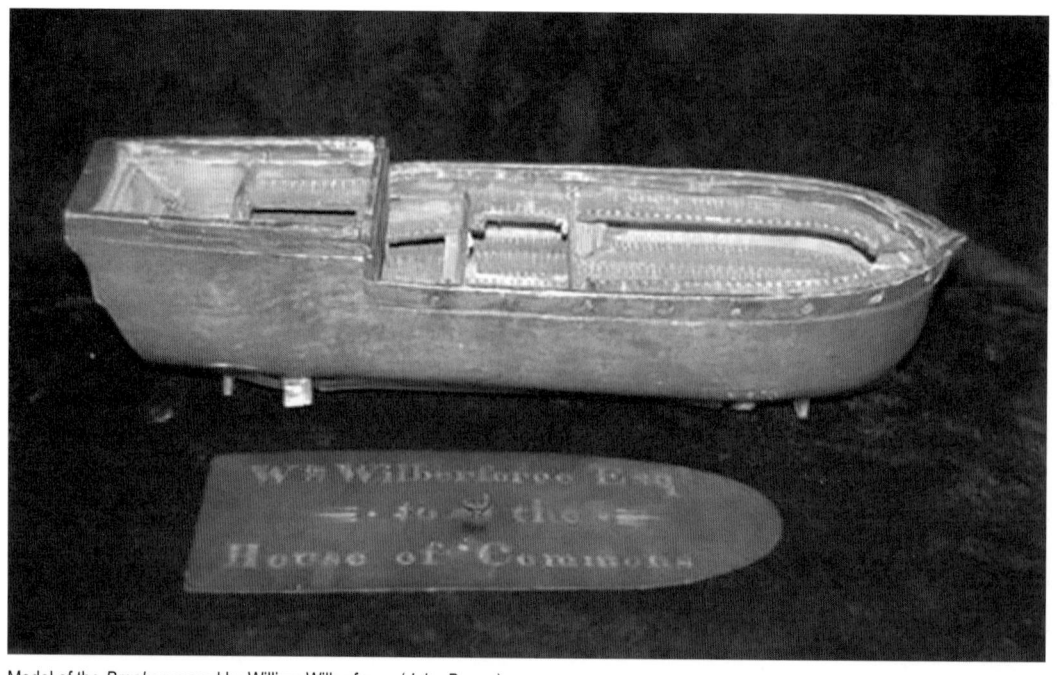

Wedgwood anti-slavery ceramic medallion, 1786.

Model of the *Brookes* owned by William Wilberforce. (*John Broom*)

tactics including organising a boycott of sugar, presenting petitions to Parliament and a speaking tour led by Thomas Clarkson, during which he would show slave chains and irons and a model of the *Brookes*.

Leaflets detailed the outrage of the slave ship *Zong*, from which the captain threw 133 Africans overboard so he could claim the insurance. Josiah Wedgwood struck a black-and-white cameo that contained the pitiful image of a chained slave and the inscription 'Am I Not a Man and a Brother?' This was to become the catchphrase of British and American abolitionists, and the image was widely reproduced on domestic objects like crockery as well as becoming a popular fashion accessory on snuffboxes, bracelets and hairpins. Clarkson wrote: 'At length, the taste for wearing them became general; and thus, fashion, which usually confines itself to worthless things, was seen for once in the honourable office of promoting the cause of justice, humanity, and freedom.'

British Africans, such as Olaudah Equiano, a former slave who had bought his freedom, formed the 'Sons of Africa', an anti-slave trade campaign group. In 1789, he published *The Interesting Narrative of the Life of Olaudah Equiano*, which went through nine editions.

Parliament passed the Act for the Abolition of the Slave Trade in 1807 and set up the West Africa Squadron of the Royal Navy to patrol the Atlantic in an attempt to stop rogue ships. Anti-slavery treaties were signed with many African rulers. However, slavery itself continued in British colonies for a further twenty-six years until a law was passed banning the practice altogether. It came at a price. Plantation owners were given £20 million worth of compensation. Nothing was given to those freed.

Historians have continued to debate the reasons for the ending of the slave trade, with some arguing that it had become unprofitable before abolition rather than its ending in British colonies motivated by the moral imperative of the abolitionists. The importance of campaigners like Clarkson and Wilberforce has been challenged as the role played by black Britons such as Equiano has been brought more to the fore.

Places to visit

- Wilberforce House in Hull contains several displays detailing the history of slavery and of the abolition movement. It is located in the house of the Yorkshire MP who did much to campaign for the ending of slavery. One of the world's earliest slavery museums, it opened in 1906.
- The International Slavery Museum in Liverpool's Albert Dock reveals the city's role in the slave trade as well as considering the issue of modern slavery.
- The Museum of London has a permanent gallery devoted to the capital's part in slavery. It is located in a former warehouse in West India Quay that once stored sugar grown and harvested by enslaved men, women and children.

Further reading

Olaudah Equiano, *The Interesting Narrative of the Life of Olaudah Equiano: or, Gustavus Vassa, the African and Other Writings* (2003).
Hugh Thomas, *The Slave Trade* (2006).
David Olusoga, *Black and British: A Forgotten History* (2017).
William Hague, *William Wilberforce: The Life of the Great Anti-Slave Trade Campaigner* (2007).

41: Tobacco Tin

This tobacco tin, made by J. & F. Bell of Glasgow and dating from the end of the nineteenth century, speaks of the continuation of the tobacco industry in the Scottish city. It was a century and a half before this tin was manufactured that Glasgow was transformed from a town of middling importance into one of the foremost cities that drove Britain's Industrial Revolution.

By the early 1600s, smoking the newly discovered New World tobacco plant was becoming part of social life in Scotland and, by the 1630s, Glasgow merchants were importing and selling tobacco to the city's consumers. Some doctors hailed tobacco for its medicinal uses and recommended smoking as a treatment for everything from arthritis, gout and epilepsy to blocked ears and panic attacks.

The 1707 Act of Union allowed Scotland access to the vast English colonial markets across the world – particularly in North America. The position of Glasgow on the river Clyde gave the city the opportunity to rival Bristol as a trading post between the Atlantic trade and that with the European mainland. In 1747, France granted Glasgow a monopoly on the importation of tobacco to French-owned territories. The conditions were ripe for Glasgow to become the epicentre of a five-decade-long economic boom.

Ships departing from the Clyde took up to twenty days less to traverse the Atlantic than those setting off from London. European demand for Virginia leaf was insatiable, and the small burgh of Glasgow, with its direct access to the North Atlantic via the Clyde, soon found itself in a hugely enviable position. Channel deepening work took place in 1768 to enable larger ships, fit for repeated Atlantic crossings, to access the port.

Tobacco became a central commodity of the triangular trade, which had slavery at its heart. Between 1740 and 1770, Glasgow's tobacco trade with the New World was at its height. Around 50 per cent of all Europe's tobacco imports arrived at Glasgow, Port Glasgow and Greenock, with the commodity accounting for 80 per cent of all Scottish re-exports. From the 1750s onwards, the Clyde was handling a larger share of Europe's tobacco than all the British ports combined. Tobacco flowed through Glasgow to France, Holland, Ireland, Scandinavia and the German states. Commercial success on this scale brought riches to the city's merchant community, stimulated urban expansion and provided the material foundations for the cultural achievements of the Scottish Enlightenment.

The Scottish Tobacco Lords amassed huge fortunes in the eighteenth century by trading in tobacco and slaves. Many gave public expression to their wealth by bestowing vast sums on large houses and ornate churches. One prominent Tobacco Lord was John Glassford, who acquired a fleet of vessels and several tobacco stores in New England. He was described in 1771 by Tobias Smollett as 'one of the greatest merchants in Europe', with a trading turnover of over half a million pounds per year.

The newly enriched Glasgow merchants were quick to ape the lifestyles of their aristocratic contemporaries. Many dressed in black silk

St Andrew's-in-the Square, Glasgow. The former Tobacco Lords' church is now Glasgow's Centre for Scottish Culture. (*Kim Traynor/Creative Commons*)

clothes topped off with black three-cornered hats and carried silver or gold-tipped ebony canes. The lavish town houses were filled with classical architectural features and mahogany furniture. An area on the western fringes of Glasgow, where their houses were built, is now known as Merchant City and includes thoroughfares such as Virginia Street and Jamaica Street. Other streets are named after individual merchants – Buchanan, Dunlop, Ingram, Wilson, Oswald, Cochrane and Glassford.

St Andrew's church was the Tobacco Lords' parish place of worship. It was built between 1739 and 1756, the first post-Reformation Presbyterian church, and is considered one of the finest churches of its era in Britain. A group of Tobacco Lords commissioned it as a manifestation of their wealth and power.

Their dominance was not to last. American colonists accused the Tobacco Lords of price manipulation and causing hardship among the planters of Maryland and Virginia. Glasgow merchants offered cheap credit to the planters, who accumulated combined debts of around £1 million, or £152 million in 2023 values. The cheap credit enabled the planters to buy European consumer goods and other luxuries before they had ready cash to do so from their harvests. Although when the time came to sell the crop, the indebted growers found themselves forced by the traders to accept low prices for their harvest in order to stave off bankruptcy.

These grievances fed into the unhappiness created by high taxes imposed from London to fuel the wars that led to American independence. One unhappy planter was the future President of the United States George Washington, who saw his liabilities swell to nearly £2,000 by the late 1760s (equivalent to £279,263 in 2023). Another was fellow founding father Thomas Jefferson, who nearly lost his farm and accused British merchants of unfairly depressing tobacco prices and forcing Virginia farmers to take on unsustainable debts.

The American War of Independence ensured that these debs were never repaid. It also abruptly halted the vast profits brought into Glasgow by the Tobacco Lords. Some, such as John Glassford, found themselves at the receiving end of the financial downswing. This once-wealthy Tobacco Lord died in 1783 with debts of £100,000. Others were quick to turn their attention to the expanding cotton trade.

Scotland's days as a major tobacco trader were over but the legacy of those heady decades remained. During the age of the Tobacco Lords, Glasgow had grown from a small town of less than 20,000 to a booming metropolis approaching 200,000 inhabitants. The city and its hinterland were to become major drivers of Britain's Industrial Revolution.

A former tobacco merchant's house, owned by Robert Findlay, at 42 Miller Street, Glasgow. (*Novoje/Creative Commons*)

Places to visit

- The Cunninghame Mansion, now the Gallery of Modern Art in Glasgow's Royal Exchange Square. William Cunninghame (1731–99) paid £10,000 for the mansion from the profits of the tobacco trade.
- St Andrew's Square was a fashionable residence for some of Glasgow's richest merchants and served as a display of their wealth and power.

Further reading

Tom Devine, *The Tobacco Lords: A Study of the Tobacco Merchants of Glasgow and their Trading Activities, 1740–1790* (1975).
Neil Oliver, *A History of Scotland* (2009).

42: Raw Cotton Bale

Cotton had been grown and converted into fabric by many civilisations across the world for several centuries before Britain's Industrial Revolution. The oldest known cotton fabric, found in Peru, dates from about 6000 BC. When Alexander the Great invaded India, his troops started wearing indigenously produced cotton garments.

Cotton fabric was known to the ancient Romans but it was only in the later medieval era that imports from Arabic-speaking lands brought cotton goods within the range of general affordability. Muslim conquests of the Iberian Peninsula and Sicily saw cotton weaving spread northwards through Italy and eventually across Western Europe. A spinning wheel was introduced *c.*1350, and by the mid-1400s, Venice, Antwerp and Haarlem were prominent cotton-trading centres.

India had been renowned for the manufacture and export of fine cotton fabrics for centuries. Marco Polo, the thirteenth-century traveller, had noted their superior quality. Indian cotton production increased up to the eighteenth century under the Mughal Empire. Twenty-five per cent of the global textile trade originated

A raw cotton bale. (*Clem Rutter/Creative Commons*)

from the Empire, with the main manufacturing centre being Dhaka.

Demand for cotton cloth increased during the periods of the Renaissance (fourteenth to seventeenth century) and the Enlightenment (seventeenth and eighteenth centuries). However, there was little reciprocal demand in India for European goods, such as woollens, metals and a few luxury items. Thus, gold and silver were transported in large quantities to Mughal India to pay for the cotton goods. By 1664, the East India Company was importing a quarter of a million pieces of calico and chintz into Britain.

Compared to other fabrics, cotton had superior qualities of cleanliness, washability and ease of colouring. Imports of calicoes, cheap cotton fabrics, were popular amongst the less wealthy. Cotton was combined with linen to make a softer, more versatile fabric, and also used to make velvet as an alternative to silk velvet. It was cheaper than silk and could be imprinted more easily than wool, allowing for patterned dresses for women. It became the standard fashion and, because of its price, was generally more accessible.

In the late seventeenth century, the East India Company established factories in South Asia to produce finished cotton goods for the British market. The imported calico and chintz garments negatively affected the livelihoods of British weavers, spinners, dyers, shepherds and farmers. The Calico Acts of 1700 and 1721 banned the importation and sale of finished pure cotton goods and the use of calicoes for clothing or domestic purposes. Raw cotton remained exempt, so bales of raw cotton were imported to Britain. The need to turn this raw product into finished goods for the domestic market stimulated the improvements in spinning and weaving technology. The Calico Acts were repealed in 1774, after the development of

Manchester from Kersal Moor, painting by William Wyld (1852). It was later rendered into a famous engraving by Edward Goodall titled *Cottonopolis* in recognition of the city's pre-eminence in the world cotton trade. (*Royal Collection/Public domain*)

cotton manufacture technology had allowed British industry to become competitive with fabrics from the East.

The era of cotton mills had begun, and by the start of the 1770s, cotton from Bengal still enjoyed a competitive advantage so the British government introduced tariffs to restrict Indian imports. The East India Company helped to deindustrialise India, creating a massive market for imported goods. Taxes raised from the Indian people after the company established direct control over the subcontinent in 1757 were invested in British industry. These factors meant that Britain overtook India as the world's leading cotton manufacturer. In Manchester, the number of cotton mills rose dramatically in a very short space of time, from two in 1790 to sixty-six in 1821. By this time, Britain imported much of its raw cotton from the USA, but during times of political upheaval in North America, imports from the Indian subcontinent came more to the fore.

The British cotton industry centred on areas with ready access to ports, particularly to the west of Scotland and Lancashire, the hinterlands of Glasgow, and Liverpool. The damp climate in those areas also helped ensure the yarn was less likely to snap.

British colonisation opened up the huge Indian market to manufactured British goods. Britain established a monopoly both in the captive Indian market and with regard to the country's raw materials. Within little over a century, India was relegated from being the primary source of finished textiles to the mere source of the raw cotton.

Given these inbuilt advantages, the British cotton industry dominated European markets, amounting to over 40 per cent of Britain's export trade in the mid-1780s. Settlers in British colonies also maintained British fashions, some of which were copied by sections of the indigenous populations.

To sum up the significance of the trade in raw cotton bales at this time, it changed India's role from being a world leader in the supply of cotton products to merely a supplier of raw materials, and fuelled Britain's Industrial Revolution by creating the need for factories and stimulating demand for coal-driven power. It also transformed Lancashire in particular into an industrial powerhouse, and caused the massive growth of Britain's inland transport network in the form of canals and, later, railways.

Places to visit

- The Museum of Science and Industry in Manchester contains a collection of textile machines that demonstrate the whole process used in a cotton mill, and a few key eighteenth-century machines.
- Quarry Bank Mill, Cheshire, has a display demonstrating the importance of the cotton trade to the area.

Further reading

Sven Beckert, *Empire of Cotton: A Global History of Capitalism* (2014).
Chris Aspin, *The Cotton Industry* (2003).

43: Glad Tidings Ship

The American ship *Glad Tidings*, pictured here in *The Illustrated London News* of 4 November 1865 approaching Liverpool, could not have been more appropriately named. Its arrival signalled the end of the Lancashire Cotton Famine, a grim and desperate period in the county's history.

The importation of raw cotton into Britain, mainly from the American cotton fields, had made Lancashire, alongside areas of Cheshire and Derbyshire, the 'workshop of the world' by the mid-nineteenth century. Eighty per cent of imported British raw cotton came from the USA. However, this meteoric rise suffered a severe dent in 1861–5, during the American Civil War. The American government placed a blockade on ports that came under the Confederacy, cutting off the supply of raw cotton to Europe. For an area as dependent on one raw material for its wealth, employment opportunities and sense of purpose as Lancashire, this came as a grievous blow. Furthermore, overproduction during a boom of 1859–60 had overheated the market. A time of contracting world markets acted as an unfortunate backdrop to the import crisis.

The Lancashire mills had wisely stockpiled a four-month supply of cotton and were able to add a further month's reserve before the blockade bit. It was hoped that America's war would be a short-lived affair but this was not to be. Without raw materials entering Liverpool, cotton production ceased by October 1861. Mills closed, previously well-paid workers became unemployed and poverty ran through the affected areas. Soup kitchens were opened to feed the poor.

The most desperate applied for relief through the Poor Law Unions and local and national

THE SHIP GLAD TIDINGS, WITH A CARGO OF AMERICAN COTTON, ENTERING THE PORT OF LIVERPOOL.—SEE NEXT PAGE.

THE COTTON FAMINE: DISTRIBUTING TICKETS FOR BREAD, SOUP, MEAT, MEAL, COAL, ETC., AT THE OFFICE OF A DISTRICT PROVIDENT SOCIETY, MANCHESTER.
SEE SUPPLEMENT, PAGE 558.

relief committees were established. Benefactors raised hundreds of thousands of pounds from across the United Kingdom and the Empire. Attendance at a self-help sewing class organised by a church might warrant a payment from the Poor Law Union. Bible Reading classes and industrial classes that taught reading, writing and simple maths with carpentry, shoemaking and tailoring followed. Receipt of benefits was usually contingent on attending these makeshift schools.

By the winter of 1862/3, three quarters of workers in Stalybridge were dependent on relief and 750 houses in the town lay empty. The local relief committee decided to halt handouts of money and instead issue tickets that could be redeemed at the shops of local grocers. This proved the last straw for many. On 20 March 1863, men refused to take the tickets and stoned the cab of the official who had attempted to distribute them.

They then broke the windows of shops owned by members of the local relief committee. A company of Hussars was despatched from Manchester, the Riot Act was read, and eighty men were arrested. Most were released the following day, but twenty-eight were committed for trial in Chester. Police and soldiers escorting them to the railway station were pelted with stones. 'Money and bread', not 'tickets' were demanded. Shopkeepers, fearful of the atmosphere, handed out bread. Resistance spread to nearby Ashton-under-Lyne, Hyde and Dukinfield. By 24 March, the local relief committee agreed to pay out money instead of tickets.

By March 1863, there were 25,000 men receiving aid but not undertaking any work in return. To the Victorian mindset, this was unacceptable. Thus, Palmerston's Liberal government passed the Public Works

(Manufacturing Districts) Act in 1864 by which local authorities could borrow money to provide public works schemes. Some areas put men to work creating public parks. One of the most splendid of these is Oldham's Alexandra Park. In other areas, large sewers were commissioned to replace the existing medieval drains. This served to improve sanitation in industrial districts. Elsewhere, canals were dug and navigations built to straighten rivers. Thus, the infrastructure of the area was improved as a side-effect of the famine.

Some mill owners employed workers who had been laid off to undertake work on their estates. In Glossop, Derbyshire, schools were established and free brass band concerts and public readings from *The Pickwick Papers* were organised. Some workers migrated to work in the woollen mills of Yorkshire, others to seek a new life in the USA or the Antipodes. Two hundred people left Glossop for Australia and New Zealand. By 1864, there were 2,000 empty houses in Stockport and 7,000 in Blackburn. Shops and beer houses began to close.

Eventually, the famine ended. In August 1864, the first large consignment of raw cotton arrived from the USA. The American Civil War ended the following spring.

The solidarity northern industrial workers had displayed for each other's needs was extended to the slaves on whose behalf the American Civil War was being fought. The Confederate states had hoped that distress in European cotton manufacturing districts would lead to political pressure on Abraham Lincoln to force the Union to negotiate peace terms. Many Lancashire cotton towns flew Confederate flags as a protest against the Union's blockade.

However, at a meeting at Manchester's Free Trade Hall on the final day of 1862, cotton workers resolved to support the Union in its fight against slavery despite their own increasing hardship. They sent a letter to Abraham Lincoln, praising his courage in removing the 'foul blot on civilisation and Christianity – chattel slavery'. Lincoln replied two weeks later, acknowledging the sufferings of the working men of Manchester but praising their 'sublime Christian heroism'. The American government sent a gift of food to the people of Lancashire.

When the ship *Glad Tidings* arrived in Liverpool, it brought more than warm words and charity relief. It brought that much sought-after raw cotton upon which the livelihoods of so many people depended during Britain's Industrial Revolution.

Places to visit

- Alexandra Park in Oldham was built as part of a public works programme to provide employment during the cotton famine. Its lavish facilities include a woodland walk, ornamental lake, bandstand and avenues.
- A statue of Abraham Lincoln stands in Brazennose Street, Lincoln Square, Manchester. It commemorates the mutual support shown between Manchester cotton workers and the American Federal government in 1862–3 and reproduces portions of the letters that were exchanged.

Further reading

Norman Longmate, *The Hungry Mills: The story of the Lancashire cotton famine 1862–5* (1978).
Jim Powell, *Losing the Thread: Cotton, Liverpool and the American Civil War* (2020).

44: Porcelain Tea Set

This attractive tea service, made in Chelsea in the 1760s, speaks of an era when taking tea became a high-fashion activity amongst the middle and upper classes. The drink was consumed in vast quantities and served via ornate tea sets like this one.

Whilst tea had been grown, drunk and traded in China for thousands of years, it only began to be imported into Europe in the early seventeenth century. The first importers were Portuguese and Dutch traders, with the tea originating in China and Japan. However, the former had strong government controls on the export of tea and a total ban on the export of the tea plant.

Due to its rarity, tea had become a fashionable luxury good. The East India Company imported tea into Britain, firstly from secondary markets, then directly from China. The fact that the Chinese would only accept payment in silver helped contribute to a trade imbalance between the two countries. This led to the East India Company smuggling opium into China to address the disparity (*see* chapter 45). Heavy taxes imposed by the British government ensured tea remained expensive. Thus, it became a focus for smuggling activities around Britain's coastline.

To undermine the smuggling trade, the 1784 Commutation Act slashed tea taxes from 119 to 12.5 per cent. The East India Company monopoly on the import of tea ended in 1834, meaning tea became far more widely available across all social classes at the height of Britain's Industrial Revolution. Promoted as one of the wholesome alternatives to alcohol by the temperance movement (*see* chapter 88), its popularity grew as the nineteenth century wore on.

(Forever Wiser/Opal Art Seekers/Creative Commons)

The Great Tea Race from China to London: the Taeping and the Ariel off the Lizard, published in *The Illustrated London News*, 22 September 1866.

Following China's defeat in the Opium Wars in 1860, the tea trade expanded substantially. New ports opened up along the Yangtze River, including Hankou, known as the tea capital of China. In Britain arose a fashion for fresh tea, the result of the first crop of the season.

In order to be the first merchants to bring in this lucrative tea, clipper ships would race across the world. The performance of these vessels could be followed in the Shipping Intelligence columns of newspapers. This information began to be reported on in the news sections, with the first ship to dock exciting considerable interest from 1857 onwards.

A Great Tea Race was held in 1866 to see which ship could bring tea to London from China in the fastest time. A premium of ten shillings per ton was paid for the winning ship's cargo. Newspaper interest was at its height, with updates and detailed reports. Many bets were placed on the outcome of the race, in London, Hong Kong, and the ports of Britain, and by the captains and crews of the vessels involved.

The race was won by *Taeping*, which docked twenty-eight minutes before *Ariel* – after a passage of more than 14,000 miles. *Ariel* had been ahead when the ships were taken in tow by steam tugs off Deal, but after waiting for the tide at Gravesend, the deciding factor was the height of tide at which one could enter the different docks used by each ship. The third finisher, *Serica*, docked an hour and fifteen minutes after *Ariel*. These three ships had left China on the same tide and arrived at London ninety-nine days later to dock on the same tide.

One of the most iconic clipper ships was the *Cutty Sark*, whose maiden voyage to Shanghai took place in 1870. John Willis, the ship's owner, wanted the *Cutty Sark* to be the fastest cargo ship afloat. The hull was made of teak and rock elm attached to a light and streamlined iron skeleton, while a sharp bow and narrow hull ensured the ship was dynamic in the water. The ship featured very tall masts, a vast sail area and wire rigging – all designed to increase speed at sea – and a

44: PORCELAIN TEA SET

The *Cutty Sark*, moored at Greenwich. (*John Broom*)

steering mechanism that freed up valuable cargo space in the hold. *Cutty Sark* was designed and built to win the tea races. She could hold about 10,000 tea chests, which would have had a value of about £6 million in today's money.

The high-water mark of tea clippers such as the *Cutty Sark* was short-lived. The Suez Canal was opened in 1869 (*see* chapter 33), reducing the journey time by steamship between Britain and China by over 3,000 miles. *Cutty Sark* completed just eight voyages to China carrying tea. Eventually, she was repurposed to work lower value, but still essential, trade routes, carrying wool from Australia to the mills of industrial Britain.

Over time, most of the tea clippers were either wrecked or scrapped. Today, *Cutty Sark* remains as virtually the sole physical reminder of the tea clipper era that was epitomised by the Great Tea Race of 1866.

Places to visit

- The *Cutty Sark*, which forms part of Royal Museums, Greenwich, is open to visitors on most days of the year.
- The Merseyside Maritime Museum has a 1:48 scale model of a typical tea clipper from about 1865, showing a cross-section of the hull.

Further reading

Steven Ujifusa, *Barons of the Sea: And Their Race to Build the World's Fastest Clipper Ship* (2018).
Peter Broadbent, *Felix Wild and the Great Tea Race* (2019).
Sarah Rose, *For All the Tea in China: Espionage, Empire and the Secret Formula for the World's Favourite Drink* (2010).

45: Opium Pipe

This ornate Chinese opium pipe, fashioned from ivory with a metal mount and terracotta bowl, is engraved with figures and scenes, and its bowl decorated with a pottery frog and enamelled flowers. Heated opium would have been placed in the top of the bowl and the fumes inhaled through the pipe. Styles of opium pipe reflected the relative wealth or poverty of their owners and ranged from bejewelled, elaborately ornamented works of art like this one to simple constructions of clay or bamboo.

Opium had long been used in limited quantities in China for the relief of tension and pain. When, during the seventeenth century, the practice of tobacco smoking spread from North America to China, opium smoking also became popular in the Far East. This quickly led to widespread addiction, to the extent that the sale and smoking of opium was prohibited in 1729. Like most prohibitions in history, this failed to stop the practice, and in 1796 its importation and cultivation was outlawed ... yet it continued to flourish.

The trade in opium was a lucrative one. The poppy was harvested by up to 1.3 million northern Indian peasants. Grown as a cash crop, a peasant might give over a half of their holding to poppies. The harvest would then be sent to two opium factories on the river Ganges to be dried and mixed, and made into cakes, which were then packed into wooden crates.

The Portuguese had begun to import opium from India and sell it in China at a considerable profit. By 1773, the British, in the shape of the East India Company, had become the leading suppliers to the Chinese market. The company established a monopoly on opium cultivation in Bengal. Other Western countries, including the newly independent USA, also took part in the trade.

Opium helped to offset the trade imbalance with China, where the demand for European manufactured goods remained low. In doing so, it also created a steady demand among Chinese addicts for opium imported by the West. The East India Company licensed private traders to take the opium from India to China. These traders would sell the opium to smugglers along the Chinese coast. Having taken their cut, the gold and silver received from these sales was

(Wellcome Images/Creative Commons)

Chinese opium smokers in a saloon experiencing various effects of the drug, 1866. (Wellcome Images/Creative Commons)

passed on to the East India Company. The company, in turn, used this gold and silver to purchase luxury items such as porcelain, silk and tea, which they sold at a profit in Britain to those who had the disposable income created from the wealth of the Industrial Revolution.

The amount of opium imported into China increased from about 200 chests annually in 1729 to roughly 1,000 chests in 1767, and then to about 10,000 per year between 1820 and 1830. The average weight of each chest was approximately 140 pounds. By 1838, for the first time, the balance of payments began to run in the British favour against the Chinese. The East India Company had 2,500 clerks working in 100 offices of the Opium Agency, monitoring farmers, enforcing contracts and exercising quality control. Exports increased from 4,000 chests per year in the early 1800s to more than 60,000 by the 1880s. It was the second most important source of revenue for the British Indian administration and one of the largest enterprises on the subcontinent. However, for the peasants growing it, once the costs of rent, manure, irrigation and hired labour were taken into account, they often operated at a loss. They were bound by contractual arrangements and annual production targets to keep on growing the crop.

Increasing levels of opium addiction from the 1820s onwards began to affect the efficiency of the Chinese state, with both imperial troops and government officials succumbing to the vice. The Qing dynasty stepped up efforts to impose the existing restrictions. Consequently, in the spring of 1839, the Chinese government confiscated and destroyed more than 20,000 chests of opium that were warehoused at Canton by British merchants.

Tensions increased in July, when some drunken British sailors killed a Chinese villager. The British government, which did not wish its subjects to be tried in the Chinese legal system, refused to turn the accused men over to the Chinese courts. This resulted in the first of two armed conflicts between China and the West, the Opium Wars. On both occasions, China was defeated. The first war (1839–42) halted Chinese efforts to stop the trade. At the end of the war, the British colonised Hong Kong in order to provide an offshore trading base. The second war (1856–60) ended with China being forced to legalise the opium trade, although able to levy a small import tax on the product.

By 1906, the importance of opium in the West's trade with China had declined, and the Qing government began to regulate the importation and consumption of the drug. In 1907, China and India signed the Ten Years' Agreement, whereby China agreed to forbid native cultivation and consumption of opium on the understanding that the export of

British and Chinese troops engage in battle at Beijing during the Second Opium War, 1860. Painting by Richard Simkin, 1900.

Indian opium would decline in proportion and cease completely by 1917. Opium smoking in China remained a problem right up until the Communist Revolution of 1949.

That opium pipe symbolised short periods of ecstasy for its user, often followed by a miserable slide into addiction. For the Indian peasants growing the crop it meant a culture of dependency and poverty. For the East India Company it meant vast profits, and for well-to-do British subjects it resulted in the fuelling of a consumer boom as the revenues generated from the Industrial Revolution were spent on the finer things in life.

Places to visit

- The National Army Museum in London contains several artefacts and documents relating to the Opium Wars.
- The British Museum in Bloomsbury has a range of Chinese-made, opium-related paraphernalia which is intermittently on display.

Further reading

William Dalrymple, *The Anarchy: The Relentless Rise of the East India Company* (2020).
Brian Inglis, *Opium War* (2020).
Mark Simner, *The Lion and the Dragon: Britain's Opium Wars with China 1839–1860* (2019).

46: David Livingstone Lithograph

This lithograph, from an image created by James Durden, shows the famous meeting between American explorer H.M. Stanley and the long-lost Christian missionary David Livingstone, which occasioned the famous quote, 'Dr Livingstone, I presume?'

(Welcome Images/Creative Commons)

The Scot was the most high profile of several missionaries who took it upon themselves to reinforce the colonisation of much of Africa and elsewhere during Britain's Industrial Revolution with the exportation of British Christian values to the colonised peoples.

In the early nineteenth century, Western colonial expansion was contemporaneous with an evangelical revival – the Second Great Awakening – throughout the English-speaking world. This led to more overseas missionary activity. The nineteenth century became known as the 'Great Century of modern religious missions'. Missionary work in central and southern Africa had begun in the early nineteenth century, before the colonisation of these regions by the European powers. Being amongst the first white people to venture forth into deepest Africa, missionaries were also often the first explorers of those lands.

The Church Missionary Society had been founded in 1799, and five years later, sent its first two missionaries to Africa. The society was richly funded by Christian patrons, with an annual income equivalent to £20 million today, and a staff of 1,300 missionaries, 375 local clergy, and 1,000 local agents and teachers. The abolition of the slave trade in 1834 (*see* chapter 40) gave missionaries a powerful motivation to increase their work in order to convert the freed slaves. The popularity of the anti-slavery movement in enlightened British circles meant that money could be raised to fund the considerable expenses of setting up a mission. The incentive of learning how to read and write at a missionary school hooked in many Africans to hearing the Word of God.

The London Missionary Society sent David Livingstone to South Africa in 1840, where he became one of the first Europeans to traverse the continent. When Europeans began to colonise central and southern Africa towards the end of the century, international coordination featured prominently in both missionary and colonial projects. Livingstone believed that the suppression of the slave trade within Africa depended upon a combination of Christianity and trade. However, the numbers of non-Christians converted were small.

Scottish factory worker Mary Slessor saw her mission as more than merely collecting converts. She spent over four decades in southern Nigeria, learning the local language and living a life of total simplicity. She dealt head-on with some of the customs of the region, such as throwing twins into the bush to die, and negotiated an end to this. Today she is still revered and loved as a local figure. Destined for a different fate was the Church Missionary Society's Bishop James Hannington, who was murdered in Uganda in 1886 and later officially recognised as a martyr.

Robert Morrison was the first English missionary to visit China, in 1807. Over the course of the next century, thousands of Protestant men, women and children would live and work in the country. Their activities were closely restricted to certain cities until the treaty ending the Second Opium War (1860) opened up the entire county to them. Protestant missionary activity exploded during the next few decades. From fifty missionaries in China in 1860, the number grew to 2,500 in 1900; more than half were British.

Life was tough for early missionaries such as Morrison. Reluctantly supported by the East India Company and actively opposed by the Chinese government and the Jesuits, he forced those working under him at the East India Company to attend Sunday services and daily meetings including prayer, Bible readings, and the singing of hymns. He gained a few native converts, despite Christianity being added to the list of banned religions in China in 1812. The death sentence was announced from 1826 for any Europeans spreading Christianity. It was only after the Treaty of Nanking in 1842, which ended the First Opium War, that missionary activity could expand.

46: DAVID LIVINGSTONE LITHOGRAPH

Li Shigong, Chen Laoyi and Robert Morrison translating the Bible into Mandarin.

In 1865, J. Hudson Taylor set up the China Inland Mission as efforts were stepped up to convert China to Christianity. Copies of the Bible were distributed and Western-style schools and hospitals were established. One of those who felt called to leave a comfortable life enjoying the fruits of Britain's Industrial Revolution was C.T. Studd, the famous cricketer who had played in the 1882 Test match that gave rise to The Ashes. Studd gave away his considerable inheritance of £29,000 to various missionary groups and spent many decades on evangelising work in China, Africa and India.

The life of an overseas missionary was hard, with a high susceptibility to tropical diseases and mental breakdowns. Converts were few – Robert Morrison could claim only twenty-five new believers after twenty-seven years of work. The first unmarried female missionary to China was Mary Ann Aldersey, who opened a school for girls in 1844. In addition to their proselytising work, women missionaries played a major role in campaigns against opium and foot binding. The widespread view in Europe and America in the late nineteenth century was that civilisation could not exist apart from Christianity.

The Boxer Rebellion of 1900 saw 189 Protestant missionaries slaughtered, as the rebels identified them as agents of Western imperialism. Missionaries trying to spread the Christian culture that underpinned the moral climate of Britain's Industrial Revolution faced danger, disease and death. They remain today inspirational figures in British Christian culture.

Places to visit

- David Livingstone's Birthplace Museum at Blantyre, South Lanarkshire, tells the story of his remarkable journeys through Africa.

Further reading

Alvyn Austin, *China's Millions: The China Inland Mission and Late Qing Society, 1832–1905* (2007).
Kathleen L. Lodwick, *How Christianity Came to China: A Brief History* (2016).
Martin Ballard, *White Men's God: The Extraordinary Story of Missionaries in Africa* (2016).

Section Three

Protesting and Reforming

47: Luddite Hammer

'Enoch hath made them, Enoch shall break them!' So went the Luddite song in praise of the large hammers they used to smash weaving frames across the north and Midlands. Enoch Taylor of Marsden near Huddersfield manufactured the massive 30-pound hammers, which colloquially bore his name. He also produced many of the shearing frames that were the targets of Luddite ire.

'Luddite' is now a term of some derision used to describe people uncomfortable with new technology, but its origins date back to an early nineteenth-century workers' movement that railed against the ways that mechanisation of the textile industry had undermined the wages of skilled craftsmen. The Luddites were workers who objected to the increased use of mechanised weaving looms and knitting frames. Most had spent years serving apprenticeships to learn their craft and feared that an unskilled machine operator could produce more fabric than they could, for a fraction of the pay.

Many Luddites were owners of workshops that had closed because factories could sell the same products for less. When they sought factory work, many were turned away and unemployment and hardship increased. The Luddites identified the new machinery as the cause of their misery, as they reduced their bargaining power in the workplace.

Times were hard during the Napoleonic Wars (1803–15), with high grain prices. The British economy was particularly struggling in the years 1810 to 1812, with high unemployment and inflation. The Napoleonic Wars were draining the country's resources, whilst the Continental System affected imports of foodstuffs. Meanwhile, escalating war against the USA caused further disruption.

A few desperate weavers began breaking into factories and smashing the textile machines.

Enoch's hammer. (John Broom)

They drew their name from a probably fictional Leicestershire youth named Ned Ludd, who was rumoured to have wrecked two stocking frames in 1779. Protestors claimed to be taking orders from 'General Ludd' and issued manifestoes and threatening letters in his name. Membership was based on the swearing of a secret oath.

The first major outbreak of Luddite machine-breaking occurred at Arnold in Nottinghamshire on 11 March 1811 and soon spread to other industrial districts over the following two years. Factories were attacked and burned, and gunfire was occasionally exchanged with guards employed to protect the machinery. In response, the government made machine-breaking subject to the death sentence.

Luddites would meet at night on the moors surrounding industrial towns to practise military-like drills and manoeuvres. The movement spread from Nottinghamshire to the West Riding of Yorkshire in early 1812, and then to Lancashire by March 1813. Amongst the machines attacked

Cartoon from 1812.

were stocking frames and cropping frames. In Lancashire, Luddites battled the British Army at Burton's Mill in Middleton, and at Westhoughton Mill. Death threats were sent to magistrates and food merchants. Activists smashed Heathcote's lacemaking machine in Loughborough in 1816. He and other industrialists had secret chambers constructed in their buildings that could be used as hiding places during an attack.

The most high-profile attack on a mill occurred near Marsden, Huddersfield, in April 1812. Four Luddites, led by George Mellor, ambushed and assassinated mill owner William Horsfall of Ottiwells Mill at Crosland Moor. Horsfall had remarked that he would 'ride up to his saddle in Luddite blood'. Mellor fired the fatal shot to Horsfall's groin, and all four men were arrested.

On the night of 11 April 1812, the Dumb Steeple at Cooper Bridge was used as the meeting place of a contingent of Luddites who were gathering to march to Cartwright's Mill at Rawfolds, near Cleckheaton, to attack the new cropping machines. There were up to 150 men present, many with their faces blackened and carrying weapons such as Enoch hammers or muskets. It is little surprise, therefore, that one of their number lost his nerve and fled the scene just before the contingent began their march across Hartshead Moor towards their target. The army was deployed to round up protestors in the following days.

In January 1813, a mass trial of over sixty men was held at York. The charges were in connection with the Marsden incident and an attack on Cartwright's Mill. One of Mellor's fellow Luddites, Benjamin Walker, turned informant, and the other three men involved in the murder were hanged. While some of those charged were actual Luddites, many had no connection to the movement. Many of the jury trials were abandoned due to lack of evidence and thirty men were acquitted.

The sentences handed down on those found guilty, including execution and penal transportation, served as a deterrent to further Luddite attacks, and incidents of machine-breaking petered out in the succeeding months and years. The Frame Breaking Act (1812) made industrial sabotage a capital offence.

Places to visit

- Colne Valley Museum at Golcar, near Huddersfield. Housed across three 1840s' weavers' cottages, one of the displays that appear on rotation concerns Luddism. A replica Enoch hammer can be seen.
- Dumb Steeple. Situated at the junction of the A62 Huddersfield to Liversedge road and A644 Brighouse to Mirfield road, the 15-foot-high column contains a blue plaque commemorating the Luddite attack of 11 April 1812.
- Sparrow Park, Liversedge, contains a statue that highlights the plight of local croppers. It stands half a mile from the site of the former Cartwright's Mill.

Further reading

Douglas Liversidge, *The Luddites; Machine-breakers of the Early Nineteenth Century* (1972).
Charles River Editors, *The Luddites: The History and Legacy of the English Rebels Who Protested against Advanced Machinery during the Industrial Revolution* (2018).
Malcolm I. Thomis, *The Luddites: Machine-breaking in Regency England* (Library of Textile History) (1970).

48: Peterloo Handkerchief

Following the shocking events that unfolded at St Peter's Fields in Manchester on 16 August 1819, the Peterloo Handkerchief was one of a range of memorabilia produced to commemorate the event and to further the cause for political reform and social justice. Other items included prints, cartoons, banners, poems, plaques, jugs, bowls and other household items, but due to the fear of a harsh crackdown on signs of dissent, many of these artefacts would have to remain hidden. The handkerchief, therefore, was a memento of radical reform that could be concealed about the person.

The handkerchief depicts a detailed scene from the Peterloo Massacre, an infamous event in which between fifteen and twenty people were killed by charging cavalry while attending a rally aimed at campaigning for political reform. Armed forces are shown using swords to fight with the crowd, leaving several protestors badly injured. Liberty caps and banners can be seen with slogans such as 'Unite and be Free'. The scroll at the top reads: 'A representation of the Manchester reform meeting dispersed by the civil and military power Aug 16th 1819.'

The scroll also acts as a key to important elements of the story. Palm branches and laurel

(Courtesy People's History Museum)

leaves on the ribbon around the outside represent the peaceful intentions of the crowd, who were respectably dressed and non-violent. The slogan on the ribbon reads: 'Universal Suffrage, Annual Parliaments and Election by Ballot.'

The St Peter's Field demonstration had its roots in the campaign for parliamentary reform that gained momentum in Britain during the late-eighteenth and early-nineteenth centuries. Radical reformers were angered by a political system that only allowed men with considerable property to vote. They argued for improvements to the political system, and leaders such as the orator Henry Hunt and journalist William Cobbett expressed these aims with clarity and force. The unemployment and lower wages caused by the economic depression that followed the end of the Napoleonic War in 1815 caused severe hardship and hunger among the textile spinners and weavers of East Lancashire. The introduction of the Corn Laws in 1815 increased this by imposing a tariff on foreign grain, which led to higher bread prices. Such harsh economic conditions enhanced the appeal of political radicalism, particularly among women, who began to set up their own reforming societies to campaign for the vote on behalf of their male relatives.

Set against the growing campaign for reform was a strong conservative element of British society that wanted to preserve the status quo. It was supported by a Tory government that was deeply suspicious of any political radicalism. In the years before 1819, the government used spies to infiltrate the reform movement and deployed troops to suppress potential unrest.

On the morning of 16 August 1819, more than 60,000 people from Manchester and

A coloured engraving by Richard Carlile which depicts the Peterloo Massacre. He dedicated it: To Henry Hunt, Esq., as chairman of the meeting assembled in St Peter's Field, Manchester, sixteenth day of August, 1819, and to the female Reformers of Manchester and the adjacent towns who were exposed to and suffered from the wanton and fiendish attack made on them by that brutal armed force, the Manchester and Cheshire Yeomanry Cavalry, this plate is dedicated by their fellow labourer, Richard Carlile.

surrounding districts gathered at St Peter's Field to demand the right to vote. Local magistrates ordered the arrest of the main speakers and the dispersal of the crowd.

A detailed depiction of the massacre at St Peter's Field is printed on the handkerchief. It shows the mounted yeomanry fighting their way through the large and respectably dressed crowd. People are trying to escape from the mayhem; in the foreground, several have been killed or injured in the crush or from a sabre blow. In the middle distance, yeomanry with raised swords surround the speakers' platform. Above the heads of the crowd are banners and placards with inscriptions such as 'Unite and be Free', 'Royton Female Union Society' and 'Liberty is the birth right of Man'. A cap of liberty sits on top of most banners. The picture includes detailed images of the buildings around St Peter's Field. At the top of the handkerchief there are titles and notes on a scroll draped among heavy clouds. These give details of particular locations such as '3 – Mess. Pickfords and Co.'s Warehouse' (where the yeomanry were mustered) and '5 – House where the magistrates sat'. Surrounding the picture there is a border of ribbon intertwined with palm branches and laurel wreaths. The ribbon is printed with the repeated slogan: 'Universal Suffrage, Annual Parliaments and Election by Ballot'.

In response to the worsening economic conditions of 1819, the Manchester Patriotic Union, a radical reform group, organised a demonstration at St Peter's Field. The demonstration would be addressed by Henry Hunt and other leading radicals. The sun was shining on 16 August as, during the morning, large groups of men, women and children from surrounding towns made their way to the centre of Manchester. Journalists later reported a peaceful and pleasant atmosphere, with people dressed in their Sunday best marching behind banners and enjoying the music of the accompanying bands. Historians estimate that 60,000 to 80,000 people had gathered by midday.

Henry 'Orator' Hunt.

The local magistrates, watching from a house on the edge of St Peter's Field, saw the crowd wave and cheer as Henry Hunt arrived at the platform at 1.20 pm. The magistrates did not believe that the demonstration would remain peaceful and feared a revolution would begin on the streets of Manchester. William Hulton, their chairman, issued an arrest warrant for Hunt and other speakers. The Manchester and Salford Yeomanry were ordered to protect the police by arresting the radical leaders and the 15th Hussars were sent in to disperse the crowd. Within ten minutes, only the wounded, their helpers and the dead were left behind. Recent research suggests that as many as eighteen people were killed and hundreds injured. The editor of the *Manchester Observer* named the tragic event 'the Peterloo Massacre' in ironic comparison with the Battle of Waterloo, which had taken place four years before.

Following the Peterloo Massacre, there was widespread public sympathy for the plight of the protesters. Newspapers reported the events in shocking detail and the radical reform movement gained support. In response, the government officially sanctioned the actions of the magistrates and soldiers. It also introduced the Six Acts, a repressive crackdown on press freedom and the right to demonstrate. This attempt to silence reformers led to an outburst of political satire, which the authorities were reluctant to prosecute for fear of creating hilarity in the courts. It also resulted in a plethora of memorabilia, like the Peterloo Handkerchief.

Places to visit

- A red plaque is sited on the wall of the Radisson Hotel, the former Free Trade Hall, and is the only memorial in the vicinity of St Peter's Square.
- A blue plaque in Middleton marks where Bamford's contingent gathered before heading to St Peter's Field.
- The People's History Museum in Manchester contains several items relating to the Peterloo Massacre.

Further reading

Jacqueline Riding & Mike Leigh, *Peterloo: The Story of the Manchester Massacre* (2018).
Robert Poole, *Peterloo: The English Uprising* (2019).
Robert Reid, *The Peterloo Massacre* (1989).

49: Old Sarum Painting

This 1829 painting by John Constable shows the windswept and deserted Iron Age hillfort of Old Sarum, Wiltshire. However, at the time that Constable painted the landscape, Old Sarum was able to return two MPs to Parliament despite having no inhabitants.

From 1801 onwards, 658 MPs, of whom 513 represented England and Wales, sat in the House of Commons. They represented two types of constituencies – counties and boroughs. County members were supposed to represent landholders, while borough members were supposed to represent the mercantile and trading interests of the kingdom. MPs elected by the counties were known as 'knights of the shire'. The right of certain boroughs to elect one or two MPs stretched back to the Middle Ages, leaving anomalies as once-important towns such as Winchelsea and Dunwich declined in relative importance whilst large industrial towns remained without an MP.

Furthermore, as each county could elect two MPs, the voter in a small county such as Rutland or Anglesey held more influence than one in Yorkshire. The parliamentary voting system that existed at the time saw that seats were unequally distributed across the country, failing to take into account population changes occasioned by Britain's Industrial Revolution. Very few people, all of them men, had the right to vote.

Places like Old Sarum, known as 'rotten' or 'pocket' boroughs, were controlled by one man, leading to agglomerations of disproportionate power in the hands of a few landowners. Most pocket boroughs were under the control of noblemen or landed gentry who could use their local influence, prestige and wealth to sway the voters. It was stated that 180 patrons controlled 370 seats, thus being able to hold a majority in the Commons. Bribery of electors in more open contests was commonplace. In the 1770s, eighty-one voters in New Shoreham had formed the

Christian Club in order to collectively sell their votes to the highest bidder. Often these bidders were merchants who had amassed vast fortunes in the expanding British Empire.

Frequently, the selection of MPs was effectively controlled by one powerful patron. For example, Charles Howard, 11th Duke of Norfolk, controlled eleven boroughs. Criteria for qualification for the franchise varied greatly among boroughs, from the requirement to own land, to merely living in a house with a hearth sufficient to boil a pot.

Previous attempts to increase the share of MPs elected by the counties at the expense of the rotten boroughs by Pitt the Elder and Pitt the Younger had failed. In 1819, large pro-reform rallies were held in Birmingham and Manchester, neither of which could elect an MP. Birmingham elected a 'legislatorial representative' but the rally in Manchester was the one that resulted in the Peterloo Massacre (*see* chapter 48).

Charles Grey, Second Earl Grey.

However, the British ruling class, with the memory of the violent overthrow of the French ancient regime still within living memory, realised that some small measure of reform was necessary. Prime Minister Arthur Wellesley, better known as the First Duke of Wellington, was resolutely opposed to parliamentary reform, although many in his Tory Party were becoming reconciled to the idea. Wellesley was ousted from power in 1830 and the new prime minister, Earl Grey, formed a Whig administration pledging to carry out parliamentary reform.

After one unsuccessful attempt to pass a Reform Bill, the Whigs won almost all the properly contested seats at the 1831 general election. A further bill was passed in the Commons but was defeated in the Lords.

Violence erupted as a result. That very evening, riots broke out in Derby, where a mob attacked the city jail and freed several prisoners. In Nottingham, rioters set fire to the castle and attacked Wollaton Hall, both of whose owners had voted down the

Old Basford Reform Act Memorial. (*John Sutton/Creative Commons*)

bill. The most significant disturbances occurred at Bristol, where rioters controlled the city for three days. The mob broke into prisons and destroyed several buildings, including the palace of the Bishop of Bristol, the mansion of the Lord Mayor of Bristol, and several private homes. Other places that saw violence included Dorset, Leicestershire and Somerset.

Grey persuaded the king to prorogue Parliament so the bill could be resubmitted without the need for a general election. He also threatened to persuade King William IV to use his constitutional powers to create additional Whig peers in the House of Lords to guarantee its safe passage. When the king proved reluctant, Grey resigned and Wellington was invited to form a new government. This created a run on the pound, as £1.8 million was withdrawn from the Bank of England in protest. Some demonstrations called for the abolition of the nobility, even of the monarchy. As Britain teetered on the brink of insurrection, Wellington gave way, and advised his peers to abstain on a further vote on the bill.

The Representation of the People Act, which was passed and received Royal Assent on 7 June 1832:

- removed the franchise from fifty-six boroughs in England and Wales and reduced another thirty-one to only one MP
- created sixty-seven new constituencies
- broadened the franchise to include small landowners, tenant farmers, and shopkeepers
- and gave the vote to all householders who paid a yearly rental of £10 or more and some lodgers.

The Act also formally excluded women from voting in any parliamentary elections.

Many historians see the 1832 Reform Act as a watershed moment in the advancement of democracy in Britain. It increased the electorate from about 400,000 to 650,000, making approximately one in five adult males eligible to vote.

Limited change had been achieved but for many it did not go far enough. The property qualifications meant that the majority of working men and all women were still unable to vote, but it had been proved that change was possible. This was a mantle that would be seized by the Chartist campaign a few years later.

Places to visit

- Old Basford Reform Act Memorial, Nottinghamshire. A plaque in the former cemetery reads: 'This memorial was erected by Thomas Bailey, the historian, in the grounds below (opposite this cemetery) to commemorate the passing of the Reform Act, AD 1832: & was removed here to mark the resting place of his much esteemed & valued friend.'
- Reform Row, Elsecar, South Yorkshire. This row of cottages, built in 1837 by Earl Fitzwilliam for his industrial workers, was named Reform Row to mark the Earl's support for the passing of the 1832 Act, during which time he served as an MP.

Further reading

Eric J. Evans, *The Great Reform Act of 1832* (1983).
Paul Foot, *The Vote: How It Was Won and How It Was Undermined* (2005).
Antonia Fraser, *Perilous Question: the Drama of the Great Reform Bill 1832* (2013).

50: Swing Riots Lithograph

This lithograph, produced in 1830 and widely distributed, shows a figure constructed from the materials for arson and emitting flames. Its body is a corn stack, its head a sheaf of corn, in which are flaming 'Fire Balls' for eyes. The right arm is a bottle of turpentine, from which burning liquid pours into a pan that is hooked onto the hand, a lighted dark lantern. The left arm is a cylinder of portable gas, emitting flame from a tap at the elbow, where it joins a firebrand with lighted matches for fingers. The right leg above the knee is an open phosphorus box, resting on a bundle of matches and with a pistol for a foot; the right leg is made of two barrels, named 'pitch' and 'tar', resting on a horn of gunpowder. Flames issue forth from the joints of the figure and the hair is made of burning ears of corn.

The context of the lithograph's construction was a series of attacks on farms that began in Kent and became known as the Swing Riots, named after a mythical Captain Swing who represented the anger of poverty-stricken agricultural workers. Many is the rural ancestor who appears on nineteenth-century census returns as an 'Ag Lab'. Behind this designation often lurked layers of misery. Against the backdrop of the wholesale enclosure of common land between 1760 and 1820 and the loss of the rights to cultivate it, landless labourers, especially in the south of England, became impoverished.

The period following the Napoleonic Wars saw economic depression. Pleas for political reform were brutally repressed. The introduction of the threshing machine had brought considerable benefits to landowners. However, their labourers were less effusive about its wider benefits. The machine reduced the demand for labour, encouraged the intensification of farms and thus stimulated further enclosing of land and the removal of rights to access common land, and transformed village agricultural peasants to transient agricultural labourers. This admixture of forces converged to produce the Swing Riots of 1830. The most visible aspect of the Swing Riots was the destruction of hundreds of threshing machines.

A run of poor harvests fuelled low wages and high unemployment in 1829–30 and agricultural workers and their families began to starve. Intimidating letters were sent to farmers and landowners, demanding an increase in wages and threatening violence to the threshing machines that were used on their land. Farm buildings and hayricks were set alight. The first letter, signed in the hand of Captain Swing, was sent to a farmer in Dover in October 1830. It warned: 'You are advised that if you doant put away your thrashing machine against Munday next you shall have a SWING,' meaning the recipient would face the gallows.

The first of the Swing Riots occurred on the night of 28 August 1830, with the destruction of a threshing machine in Lower Hardres, near Canterbury. Further fires, machine-breaking and meetings demanding wage increases continued in Kent through to November.

Initial sentences handed down to the machine-breakers were lenient. In the Canterbury and East Kent quarter sessions in October 1830, Sir Edward Knatchbull imposed a light three-day imprisonment on seven guilty men. As the deterrent nature of such punishment was negligible, penalties increased. On 24 December, William and Henry Packham were hanged at Penenden Heath, Maidstone, for committing arson on a barn belonging to William Wraight. A petition asking for clemency was rejected by Mr Justice Bosanquet of Maidstone, as was the jury's recommendation for mercy.

The riots saw 992 criminal cases being heard across Berkshire, Buckinghamshire, Dorset, Hampshire and Wiltshire: 227 death sentences were handed down, although just nineteen of these were carried out; 359 individuals were transported to New South Wales or Van Diemen's Land; 254 people received jail terms and two were fined.

Although the great mass of riots subsided in 1831, occasional outbreaks of violence against threshing machines continued through the rest of the decade. The rural agitation led the new Whig government to establish a Royal Commission on the Poor Laws and its report provided the basis for the 1834 Poor Law.

Further reading

Eric Hobsbawm & George Rude, *Captain Swing* (2001).

51: Tolpuddle Martyrs Tree

In the centre of the quiet Dorset village of Tolpuddle there stands a 320-year-old sycamore tree. It is easy to pass by without giving it a second glance. However, in 1833 the tree was the site of a meeting that would have reverberations across the world.

Six agricultural labourers, ground down by years of falling wages and spiralling food costs, met under the tree to swear a secret oath as a presage to forming the Friendly Society of Agricultural Labourers. One demand of the society was a minimum wage of ten shillings per week, in contrast to the seven shillings then on offer.

The society was led by George Loveless, a Wesleyan Methodist preacher, and they met

(John Broom)

at the house of Thomas Standfield. Loveless had previously represented Dorset agricultural labourers in discussion with farmers, the outcome being that a wage of ten shillings per week was agreed. However, Tolpuddle landowners only agreed to pay nine shillings, and later reduced this to seven, with a threat to further reduce to six. James Hammett apart, Loveless and the other four Martyrs were bound by ties of blood, marriage and Methodism.

In 1834, local magistrate and landowner James Frampton wrote to the Home Secretary, Lord Melbourne, to complain about the union's activities. Melbourne advised him to invoke the Unlawful Oaths Act of 1797. On 24 February, having set off for another day's agricultural toiling, 37-year-old George Loveless was served with a warrant for his arrest. Landowners such as Frampton were wary of a repeat of the Swing Riots and, worse for them, a series of revolutions as had occurred in France from 1789 onwards.

The six society members – James Brine, James Hammet, George Loveless, James Loveless, Thomas Standfield and John Standfield – were arrested and tried in front of Sir John Williams in the case of Rex v Lovelass [*sic*] and Others. They were sentenced to transportation to Australia to face seven years' penal servitude. While incarcerated in prison, George Loveless wrote these words: 'We raise the watchword, liberty. We will, we will, we will be free!' Five of the men sailed on the convict ship *Surry* to New South Wales, arriving on 17 August 1834. Loveless, delayed by illness, landed in Hobart on 4 September. All were assigned farm labouring work.

The fledging Trade Union movement was not prepared to stand aside and see their comrades treated in this harsh manner. A London Central Dorchester Committee formed to agitate for their pardon. Meanwhile, a petition demanding their release was circulated and a march organised by the Grand National Consolidate Trades Union took place, comprising 50,000 to 100,000 people, in London. They met at Copenhagen Fields near King's Cross, on 21 April 1834. The government feared disorder and swore in more than 5,000 special constables. A

Martyrs Memorial and Museum, Tolpuddle. (*John Broom*)

grand procession with banners flying marched to Parliament with good discipline amidst cheers from the Londoners they passed. The petition was taken to the office of Lord Melbourne, who refused to accept it.

Radical MPs such as William Cobbett continued to raise the Martyrs' cause in the Commons and petitions flooded in from all across Britain, eventually numbering 800,000 signatures. In March 1836, they were pardoned, on condition of good conduct. Lord John Russell, the current Home Secretary, had bowed to a successful political campaign. News was slow to reach the six men, and Loveless further delayed his return while awaiting news that his wife was not still planning to sail to Van Diemen's Land to join him. He left the island on 30 January 1837, arriving in England on 13 June.

Administrative issues delayed the release of the other five, of whom, four – James Loveless, Thomas and John Standfield, and James Brine – left Sydney on 11 September 1837. James Hammett was delayed due to an assault charge, eventually reaching England in August 1839.

During their three years of state-sanctioned isolation, the Martyrs' families had been sustained by voluntary donations of well-wishers, and funds were available to transition them back into life in England. The Lovelesses, Standfields and Brine settled in farms near Chipping Ongar, Essex. Later they emigrated to London, Upper Canada, to form an affordable housing co-operative and trade union complex. George Loveless and James Brine died in Ontario.

Today, the Tolpuddle Martyrs Tree is under the care of the National Trust and forms the focal point of a tour of this fascinating village, which played such an important role in the progression of the rights of ordinary people in the workplace. A shelter was erected by the tree to commemorate the Martyrs' centenary in 1934 and a memorial service, attended by Labour Party leader George Lansbury, was held at the grave of James Hammet, the only one of the six to resettle permanently in Tolpuddle. There is an annual cultural festival in July that celebrates the lives of the Martyrs.

Places to visit

- The Tolpuddle Martyrs Museum is housed in one of the Tolpuddle Martyrs Memorial Cottages and contains various artefacts, documents and memorabilia relating to the history of the Tolpuddle Martyrs.
- The Shire Hall Courthouse Museum in Dorchester includes the cells in which the Martyrs were held before trial, and the courtroom in which they were found guilty and sentenced.

Further reading

Alan Gallop, *Six for the Tolpuddle Martyrs: The Epic Struggle for Justice and Freedom* (2017).
Joyce Marlow, *The Tolpuddle Martyrs* (1972).
Andrew Norman, *The Story of George Loveless and the Tolpuddle Martyrs* (2008).
Trades Union Congress, *The Book of the Martyrs of Tolpuddle 1834–1934: The Story of the Dorsetshire Labourers Who Were Convicted and Sentenced to Seven Years Transportation for Forming a Trade Union* (TUC, 2000).

52: Richard Oastler Medal

DWELL IN THE LAND & VERILY THOU SHALT BE FED/ LIVE AND LET LIVE

(Courtesy Tim Millett Historical Medals)

So reads the inscription on an 1838 medal, struck to raise funds for a national testimonial in aide of Richard Oastler MP. Containing Oastler's profile on one side and a pastoral scene with a cottage, church and a man ploughing on the reverse, the medal commemorates the occasion when Oastler was dismissed from his post as steward of Thomas Thornhill's Fixby Estate near Huddersfield. His sacking had an air of theatricality about it, as his supporters formed a procession, headed by gentlemen on horseback, with white wands decorated with Oastler's medal suspended from a white ribbon.

But how had a high-profile Tory come to be dismissed in such a manner, and why was there an upsurge of support for him in his hour of need? The son of a Leeds estate steward who had moved from Thirsk having been disowned by his own father for converting to Methodism, Oastler worked as a merchants' agent until 1820, when he was appointed as a land steward for Thornhill. Politically, he was a Tory, opposed to parliamentary reform and trade unions. However, he also railed against the overt exploitation of working people.

In 1830, Oastler, an opponent both of slavery and of domestic political reform, visited a Bradford industrialist who bemoaned the practice of fellow mill owners ignoring existing Factory Acts. Children as young as 6 were frequently employed and the maximum hours of work for children were often exceeded. In Oastler's mind, such conditions amounted to slavery, and he contrasted the noble words of many Yorkshire abolitionists with their treatment of their workforce. Under the heading 'Yorkshire Slavery', he wrote to the *Leeds Mercury*:

> Thousands of our fellow-creatures and fellow-subjects, both male and female, the miserable inhabitants of a Yorkshire town, (Yorkshire now represented in Parliament by the giant of anti-slavery principles) are this very moment existing in a state of slavery, more horrid than are the victims of that hellish system 'colonial slavery'.

John Cam Hobhouse MP proposed to introduce a bill limiting working hours for under-18s in the cotton mills to eleven and a half hours per day. The bill was then watered down, with few enforcement measures in place, so Oastler took the lead in forming local committees of workers agitating for a ten-hour day. He maintained a close contact with Michael Sadler MP, one of the key parliamentarians to maintain the momentum of the Ten Hours Movement. Anthony Ashley-Cooper (later Lord Shaftesbury) was another leading MP in the Ten Hours Movement. An 1833 Factory Act introduced this measure, which applied to older woollen-producing communities in Yorkshire that had been ignored in previous legislation. Children under 9 were prohibited from working in factories and a maximum working week of forty-eight hours for those aged 9 to 13 was enacted, limited to eight hours per day. For children aged 13 to 18, the daily limit was twelve hours. In addition, children under 13 were to receive elementary education for two hours per day.

To address the main deficiency of previous acts, a team of inspectors was appointed with the power to impose penalties for infringements. However, this body only amounted to four men to cover about 4,000 mills so was widely ignored.

Oastler, now known as the 'Factory King', continued to campaign on the issue of the working day. In 1836, in a throwback to the tactics of the Luddites, he advocated sabotage of machinery by factory children. He also turned his attention to campaigning against the New Poor Law from 1834 onwards, and spoke at various public meetings. As a result of his anti-Poor Law activities, Thornhill saw fit to dismiss Oastler and pursue him for debt. Unable to pay, Oastler was thrown into the infamous Fleet Prison for three and a half years. From here, he was still able to write newspapers and pamphlets, called the *Fleet Papers*.

Due to his popularity, a subscription was established, of which the medal played a part, and his debts were paid off by well-wishers. Oastler continued his campaign for a shortened working day and eventually, in 1847, the Ten Hours Act was passed. Finally, the working day for women and young people under the age of 18 was restricted to ten hours. A fifteen-year campaign, one of the great radical causes of the 1830s and 1840s, was at an end. Oastler had been a prominent and early advocate. Anthony Ashley-Cooper had done much of the work inside Parliament whilst John Doherty had mobilised support amongst millworkers. It was John Fielden, the radical MP for Oldham, who had piloted the 1847 Act through the Commons. In doing so, he faced opposition from Anti-Corn Law luminaries such as John Bright, whose free trade principles led them to objecting to the government restricting the terms on which a person's labour might be bought and sold.

Places to visit

- Quarry Bank Mill in Cheshire, under the care of the National Trust, gives a unique insight into the working lives of children in a textile mill.

Further reading

Hilary Haigh & John Hargreaves, *Slavery in Yorkshire: Richard Oastler and the campaign against child labour in the Industrial Revolution* (2012).
John Pollock, *Shaftesbury: The Poor Man's Earl* (1990).
Sue Wilkes, *The Children History Forgot: Young Workers of the Industrial Age* (2011).

53: Anti-Corn Law League Membership Cards

The first membership card was issued to John Lomas, member No. 1,362. It shows a poor family eating dear bread (protection) and a prosperous family eating cheap bread (free trade). They are separated by the Anti-Corn Law League symbol of a sheaf of wheat, beneath a banner that says: 'He that withholdeth corn, the people shall curse him.'

The second, a card for John Bailey, No. 7846, shows a starving family huddled beneath a quote from the Lord's Prayer: 'Give us this day our daily bread.'

The 1815 Corn Laws were taxes on imported grain. They served to keep prices high for landowners in Britain. The raising of food prices became the focus of opposition from urban areas, which had less political power than rural Britain. The Corn Laws initially prohibited foreign corn completely from being imported at below eighty shillings a quarter. The result was to safeguard the interests of Britain's landowning class, traditionally the repository of wealth and political power, at the expense of the rising industrial capitalists and their urban workforces.

In 1828, an amendment to the Corn Laws introduced a sliding scale of duties on imported wheat, causing fluctuation of bread prices during a period of high unemployment and poor harvests. The Corn Laws aroused considerable but intermittent protest, with Anti-Corn Law associations formed in a number of cities, including Sheffield (1831), Dundee (1834), and London (1836).

In March 1839, the Anti-Corn Law League was set up to co-ordinate the work of organisations that were campaigning for the repeal of the legislation. Its Manchester base gave the movement particular resonance. The city and its surrounding towns were major importers of raw materials and were Britain's manufacturing powerhouse. The Peterloo Massacre two decades previously had demonstrated the callousness and disdain with which arguments for reform were treated.

Many historians have claimed that the ACLL formed the template for the modern-day pressure group. Parliamentary motions were moved annually to call for a full enquiry into the operation of the Corn Laws. It became apparent that the Whig government did not share the ACLL's desire of complete repeal of the laws. Thus, it set out to secure the election to the Commons of several of its members. The cotton manufacturer Robert Hyde Greg, a member of the Unitarian family that had established Quarry Bank Mill, was elected as an MP for Manchester in September 1839. At the 1841 general election, Richard Cobden, founding member and leader of the ACLL, was elected as MP for Stockport. He was joined in the Commons in 1843 by the Quaker Rochdale cotton spinner John Bright, who was returned by the Durham constituency. Bright was a passionate and captivating orator and toured the length and breadth of the UK spreading the free trade message.

Among the multifarious arguments against the Corn Laws were that they impeded political and economic progress and harmed Britain's export trade in manufactured goods by restricting the ability of foreign traders to acquire British currency through the sale of foodstuffs. Protectionism was only benefiting a small section of the British population.

In addition to parliamentary pressure, the ACLL used a range of campaigning techniques that would become staples of reformers for the next century and a half. Petitions, mass meetings and strikes were utilised in order to

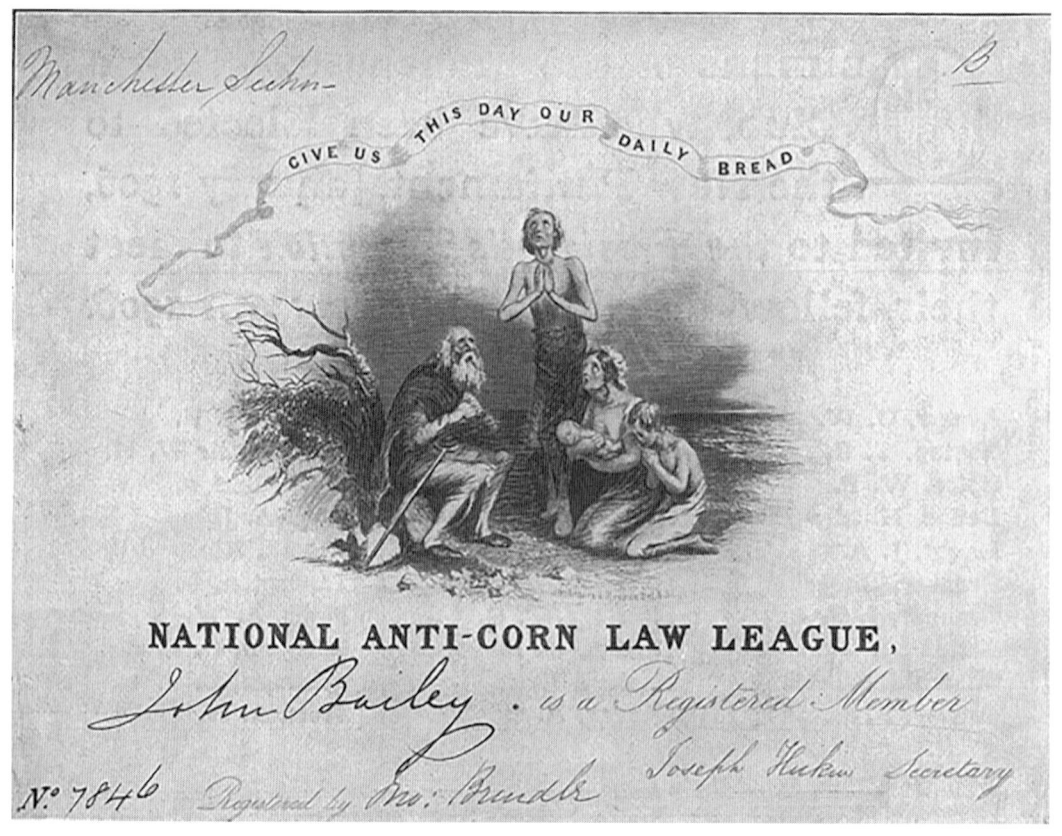

BRITAIN'S INDUSTRIAL REVOLUTION IN 100 OBJECTS

(Author's Collection)

53: ANTI-CORN LAW LEAGUE MEMBERSHIP CARDS

Richard Cobden.

Sir Robert Peel's new Tory administration of 1841 chose to reintroduce income tax and lower the sliding scale on imported corn. Nevertheless, the ACLL continued to push for total repeal, arguing that protectionism was a tool of repression used by the aristocracy. They set the interests of the landed class against those of industrialists and the working population. As the Chartist campaign for wholesale electoral reform seemed an increasingly forlorn hope, the League gained further support from several industrialists as a clear, one-issue campaign.

The ACLL sought to have more members elected as MPs. Every voter in the country received a pack of publications advocating free trade and local committees ensured that anyone with the right to vote appeared on the electoral register. Like smaller political parties of a more recent hue, a list of target seats was drawn up so campaign resources could be effectively targeted.

spread antipathy towards the Corn Laws. They highlighted the unjust nature of protection, harming the interests of working people by artificially inflating the cost of bread, a staple part of the ordinary family's diet.

A weekly publication, *The League*, was launched in 1839. In addition, hundreds of books and pamphlets on the merits of free trade were issued; using the latest means of communication – the pre-paid postal system introduced by Rowland Hill in 1840 – these could be easily and cheaply distributed around the country. Subscriptions, such as those paid by the holders of the membership cards opposite, also allowed for hundreds of paid public speakers to use the railway network to travel the county to address public meetings. Thus, the League's representatives were professional and had a consistent message.

Anti-Corn Law songs were composed and anti-Corn Law dances held. An Anti-Corn Law Bazaar was held at Manchester's Theatre Royal in 1842 and a Great Exhibition-style event organised at Covent Garden in May 1845.

Statue of John Bright in Albert Square, Manchester. (*John Broom*)

Opponents accused the League of bribery and corruption at elections, but this was the common currency in an era of restricted suffrage and open ballots.

In 1845, Lord John Russell, leader of the Whigs, declared in support of repeal of the Corn Laws. Severe famine in Ireland had made high bread prices an acute issue. Prime Minister Peel, having been won over by the personal persuasion of Richard Cobden, recalled Parliament in January 1846 and split his own Tory Party in order to force through repeal. On 15 May 1846, the Commons voted by 327 votes to 229 in favour of repeal. Peel was ousted from office by his party, with those Tories who supported him becoming known as the Peelites, who eventually merged with the Whigs in 1859 to form the Liberal Party. Peel died in 1850 following a fall from a horse.

The ACLL had been central in the removal of damaging laws and indirectly helped to reshape British politics.

Places to visit

- Statues of John Bright stand in Albert Square, Manchester, and Rochdale and Birmingham.
- Richard Cobden is honoured with a statue in St Ann's Square, Manchester. A blue plaque is located at his former home at the corner of Byrom Street and Quay Street.
- Manchester Free Trade Hall was built in 1853–6 on land donated by Richard Cobden. Located in St Peter's Field, the site of the infamous 1819 massacre, it is now an upmarket hotel. A former building on the site had served as an office of the Anti-Corn Law League.

Further reading

E.G. Power, *Robert Peel, Free Trade and Other Corn Laws* (1975).
Bill Cash, *John Bright: Statesman, Orator, Agitator* (2012).
Wendy Hinde, *Richard Cobden: A Victorian Outsider* (1987).

54: The People's Charter

In the 1830s, despite the previously rising tide of national prosperity that technological and industrial change was providing, Britain entered a national depression, with the labouring classes naturally bearing the brunt of its negative consequences. Too often, deplorable factory conditions added to the possibility of unemployment and thus recourse to the meagre level of poor relief available. Against such a backdrop, working-class radicalism grew. The 1832 Reform Act, which had promised much, had turned out to be a damp squib in terms of extending the franchise to the labouring classes. Adequate political representation in Parliament to address the issues of poor working and living conditions failed to materialise.

In May 1838, William Lovett, leader of the London Working Men's Association, drafted a People's Charter. It contained six points, many of which had circulated previously on the radical left. What Lovett brought was a coagulation of demands, under a snappy nomenclature with overtones of the Magna Carta, a document often seen as the departure point for political representation. The six points were:

1. A vote for every man over the age of 21.
2. Secret ballots.
3. No property qualification for MPs.
4. Payment of MPs.
5. Constituencies of equal size.
6. Annual parliaments.

The idea of combining this admixture of demands, which had been in circulation for some decades, quickly caught the public imagination. The message was spread by travelling orators and the radical press. Feargus O'Connor's *Northern Star* newspaper outsold *The Times* at its peak and would frequently be read out in pubs for the benefit of those unable to read.

The Six Points of the PEOPLE'S CHARTER.

1. A VOTE for every man twenty-one years of age, of sound mind, and not undergoing punishment for crime.
2. THE BALLOT.—To protect the elector in the exercise of his vote.
3. No PROPERTY QUALIFICATION for Members of Parliament —thus enabling the constituencies to return the man of their choice, be he rich or poor.
4. PAYMENT OF MEMBERS, thus enabling an honest tradesman, working man, or other person, to serve a constituency, when taken from his business to attend to the interests of the country.
5. EQUAL CONSTITUENCIES, securing the same amount of representation for the same number of electors, instead of allowing small constituencies to swamp the votes of large ones.
6. ANNUAL PARLIAMENTS, thus presenting the most effectual check to bribery and intimidation, since though a constituency might be bought once in seven years (even with the ballot), no purse could buy a constituency (under a system of universal suffrage) in each ensuing twelvemonth; and since members, when elected for a year only, would not be able to defy and betray their constituents as now.

To maintain the momentum of the campaign, a mass petition was presented to the government in July 1839 but was rejected decisively. Occasionally, those purporting to be in favour of the Charter would lapse into violence, leading scholars to distinguish between 'moral force' Chartism – petitioning, mass meetings, attempting to gain election to Parliament – and 'physical force' Chartism, which implied a readiness to take up arms against the state. There were riots in Birmingham in February 1839, and the Newport Rising occurred on 4 November. Thousands of local Chartists gathered in Newport, South Wales, and marched on the town's Westgate Hotel, where the police and mayor had already taken several prominent Chartists prisoner.

The hotel was defended by a small detachment of infantry. As the demonstrators massed outside, seeking to free the prisoners, a

The Chartist demonstration on Kennington Common, 1848.

gun went off, prompting the soldiers to fire into the multitude, causing injury and confusion. Some Chartists managed to break into the hotel, where they were met with further shots. The crowd eventually dispersed, leaving dozens wounded and at least twenty-two dead. The exact number is not known as the corpses were buried in unmarked graves. The leaders were rounded up and arrested, and put on trial in Monmouth. They were sentenced to be hanged and quartered, but a public campaign, drawing on the success of that which had seen the Tolpuddle Martyrs pardoned, saw the sentence changed to transportation to Tasmania.

A second petition, with 3.3 million signatures, was presented to the Commons in 1842. Again it was rejected, triggering a wave of strikes across northern England. A third petition, this time of 6 million signatures, was collected in 1848 – a fateful year across much of mainland Europe. Revolutionary insurrections broke out in Paris, Berlin and Vienna. Meanwhile, a large Chartist march was planned on 10 April to proceed from Kennington Common to Westminster. Some 115,000 people turned up to listen to addresses by Chartist leaders. On the front of the stage a banner read 'Labour is the source of all wealth'.

Fearful of what such a large crowd might do, the government took precautionary measures. The Queen and Prince Albert evacuated to the Isle of Wight and troops were stationed on London's bridges to prevent Chartists arriving at Westminster en masse. This meant that the petition had to be sent to Parliament in a fleet of Hansom Cabs. There it occasioned even less support than its predecessors, receiving only fifteen votes when MPs came to discuss its demands. Following this setback, the economy improved and the movement ran out of steam, eventually ending in 1858.

Although none of the six demands had been met, Chartism had shown how to run a nationwide political campaign. It raised awareness of the many iniquities that faced ordinary people, and educated and radicalised a significant core of the working class. Governments of the 1850s, 1860s and 1870s became more reformist in nature, with Parliamentary Acts passed to improve working conditions, and health and education provision and outcomes for the masses.

Eventually, five of the six points of the People's Charter were passed into law, with only the demand for annual parliaments never enacted.

The attack of the Chartists on the Westgate Hotel, Newport, Mon, Nov, 4,th, 1839. W. W. & C.

Places to visit

- Newport Museum owns a collection of nationally significant Chartist objects. It stands a few yards from the Westgate Hotel. The hotel, which was demolished and rebuilt in 1886, contains pillars from the previous building, complete with bullet holes which research has shown to have been made by Chartist gunfire in 1839.
- Blackstone Edge, a dramatic rocky outcrop on the Pennine Way footpath, staged several huge Chartist rallies between 1838 and 1850 that were attended by up to 100,000 people. It was chosen for this purpose because of its location midway between the industrial towns of East Lancashire and the West Riding of Yorkshire. Being up in the hills also made it less likely that the authorities would interfere. The rallies had something of a carnival atmosphere, with music, sideshows and games as well as speaker podiums.
- Rosedene, Dodford, Worcestershire. Chartism was about more than just political demands. Prompted in part by the failure of the second petition, Feargus O'Connor established a land plan that was adopted by the Chartists in 1845. The scheme aimed to buy country estates and turn them into colonies for industrial workers. Only five Chartist colonies, containing 234 smallholdings, were ever created. One of these was at Dodford, where the National Trust has restored the Rosedene cottage to its 1840s' appearance.

Further reading

Malcolm Chase, *Chartism: A New History* (2007).
Richard Brown: *Radicalism and Chartism* (2019).
Stephen Roberts, *Images of Chartism* (1998).

55: Co-operative Wholesale Society Cigarette Card

This cigarette card, depicting the CWS biscuit works, was issued in 1905. Crumpsall Biscuit Works opened in Lower Crumpsall, near Manchester, in about 1873. Established on the principles of the Co-operative Movement, one of the more enlightened innovations of Britain's Industrial Revolution, the Crumpsall Works boasted being 'the only 8 hour day biscuit works in England'.

The earliest co-operative society for which records survive was formed by the Fenwick Weavers in 1761. As Britain's Industrial Revolution brought the rapid growth of towns and fewer people producing their own food, so people became reliant on buying their sustenance from shopkeepers. Sometimes sharp practices were in operation, such as adulterating flour and other consumables and using false weights and measures.

Robert Owen, often regarded as the founder of the Co-operative Movement, believed that character is formed by positive environmental influences such as educational opportunities and negative ones such as poor working conditions. Owen's vision was for villages of co-operation in a New World Order of mutual help, social equality and brotherhood. His followers were called co-operators or socialists. Owen had established a model community in the early 1800s around his cotton mill at New Lanark. He paid higher wages for fewer work hours than his competitors, and provided housing and education. Owen's ideas were taken up by William King of Brighton, who founded a monthly periodical, *The Co-operator*, in 1827, urging the formation of small local co-ops to tackle poverty.

Rising food prices had resulted from the marketisation of the economy and from the lack of political representation for the working class during this period. Early co-ops often focused on the provision of essential services – notably food – to members where the market was either unable to provide these services sufficiently or was considered unjust. The provision of food was

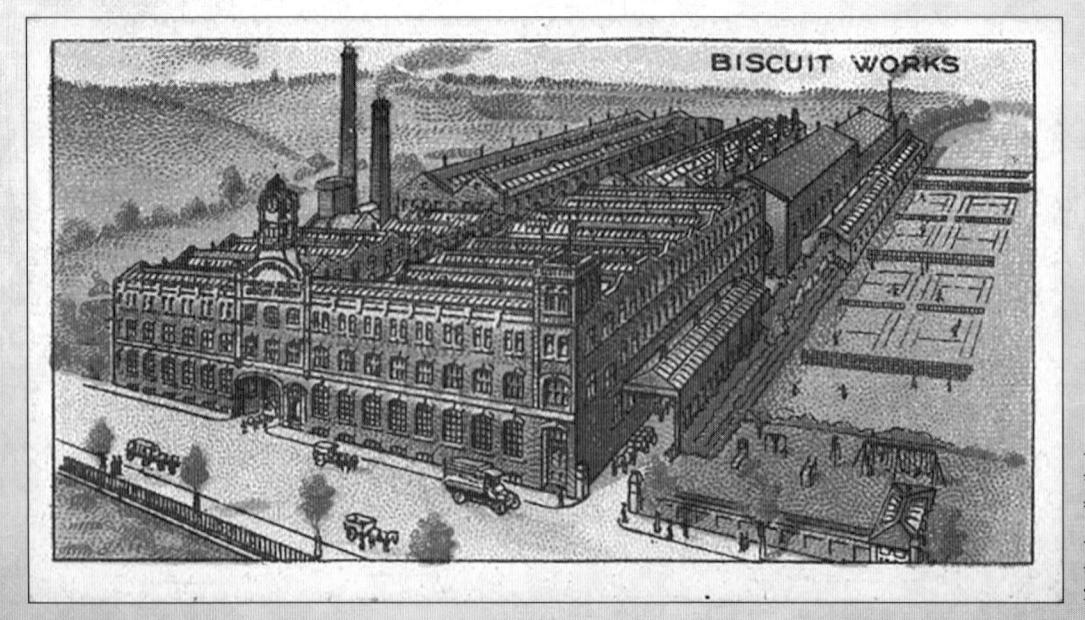

(Author's collection)

55: CO-OPERATIVE WHOLESALE SOCIETY CIGARETTE CARD

1865 photograph of thirteen of the original twenty-eight Rochdale Pioneers.

a highly successful area for co-ops, with many becoming involved in milling flour and baking bread. The Hull Anti-Mill Co-op, which was established in 1795 and traded for a century, provides an example of such a successful society.

By the 1840s, the Lancashire mill town of Rochdale was third only to Manchester and Leeds as a centre of working-class activity. The many strikes against the falling wages of cotton and woollen workers failed to improve wages and conditions. The Rochdale Society of Equitable Pioneers was a group of twenty-eight men that formed in 1844. Around half were weavers. As the mechanisation of Britain's Industrial Revolution forced increasing numbers of skilled workers into poverty, the Pioneers decided to pool their funds to open their own shop selling food items they could not otherwise afford. Mindful of lessons from previous failed attempts at co-operation, they designed the notable Rochdale Principles:

1. Democratic control: one member, one vote.
2. Open membership.
3. Fixed or limited interest on capital.
4. Dividend on purchases.
5. Trading strictly cash.
6. Selling of pure and unadulterated goods.
7. Provision of education of members in co-operative principles.
8. Political and religious neutrality.

Over a period of four months, they raised £1 per person for a total of £28 of capital. On 21 December 1844, the Toad Lane shop opened with the following stock:

Butter, 1 qr 22lb
Sugar, 2 qrs
Flour, three sacks at 37*s* 6*d* and three at 36*s*
Candles, 2 doz
Oatmeal, one sack
The total cost of the goods was: £16 11*s* 11*d*

Rochdale Pioneers Museum, 31 Toad Lane, Rochdale. Frontage of the original shop, which is now the entrance to the museum. (*Chemical Engineer/Creative Commons*)

Within three months, the stock had diversified to include tea and tobacco. The Pioneers' integrity meant that shoppers knew that high-quality, unadulterated goods were being sold. After a year of trading, the Rochdale Pioneers had eighty members and £182 of capital.

Inspired by trading principles set out by visionary socialists such as Robert Owen, members received profits from the shop in the form of a dividend. Also drawing from Owen and other reformers, the importance of education was emphasised, with the upstairs room at Toad Lane used to provide members with further education.

The Rochdale Pioneers opened new branches over the following years, and many other societies were established. By 1854, the British co-operative movement had taken up the Rochdale Principles and over 1,000 such stores were open. By 1900, there were 1,439 different co-operative societies and about 2 million members. In order to be able to buy in the best markets, the North of England Wholesale Society was set up in 1863. It became the Co-operative Wholesale Society (CWS) and extended its activities into manufacturing, farming and importing.

The Rochdale Principles had changed the world forever, bringing a social conscience to business that echoes loud into the modern world as, all around the globe, co-operatives use the rules set down by those original Pioneers as a basis for their own trading. Although other co-operatives preceded them, the Rochdale Pioneers' co-operative became the prototype for societies in Great Britain. They started a revolution in shopping that resonates to this day.

Places to visit

- The Rochdale Pioneers Museum stands in the original co-operative shop on Toad Lane in Rochdale. The Pioneers moved out in 1867 but the co-operative movement later purchased the premises and opened it as a museum in 1931. The ground floor faithfully recreates the original shop, together with its rudimentary furniture and scales.
- New Lanark Mills in Scotland includes the site of the village store established by Robert Owen in 1813. Run for the benefit of the community, it was regarded as an inspiration for the Rochdale Pioneers. Owen's village store sold good-quality, fresh and affordable products; workers could be paid in tokens or tickets, which they would use at the store, encouraging the villagers to shop locally.

Further reading

Johnston Birchall, *Co-op: The People's Business* (1994).
George Jacob Holyoake, *The History of the Rochdale Pioneers* (2009).

56: A Sheffield Saw

Saw grinders in Sheffield, 1866. (*Wellcome Collection*)

This 1860 engraving, depicting saw grinders from Sheffield hard at their dangerous work, reminds us of a turbulent episode in the city's past. It was the attempt by a handful of employers to bypass apprenticeship requirements, ignore trade unions and undermine the pay and conditions of Sheffield saw grinders, which led to violent disorder. A series of explosions and murders carried out by a small group of trade unionists in the 1850s and 60s have become known as the Sheffield Outrages.

Whilst the rapid growth of the Sheffield steel industry had brought wealth to the city in general, for many workers conditions were harsh. Friedrich Engels, when researching his *The Condition of the Working Class in England* in 1844, interviewed Sheffield medic Dr Knight, who told him of the local condition – Grinder's asthma – suffered by Sheffield cutlery workers.

They usually begin their work in the fourteenth year, and if they have good constitutions, rarely notice any symptoms before the twentieth year. Then the symptoms of their peculiar disease appear. They suffer from shortness of breath at the slightest effort in going up hill or up stairs, they habitually raise the shoulders to relieve the permanent and increasing want of breath; they bend forward, and seem, in general, to feel most comfortable in the crouching position in which they work. Their complexion becomes dirty yellow, their

William Leng.

William Broadhead, the man thought to have been the driving force behind the Sheffield Outrages.

features express anxiety, they complain of pressure on the chest. Their voices become rough and hoarse, they cough loudly, and they sound is as if air were driven through a wooden tube.

By the mid-1860s, living and working conditions in industrial England were not showing any significant improvement and trade unions struggled to advance the interests of their members. Despite being illegal, trade union membership and activity grew during the period. The steel city of Sheffield was a hive of union activity during this decade. With working conditions dangerous and wages low, many saw union membership and mutual solidarity as literally a matter of life and death.

In such conditions great discontent arose, which led to militant action. Some workers used violence against employers and fellow workers who would not become union members. Workers who refused to pay their union fees were 'rattened' – the belt that drove their grindstone would be removed or cut so they could not work. In the late 1850s, the conflict between employers and workers reached new heights, culminating in a series of explosions and murders carried out by union militants. As a later justification of the actions, they argued, 'When strikes are criminal offences, and unions are smashed with all the might of law, what method is there left but outrage?'

Thomas Fearnehough, a saw grinder, was accused of taking on unlawful apprentices. In retribution, he had a can of gunpowder thrown into his cellar in 1866. Less fortunate was James Linley. Accused of the same anti-union action, there had been several previous attacks on his person and property. On 11 January 1859, there was an attempt to blow up the house of Mr Poole, a butcher living on The Wicker, in which Linley was living. On 1 August the same year, he was shot in the head while drinking in the snug in the Crown Inn on Scotland Street and he died several months later from his wound. Linley had drawn the particular ire of the union members as he traded as a saw grinder despite having trained as a scissor grinder. Furthermore, he had taken on more apprentices than he could possibly train and educate, sacking them as soon as they completed their apprenticeships and reached adulthood.

Between 1857 and 1867, there were 200 incidents. William Leng of the *Sheffield Daily Telegraph* investigated the Outrages, concluding that local trade union leaders were complicit. He, too, received threatening letters, some signed 'Mary Jane', the name of Broadhead's wife, and had to carry a revolver for protection.

To establish the full facts, a trade union delegation made up of members from Sheffield and London requested that the Home Secretary set up an official investigation. A Special Commission of Enquiry was established in May 1867, with immunity offered to all those who gave evidence. William Broadhead, Secretary of the Saw Grinders Union and landlord of the Royal George Inn on Carver Street, dramatically described how he had paid two workmen £5 to attack Linley. Broadhead declared:

> I had a right to take these courses in the absence of the law … if the law could give [trade unions] some power … to receive contributions without having recourse to such measures there would be no more heard of them … it would destroy these acts that have taken place and which place me in this painful position.

It was found that Samuel Crooks was employed by Broadhead to carry out the attacks, as was James Hallam, who admitted before the commission his part in the murderous assaults incited and funded by William Broadhead.

The Commission's report led to the passing of the Trade Union Act by Gladstone's Liberal government in 1871, which gave the organisations a more secure footing.

William Broadhead emigrated to America in 1869, returning to Sheffield the following year to begin a new and quieter career as a grocer. Grateful Sheffield businessmen who had suffered at the hand of Broadhead's trade unionists subscribed 600 guineas and presented the sum and a privately commissioned portrait to the newspaper proprietor and editor William Leng, who had waged a campaign against the unions.

Places to visit

- The Kelham Island Museum in Sheffield tells the story of the Sheffield Outrages.

Further reading

Mick Drewry, *Intimidation: The History, The Times And The People Of The Sheffield Outrages* (2017).

57: The Communist Manifesto

The Communist Party Manifesto was published in London in 1848 by Karl Marx and Friedrich Engels, two German political philosophers based in England. Commissioned by the Communist League, it appeared in the same year that revolutions broke out across much of mainland Europe. However, despite the threat that the large Chartist demonstration on Kennington Common posed to public order, the ideas propounded in the Communist Manifesto never took hold in Britain to the same extent that they did elsewhere in Europe.

The manifesto analysed the history of class struggle and examined how capitalist modes of production had affected society over the past century. 'A spectre is haunting Europe—the spectre of communism. All the powers of old Europe have entered into a holy alliance to exorcise this spectre,' began the work. Therefore, communists needed to have a clear manifesto of their beliefs.

In the first section of the manifesto, 'Bourgeois and Proletarians', the materialist concept of history is outlined: 'the history of all hitherto existing society is the history of class struggles.' Throughout time, the majority has always been exploited and oppressed by a minority elite. In the modern society created by Britain's Industrial Revolution, the industrial working class, or proletariat, was engaged in class struggle against the owners of the means of production, the bourgeoisie. According to Marx and Engels, revolutionary reordering of society was bound to result from this struggle. In accumulating vast capital, the bourgeoisie would become their own 'grave diggers' as the proletariat would achieve consciousness of their collective power and overthrow their masters.

The second section, 'Proletarians and Communists', stated that the role of communists was to take an international view whilst not

The title page from the original *Communist Manifesto*, printed in London, February 1848.

opposing indigenous working-class political parties in different countries. A set of demands was made – a progressive income tax; abolition of inheritances and private property; abolition of child labour; free public education; nationalisation of the means of transport and communication; centralisation of credit via a national bank; and expansion of publicly owned land. These were precursors to a classless and stateless society.

The third section, 'Socialist and Communist Literature', dismissed other contemporary variations of socialism as being reformist and failing to recognise the pre-eminent revolutionary role of the working class. The final section, 'Position of the Communists in Relation

Karl Marx's tomb, Highgate Cemetery.

to the Various Opposition Parties', predicts a world revolution and ends with the stirring call, 'Working Men of All Countries, Unite!'

In late 1847, Marx and Engels met at the London headquarters of the German Workers' Education Association to attend a congress. They were commissioned to draw up a manifesto for the League of Communists, with Marx writing the main body of the manifesto over a six-week period in early 1848. The twenty-three-page document, which was written in German, was published by the Workers' Educational Association at Bishopgate, London. It was serialised in the *Deutsche Londoner Zeitung*, a newspaper for German *émigrés*.

The manifesto appeared in English for the first time in 1850, serialised in the Chartist magazine *The Red Republican*. Following the failed revolutions of 1848 in Europe, Marx was expelled from Prussia and sought refuge in London, making the city his home from 1849 until his death in 1883. The manifesto fell into obscurity for two decades.

Events on the Continent in the early 1870s revived the manifesto's fortunes. Because of the rise of social democratic parties across the world, it was translated into thirty languages. When the Bolsheviks seized power in Russia in 1917, the effects of Marx and Engels' manifesto were to reverberate throughout the twentieth-century world stage. Several historians have argued that the manifesto is the single most influential text written in the nineteenth century.

Places to visit

- Highgate Cemetery in London contains the grave of Karl Marx and his family in a spot where, in 1954, they were reinterred after being moved from another part of the cemetery. In 1956, an impressive bronze bust of Marx was unveiled at the grave by Harry Pollitt, General Secretary of the Communist Party of Great Britain. Over the past several decades, the tomb has been a site of both pilgrimage by Marxists and desecration by those who reject his theories.
- A statue of Friedrich Engels, standing in First Street, Manchester, relocated from Ukraine, honours the former resident of the city.

Further reading

Tristram Hunt, *Marx's General: The Revolutionary Life of Friedrich Engels* (2009).
Francis Wheen, *Karl Marx* (2010).
Karl Marx, Friedrich Engels, *Manifesto of the Communist Party* (1848).

58: Trade Union Banner

This striking banner, created in 1869 for the Operative Bricklayers Society emblem, demonstrates the ethos of the emerging trade union movement during the High Victorian era. The slogans include 'By Industry We Flourish', 'Unity is Strength' and 'Industry is the Source of Prosperity'. Various tableaux of hard work adorn the banner, which also features classical female figures. Over the course of Britain's Industrial Revolution, workers overcame great barriers in order to organise themselves for mutual protection against the vagaries of rapid technological and industrial change which radically altered their workplaces and conditions of employment.

Skilled workers in Britain had begun organising themselves into trade unions back in the seventeenth century. Changes in working practices in the late eighteenth century caused a new wave of trade disputes. Consequently, Pitt the Younger's government passed the Combination Acts of 1799 and 1800, making any sort of strike punishable by up to three months' imprisonment and prevented workers in England collectively bargaining in groups or through unions for better pay and improved working conditions. Despite these restrictions, the disruption as well as huge rises in food prices caused by the wars with France (1793–1815) saw trade unions grow rapidly, resulting in the repeal of the Combination Acts in 1824 and 1825.

Nevertheless, unions frequently found it hard to get a hearing from employers, who in a time of economic hardship could simply dismiss any men or women they saw as troublemakers and hire new workers. In the 1830s, collective action reached new levels, with the formation of Robert Owen's Grand National Consolidated Trades Union (1834) and the Swing Riot protests (*see* chapter 50) against agricultural distress. However, the harsh treatment meted out to the Tolpuddle Martyrs (*see* chapter 51) saw many unions, including Owen's, collapse. The campaign for the improvement of the working classes found other outlets. In addition to the Chartist movement (*see* chapter 54), short time committees demanded the regulation of working conditions in factories and opposition also became focussed on the hated Poor Law Amendment Act of 1834.

As Chartism subsided after 1848, and given the improved economic conditions of the 1850s and 1860s, trade unionism began to embed itself amongst industrial and agricultural workers. Trade union membership rose to around

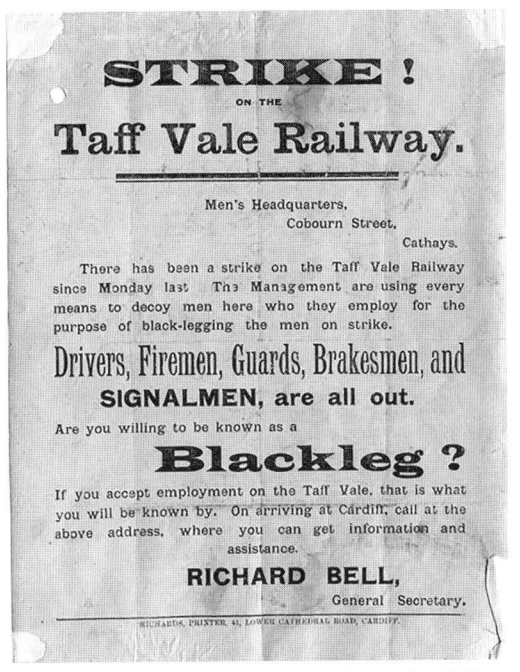

Poster warning men against breaking the Taff Vale strike, 1900.

1 million by 1874. This era of 'New Model' unionism saw workers from skilled trades and crafts forming unions. The Amalgamated Society of Engineers (1851) benefitted from a centralised national organisation. The ASE and similar unions levied high membership dues so were able to employ full-time officials and offer friendly society benefits. Employers saw such unions as more respectable, and negotiation and arbitration became a more common way of achieving improvements in conditions than strike action. Although mostly excluded from these craft unions, women continued to organise in the weaving industry. Attempts to organise female workers came from outside the labour movement. The Women's Protective and Provident League of 1874 became the Women's Trade Union League. It was not until the Bryant & May strike of 1888 (*see* chapter 59) that women's trade unionism gained widespread recognition.

The 1867 Reform Act, which extended the franchise to millions of working men, saw both Liberal and Tory governments showing an increased interest in trade unions. The new unions combined to form regional trade organisations, with the Trades Union Congress (TUC) founded in Manchester in 1868. An act passed in 1871 by Gladstone's Liberal government established the legal status of trade unions, albeit making strike organisation difficult and picketing illegal. The latter practice was legalised in 1875 by Disraeli's Tory government. In 1875, the old Master and Servant Law was modified by the Employers and Workmen Act so that employees too could sue for breach of contract. A ten-hour limit was set on the working day during this period.

By the 1880s, a strong, albeit narrowly based, trade union movement had been created, although an economic depression challenged the efficacy of the self-help ideal. Some union leaders, such as Thomas Mann, one of the organisers of the London dockers' strike of 1889, argued that the trade union movement needed a much broader base and unskilled workers and women's trade societies should be brought within the TUC's fold. Emphasising the link between organised labour and its political expression, Mann became the first secretary of the Independent Labour Party (*see* chapter 60). The dockworkers' strike of 1889 captured the public imagination. Their strike, which lasted five weeks, won the concession of 6*d* per hour pay and emphasised inter-union solidarity, as a strike fund and even a £30,000 donation from Australia allowed the strike to hold.

The Taff Vale case of 1900–1, in which the House of Lords supported the right of the Taff Vale Railway Company to sue the Amalgamated Society of Railway Servants for loss of earnings, further demonstrated to the trade unions the importance of political representation in Parliament. Many unions affiliated to the Labour Representation Committee, forming a link that exists to this day. Emboldened by growing industrial and political power, trade unionism was to enter a more militant phase during the Great War and beyond.

The Grand National Consolidated Trade Union leads a march of 30,000 people at Copenhagen Fields, London, to appeal for clemency for the Tolpuddle Martyrs.

Places to visit

- The People's History Museum in Manchester has over 450 historic and contemporary banners, including the largest and most important collection of trade union and political banners in the world. This includes the world's oldest trade union banner, the Tin Plate Workers Society banner of 1821. It also has extensive displays on trade union history through the ages.

Further reading

John Gorman, *Banner Bright: An Illustrated History of Trade Union Banners* (1986).
Keith Laybourn, *A history of British Trade Unionism c.1770–1990* (1992).
Ben Pimlott & Chris Cook, *Trade Unions in British Politics: The First 250 Years* (1991).

59: Bryant & May Matchbox

These simple matchboxes were made by leading British match manufacturer Bryant & May in the early 1890s, in the aftermath of one of the most famous examples of female workers' solidary of Britain's Industrial Revolution.

At that time, there were twenty-five match factories in Britain, employing just over 4,000 people. Twenty-three of these factories used white phosphorous in the matchmaking process, a product that caused a condition technically known as phosphorous necrosis of the jaw, popularly 'phossy jaw'. The sufferer would experience toothache and flu symptoms before then loosing teeth and having swelling of the gums and abscesses. The condition was fatal in about 20 per cent of cases.

Matchstick manufacture involved the dipping of sticks, made from poplar or pine wood, into a solution that included white phosphorous. Red phosphorous, a less damaging concoction, had been discovered in the 1840s but was not as readily available as the white, so the workers at Bryant & May continued to risk facial disfigurement and worse.

The Bryant & May company had been formed in 1843 by two Quakers. In 1850, they moved into the match market in Britain, which sold 250 million matches per year. Growth for the company was rapid over the next decade, with sales increasing from 231,000 boxes in 1850 to 27.9 million boxes per year by 1860. The following year, the company opened a new match factory on a 3-acre site in Bow, in London's East End.

The factory employed about 2,000 people by 1895, a proportion of whom were Irish or of Irish descent. The majority of these were female, some as young as 13. In order to avoid factory legislation, domestic workers were contracted to produce the boxes, with a piece rate of 2½d per gross.

Inside the factory, wages varied depending on the level of responsibility, and fines were levied for any workplace misdemeanours, including lateness, talking, dropping matches or having dirty feet, despite the fact that many of the workers were too poor to afford a pair of shoes. Bryant & May took a dim view of any worker contracting phossy jaw; they were told to have their teeth removed immediately or face the sack. Working days were exhausting, lasting up to fourteen hours. Workers would be required to stand all day long, with only two scheduled short breaks. Impromptu toilet breaks were deducted from their wages. Each penny the company saved by such punitive measures could be pumped into keeping the dividends of shareholders as high as 20 per cent.

The matchmakers had previously been involved in political activism. In 1871, they had helped to overturn a tax on matches proposed by the Gladstone administration. They had also been on strike three times already in the 1880s over low wages and the punitive fine structure. The major strike of 1888, which has

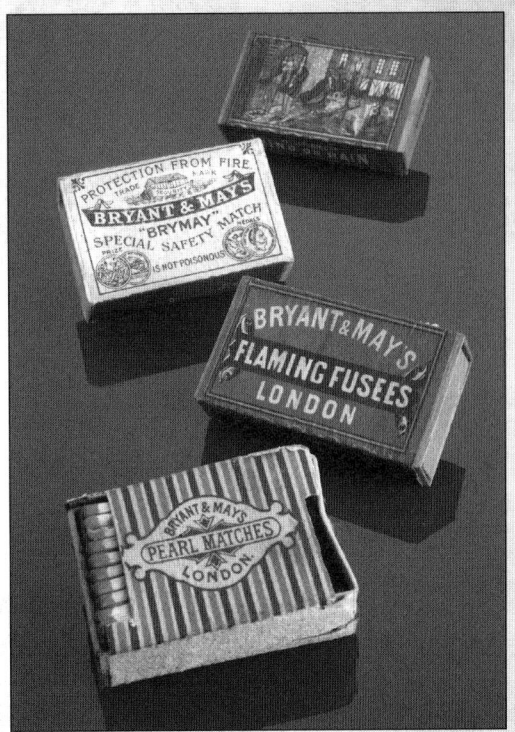

(Wellcome Images/Public domain),k

Herbert Burrows and Annie Besant, together with the matchgirls' strike committee in 1888.

made the matchmakers famous in the history books, therefore had the underlying causes of long working days of up to fourteen hours, low pay, excessive fines and unhealthy working conditions. Its spark came with the dismissal of one of their number in July 1888.

Social activists Herbert Burrows and Annie Besant had published an article in *The Link* newspaper of 23 June criticising working practices at the factory. The Bryant & May management insisted the workforce sign a paper contradicting Besant's allegations. They refused to do so and one of their number was dismissed on another pretext, resulting in 1,400 women and girls immediately going on strike. Fearing the power of such swift solidarity, the management offered to reinstate the worker, but the women, now on the offensive, demanded further concessions. The management rejected these concessions and by 6 July, the factory had ground to a standstill.

Charles Bradlaugh, the radical MP, spoke in the strikers' favour in Parliament and the London Trades Council became involved in organising fundraising activities to support them. A march was organised on Parliament to present a petition on their behalf. On 16 July, at a meeting attended by Annie Besant and representatives of the newly formed Union of Women Matchmakers, terms to end the strike were agreed. These included the taking of grievances straight to the management rather than mediation through a foreman; meals to be taken in a separate room to minimise the risk of contamination of food; and a removal of unfair fines.

The bad publicity the strike had caused for Bryant & May continued. The Salvation Army opened a match factory in Bow, which paid better wages and used the less toxic red phosphorous. Several children had died from putting the white phosphorous-tipped matches in their mouths, while helping their parents who had taken on domestically outsourced work. In 1901, Bryant & May announced that they were discontinuing the use of white phosphorous. In 1908, the

Procession of Match-Makers to Westminster, July 1888, print by W.D. Almond.

government passed legislation to prohibit the use of white phosphorous in matches from 1911 onwards.

The production of such a commonplace everyday item as the Bryant & May matchbox had helped to trigger misery for so many, and the eventual reform of working conditions in the factories that produced them. It also led to the creation of a new union for the women to join, acting as an impetus for other unskilled worker unions to emerge in a 'New Unionism' wave.

Places to visit

- The Bryant & May match factory in Bow is still standing. Today it is a gated community known as the Bow Quarter.
- The People's History Museum in Manchester has a gallery in which visitors can play an arcade-style game about the Bryant & May factory, where players' progress is hampered by sickness and unfair fines.

Further reading

Patrick Beaver, *The Match Makers: The Story of Bryant & May* (1985).
Reg Beer, *The Match Girls Strike, 1888* (1983).
Louise Raw, *Striking a Light: The Bryant and May Matchwomen and their Place in History* (2011).

60: Keir Hardie Election Poster

This election poster, issued in 1895 in support of Keir Hardie, gives clear articulation of the policies upon which he was standing as an Independent Labour Party candidate in the parliamentary seat of West Ham South. Hardie had begun work at the age of 7 and went on to become a preacher and talented public speaker. He rose through the ranks of a miners' union, leading strikes, and became a full-time union organiser and journalist.

Having initially supported Gladstone's Liberal Party, Hardie became convinced of the need for the working class to have its own political party to represent their interests in Parliament. He stood as an independent in 1888 and formed the Scottish Labour Party in the same year. Having won the West Ham South seat as a Liberal-Labour candidate in 1892, he lost it in the year the poster was issued, but regained his place in the Commons in 1900 by winning the seat of Merthyr Tydfil. That year also saw the formation of the Labour Representation Committee, later to be renamed the Labour Party.

The Labour Party came into being as a result of Britain's Industrial Revolution creating an urban proletariat with a distinctly separate set of interests to those of their employers. Most of the male urban working class had gained the right to vote in parliamentary elections due to the extension of the franchise in 1867 and 1884, thus belatedly meeting one of the demands of the People's Charter (see chapter 54). The Liberal Party endorsed a handful of trade union sponsored candidates from 1870 onwards. However, the desire for a distinctly working-class party saw an Independent Labour Party field twenty-eight candidates in the 1895 general election.

A range of small socialist groups had formed since the extension of the franchise with the intention of promoting practical political policies to improve the lot of working people. Among these were the Independent Labour Party, the intellectual and largely middle-class Fabian Society, the Social Democratic Federation and the Scottish Labour Party.

Many of the Labour movement's early electoral successes came in local government. In 1889, a Progressive Party composed of Fabians and Liberals took control of London County Council. They used this position to build social housing and increase spending on public services such as the fire brigade. Further parks and public

Membership Card for the Scottish Labour Party. Dated May 1892, it belonged to William Baddow. The inscription reads: *Nemo me impune lacessit* (No one provokes me with impunity); No Monopoly; No Privilege; No Noble Task Was Ever Easy.

The Sixth Annual Meeting of the Labour Representation Committee, Congregational Hall, London, 15–17 February 1906.

baths opened, the sewerage system was improved, and the Blackwall Tunnel constructed. In 1892, Independent Labour Party member Fred Jowett was elected to Bradford City Council. His influence led to the city becoming the first in the county to offer free school meals as well as a campaign to improve the quality of food given to children in the Bradford Workhouse. Slum areas were cleared and new houses erected.

West Ham Borough Council was taken by the Labour interest in 1898. It took a large number of municipal workers onto its payroll to improve job security, working conditions and pay for its workers. This included an eight-hour day, a minimum wage and a paid fortnight's annual holiday.

Hardie's roots as a lay preacher saw the early ILP imbued with a strong strain of Nonconformist Christianity, with it being said that 'Socialism in Britain owed more to Methodism than Marx'. On 26 and 27 February 1900, a special conference was held at the Congregational Memorial Hall in London, where several of the above political and workplace-based groups met. A motion, proposed by Hardie, to establish a distinct Labour group in Parliament, was passed. Two MPs – Hardie and Richard Bell – were successful in the 1900 general election.

Support for the fledgling LRC grew after the Taff Vale Case of 1901 demonstrated that the courts, employers and Conservative and Liberal interests would unite to make future strikes illegal. At the next general election, in 1906, the LRC won twenty-nine seats. The new MPs voted to adopt the name 'The Labour Party' on 15 February 1906, with Hardie elected as Chairman of the Parliamentary Labour Party, the de facto leader.

The first party conference was held in Belfast in 1907, with the principle being established that party sovereignty lay with that body, rather than the PLP. In the general election of December 1910, the number of Labour MPs increased to forty-two, and in 1913, the Liberal government introduced a salary for MPs, fulfilling another demand of the People's Charter. This was an attempt to try to minimise the reliance of Labour MPs on funding from trade unions. However, the Trades Disputes Act of 1913 established the principle, still in place today, that unions could sponsor individual MPs.

The party that formed to represent the interests of those who kept the wheels of Britain's Industrial Revolution turning stood poised to exert a major influence in politics over the next century, quickly surpassing the Liberals to become one of Britain's two main parties of government.

Places to visit

- The People's History Museum in Manchester has on display the minutes of the first Labour Party meeting. It also contains a vast archive of material relating to the early years of the party.
- The Baird Institute in Cumnock, East Ayrshire, has a room dedicated to Keir Hardie, containing many of his personal belongings.

Further reading

Bob Holman, *Keir Hardie: Labour's Greatest Hero?* (2010).
Martin Pugh, *Speak for Britain!: A New History of the Labour Party* (2011).

Section Four

Living and Learning

61: A Piece of Old Rope

If you were unfortunate enough to fall on temporary or long-term hard times due to the turmoil and vagaries of industrial and social change, there was a fair chance of ending up in a Victorian workhouse.

In these morose, bleak institutions, inmates would often spend long dreary days unpicking the oakum from old pieces of rope. Rope-making peaked as an industry in the nineteenth century as the Royal Navy's ships required several thousands of miles worth of the product. HMS *Victory* alone had 27 miles of rigging rope. The unpicked oakum was used to caulk up the seams of wooden ships and seal joints on lead water pipes to make them watertight.

Oakum picking was a punishment for errant sailors and prison inmates, but a ready supply of free labour was also to be found in Britain's workhouses. In 1834, the Poor Law Amendment Act scrapped the provision of some outdoor relief via the old Parish Poor Law system to decree that the old, the infirm, the disabled, the unemployed, the unmarried or widowed mother and their children could only receive government support inside a workhouse. Those physically capable of work were made to break rocks, walk to power a treadmill or pick oakum. The repetitive rubbing of the fingers could cause them to bleed. Long-term effects included tendonitis, bursitis and nerve damage.

Under the 1834 Act, the 15,000 parishes in England and Wales combined into over 600 Poor Law Unions, each managed by a locally elected Board of Guardians. Hundreds of new union workhouses were erected across the country, designed to facilitate the segregation of different categories of inmate. Workhouses were meant to act as a deterrent to the able-bodied

LARGE OAKUM-ROOM (UNDER THE SILENT SYSTEM) AT THE MIDDLESEX HOUSE OF CORRECTION, COLDBATH FIELDS.

The former Andover Workhouse, site of the 1845 scandal. (*Keristrasza/Creative Commons*)

pauper. If he entered the workhouse, his whole family would have to enter with him and were then segregated from each other.

Workhouse diet was monotonous – gruel was immortalised in Charles Dickens's *Oliver Twist*, whilst bread and cheese was also a staple. Inmates had to wear a rough uniform and sleep in dormitories. A supervised bath was allowed once a week. Segregated families might typically be only allowed an hour of contact on a Sunday. Entering the workhouse as an able-bodied male became the ultimate social humiliation and degradation. The largest workhouses could accommodate a thousand inmates, who could in theory leave at any point should they be able to be supported in the community.

Sometimes, individual workhouses were hit by scandal. In August 1845, it was revealed that inmates at Andover Workhouse had been driven by hunger to eat the marrow and gristle from the putrid bones they had been tasked to crush in order to make fertiliser. Workhouse master Colin McDougal was apparently diverting the meagre funds allocated for a subsistence diet for private gain. It was also alleged that he was persistently drunk and was sexually abusing female inmates. The reluctance of the authorities to install an appropriate replacement led to the passing of the Poor Law Commission Act in 1847, with a Poor Law Board that included Cabinet ministers. Ironically, the former Andover Workhouse building is now a series of luxury residential apartments known as 'The Cloisters'.

Sanitation in other workhouses was frequently criticised, with women such as Florence Nightingale and Louisa Twining lambasting workhouse conditions. *The Lancet* took a dim view of the treatment of the sick, with nursing care provided by untrained female inmates. Eventually, the Metropolitan Poor Act required separate workhouse hospitals.

Conditions gradually improved as the nineteenth century wore on, and special schools or cottage homes were established in order to give children the chance of a decent education and to learn a trade. The author's great uncle, Alfred Broom, and his wife Margaret, ran such a home, which instructed boys in the trade of tailoring in the early twentieth century.

Places to visit

- Gressenhall Farm and Workhouse, Norfolk. Built as a 'House of Industry' in 1775, this splendid Georgian building was reconstituted in 1834 as the Mitford and Launditch Workhouse. Its display rooms, working farm and the old schoolroom can be seen as part of an extremely informative and evocative visit. The final inmates left Gressenhall in 1929.
- Southwell Workhouse, Nottinghamshire, now under the custodianship of the National Trust, was built in 1824 and designed to segregate the poor into 'blameless' and those capable of work but unemployed, labelled 'idle and profligate able-bodied'. This model attracted much attention and heavily influenced the 1834 Act. It is the best-preserved nineteenth-century workhouse in the country.
- The Weaver Hall Museum and Workhouse, Northwich, Cheshire. Formerly the Northwich Union Workhouse, dating from 1839, displays include coverage of the building's previous purpose.

Further reading

www.workhouses.org.uk – a comprehensive website with information on every workhouse in England, Scotland, Wales and Ireland. There is also a wealth of information on matters such as workhouse rules, inspections, education, buildings and staff.

Anne Digby, *Pauper Palaces* (1978).

62: Carbolic Steam Spray Device

This carbolic steam spray device, of a type devised by Joseph Lister in 1867, revolutionised the chances of surviving a visit to a hospital during Britain's Industrial Revolution. The steam spray covered everyone and everything in the operating room or hospital ward with a vapour of carbolic acid or phenol, creating an antiseptic environment.

At the beginning of the period of Britain's Industrial Revolution, rather than being regarded as places of healing, hospitals were frequently viewed as gateways of death. Overcrowded wards and lack of anaesthetics and hygiene meant that both patients and staff were at risk of spreading and catching deadly viruses and infections.

(Wellcome Collection)

Whilst the wealthy would pay privately for a doctor to attend to them at home, the poor had little choice but to enter a charitable hospital, which were few and far between, or a workhouse infirmary. Prior to the pioneering research of Dr John Snow (*see* chapter 67), it was believed that foul air, or miasma, caused infection. The idea that germs lurking on surfaces and in water did not present itself until the 1850s.

Some hospitals had small rooms emanating from a main corridor as it was thought that smaller wards would reduce the spread of disease and infection. However, these wards were overcrowded. Little surgery was attempted as the success rate was very low and, prior to the development of anaesthetics, very painful, so the patient would frequently die of shock, if not post-operative infection.

Like most aspects of life in Victorian Britain, advances in science and technology improved life for millions. In 1867, Lister, the 'father of modern surgery', successfully introduced carbolic acid to sterilise surgical instruments and clean wounds. The chemical became the first widely used antiseptic in surgery. Lister first suspected it would prove an adequate disinfectant after seeing it used to ease the stench from fields irrigated with sewage waste. He presumed it was safe because the livestock that later grazed upon the fields treated with carbolic acid suffered no ill effects. Post-operative infections declined.

A General Medical Council formed in 1858 to establish and maintain a register of those qualified to practise medicine. Before this, doctors were elected by a commission, with no control or defined standard of qualification. Hospitals varied in their designation and scope – voluntary hospitals, specialist and cottage hospitals, Poor Law infirmaries, hospitals for infectious diseases and asylums for the mentally ill.

Joseph Lister, c.1855.

Voluntary hospitals were charitable institutions funded by donations, subscriptions and bequests from wealthy benefactors. A committee of these benefactors appointed the staff and oversaw the running of the hospital as they saw fit. Treatment was free at the point of delivery for the poor and admission decided upon by receipt of a letter of recommendation by a benefactor, who would screen for those she or he felt worthy of treatment. This 'letter system' was eventually discontinued, as it was not meeting the needs of those requiring urgent treatment. The doctors then became the arbiters of what medical attention was necessary, before a financial assessment was made.

The destitute were often turned away, as were those who could afford to pay, as the Victorian notion of the 'deserving poor' came into play (*see* chapter 77). Those with incurable conditions were also refused treatment, as it was not considered efficient use of resources. Patients injured in industrial accidents were given priority treatment as businesses would often make a donation to the hospital as compensation.

Medical advances from the mid-1850s onwards made hospitals more attractive places in which to receive treatment, so increasing numbers of the wealthy sought to have operations conducted in them. Operating theatres were added, along with pharmacies, a kitchen, laundry and chapel. Richer patients were required to contribute towards the cost of their treatment. Hospitals would also arrange fundraising drives to help finance the increased demand for treatments.

As medical knowledge advanced, from 1860 onwards, several Specialist Hospitals were established. These might be inaugurated by someone whose family member had suffered from a particular condition, or perhaps by a doctor with a specialised interest. The benefits of concentrating treatment of one particular disease to a regular body of medics enabled further specialist understanding of certain conditions. The rise of the specialist, rather than generalist, doctor can be traced to this period. There was some resistance. The *British Medical Journal* ran a campaign against specialist hospitals, arguing that they drew away interesting cases from general hospitals, restricting the education of medical students in those institutions.

Cottage hospitals sprang up in rural locations, reducing the distance people had to travel to receive medical attention. Typically containing up to two dozen beds, the first cottage hospital opened at Cranleigh, Surrey, in 1859. By 1877, there were 148 such institutions.

Poor Law Infirmaries were set up within workhouses. These typically housed the aged and incurably infirm who were unable to care for themselves. Poor Law Guardians employed salaried doctors to visit the infirmary on a periodic basis. Under the Metropolitan Law Amendment Act of 1867, infirmaries had to be removed from workhouses to become independent institutions.

Specialist hospitals for infectious diseases were established in order to isolate potentially contagious patients. Sometimes these were housed on ships. Hulks moored in the Thames acted as floating hospitals during smallpox epidemics in the 1870s and 1880s. Another kind of isolation hospital was the tuberculosis sanatorium.

Mentally ill patients were often accommodated in asylums, as per the 1808 County Asylums Act. From 1845, legislation made the provision of county asylums mandatory, funded from the local poor rate, and lunacy commissioners carried out regular inspections. For efficiency reasons, several harmless mentally ill people were kept in workhouse provision whilst the dangerously insane were sent to the asylums.

Places to visit

- The Thackray Museum of Medicine in Leeds explores conditions in Victorian hospitals. Housed in a former hospital, it includes a recreation of a nineteenth-century operating theatre.
- The Bethlem Museum of the Mind, situated within the grounds of the centuries-old Bethlem Royal Hospital in Beckenham, tells the story of the famous institution and displays artwork of former and current patients.
- The Wellcome Collection, Euston, London, is the legacy of Sir Henry Wellcome, a pharmaceutical entrepreneur who was also a keen traveller and avid collector. The permanent gallery 'Medicine Man' highlights the most remarkable objects in his collection.

Further reading

Lindsey Fitzharris, *The Butchering Art: Joseph Lister's Quest to Transform the Grisly World of Victorian Medicine* (2018).
Michelle Higgs, *Life in the Victorian Hospital* (2009).
Lavinia Mitton, *The Victorian Hospital* (2008).

63: Everlasting Pill

One popular product found in pharmacies during the earlier decades of Britain's Industrial Revolution was the Everlasting Pill. Also known as the Antimony Pill, and stored in containers such as the one pictured, it was a way to clear the body. Working on the theory that a person could feel unwell due to an imbalance of bodily humours, the pill would seek to purge the body of unwanted liquids, gases and solids. The early Victorians maintained the popular belief that getting rid of all badness in the body would cure you of various ailments.

The Everlasting Pill itself was small and made of antimony, a metal now known to be toxic. Swallowing the pill would induce severe vomiting and diarrhoea, thus giving the body what they thought to be a healthy cleanse. The Antimony Pill earned the soubriquet 'Everlasting' because it could be retrieved from the excrement it produced; thus, it was marketed to be reusable: a quick wash and it could be kept on the shelf ready for its next user.

The pharmacy, where Everlasting Pills could be purchased, was the place where many people

Antimony or Everlasting Pill container. (*Wellcome Collection*)

during Britain's Industrial Revolution accessed cures and remedies for illness. In an era where few could afford the regularity of medical treatment from a qualified doctor, the facility to buy medicines directly from a shopkeeper with a modicum of medical knowledge proved extremely attractive.

Interior of Plough Court Pharmacy, 1897.

63: EVERLASTING PILL

> When illness oppresses, maladies seize,
> 'Tis the Surgeon or Druggist restores us to ease,
> But what tho' our health be the care of his art,
> He cannot from Love's pangs secure his own heart;
> And if that be wounded, he then must apply,
> To the fair one for cure, who Love's cure can supply.
>
> J. T. WOOD, 278, Strand, London.

A pharmacist making up prescriptions in his shop, mid-1800s.

A Victorian chemist's shop would contain a huge range of pre-packaged sprays, syrups, pills, sachets, ointments, capsules, lozenges, pastilles, emulsions and tinctures to cure or alleviate thousands of everyday ailments. Ointments, lotions and plasters were applied externally, whilst enemas, suppositories, pessaries and inhalations were all to be taken via a bodily orifice. They would be stored in apothecary jars on immense rows of wooden shelving. Latin names would abound and the pharmacist would keep a store of herbs, plants and even animal parts in order to be ready to mix up bespoke products. To that end, a set of scales would be a common sight, as well as pill-rolling devices, a pestle and mortar, measuring instruments and a large volume containing recipes of the various remedies and potions.

In the early phase of Britain's Industrial Revolution, much of the pharmacy was based on traditional herbalist knowledge and methodology. One advantage of this was the free and ready availability of the ingredients with which to make the cures. Despite the degree of specialist knowledge and care needed to blend the right amount of the various elements of a medicine, no formal qualifications were required in order to set oneself up as a pharmacist.

Right up to the early years of Queen Victoria's reign, leeches were still in use. Victorians believed that when a person was unwell, it was down to an excess of certain 'humours', one of which was blood. This blood could be sucked out of the body by the application of leeches. Plantain was another common remedy. This herb was used to treat hay fever and other allergies and to sooth irritations in the lungs caused by common coughs. It was frequently mixed in tea (*see* chapter 44).

Plasters sold at Victorian pharmacies were also used to draw bad humours from the body rather than provide protection over a wound. They were made from a thin piece of leather, smothered with a blend of wax and other ingredients such as lead, opium or frankincense for application to various parts of the body – the forehead, chest or behind the ears. They could be up to 12 inches in diameter. A cough might be treated by applying a plaster to the chest with warm water to make it stick better. Thus, half-melted wax would often stick to the skin for a period of days for the plaster to take effect.

The European Enlightenment gradually seeped through into the everyday practice of dispensing medicines. Chemical analysis of the properties of various substances was scientifically undertaken. Attempts were made to isolate the active ingredients and identify their precise effects on the body, including unwanted side effects. Pharmacy grew into a scientific discipline, with the production of medicines moving from the individual shop to industrial pharmacies with specialist machinery and larger budgets. The herbal medicine store founded by John Boot in Nottingham in 1849 was reformed as the Boots Pure Drug Company Limited in 1888.

Drugs that were isolated during the first half of the century included alkaloids such as strychnine, emetine, morphine, quinine and caffeine. Salicylic acid and, later, salicin were also isolated from willow bark. By the 1880s, synthetic chemicals were increasingly common in the pharmacist's shop. However, the practice of medicines made in-house continued well into the twentieth century.

Places to visit

- The Science Museum in London contains a recreation of John Gibson's pharmacy, founded in 1834, which formerly served the people of Hexham. The museum contains the original fixtures and fittings from the shop and describes the immersive exhibit as 'an atmospheric place with dark-wood panelling, colourful glass decanters and a cornucopia of herbs, compounds and potions'.
- Blists Hill Victorian Town near Telford includes Bates & Hunt, a recreated nineteenth-century chemist's shop.
- The Royal Pharmaceutical Museum, Lambeth, established in 1842, contains a unique collection of about 45,000 objects covering all aspects of the history of British pharmacy. These include traditional dispensing equipment; drug storage containers; proprietary 'brand name' medicines dating from the eighteenth century to the present day; bronze mortars; medical caricatures; and a photo archive.

Further reading

Nigel Tallis & Kate Arnold-Forster, *Pharmacy History: A Pictorial Record* (1991).
Stuart Anderson, *Making Medicines: A Brief History of Pharmacy and Pharmaceuticals* (2005).

64. Prison Treadmill

The treadmill, or treadwheel, invented by William Cubitt in 1818, was the most hated form of hard labour in prisons during much of the period of Britain's Industrial Revolution. The prisoner had to lift his body up 3 feet at each step. The Prison Discipline Society advised that each male individual should complete 12,000 feet of ascent per day. Treadmills were usually unproductive and part of the Victorian prison's aim to deter criminals, rather than rehabilitate them, and were eventually banned in 1902. This engraving shows prisoners at Brixton Prison in London engaged in grinding corn. Up to twenty-four prisoners could work at once, each moving from left to right as a new prisoner joined at the far end. Each prisoner would get twelve rest minutes per hour.

Before Britain's Industrial Revolution, sanctions for criminal behaviour tended to be public events that shamed the criminal and acted as a deterrent to others. They included the ducking stool, the pillory, whipping, branding and the stocks. The sentence for many other offences was death. In general, prisons were temporary lock-ups for those awaiting trial or sentencing – rarely used as a punishment in themselves. Men and women, boys and girls, debtors and murderers, were all held together. Many died of diseases such as gaol fever, a form of typhus.

Prison hulks were also used from 1776 – ships anchored in the Thames and at Portsmouth and Plymouth, where prisoners would be put to hard labour during the day and then chained up in the ship at night. The appalling conditions on the hulks eventually led to the end of this practice in 1857.

John Howard, the first penal reformer, in 1777 condemned the prison system as disorganised, barbaric and filthy. He called for wide-ranging reforms including the installation of paid staff, external inspection, improved sanitation and a nutritious diet for prisoners.

In 1791, Jeremy Bentham designed the 'panopticon'. This prison design allowed a

Treadmill at Brixton Prison.

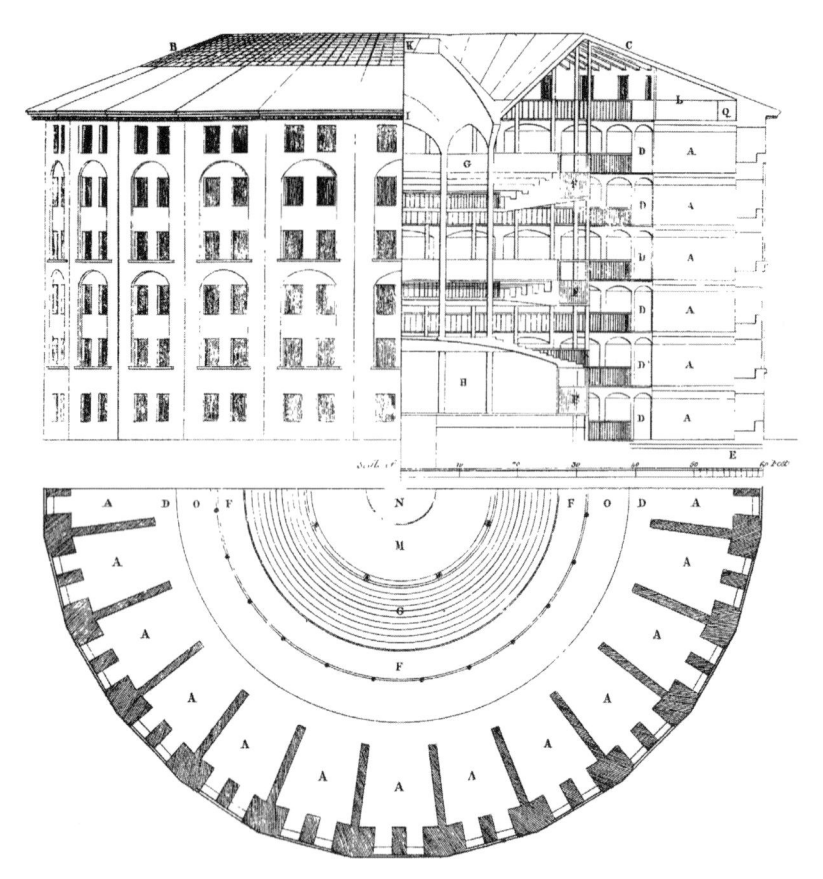

Plan of Jeremy Bentham's panopticon prison, drawn by architect Willey Reveley in 1791.

centrally placed observer to survey all the prisoners, as prison wings radiated out from this position. Bentham's panopticon became the model for prison building for the next half-century. The 1799 Penitentiary Act specified that gaols be built for one inmate per cell and operate on a silent system with continuous labour.

As doubts about the efficacy of the transportation system increased (*see* chapter 65), ninety prisons were built or significantly expanded during the period 1842 to 1877, as part of a concerted building programme. Many prisons were based on the Bentham design, with wings of cells organised around a central hub. All had small cells intended for single occupancy, arranged along landings stacked three or more storeys high. This gave staff clear sight lines.

Cells typically had low, narrow doorways that fitted the average Victorian body. Candle alcoves were provided so that prisoners could read the Bible, and some cells with larger windows provided fresh air for prisoners with respiratory conditions. Between 1837 and 1901, there were more than 15 million prison admissions, with the majority of prisoners serving sentences of less than one month.

The first government-built prison opened at Millbank in London in 1816. It held 860 prisoners in separate cells, although association with other prisoners was permitted during the day. Work in prison included picking 'coir' (tarred rope) and weaving. In 1842, Pentonville prison, constructed to Bentham's panopticon design, held 520 prisoners, each in a cell measuring

13 feet long, 7 feet wide and 9 feet high. It operated the separate system – basically, solitary confinement. Over the next six years, fifty-four new prisons were built using this template.

The separate system was widely used, aiming to reform prisoners through silent, solitary contemplation. Communication between prisoners was forbidden, even when performing work tasks out of their cells. Rather than leading people closer to Christian contemplation, the system led to increased rates of mental illness.

Hard labour was a common sentence handed down by magistrates. Adult males over the age of 16 were expected to work for no less than six and no more than ten hours a day. The terms of the Prisons Act 1865 decreed that 'the treadwheel, crank, capstan, shot-drill and stone-breaking' were appropriate types of hard labour. Assistant Director of Prisons Sir Edmund du Cane promised the public that prisoners would get 'Hard Labour, Hard Fare, and Hard Board'.

Gradually, attitudes to imprisonment, and thus prison conditions, improved. Penal reform became increasingly popular. Christian groups like the Quakers and the Evangelicals were highly influential in promoting ideas of reform through personal redemption. Prisoners were God's creatures who deserved humane treatment. In 1866, admirers of John Howard founded the Howard Association – later renamed as the Howard League for Penal Reform. For these rational improvers, the purpose of prison was to reform and rehabilitate as well as punish. Food improved in many prisons and libraries were established in accordance with the idea of 'Self-Help' (*see* chapter 77). In 1877, prisons came under the control of the Prison Commission. For the first time, all prisons came under central control.

The Prison Act of 1898 reasserted reformation as the main role of prison regimes and, in many ways, this legislation set the tone for prison policy today. The separate system was diluted and hard labour abolished. Work was to become productive. The Church of England Temperance Society appointed missionaries to the London Police Courts. Offenders were released on condition they kept in touch with their missionary, this system being formalised with the Probation Order, introduced in 1907. The borstal system was introduced in the Prevention of Crime Act 1908, recognising that young people should have separate prison establishments from adults. Young convicts would be subject to hard physical work, technical and educational instruction, and a strong moral atmosphere.

Thirty-two Victorian prisons are still in operation in England and Wales, holding 22,000 prisoners – a quarter of the prison population.

Places to visit

- Lincoln Castle grounds contains its original Victorian prison, complete with chapel with separate pews to keep inmates apart.
- Prison and Police Museum, Ripon. Many hands-on activities recreate the horror of the Victorian prison regime.

Further reading

Neil Storey, *Prisons and Prisoners in Victorian Britain* (2010).
Michelle Higgs, *Prison Life in Victorian England* (2007).
Trevor May, *Victorian and Edwardian Prisons* (2006).

65: Convict Ship

This engraving of a convict ship, showing prisoners caged like animals en route to Australia, tells us of one feature of the Industrial Revolution employed to remove those who fell foul of the law, and so rendering them unable to share in the benefits of that revolution.

Transportation was introduced as a punishment for many criminal offences by the Elizabethan Act of 1597, 'For the punishment of Rogues, Vagabonds, and Sturdy Beggars – to be banished out of this Realm and all other Dominions thereof'. From this time onwards, convicts were dispatched across the Atlantic to Virginia, Jamaica and Barbados. The American War of Independence precluded the use of these destinations; therefore, another destination point had to be found.

For about a decade following the American Declaration of Independence in 1776, transportation fell into disuse. Criminals who would have previously been transported were sentenced to hard labour. This resulted in the overcrowding of prisons and the necessity for prison hulks, disused warships moored at Woolwich, Chatham, Portsmouth and Plymouth.

Prison conditions deteriorated and consideration was given to using Gibraltar or parts of Africa as penal colonies. Both were found to be unsuitable. It was then decided to elide the policies of transporting convicts and settlement of the southern hemisphere. Botany Bay in New South Wales was the new destination of the authorities' choice.

Captain James Cook's voyages to the South Pacific, during which he stumbled across Australia, provided a perfect venue for Britain's unwanted convicts. Transportation to Australia began in 1787, when eleven ships left Portsmouth bound for Botany Bay, via Tenerife, Rio de Janeiro and Cape Town. Six transport vessels were under contract from private owners: *Alexander*, *Charlotte*, *Friendship*, *Lady Penryn*, *Prince of Wales* and *Scarborough* carried the convicts, whilst three store ships and two Royal Navy escort ships formed the rest of the convoy.

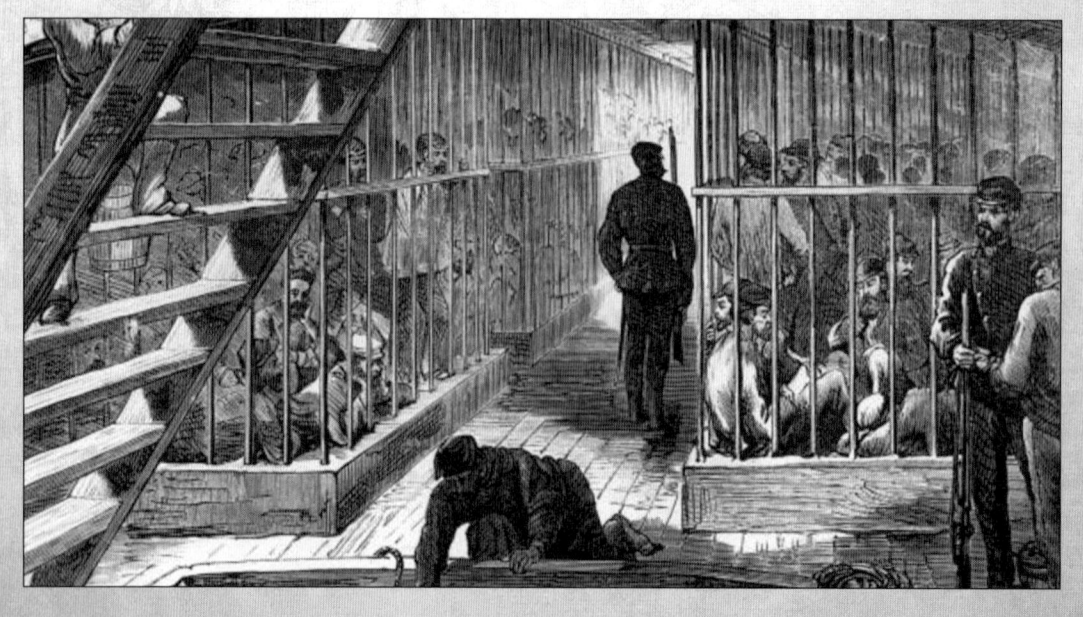

The first ship arrived at Botany Bay on 18 January 1788.

Admiral Arthur Phillip was tasked with establishing a settlement there for convicts and free settlers. Phillip became the first governor of New South Wales. He explored the Australian coast for a good place in which to establish a settlement for the convicts and their guards. He found what was 'without exception, the finest and most extensive harbour in the universe and at the same time the most secure, being safe from all winds that blow'. The rest of the fleet landed at the newly named Sydney Cove, in honour of Viscount Sydney, who had chosen Phillip to lead the expedition. Phillip was a far-sighted governor, who realised that New South Wales would need both a full civil administration and a system of emancipating convicts who had served their time. Of the 737 convicts who left the Hampshire port, forty died during the eight-month journey.

Eighty per cent of those transported over the following century had been found guilty of theft, many of them repeat offenders. Protestors or those who otherwise fell foul of various governments' repression of working-class movements also made the long trip to the Antipodes. Some of those involved in the Luddite movement, the Rebecca Riots, the Merthyr Rising and the Swing Riots were transported, as well as the six Tolpuddle Martyrs and some Chartists. During the times of the Bloody Code, when up to fifty offences carried the death penalty, many judges used transportation as an alternative. John Frost, the Welsh Chartist leader, was one of those whose death sentence was commuted to transportation.

There were three levels of transportation sentence – seven years, fourteen years and life

Engraving depicting the First Fleet arriving at Botany Bay in January 1788, with indigenous Australians in canoes witnessing the arrival. Bare Island is in the background.

Government gaol gang, from *Views in New South Wales and Van Diemen's Land: Australian scrap book* (1830).

– and 15 per cent of transported convicts were female. Sixty-nine per cent were from England, 25 per cent from Ireland, 5 per cent from Scotland and 1.2 per cent from Wales.

In Australia, some convicts were sent to work on the farms of free settlers whilst others were set on road building or breaking rocks. Punishments were harsh and convicts who disobeyed rules were whipped. Those who refused to follow the rules were posted to the more remote settlements to work in chain gangs.

Transportation to New South Wales continued until the 1830s. It became the practice to transfer convicts from New South Wales to Van Diemen's Land (Tasmania). The authorities and free settlers in New South Wales were relieved to have the worst miscreants removed from their society, a practice that continued up to 1853. From 1850, convicts were also sent to Western Australia.

Having completed a sentence, a convict would achieve a certificate of conditional freedom. Occasionally, convicts could secure early release after four years of good conduct through a ticket-of-leave. Others received a 'conditional pardon' and were then able to find paid work of their own for the remainder of their sentence. Some entered government service, including staffing prisons. Up to 1834, anyone attempting to end his or her sentence by escaping risked the death penalty. Once freed, many convicts settled in Australia, partly because of the prohibitive cost of the return journey home.

The transportation of convicts continued uninterrupted until 1836, when the harsh treatment of the Tolpuddle Martyrs caused a re-examination of the practice. A House of Commons Select Committee was established, which determined that those sentenced to seven years or less should remain in Britain or be sent to Bermuda or Gibraltar. As an alternative, able-bodied young men could join the Army or Royal Navy.

Finally abolished in 1868, transportation was superseded by a system of penal servitude. Around 170,000 convicts had been sent to Australia between 1787 and 1868. About 40 per cent of the population of Australia in its first fifty years as a colony consisted of transported convicts.

Places to visit

- The Down County Museum in Northern Ireland is housed in the old County Gaol of Down, which used to house prisoners prior to transportation. It holds extensive records about the approximately 50,000 Irish felons transported to Australia.

Further reading

Lucy Williams, *Convicts in the Colonies: Transportation Tales from Britain to Australia* (2018).
Graham Seal, *Great Convict Stories: Dramatic and moving tales from Australia's brutal early years* (2017).
Deborah J. Swiss, *The Tin Ticket: The Heroic Journey of Australia's Convict Women* (2010).

66: Punch Cartoon: A Court for King Cholera

A Court for King Cholera, a famous cartoon by John Leech that appeared in *Punch* magazine in 1852, offers a satirical look at the urban impact of the Industrial Revolution. Its punning caption makes a mistaken link between overcrowding and the spread of cholera, rather than the root cause of impure water. However, Leech lays bare the overcrowding, poor-quality housing, lack of sanitation and lack of hygiene that blighted the lives of the urban impoverished during Britain's Industrial Revolution.

Between 1800 and 1850, the population of England doubled. At the same time, people were being forced from agriculture into factory-based industries. National census returns showed that in 1801, 70 per cent of the population lived in the country but by 1851, half the nation's citizens were urban dwellers.

Cities swelled with new inhabitants, as people were either thrown off the land or were seeking better-paid work with prospects of improvement and promotion. Existing housing stock in cities and large towns was inadequate to deal with the sudden increased demand.

Before Britain's Industrial Revolution occasioned a change in the distribution of urban housing, the rich and poor had lived in the same districts: the rich in the main streets, the poor in the service streets behind. With the coming of smoky factories to city centres, the prosperous moved out to fashionable suburbs, often located

A COURT FOR KING CHOLERA.

to the west of a city in order to avoid the prevailing westerly wind carrying smoke over their neighbourhoods.

Where the poor had lived, houses were often torn down to make way for commercial premises or railway lines and stations. The reshaping of Britain's urban spaces was termed 'improvement'. However, for those whose rented spaces had been demolished to make way for industrial expansion, there was little option but to move to already crowded districts, causing a diminution in the quality of living for all the inhabitants of those areas.

Cheap housing was hastily erected. The term 'slum' was first used in 1825 to describe the new housing. The incentive for house builders was to erect as many dwellings as they could on their land. The incentive for tenants was to live within walking distance of their place of work. These two factors led to overcrowding.

Social attitudes in educated Britain polarised, between those such as Charles Dickens who deplored the overcrowded and insanitary slum conditions, and those who sought to apportion blame to the victims of poor housing. Slum inhabitants were characterised as drunkards and thieves. The police claimed that slums were often too dangerous for them to enter. However, Dickens felt no such qualms, writing, 'I ... mean to take a great, London, back-slums kind of walk tonight, seeking adventures in knight errant style.' In 1838, Dickens conjured up an image of life in a Bermondsey slum, Jacob's Island, in *Oliver Twist*:

Crazy wooden galleries ... with holes from which to look upon the slime beneath; windows, broken and patched ... rooms so small, so filthy, so confined, that the air would seem too tainted even for

Artistic representation of overcrowded housing in London, from *London, a Pilgrimage* by William Blanchard Jerrold with illustrations by Gustave Doré, 1872.

the dirt and squalor which they shelter ... dirt-besmeared walls and decaying foundations.

Journalist Henry Mayhew, who co-founded *Punch* magazine in 1841, recorded: 'The water of the huge ditch in front of the houses is covered with a scum ... and prismatic with grease ... Along the banks are heaps of indescribable filth ... the air has literally the smell of a graveyard.'

Sordid stories about life in slums became entertainment for readers who enjoyed the tales at a safe distance. 'Slum tourism' developed, where members of polite society went to see for themselves what the slums were like. The press reported on an unnamed young girl from a wealthy background who had gone missing. Detectives eventually located her in a slum dwelling in East London. She claimed to have been so 'enthused' by Walter Besant's *All Sorts and Conditions of Men (*1882) that she had decided to visit the area to see how the poor really lived. After telling one resident about her rich parents, she had been abducted in the hope that her father would pay a ransom for her release.

Much slum housing was down narrow alleys which gave access to a courtyard. Some houses only had one window, facing onto the yard, others none at all. Some large families living in a one or two-room dwelling might be forced to take in extra lodgers to make ends meet. Some people lived in cellars, into which the liquids from cesspools would seep.

Few houses had the luxury of drainage and there were scarcely any privies – often two for a whole courtyard. Several hundred people living in a court would share the use of one standpipe. Due to overcrowding, the sick and dying lived side by side with the (for now) healthy.

Victorian slums were the consequence of the rapid industrialisation and urbanisation of the country and led to a more dramatic spatial separation between the rich and the poor. This was known as the two-nation divide, embracing widely different lifestyles and living standards. Through the work of social campaigners and the recorded experiences of the curious well-to-do, the public gradually became aware that slum conditions were not caused by the immorality and deviancy of their inhabitants, but rather, afflicted by the economy and circumstances, and that reform was possible given progressive economic, social and cultural policy.

Places to visit

- The Museum of Liverpool recently undertook an excavation of the remains of an old slum court, Missionary Buildings, which in the 1830s was nicknamed 'Little Hell'. Some of the personal objects uncovered are on display in the People's Republic gallery of the museum.

Further reading

Sarah Wise, *The Blackest Streets: The Life and Death of a Victorian Slum* (2009).
Dean Kirby, *Angel Meadow: Victorian Britain's Most Savage Slum* (2020).
Elizabeth J. Stewart, *Courts and Alleys: A History of Liverpool Courtyard Housing* (2019).

67: Broad Street Pump

Cholera, a disease that saw epidemic outbreaks in nineteenth-century Britain, brought in its midst illness, death and fear to the inhabitants of industrial towns and cities. First reported in 1831, it had London firmly in its grip by the 1850s. Cholera is a deadly disease. The primary symptom is acute diarrhoea, which drains the body of nutrients and fluids. The 1831 outbreak had originated in India and killed over 6,000 people in London. At the time, the cause of the disease was a mystery.

Some suspected there was a link between the disease and the contamination of drinking water by human sewage. It was obvious that Thames water, when seen through a microscope, was far from clean and it was a subject of wonderful campaigning cartoons in the London newspapers and the satirical magazine *Punch*. However, the dominant scientific opinion of the time was the miasmatic theory that the disease spread by foul air. It was not thought that the polluted water was deadly, but rather the very smell of it. Despite their best endeavours, scientists were in the dark as to how and why cholera spread.

During a severe outbreak in the late summer of 1854, which killed about 600 people in the area around Broad Street in Soho, Dr John Snow, a local GP and surgeon, managed to prove his previous suspicion that cholera was not spread through the air by foul smells or miasmas, but by an infected water supply. In particular, Snow had suspicions about a water pump that sat at the heart of the outbreak. He noted that none of the workers at a Soho brewery developed cholera as they either drank water from the brewery's own independent source or just the beer, which had gone through the brewing process. Snow traced all the cholera patients in the area and asked if they had drunk water from the Broad Street pump, creating a dot map to illustrate the spread of cases linked to the suspicious source. 'Within 250 yards of the spot where Cambridge Street joins Broad Street there were upwards of 500 fatal attacks of cholera in 10 days,' Snow recorded. He persuaded officials to remove the handle from the pump so that water could no longer be drawn from it. The outbreak declined and shortly ended.

Broad Street pump. (*Jack Foster*)

Punch cartoon, A Drop of London Water, *published in 1850.*

It was later discovered that the source for the pump stood a few yards from a cesspit into which contaminated human excrement had leaked. It took a further decade for Snow's theory that contaminated water supplies caused cholera outbreaks to be accepted.

Across much of the capital, which had a population of well over 2 million, much of the city's sewage was still recycled as fertiliser. Individual houses had cesspits from which solid waste, known as 'night soil', was collected by nightmen, who transported it on stinking carts to the market gardens on London's outskirts. Waste water from the cesspits seeped through the ground, or flowed on the surface of the streets into London's system of ancient rivers, which had become de facto sewers, and into the Thames.

In 1848, the government established a Metropolitan Commission of Sewers. After issuing a general invitation to engineers to submit proposals for dealing with London's sewage, an engineer with a background in land drainage methods, Joseph Bazalgette, was hired. In 1855, the Metropolitan Board of Works was established, one of whose duties was to 'make such sewers and works as they may think necessary for preventing all and any part of the sewage of the Metropolis from flowing into the river Thames in or near the Metropolis'. Bazalgette was appointed chief engineer for the Board of Works and produced a detailed plan for a scheme of intercepting sewers to collect London's sewage and discharge it into the Thames 10 miles further downstream.

Dr John Snow died of a stroke in 1858 at the age of 45, but Londoners are reminded of his legacy by a 1992 replica of the original Broad Street pump as well as a plaque affixed to the side of the pub a few yards away, also named in Snow's honour.

The year of Snow's death also saw the Great Stink pervade summer in London. The stench from effluent floating in the Thames wafted into the Houses of Parliament. Sheets soaked in disinfectant were hung to disguise the smell but serious consideration was given to moving the sitting upstream and out of London. Thus, a bill for the construction of a new sewage system for London was voted through in just eighteen days. The total cost would be £2.5 million (approximately £300 million in today's money) and financed from the public purse.

Joseph Bazalgette set to work constructing his intercepting sewer system, which would gather waste and carry it eastwards and southwards outside the city for discharge into the Thames. Principally, natural gravity would carry the effluent but at certain points, pumping stations were built to move it to a higher level. Steam pumps installed at Deptford in 1864 were at the time the largest in the world. As the scheme was also a demonstration of the technical brilliance of engineering, several of the buildings above ground were lavishly decorated.

The building of 1,100 miles of new sewers involved the excavation by hand of 3.5 million cubic yards of earth and the use of 318 million bricks, resulting in a shortage for housebuilding. Members of the Royal Family formally opened most of the pumping stations. Although further

Crossness Pumping Station. (*Peter Scrimshaw/Creative Commons*)

refinements were needed to disperse solid and liquid waste in different ways, the infrastructure that still serves the United Kingdom's capital city today was firmly in place.

Unlike Snow, who died without great public accolade, Bazalgette was richly rewarded for his immense work, being knighted in 1875 and retiring a wealthy man.

Places to visit

- Broad Street Pump – a replica of the original source of the 1854 cholera outbreak, on the now renamed Broadwick Street in Soho. Symbolically, the pump has no handle, to replicate its removal in 1854 to prevent further spread of cholera.
- Crossness Pumping Station Museum. Built in 1865, the Grade I Listed industrial heritage site is a fine example of High Victorian decoration as well as the ideal place to learn about the history of toilets and sewage systems.
- Joseph Bazalgette Memorial on Victoria Embankment, another engineering project for which he was responsible.

Further reading

Stephen Halliday, *The Great Stink of London: Sir Joseph Bazalgette and the Cleansing of the Victorian Metropolis* (1999).
Sandra Hempel, *The Medical Detective: John Snow, Cholera and the Mystery of the Broad Street Pump* (2007).
Amanda J. Thomas, *Cholera: The Victorian Plague* (2015).

68: The War Cry, 6 August 1887

This edition of the *War Cry*, a newspaper founded in 1879 by General William Booth of the Salvation Army, was vociferous in arguing against an increase in the number of bank holidays. Rather than object to an increase in leisure time for the working person, the *War Cry*'s concern was that the days would be spent drinking, smoking and enjoying immoral entertainments. However, the Salvation Army was no mere killjoy organisation, but a group that strove to improve the lives of the most destitute and downtrodden subjects who had not benefitted from the fruits of Britain's Industrial Revolution.

In 1865, William Booth and Catherine Booth, members of the Methodist Church, founded the Christian Revival Association, an evangelical movement based in London's East End. In 1870, it became the East London Christian Mission and in 1878 was reorganised to form the Salvation Army. Their doctrine was one of practical Christianity – characterised as soup, soap and salvation – to achieve social and spiritual transformation amongst the vulnerable and marginalised in society.

Distinctively amongst Christian denominations, the Salvation Army developed military-style titles and a uniform, with General Superintendent William Booth at its head. Its Articles of War, which all members pledged to try to abide by, included the renunciation of alcohol and religious sacraments such as baptism and communion, considering the former a great evil and the latter unnecessary. Grace was to be sought via the inner soul, rather than outward manifestations of religiosity.

In 1884, the Salvation Army branched out into the establishment of a women's refuge in Whitechapel, part of a campaign to rescue young women from prostitution. In 1888, after witnessing several individuals sleeping rough on bridges on the Thames, Booth began his mission to the homeless. Sleeping rough was a punishable offence under the Vagrancy Act of 1824, but a vagrant could escape prosecution if they could

General William Booth.

demonstrate visible means of subsistence. To that end, the Salvation Army began to operate night shelters and food depots, accessible for a penny per night. Those using them would be treated with Christian kindness and respect, unlike when entering a workhouse casual ward.

Two years later, Booth published *Darkest England and the Way Out*, in which he estimated the number of paupers, homeless, starving and very poor people in London. The figures made for grim reading, amounting to a little under a million souls. Nationwide he judged the number of what he termed the 'submerged classes' to be 3 million, 10 per cent of the population. To alleviate such distress, Booth proposed the creation of City, Farm and Overseas Colonies, each designed to provide work in urban and rural settings. These schemes would be underpinned by 'a course of regeneration by moral and religious influences'.

Booth's book sold well, with the profits being put towards opening a City Colony, night shelters, working men's homes, hostels, workshops, and a home for single mothers. The first Salvation Army night shelter opened in 1888 in Limehouse. This facility and others provided a warm place to stay the night with basic refreshment for the cost of a penny.

A more comprehensive service could be obtained from The Ark in Southwark Street and The Harbour in Stanhope Street. Known as 'Metropoles', a resident could access a bed in a four-bedded room for 4*d* per night, or a separate cubicle for 6*d*; a supper of bread, cold meat and tea cost an additional 3*d*. Residents were able to come and go as they pleased, although were encouraged to attend a religious service at 7 pm each day.

Salvation Army officers would scour the streets seeking out rough sleepers, offering them a voucher for a free breakfast at a shelter in return for attendance at a subsequent Salvation Army service. Booth's vision was to convert prostitutes, gamblers and alcoholics to Christianity. Catherine Booth, meanwhile, would seek to raise funds from wealthy patrons. She also served as a minister, an unusual position at the time for a female in a Christian church.

In 1890, the Salvation Army opened its first Elevator, a building combining a factory workspace with hostel accommodation above for those who worked there. They operated on the principle of men and women earning their keep via the work, while learning practical skills that would keep them away from vagrancy in the future. Trades on offer included basketmaking, carpentry, cabinetmaking, tinsmithing, tambourine making, carpet weaving, mattress making, signwriting, woodcarving, tailoring and bakery.

Booth established a farm colony at Hadleigh, Essex. Allowing its members to escape from the London slums, it included a market garden, an orchard and facilities for producing milk. Men would also be trained in building trades and household work. The movement soon spread to the USA, Australia and elsewhere.

Members of the Salvation Army were discouraged from drinking alcohol, smoking and gambling. Thus, the movement proved unpopular amongst some pub landlords, who began to lose trade. A body known as the Skeleton Army was set up, which sought to disrupt Salvation Army service, throwing rocks, bones, rats and tar as well as assaulting Army members. Despite such low acts, the Salvation Army turned around thousands of lives that had been damaged because of Britain's Industrial Revolution.

Places to visit

- The Salvation Army International Heritage Centre tells the story of the organisation from its origins in 1865. It comprises two museums, one in London, and one in Nottingham at the birthplace of William Booth.
- A statue of William Booth stands outside the William Booth Memorial Training College in Camberwell.

Further reading

Andrew M. Eason & Roger J. Green, *Boundless Salvation: The Shorter Writings of William Booth* (2012).
Pamela J. Walker, *Pulling the Devil's Kingdom Down: The Salvation Army in Victorian Britain* (2001).

69: Victorian Tinplate Bath

This tin bath, measuring approximately 4 feet by 2 feet, would herald the weekly bath time in the average British Victorian household. Pots and kettles on the range heated the water to fill it. Then each family member would bathe, in turn, in front of the fire, using the same water. Some wealthier families could afford a separate bathroom, but with plumbing not becoming widely available until the 1880s, a chambermaid would be required to carry hot water up the stairs to fill the bath. This bath symbolises the ever-improving levels of domestic comfort that the working and middle classes could expect during Britain's Industrial Revolution as services and facilities we now regard as essential were gradually introduced into people's homes.

Between 1851 and 1911, Britain's urban population increased threefold, so by the time of the 1911 census (*see* chapter 92), 79 per cent of Britons lived in towns. To house this growing population, new Victorian and Edwardian suburbs were typically situated close to places of work, but increasingly, towards the end of the era, within reasonable commuting distance for those with access to trams or private means of transport. Housing for the more affluent tended to be built on the western edge of towns, meaning the prevailing British weather drift of west to east would mean the smoke and smog of industry would be carried across the poorer districts to the east.

Large semi-detached or detached villas were built for the well off. Privacy and comfort were the objectives, with many separate rooms being created rather than the open-plan living more fashionable today. Separation of activities into different rooms was important to the Victorian mind.

The styles of housing in which those who had achieved a comfortable standard of living or better from Britain's Industrial Revolution changed during the nineteenth century. In the

Victorian gas kitchen range. (*David Dixon/Victorian Range, Sudbury Hall Kitchen/CC BY-SA 2.0*)

early Victorian period, the classical Regency style continued to influence most house designs. During the 1850s, the Italianate style, with its stucco, began to dominate. Thence onwards, the Gothic Revival movement, which influenced the design of many great public buildings, was also seen in the domestic sphere as pointing, projecting porches prevailed, complete with bay windows and grey slate from the Welsh mines (*see* chapter 17).

The abolition of tax on bricks in the 1850s made these elements more affordable and the development of the railway network meant they could be transported quickly and cheaply around the country. Standard sizes and shapes became the norm so several houses of the respectable working classes and the middle classes had very similar features.

As the Victorian decades wore on, facilities that had been considered luxuries at the beginning of the grand Queen's era became more commonplace. This meant the introduction of sanitation features such as effective drains, waste collection, and outside privies or indoor water closets. Hot and cold running tap water, the former heated up by a boiler, became common features. Many houses were built with a cellar in which to store the coal required to heat open fires and water. In order to access a reliable supply of clean water in an era before mains water supply from private or municipal water companies, developers sank wells to determine ready access to spring water. Rainwater was used for the weekly wash and other scullery uses. An average sized roof yielded between 21,000 and 35,000 gallons of water per year and so many good-quality houses were equipped with large rainwater storage tanks in the basement from which the water was drawn by a hand pump.

From the 1870s onwards, many middle-class houses could afford fixed bathroom appliances with hot and cold running water. The advent of a discrete bathroom on the first floor radically altered upper floor plans. Cleanliness and hygiene were also improved. It could take half an hour for the water to heat up but following the invention of the geyser by Benjamin Waddy Maughan in 1868, scalding hot water could be had instantaneously. The geyser consisted of a copper cylinder in which finely divided streams of water were heated by the rising hot gasses from rows of gas jets in the base. Although initially the preserve of the more affluent classes, as the decades wore on the solidly respectable working classes could also find the space and cost of such luxuries.

Gas lighting became available in many towns, before being rolled out to individual dwellings. Eventually, gas cooking facilities on large or smaller ranges became available for many families. Sash windows with larger panes of glass gradually replaced the Regency style of small panes on a grid pattern. Brick chimneys spread out across the new urban centres and terraced houses lined the streets of industrial areas. Small gardens or vegetable patches reflected the later Victorian ideal of the love of nature.

More wealthy families tended to have live-in servants, their accommodation frequently being up in draughty attic rooms. People began to follow trends and styles in interior design and decoration. Heavy curtains, flowery wallpaper and richly patterned carpets and rugs became de rigueur. Ornaments, well-crafted furniture, paintings and houseplants would adorn living and sleeping areas.

Places to visit

- Mr Straw's House, a National Trust property in Worksop, Nottinghamshire, is an Edwardian semi-detached, red-brick villa previously owned by grocer William Straw. Its wallpaper, carpets and ornaments reflect the contemporary style.
- Moorside House, part of the Bradford Industrial Museum, is a former mill manager's dwelling restored to its 1900s glory and set within the grounds of a cotton mill. It includes stunning antique furniture, authentic contemporary light fittings and a recreated bathroom and kitchen.
- Lindley Sambourne House in Kensington, London, is a late Victorian/early Edwardian house crowded with ornaments, pictures and furniture. The grand hallway contains a fireplace and stained-glass windows echoing the elaborate Victorian upper-middle-class taste in interior design.

Further reading

Trevor Yorke, *The Edwardian House Explained: A Brief History of British Architecture from 1900–1914* (2006).
Pamela Horn, *Life in a Victorian Household* (2011).
Judith Flanders, *The Victorian House: Domestic Life from Childbirth to Deathbed* (2004).

70: William Morris Wallpaper

This wallpaper sample, taken from a book of designs made by William Morris and Co., represents the Arts and Craft style of design that became popular in the late nineteenth century, not so much as a product of Britain's Industrial Revolution, but more as a rejection of many of its principles.

'Have nothing in your house you do not know to be useful or believe to be beautiful,' William Morris said. Britain's Industrial Revolution found its critics in terms of the impersonalisation and mechanisation of society. The damaging effects of machine-dominated production on both social conditions and the quality of manufactured goods had been recognised since about 1840.

The Arts and Crafts movement in Britain was established on the principle that society needed to adopt a different set of priorities in relation to the manufacture of objects. Its leaders wanted to develop products that not only had more integrity but were also manufactured in a less dehumanising way.

Arts and Crafts adherents used high-quality materials and strove for an emphasis on utility in design. They believed that machinery had stunted creative processes and hand-produced work was the key to both human fulfilment and aesthetic beauty. The movement was heavily influenced by the imagery of nature and medieval art forms, especially the Gothic style.

William Morris, c.1887.

The Arts and Crafts movement was a loose collection of different artistic societies, such as the Exhibition Society, the Art Workers' Guild, set up in 1884, and other craftspeople in both small workshops and large manufacturing companies.

The movement took its name from the Arts and Crafts Exhibition Society, a group founded in London in 1887. The Society's chief aim was to assert a new public relevance for the work of decorative artists. The Refreshment Rooms of the South Kensington Museum, later the Victoria and Albert Museum, had previously given decorative artists a chance to showcase their work. The Arts and Crafts Exhibition Society mounted its first annual exhibition in 1888. It included examples of ceramics, textiles, metalwork and furniture in the hope that it would elevate these crafts to an art form.

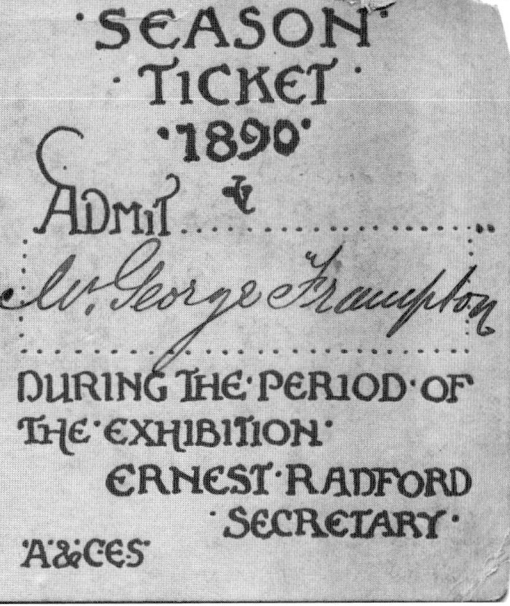

The work of William Morris was hugely influential amongst Arts and Crafts devotees. Morris believed passionately in the importance of creating beautiful, well-crafted objects for everyday use that were created in a way that allowed their makers to remain connected both with their product and with other people. Looking to the past, particularly the medieval period, for simpler and better models for both living and production, Morris argued for the return to a pre-industrial system of manufacture based on small-scale workshops. He particularly disliked the division of labour in modern industrial manufacture, where the making of an object was broken into small, separate tasks, meaning individuals had a very weak relationship with the product of their labour. As a socialist, he wanted to free the working classes from the frustration of a working day focused solely on repetitive tasks, and allow them the pleasure of craft-based production in which they would engage directly with the creative process from beginning to end.

Morris had his residence, the Red House, designed by architect Philip Webb to showcase the Arts and Craft style. Built within commuting distance of London but situated at the time in the countryside, it featured an asymmetrical, L-shaped plan, pointed arches and picturesque set of masses with steep rooflines in the Gothic style. Its tiled roof and brick construction, largely devoid of ornament, spoke of the simplicity that Morris preached and its function as a mere residence. The interior, however, demonstrated the richness of Arts and Crafts design, with murals painted by Edward Burne-Jones. Partly inspired by their socialist beliefs, Webb and Morris included large servants' quarters.

However, five years of commuting into London proved too much for Morris and he sold the house and moved closer to the capital.

Towards the end of the period of Britain's Industrial Revolution, the Arts and Crafts movement flourished in large cities such as London, Birmingham, Manchester, Edinburgh and Glasgow. Exhibition societies inspired by the original one in London helped establish the Movement's public identity. Members of the Arts and Crafts community felt driven to spread their message, convinced that a better system of design of manufacture could actively change people's lives.

Between 1895 and 1905, this strong sense of social purpose drove the creation of over a hundred organisations and guilds that centred on Arts and Crafts principles in Britain. These included art schools and technical colleges, which taught skills such as enamelling, embroidery and calligraphy. Goods could be sold through Morris and Co. in Oxford Street.

The Arts and Crafts movement marked the beginning of a change in the value society placed on how things were made, and reformed the design and manufacture of everything from buildings and stained glass to jewellery.

Places to visit

- The Red House, in Bexleyheath, is under the custodianship of the National Trust.
- Wightwick Manor in Wolverhampton, now run by the National Trust, built between 1887 and 1893 in Arts and Crafts style, contains several Morris wallpapers and fabrics.
- The Church of All Saints in Brockhampton, Herefordshire (commissioned by Alice Foster and built between 1901 and 1902), is considered among the best examples of the works of the Arts and Crafts movement.

Further reading

Mary Greensted, *The Arts and Crafts Movement in Britain* (2010).
Rosalind P. Blakesley, *The Arts and Crafts Movement* (2006).
Fiona MacCarthy, *William Morris: A Life in Our Time* (2010).

71: Great Exhibition Telescopic View

This telescopic view, printed and published by C.A. Lane of Hampstead, depicts Queen Victoria opening the Great Exhibition of 1851. It is made of printed paper and card, and supplied in a slip-in card box. When removed from the box, it opens with a concertina action. Looking through the little peephole, the viewer can see a three-dimensional interior view of the Crystal Palace, which housed the exhibition.

To give it the full title, the Great Exhibition of the Works of Industry of All Nations of 1851 was the brainchild of Prince Albert, consort to Queen Victoria, and Henry Cole. The pair were both associated with the Royal Society for the Encouragement of Arts, Manufactures and Commerce. Cole persuaded Prince Albert that an international exhibition in London would educate the public and inspire British designers and manufacturers, and so a royal commission was established, meeting for the first time in 1850 to organise such an event.

The vast Crystal Palace, extending 1,851 feet in length and 128 feet high, incorporated several elm trees to prevent their removal. The building's architect, Joseph Paxton, had previously designed greenhouses on the great Chatsworth estate of the Duke of Devonshire. The building's cast-iron framework and glass were constructed in the Black Country powerhouses of Birmingham and Smethwick.

As well as performing the opening ceremony, Queen Victoria took her family for further visits and herself attended on thirty-four occasions. Other famous visitors included W.M. Thackeray, Charles Darwin, Karl Marx, Michael Faraday, Lewis Carroll, Alfred Lord Tennyson, Charles Dickens, George Eliot and Charlotte Brontë.

More than 6 million people, many making use of the rapidly developing railway network, poured into Hyde Park to view the exhibition. Admission prices varied from three guineas – about £300 in 2023 money – for a season ticket, to one shilling per weekday after 22 May. The one-shilling ticket proved most successful amongst the industrial classes – 4½ million of whom attended.

The newly expanding railways offered highly discounted tickets for people travelling from distant parts of the country and special rates were offered to parties, often led by the local vicar. Those too poor to travel lined up by the rail tracks to watch the long trains of open carriages steaming past. The exhibition ran from 1 May to 11 October, with an average daily attendance of 42,831 and a peak attendance of 109,915 on 7 October.

In addition to the exhibits, visitors were able to enjoy the use of the first public flushing toilets, invented by George Jennings. Access to the Retiring Rooms at Crystal Palace, which included use of a toilet, towel, comb and a

Crystal Palace terraces, Sydenham Hill. (*Mrs Ellacot/Creative Commons*)

shoeshine, came at the cost of a penny. Many of the 827,280 visitors who 'spent a penny' may have visited them after drinking Schweppes, the world's first commercially available soft drink and the official sponsor of the event.

More than 100,000 objects were displayed by over 14,000 exhibitors from, according to the catalogue, Britain, its 'Colonies and Dependencies', and forty-four 'Foreign States'. The exhibits were grouped into themes of Machinery, Manufactures, Fine Arts and Raw Materials. Of particular interest were the Russian exhibits, which included huge vases and urns made of porcelain and malachite more than 10 feet tall, furs, sledges, and Cossack armour.

The British Empire representation included Canada sending a fire engine with painted panels showing Canadian scenes, and a trophy of furs. India contributed an elaborate throne of carved ivory, a coat embroidered with pearls, emeralds and rubies, and a magnificent howdah and trappings for a rajah's elephant. Two of the most popular exhibits also originated from the subcontinent – the Koh-i-Noor diamond, and the Daria-i-Noor, one of the world's rarest pale pink diamonds. C.C. Hornung of Copenhagen, Denmark, showed his single-cast-iron frame for an upright pianoforte, the first made in Europe.

Although the exhibition highlighted the superiority of British goods, Prince Albert, himself of Germanic extraction, had an internationalist outlook. As many European states had recently come through the revolutions of 1848, he wanted to emphasise the use of technology as providing the world with a better future. Visitors could watch the whole process of cotton production from spinning to finished cloth. There were displays of scientific instruments, including electric telegraphs, microscopes, air pumps, barometers and surgical instruments.

The Great Exhibition had generated a profit of £186,000 – over £18 million in today's money. Enduringly positive use was made of the funds to inaugurate the Science Museum, Natural History Museum, and Victoria and Albert Museum in London. Cole became the first director of the V&A, ensuring the principle of free access in order to become, in his words, 'a schoolroom for everyone'.

Ten years after the fulfilment of his vision of a Great Exhibition, Prince Albert died. His Hyde Park memorial depicts the exhibition catalogue in his right hand, inscribed with statistics from the exhibition.

After the structure was dismantled piece by piece, the 294,000 glass panes were relocated to Sydenham Hill, to the south-east of London, to an area that then became eponymous with the great building. A horrendous fire in 1936 destroyed the edifice, so all that remains is the Italianate terrace, which serves as a picturesque reminder of an event that demonstrated Britain's cultural, technological and industrial might at the height of its Industrial Revolution.

Places to visit

- The Albert Memorial in Hyde Park stands a few hundred yards from the site of the Prince Consort's Great Exhibition.
- The Sydenham Hill site of the reconstructed Crystal Palace can still be visited.
- The Victoria and Albert Museum in South Kensington houses many items related to the Great Exhibition.

Further reading

Anthony Burton & Elizabeth Bonython, *The Great Exhibitor: The Life and Work of Henry Cole* (2003).
Jonathon Shears, *The Great Exhibition, 1851: A sourcebook* (2017).
Heritage Hunter & Andrew Chapman, *The Great Exhibition in Colour* (2016).

72: Board School Slate

In Victorian Britain, the use of writing slates was extensive in all schools. The hard, quarried slate material was generally set in a wooden frame, with writing done with the aid of a slate pencil, which was sharpened to a point. Often an awful screeching sound was heard when the pencil marked the slate. A grey-silver mark was left on the slate and cleaned with a rag or sleeve, hence the phrase 'to wipe the slate clean'.

Daisy Cowper attended school in Liverpool in the 1890s. She recalled: 'One horrid thing about those days was the use of slates ... it was disgusting to see them being cleaned by spitting and rubbing with a slate-rag; if no slate-rag was to hand, the bare wrist would serve!'

With paper being too expensive for everyday use in most schools, children would have no record of previous work done, and the slate could easily break if dropped. Very young children first learned to write their letters in sand trays using their fingers or a stick before progressing to writing on slates.

Most children in nineteenth-century Britain would have been very familiar with the school slate as education provision expanded to meet industry's need for a more literate and numerate workforce able to fulfil an expanding range of technical roles. Before 1833, the spread of schools had been erratic, but in that year, Parliament authorised that money should be provided for the construction of schools for poor children of England and Wales.

Before this date, the type of education children received depended on the social class of their parents. While sons of the wealthy were educated at public schools, a governess taught their daughters at home. For parents who could afford it, there were 'dame' schools, usually run by a mistress in her own home who took in a number of children. This service was similar to childminding and attending children typically learned very little, often being left to their own devices. From the 1780s onwards, children of working-class families might attend a Sunday school. For children who worked during the week, these schools provided the only education they received in literacy, numeracy and Bible instruction.

There were also 'ragged' schools providing free education for the poorest children and orphans. First introduced in 1818, these developed quickly after the Ragged School Union formed in 1844. From 1833, children working in factories were to be provided with two hours of schooling each day, although this was not always adhered to. This was extended to three hours a day from 1844. Child inmates of workhouses were also educated, in order to prevent them lapsing into cycles of poverty when older and being a drain on the public purse.

Learning in state-funded schools was mainly by rote, including memorising times tables and sections of the Bible and poetry. Instruction in the 'three Rs' was paramount – reading, writing and arithmetic. Many teachers had risen through the state system, employed as apprentice

The Monitorial System in action, with an older pupil teaching his younger peers.

teachers while undertaking their training and qualifications. School attendance was often patchy, as poor families frequently needed their children to work, especially at harvest times. Some schools asked parents for a donation towards their child's education, or to supply paper and ink should they wish their child to have those luxuries.

Before 1870, religious bodies provided much of the elementary education. The National Society for the Promotion of Education, founded in 1811, was a Church of England organisation. About 6,000 such schools existed by the 1860s. Many Church of England schools today in the UK are still voluntary aided and voluntary controlled. The floridly named 'British and Foreign School Society for the Education of the Labouring and Manufacturing Classes of Society of Every Religious Persuasion' worked on broadly the same principles as the National Society, but with a non-Anglican focus. The Methodist and Roman Catholic churches also established schools, all funded from public subscription before 1833.

Most schools operated the Monitorial System, whereby one teacher would instruct a handful of senior pupils who would then teach a class of younger pupils. Thus, many children rarely received direct education from a qualified teacher.

The Forster Elementary Education Act of 1870 was a major turning point in British state education. It allowed local school boards to raise money from the rates in order to build schools in the rapidly expanding towns and cities, where the National Society and British Society schools could not expand quickly enough to meet the demands of a surging population. Church schools could also receive state funding and doubled in number to about 12,000 by the mid-1880s. Elsewhere, thousands of Board Schools were built, many of which still stand today, albeit several of them having been converted into flats or other uses.

Board schools could charge parents for attendance, often known as the 'school penny', but this was waived in certain cases. For the first time, some degree of standard education was provided across the country, with education for all children now not only available but actively encouraged. Pupil teachers could train, from the age of 13, to become fully qualified and thus provide a good standard of education.

An 1880 Act made school attendance compulsory between the ages of 5 and 10, with fines issued to the parents of non-attenders. In

Wheeler Street School, Hull – one of many Board School buildings retaining their original use. (*John Broom*)

1893, this was raised to age 11 and in 1899, to 13. By April 1900, higher elementary schools were providing education up to the age of 15.

The school day stretched to five or six hours with an extended lunch break. Added to the curriculum were extra subjects such as singing, physical training, science, history and geography.

There were regular inspections of schools and some funds withheld from those not reaching the required standards. The cane was used to discipline unruly children and sometimes to incentivise different-style learners to achieve the required level.

Places to visit

- The Wilderspin National School Museum in Barton-upon-Humber, North Lincolnshire, has a recreated late Victorian schoolroom and displays that relate the history of the National Society. An infant school and playground portray school life from the mid-1840s, when the school was built.
- The Ragged School Museum in Tower Hamlets, London, has a Victorian classroom, which runs replica lessons from the era. It is located in one of Dr Barnardo's original classrooms and features authentic school desks, slate boards and even a dunce's hat.
- British School Museum, Hitchin, Hertfordshire, has regular recreations of Victorian classrooms and detailed displays.

Further reading

Bob Mealing, *Life in a Victorian School* (2013).
G.D. Nash, *Victorian School Days in Wales* (1991).
Mandy Ross, *Victorian Schools* (2005).

73: Ragged School Door

This striking door, which was formerly the entrance of the Charter Street Ragged School and Working Girls Home in Manchester, was the gateway from a life of poverty, crime and destitution. Generations of Mancunian children passed through it as philanthropists sought to plug the gaps in a wealthy nation's provision of education for the masses. The school provided food, clogs and clothing for children and a Sunday breakfast for destitute men and women.

Ragged schools were charitable organisations dedicated to the free education of children made destitute during Britain's Industrial Revolution. Mainly located in industrial areas, they aimed to educate children commonly excluded from Sunday schools due to their unkempt appearance and challenging behaviours.

Before the foundation of the London Ragged Schools Union in 1844, there had been established several independent schools for the poor. Thomas Cranfield, a tailor who had studied at a Sunday school in Hackney, set up a free children's day school near London Bridge in 1798. Over the subsequent four decades, Cranfield expanded this provision to nineteen schools across the poorer boroughs of England's capital city. Education for destitute children could be accessed variously during the day, in the evening and on Sundays.

Another early pioneer of free education for poor children was John Pounds, a shoemaker from Portsmouth. At the age of 15, while serving an apprenticeship with a shipwright, he had fallen into a dry dock and sustained a life-crippling thigh injury. He switched trades to shoemaking, earning the title the 'Crippled Cobbler', and from 1818 began to teach poor children for free from his shop in St Mary Street, Portsmouth. Focusing on literacy and numeracy skills, Pounds soon had more than forty pupils attending. He was able to expand the curriculum to include industrial skills such as cooking, carpentry and shoemaking.

Of a slightly different ilk was the school established by Sheriff William Watson in Aberdeen. In his legal position, Watson came across children who had committed petty crimes. As an alternative to prison, he would force them to enrol in a place of learning he had established – the Industrial Feeding School. Watson believed that a grasp of basic education – with the addition of subjects like geology, shoemaking and printing – would help the boys rise above the dregs of society. The school provided three meals a day. In 1843, Watson set up the Female School of Industry, merging both institutions in 1845. Watson's movement spread to other Scottish towns and cities.

(Pete Birkinshaw/Creative Commons)

Women teachers taking a class for female pupils at the Lambeth Ragged School, 1846.

By 1844, there were at least twenty free schools for the poor in London, funded by philanthropists, with church missions supplying many of the volunteers. It was suggested that a common organisation could share resources and collectively promote their cause. Thus, in April 1844, the London Ragged School Union was founded during a meeting of four men to pray for the city's poor children. Amongst them was S.R. Starey, secretary of the Field Lane school, who had coined the term 'ragged' in an advertisement he took out in *The Times* which is thought to have referred to children raggedly clothed. Many had no shoes and attended school barefoot. Charles Dickens visited Field Lane and was inspired to write *A Christmas Carol*, showing how childhood trauma could warp a man in later life. He donated funds to the schools on several occasions.

All school patrons shared the aim of crime prevention rather than punishing wrongdoers after the event. The eminent social reformer Anthony Ashley-Cooper, 7th Earl of Shaftesbury, assumed the presidency of the

Dr Thomas Barnardo, pictured with some of his ragged school pupils, c.1866.

Ragged School Union in 1844, a post he filled for thirty-nine years.

Poor children received food, clothing, lodging and other missionary services in addition to a free education. The union's publications helped to spread the idea of ragged schools across the country. Ragged school teachers were often working people who freely volunteered their time, or females from well-to-do families with spare time on their hands, which their consciences led them to utilise for the benefit of the less fortunate. Teachers commandeered any available space in which to hold their classes – such as stables, lofts or railway arches.

The basic curriculum included the classic 'three Rs' – reading, writing and arithmetic – as well as Bible study. Many schools added industrial and commercial subjects. By 1861, there were 226 Sunday ragged schools, 204 day schools and 208 evening schools providing learning for 26,000 students. In 1867, Dr Thomas Barnardo set up his first ragged school in the wake of a devastating cholera epidemic. Many of the volunteer teachers were female and by the time of Forster's Education Act of 1870, there were 350 ragged schools. An estimated 300,000 children went through the London Ragged School system between 1844 and 1881.

The success of the ragged schools demonstrated that there was a demand for education among the poor and led to public funding for elementary education for all from 1870 onwards. Paradoxically, their success was the incubator of their decline as the provision of a basic education no longer relied on the ethics and drive of those with a conscience. Ragged schools were phased out or incorporated into the state system.

Places to visit

- The Ragged School Museum in Tower Hamlets is housed in buildings previously used by Dr Thomas Barnardo to accommodate the largest ragged school in London.

Further reading

Laura Mair, *Religion and Relationships in Ragged Schools: An Intimate History of Educating the Poor, 1844–1840* (2019).
Wendy Prahms, *Newcastle Ragged and Industrial School* (2006).

74: Metamorphic Library Steps

These metamorphic library table-steps, dating from the end of the eighteenth century, fold out into a small ladder to reach higher shelves. As the provision and size of publicly accessible libraries grew in Britain during the Industrial Revolution, so did the demand for furniture to facilitate their safe and efficient use.

For over a century and a half, public libraries have been at the heart of English life; in cities, towns and villages across the land they were and are places of learning, leisure, enlightenment and betterment, open to all. However, the story of the public library stretches back over several centuries.

In 1598, Francis Trigge established a library in a room above St Wulfram's Church in Grantham, Lincolnshire, and decreed it should be open to the clergy and residents of the surrounding neighbourhood. The books were chained to stalls and had to be read in situ.

The seventeenth century saw the opening of the Bodleian Library in Oxford in 1602, the Norwich City Library in 1608, and Chetham's Library in Manchester in 1653. From the early eighteenth century, more libraries started to lend out books rather than keeping them chained. The British Museum opened in 1751 with a library of more than 50,000 books. It operated on a pass system, which meant a three or four-week wait to view a book.

As Britain's Industrial Revolution gathered pace, Chetham's Library remained freely and fully accessible to the public. Several booksellers rented out extra copies of their books, creating de facto commercial libraries. Concern was expressed at the 'villainous, profane and obscene' nature of perennially popular romantic fiction at a time when reading was fast becoming a social activity undertaken for pleasure, not merely for those seeking academic wisdom or spiritual enlightenment. These businesses were known as circulating libraries as books were recycled between different readers. In addition, there were subscription libraries, where members paid an annual fee.

The price of books increased in the final two decades of the eighteenth century and they were difficult to obtain outside London as booksellers could not afford to carry vast stocks. Thus, the popularity of borrowing, as opposed to buying, increased. Still, reading for leisure was a pastime for only those with the means to pay for the borrowing and had the daylight time in which to read.

Towards the end of the eighteenth century and in the first decades of the nineteenth, the demand for books and general education grew

Carnegie Library, Hull (1905), where the author spent many childhood hours. (*Paul Lakin/Creative Commons*)

due to Britain's Industrial Revolution. There was an increase in subscription libraries intended for the use of tradesmen. For example, an Economical Library 'for the use and instruction of the working classes' was established in Kendal in 1797.

There were over 500 subscription libraries in Britain by the mid-nineteenth century. Nevertheless, Chartist agitation had led to a realisation that reform was needed to improve the fabric of public life. The Public Libraries Act of 1850, which grew out of the Free Library Movement, was one of several initiatives during the high-water mark of Britain's Industrial Revolution that sought to raise the educational level of the masses and therefore improve their workplace skills and morals. It formed part of the general liberal drive for enlightened progress to offset the more egregious side effects of industrial capitalism.

The Free Library campaign had been led by Liberal MPs William Ewart and Joseph Brotherton and the Chartist Edward Edwards. Edwards was a former bricklayer who had educated himself in mechanics' institute libraries. In 1845, William Ewart's Museums Act provided the first opportunity for local authorities to provide 'free' libraries, albeit in or as annexes to buildings ostensibly designed for a different purpose; Canterbury, Warrington and Salford each exploited the Act to attach free libraries to local museums.

Despite their noble ideals, there was considerable opposition in Parliament to the establishment of free libraries, with MPs alarmed at both the cost of providing them and the unwanted effects of ordinary people being educated beyond their natural station in mid-Victorian life.

Ewart was forced to make several concessions to get his bill passed. Only boroughs with populations of more than 10,000 could open libraries; local referenda would be required, with the support of two thirds of ratepayers needed to approve plans. Local rates could be increased by no more than half a penny in the pound to pay for the service, with that money unable to be spent on books. The first free public library opened in Campfield, Manchester, in 1852, and the Act's scope extended to Scotland and Ireland in 1853.

Although the rate that boroughs could charge for libraries increased to one penny in 1855, it was not enough for councils to fund new libraries. Queen Victoria's Golden Jubilee in 1887 gave further impetus to library building, seeing the

Chetham's Library Reading Room, Manchester. (*Michael D. Beckwith/Creative Commons*)

erection of public buildings and monuments to mark the occasion. However, the growth of libraries up to the Great War was heavily dependent on the donations of philanthropists, such as John Passmore Edwards, Henry Tate and Andrew Carnegie. Edwards was a Cornishman who became a Liberal MP and made his fortune in newspapers. He endowed fifteen libraries, known as 'Passmore Edwards Institutes', in Cornwall alone.

Scottish-American steel magnate Andrew Carnegie invested around $5.2 billion, in today's money, of his extensive wealth to philanthropic and educational causes. His 1889 article proclaiming 'The Gospel of Wealth' called on the rich to use their money to improve society. Carnegie established libraries in well over 600 towns and cities across Britain, many of which are still in use today, whilst others remain, but their function turned over to a range of community uses.

Generations of British children and adults were to derive countless hours of education, elevation and entertainment from Britain's public libraries for over a century and half. Sadly, their future remains in doubt.

Places to visit

- Chetham's, Britain's oldest continuous-use public library, occupies a beautiful sandstone building dating from 1421. The library's entire collection is designated of national and international importance. It is also an accredited museum, attracting visitors from all over the world.

Further reading

Alistair Black & Peter Hoare, *The Cambridge History of Libraries in Britain and Ireland* (2006).
Robert Milton, *Andrew Carnegie: The Biography of America's Most Successful Robber Baron and Business Tycoon* (2020).

75: Mechanics' Institute Poster

This 1858 poster, inviting the inhabitants of the north-eastern coastal town of Hartlepool to a lecture on 'The Literary Constellation of the Seventeenth Century', demonstrates how opportunities for adult education were disseminated during the period of Britain's Industrial Revolution. For the privilege of hearing the Reverend H. Jones expound on the topic, an attendee would pay 6*d* for a front seat or 3*d* for one at the back. Monies raised would go to furthering the work of the Institute.

The term mechanics' institute is somewhat misleading to the twenty-first-century reader, conjuring up images of someone building or fixing machinery. The Industrial Revolution had created a demand for a mechanically minded workforce to manage, repair and improve the increasingly complex machinery used in factories, furnaces, mines and elsewhere. Mechanics' institutes, however, provided a broader education for the worker, with lending libraries, lectures, classrooms and laboratories. Courses and lectures enabled workers to learn and better themselves, both in their own trade and in the arts, humanities and sciences, in the self-help spirit of the age (*see* chapter 77).

Mechanics' institutes formed part of a plethora of organisations aimed at improving the education of adults, such as Literary and Scientific Institutes, Reading Rooms, Useful Knowledge Societies, Athenaeums and Lyceums. The institution founded by John Anderson in Glasgow in 1795 and billed as a 'university open to all' is generally regarded as the precursor to the great wave of mechanics' institutes that swept across Industrial Revolution Britain. Now the University of Strathclyde, one of the Anderson Institution's earliest lecturers was Dr George Birkbeck. He gave lectures aimed at mechanics and other tradesmen, which continued after his departure. In 1823, those tradesmen split from the existing institution to form the Glasgow Mechanics' Institution – the first time that such an appellation was used.

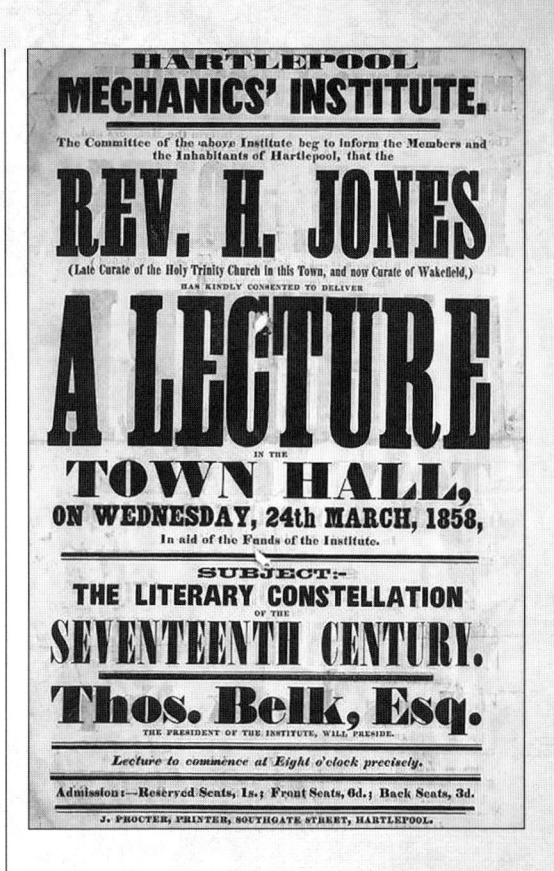

Also the same year, J.C. Robertson founded *The Mechanics' Magazine*, and Robertson, George Birkbeck and William Cobbett founded the London Mechanics' Institute, which eventually became Birkbeck College.

Meanwhile, October 1821 had seen the establishment of the School of Arts of Edinburgh, now Heriot-Watt University, with the provision of technical education for working people and professionals. The first mechanics' institute in England opened in Liverpool in 1823.

The highest concentration of mechanics' institutes was to be found in Yorkshire's West Riding industrial powerhouse, which boasted 125. Others sprung up in small towns and rural areas. Many institutes were sponsored by local industrialists, such as that in Saltaire, one of many public buildings erected by the forward-

Marsden Mechanics' Institute. (*Stevekraken/Creative Commons*)

thinking mill owner Titus Salt. It was often the desire to provide a wholesome alternative to the temptations of the public house, rather than a passion of adult self-improvement, which motivated such ventures.

In addition, the prevalence on the governing committees of most mechanics' institutes of industrialists and members of the professional classes ensured that they did not become loci of the promotion of radical political ideas. Friedrich Engels averred in 1850: 'Mechanics Institutes offer classes in that brand of political economy which takes free competition as its God. ... The students are taught to be subservient to the existing political and social order.'

Engels' cynicism was not totally justified, as in 1868, the inaugural meeting of the Trades Union Congress was held at the Manchester Mechanics' Institute. The building also saw the foundation of the University of Manchester Institute of Science and Technology (UMIST) and the Co-operative Insurance Society.

Some employers enrolled their male workforce en masse. Female participation was less encouraged until the end of the nineteenth century. In Shrewsbury, women paid half subscriptions and could only attend lectures. By 1851, there were approximately 700 mechanics' institutes and by the late nineteenth century there were about 1,200 such organisations and similar institutions spread across Britain's towns and cities, many of them purpose-built in fine Victorian Gothic style. The monies for their construction generally came from a blend of public subscription or wealthy benefactors. In general, the layout included a large lecture and demonstration hall, classrooms and a library-cum-reading room. Some later iterations included social and welfare facilities.

Institute subscriptions typically ranged from ten shillings to £1 per year, a considerable amount for most manual workers. There was often a local flavour to the curriculum, with decorative arts taught to workers from the local pottery industry. Regional Unions of institutes would share books and teachers. A lending library was often included in the subscription.

Later institutes, often minus the 'mechanics' moniker, sometimes catered for children. Concerts and dances became more popular in the twilight of Victoria's reign and refreshment rooms and public baths were occasionally included. When the Technical Instruction Act of 1889 gave local authorities responsibilities to promote and fund adult education, they often took over existing institutions such as mechanics' institutes.

75: MECHANICS' INSTITUTE POSTER

Manchester Mechanics' Institute. (*KJP1/ Creative Commons*)

As public funding for child and adult education and libraries increased towards the end of the nineteenth century, so the educational role of mechanics' institutes declined. Sadly, many fine buildings were demolished, others repurposed for accommodation or retail use. However, several were taken over by technical colleges or appropriated as council libraries or community rooms and still fulfil the original educational vision of their founders, a century and a half or more after their foundation. Today, about seventy-five mechanics' institute buildings have listed status, with around a third of these being used for purposes broadly in line with their original intention.

Places to visit

- Marsden Mechanics' Institute building, near Huddersfield, is now owned by a local community trust and contains rooms for meetings and adult classes, together with a public library and the offices of a theatre company. Functions and concerts take place in the original main hall.
- The Witham, in Barnard Castle, is in the old Witham Testimonial Hall. Again, owned by a local trust, it contains an arts centre, gallery and classrooms. The 1860s music hall has been restored as a theatre.

Further reading

Martyn Walker, *The Development of the Mechanics' Institute Movement in Britain and Beyond: Supporting further education for the adult working classes* (2016).

76: Friendly Society Banner

This striking banner, created for the Independent Order of Oddfellows in 1875, demonstrated the core values of this friendly society. The Order had been founded in Manchester in 1810 to protect and care for members and their communities at a time when there was no welfare state or National Health Service. The aim was to provide help to members and communities when they needed it. Such societies were non-profit mutual organisations owned by their members, with all income passed back to the members in the form of services and benefits.

As Britain's Industrial Revolution broke up longstanding rural communities with their networks of mutual support based on ties of family and working associations, urban industrial workers had no state provision to

(Author's collection)

fall back on during hard times. Thus, mutual aid organisations known as friendly societies were created to help families through economic distress caused by illness, injury or death.

Most friendly societies started out as locally based groups of people who knew each other. Members would contribute a small monthly payment to ensure a lump sum payout in times of need and the money was invested for future use. As well as insuring against the cost of a funeral or work-restricting sickness, another misfortune that could be indemnified was the death of a valuable animal such as a cow or horse.

The first friendly society law, Rose's Act, was passed in 1793. It created a system of local registration. In 1829, Parliament appointed barristers throughout the United Kingdom to assist local Justices of the Peace in verifying the rules of individual societies. Friendly societies sometimes worked to influence legislation, appointing parliamentary agents to protect their interests. The Chartists and trade unions used the societies as ideological and financial resources, as did the Anti-Corn Law League. Later, some societies affiliated themselves with the cause of temperance (*see* chapter 88).

Between 1800 and 1825, to avoid the restrictions of the Combination Acts, skilled workers organised trade unions disguised as friendly societies. In doing so, they were able to present themselves to the public as meeting the test of respectability and legality.

Common from the late eighteenth to early twentieth century in the west of England – particularly Somerset and surrounding counties – was the use of brasses as friendly society or club emblems. Some societies served specific groups, for instance the York Female Friendly Society, founded in 1788 by Faith Gray and Catherine Cappe, which provided education for girls.

If members became sick, they would receive an allowance to help them meet their financial obligations. The society might have a doctor whom the member could consult for free. Some societies went further than financial transactions; other members would visit to provide emotional and other support in times of need. In a recreational capacity, some friendly societies held social functions such as dances and sports events.

Employers would sometimes become patrons of these societies, as encouraging their workers to fund their own health insurance helped reduce their obligation to provide relief. Moreover, gatherings of working men aroused suspicion among employers, as fears of trade union activity were never far away. By becoming a society patron, an employer could both demonstrate his benevolence and keep an eye on his workforce.

The Emblem of the Order of Druids, founded in England in 1858. (*Chartix/Creative Commons*)

Membership of a friendly society did come with some level of risk. To stop an individual treasurer absconding with society funds, many possessed boxes with three locks and three key-holders – an early example of the triple-lock concept. Further peril would arise if a place of work closed, rendering all its workers unemployed. There would be insufficient funds to pay unemployment benefit to all its members. If a contagious illness swept through a community or a sufficient number of young men could not be persuaded to join, the elderly and sick membership might become destitute. As a result, national and international societies were established. These helped spread the risks and enabled members to move to other towns and countries and build bonds with other society members.

Two of the more notable societies were the United Ancient Order of Druids, founded in 1833, and a splinter group, the Order of Druids, created in 1858. The former was structured as a benefit society and registered by government. Their motto, 'United to Assist', affirmed the ethos of the society. Similar societies had passwords and handshakes which only paid-up members would know, and elaborate rituals, dramas and oaths. Ceremonies, singing, parades, graveside duties, symbols and allegory turned such friendly societies into quasi-religious organisations as well as providing mutual aid. The Nottingham Imperial Oddfellows dressed in full-length fake medieval costume whilst the regalia of the Ancient Order of Foresters included horns and axes. National friendly societies would send delegates to annual conferences, often at the seaside, giving men without the vote in general elections opportunity to reach democratic decisions and demonstrate their civic credentials.

The government acknowledged the role of friendly societies and membership was encouraged as part of the High Victorian notion of self-help (*see* chapter 77). The Friendly Societies Act of 1875 called for a system of auditing and registration to ensure a consistency of security amongst organisations with vastly different aims and remits.

By the end of the nineteenth century, there were approximately 27,000 officially registered friendly societies providing most insurance, life and work benefits, and pensions across the UK. Without their presence, tens of thousands more people would have ended up in the dreaded workhouses. Although the National Insurance Act of 1911 removed the overall need for friendly societies, some survive to this day.

Places to visit

- The Museum of English Rural Life at the University of Reading has a collection of over 900 friendly society brasses aka poleheads. The design of the brasses was sometimes conventional or could represent an interest of the club such as the inn in which the meetings were held.

Further reading

Victoria Solt Dennis, *Friendly and Fraternal Societies: Their Badges and Regalia* (2008).
Simon Cordery, *British Friendly Societies, 1750–1914* (2003).
Daniel Weinbren, *The Oddfellows, 1810–2010: 200 Years of Making Friends and Helping People* (2010).

77: *Self-Help* by Samuel Smiles

This 1905 edition of Samuel Smiles's seminal book, published a year after his death, demonstrated the enduring nature of the principles he had set out in the first edition of 1859. His ideas formed the cornerstone of much of the thinking that informed attitudes to poverty and educational reform in the final third of the period of Britain's Industrial Revolution, as reformers sought to mediate between the poverty that resulted from such dynamic societal change and the responsibility of each person for their own welfare.

Smiles was a reformist Scottish journalist who had previously advocated the Chartist cause. However, by the late 1850s, his attention had turned from achieving progress through reform of political representation to the promotion of personal thrift, claiming that irresponsible habits caused poverty. Nevertheless, he had no truck with materialism and laissez-faire government.

Smiles was one of eleven surviving children of a strict Reformed Presbyterian family. Leaving school aged 14, he was apprenticed to a doctor and studied medicine at the University of Edinburgh. Although his father died in the 1832 Cholera epidemic when Samuel was 19, his mother supported his studies with the proceeds of her small general store, believing in the maxim that the 'Lord will provide'. This strong example of determined self-reliance had a strong influence on Samuel's outlook.

During the 1830s and 1840s, Smiles was a prominent advocate of the Chartist cause, becoming editor of the *Leeds Times* and secretary of the Leeds Parliamentary Reform Association. Through his editorials, he also advocated radical causes such as women's suffrage and free trade. Smiles drifted away from Chartism due to the prominence of the physical force advocates.

After a period working as secretary of the Leeds and Thirsk Railway, he abandoned his interest in parliamentary reform, turning instead to the importance of self-help as the most important piece of reform. Hence the writing of the book which forms this object of Britain's Industrial Revolution. His book proposed that knowledge is one of the highest forms of human enjoyment, and education the imperfect means of attaining that knowledge. Crucially, he put the onus of acquiring that education on the individual rather than the state.

In doing so, Smiles was encouraging those who had not benefited from the wealth of Britain's Industrial Revolution to educate themselves and strive for upward mobility. Everyone could improve their lot by hard graft and perseverance.

Samuel Smiles, *Vanity Fair* cartoon, 1881.

Smiles's original first edition of *Self-Help* was privately published at his own expense. Within a year, it had sold 20,000 copies. Its success came as a surprise to him and he became an unexpected influencer in the worlds of business and education. Capitalists appreciated the notions of the 'deserving' and 'undeserving' poor – concepts that still frame much political debate around social welfare today. The deserving poor might be able to draw upon assistance in occasional times of need, having satisfied those in charge of dispensing support that they were worthy of aid. The undeserving poor, in contrast, needed a withdrawal of all state and charity support in order to incentivise them to fend for themselves.

Smiles claimed that men of any class could attain refinement: 'Riches and rank have no necessary connexion with genuine gentlemanly qualities ... diligent self-culture, self-discipline and self-control – and above all ... that honest and upright performance of individual duty which is the glory of manly character.' Elsewhere he argued for the nationalisation of the railways, about a hundred years ahead of the idea's fruition. In an 1861 book titled *Workmen's Earnings, Strikes and Savings*, Smiles claimed poverty was often the result of habitual improvidence.

Smiles pointed out that when wages were high, it was not mechanics' institutes and schools that flourished, but publicans who prospered. He accused some workers earning fifty to sixty shillings a week, a decent wage at that time, of being happy to have their families inhabit a one-room dwelling in a slum while spending money on frivolities.

In 1875, he wrote a further book, *Thrift*, in which he argued: 'Riches do not constitute any claim to distinction. It is only the vulgar who admire riches as riches.' He also strongly criticised laissez-faire policies, which saw governments abdicate responsibility for providing the social infrastructure within which individuals could strive for self-improvement. In 1881, he claimed that those who lived off the labour of others were

(*Wikimedia Commons/Tim Green*)

'enemies'. So too were those who fawned upon the wishes of the masses, telling them that others were to blame for their problems.

By the time of Smiles's death in 1904, *Self-Help* had sold over a quarter of a million copies. It had made him a Victorian celebrity, a much-consulted guru on various matters and the type of person in demand to lay foundation stones of public buildings.

Smiles's speculative self-published work continued to hold resonance over a century after its appearance. Conservative Prime Minister Margaret Thatcher wanted to give *Self-Help* as a gift to every schoolchild in Britain. George Osborne, when serving as Chancellor of the Exchequer, spoke at the 2012 Conservative Party Conference of 'the fairness … for the shift-worker, leaving home in the dark hours of the early morning, who looks up at the closed blinds of their next-door neighbour sleeping off a life on benefits'. This contrast between Smiles's deserving and undeserving poor frames public welfare policy into the twenty-first century.

Places to visit

- Samuel Smiles's old residence at 11 Granville Park, Lewisham, has a blue plaque in his honour.
- A further blue plaque in Cookridge Street, Leeds, was installed in honour of Smiles's contribution to the city. He was the first president of the Woodhouse Mechanics' Institute and taught at the Zion School at Wortley.

Further reading

Asa Briggs, 'Samuel Smiles and the Gospel of Work' in *Victorian People. A Reassessment of Persons and Themes. 1851–67* (1955).
Samuel Smiles, *Self-Help* (2002 OUP Edition with Introduction by Peter Sinnema).
Aileen Smiles, *Samuel Smiles and His Surroundings* (1956).
Adrian Jarvis, *Samuel Smiles and the Construction of Victorian Values* (1997).

78: Punch Magazine Cover

This magazine cover, the first edition of *Punch or The London Charivari*, saw the light of day on 17 July 1841. Full of cheerful humour and biting satire, '*Punch*' came from Punch and Judy, while '*Charivari*' meant a hideous racket made by groups of people clanging kettles, pans and other metal objects outside the homes of people they disliked, feared or disapproved of. *Punch* launched attacks on Prince Albert for being a foreigner, Roman Catholics for demanding special treatment and the Pre-Raphaelites for abandoning the traditions of English art. *Punch* became a household name and a treasured element of the English scene. Sales reached 40,000 copies a week by 1850, and rose above 100,000 by 1910.

One side effect of increasing levels of literacy made possible by the expansion of education to the masses of Britain's Industrial Revolution was the growth of the printed periodical. About 100,000 different titles were published; some achieved only short runs, whilst others, such as *Punch*, became enduring favourites. They covered a vast array of topics – from politics to science, music to sport.

Prior to the 1830s, periodicals targeted those with disposable income and a high level of literacy. However, from that decade onwards, less expensive magazines, aimed at a wider public, began to appear. Initially the focus was on improvement, enlightenment and family entertainment, but eventually it evolved into popular versions that aimed at providing amusement.

Charles Knight served as the publisher for the Society of the Diffusion of Useful Knowledge, producing the weeklies *The Penny Magazine* and *Penny Cyclopaedia* in the 1830s, '40s and '50s. Some well-known publishing names entered the fray during this period. William and Robert Chambers achieved a circulation of 90,000 with their *Chambers' (Edinburgh) Journal* whilst teetotaller John Cassell launched the *Working Man's Friend and Family Instructor* (1850–3).

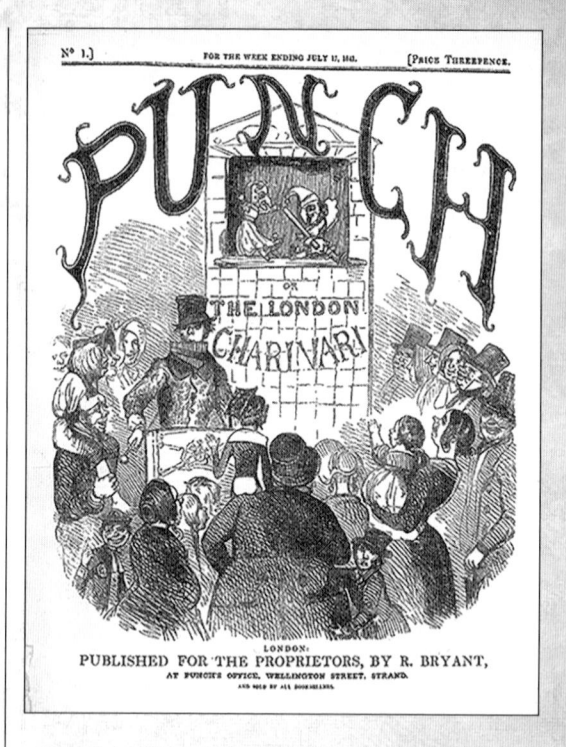

By the final decades of the nineteenth century, compulsory education had greatly expanded the potential market for periodicals. George Newnes turned his habit of cutting out any paragraph that appealed to him into a penny magazine in 1881, *Tit-Bits from all the Most Interesting Books, Periodicals and Contributors in the World*, later shortened to *Tit-Bits*. Newnes's empire would eventually include *Country Life*, founded in 1897, and *The Strand Magazine*, which ran from 1891. The latter was most famous for its serialisation of Arthur Conan Doyle's Sherlock Holmes stories.

Alfred Harmsworth, later owner of the *Daily Mail* and *Daily Mirror*, also cut his teeth in magazine production. His publications included competitions to encourage ongoing reader loyalty. Herbert Ingram, a Nottingham newsagent, noted the effect of illustrations on periodical sales. On moving to London in 1842, he published *The Illustrated London News*, the first illustrated weekly news magazine, which comprised sixteen pages and included thirty-two woodcuts. In due course, the *ILN* sent artists to cover the Boer Wars, making drawings on the spot.

Magazines aimed at women reflected the Victorian ideal of peaceful domesticity. Examples included *The Ladies' Pocket Magazine*, *The Ladies' Cabinet* and *The Ladies' Treasury*. They would typically include lines of verse, pieces of fiction and articles of high moral tone. *The Female's Friend*, which enjoyed a short existence in 1846, was unusual in espousing women's rights. In 1852, Samuel Beeton launched *The Englishwoman's Domestic Magazine*. Priced at 2d, the periodical concentrated on household management and offered practical advice rather than entertainment to fill idle hours. Samuel's wife, Isabella, later to write her own famous book of household management tips, was a regular visitor to Paris, where she acquired fashion plates that featured in the magazine as the Practical Dress Instructor, giving patterns and plans on making one's own outfits. This feature was taken up by *Myra's Journal of Dress and Fashion* and *Weldon's Ladies' Journal*.

Cheap weeklies such as *Home Notes* (1894), *Home Chat* (1895) and *Home Companion* (1897) gave information to women about childcare, nutrition and hygiene.

Magazines also became a forum in which to discuss the great political, literary, artistic and scientific issues of the era of Britain's Industrial Revolution. The *Edinburgh Review* was a strong supporter of the Romantic movement, Whig politics and calls for reform. In contrast, the *Quarterly Review*, founded by John Murray, espoused Tory causes. *The Westminster Review* was founded in 1823 by radical reformer Jeremy Bentham, with John Stuart Mill an early contributor. *The Spectator*, still in circulation, was a conservative-leaning political weekly that nevertheless supported parliamentary reform and the anti-slavery cause during the American Civil War.

Blackwood's *Edinburgh Magazine* was an early literary magazine that spawned *The London Magazine*. The rivalry between them led to a duel in which John Scott, editor of the latter, was mortally wounded. *The Examiner* introduced the poetry of Shelley and Keats to the public whilst *Bentley's Miscellany* had Charles Dickens as its first editor and serialised *Oliver Twist*. Another eminent Victorian novelist, W.M. Thackeray, founded *The Cornhill Magazine*, the first literary journal to achieve a circulation of over 100,000.

Nature, launched in 1869, propagated new scientific ideas and boasted Charles Darwin and Thomas Huxley amongst its contributors. Specialist professional magazines also flourished in this era. They included *The Lancet* (1823), *The Mining Journal* (1835), the *British Medical Journal* (1840) and the *Solicitors' Journal* (1857).

Places to visit

- The British Library in London houses a copy of every periodical printed in Britain. Several historical periodicals are available online via various subscription services.

Further reading

David Butterfield, *10,000 Not Out: The History of The Spectator, 1828–2020* (2020).
Dolores Marsh, *British Literary Magazines 1837–1913: The Victorian and Edwardian Age* (1984).
J. Don Vann & Rosemary T. VanArsdel (eds.), *Victorian Periodicals and Victorian Society* (1993).

79: The Illustrated London News, 14 May 1842

This inaugural edition of *The Illustrated London News*, published on 14 May 1842, depicts the contemporary London skyline in its header, with St Paul's Cathedral looming large over the city. At the bottom of the page is an illustration of the fire that destroyed much of the city of Hamburg. With an extent of sixteen pages that included thirty-two wood engravings, the reader was well served for their 6d. The paper covered topics such as the war in Afghanistan, the Versailles rail accident, a survey of the candidates for the US presidential election, extensive crime reports, theatre and book reviews, and a list of births, marriages and deaths. Its publisher, Herbert Ingram, hired 200 men to carry placards through the streets of London promoting the first edition of his new newspaper. It sold 26,000 copies and by 1855, circulation stood at 200,000 copies per week.

Newspapers in Britain had first appeared in the seventeenth century, after a relaxation of censorship. These publications both told the news and informed the readers of rumours. Published at regular intervals, they became known as periodicals. The Civil Wars across Britain and Ireland stimulated the demand for news and periodicals generally reported events from a Royalist or Parliamentarian perspective.

In 1702, *The Daily Courant* became the first daily newspaper reporting on events in London. By the 1720s, there were twelve London newspapers and twenty-four provincial ones. Successive governments found their increasing popularity problematic as criticism of their policies spread to a wide audience. Consequently, in 1712, a penny tax was levied on papers of between half a sheet and a full sheet in size. Nevertheless, the rise of the newspaper continued apace, with 7,411,757 sold in the year 1753, 9,464,790 by 1760 and 11,300,980 by 1767. *The News Letter*, printed in Belfast, came out in 1737 and remains the oldest surviving English language newspaper. In 1772, a campaign organised by John Wilkes led to the right to publish parliamentary reports, as the notion of the freedom of the press spread through Industrial Revolution Britain.

The Times began publication in 1785 and rose to become the leading British newspaper of the nineteenth century. *The Observer*, first published in 1791, became the world's first Sunday newspaper as the demand for news of the ongoing French Revolution increased. A lifting of taxes on newspapers and technological innovations led to a boom in newspaper publishing in the late nineteenth century. From the 1830s onwards, a combination of circumstances led to a massive increase in the circulation of British newspapers. The development of the railway network meant that newspapers printed in London in the late evening could reach the provinces by the following morning. A national postal system was developed. A reduction in stamp duties and taxes on paper kept down costs, and an insatiable desire amongst the public to be kept up to date with the latest news saw Britain's Industrial Revolution usher in a new information age.

Newspaper editorials and content reflected a range of political biases. Between 1831 and 1835, several newspapers, of fiercely anti-government tone, appeared and their publishers refused to pay any taxes on them. After pressure from Richard Cobden and others, these taxes were reduced from 1836 onwards and eventually repealed in 1855. In doing so, the British establishment demonstrated a willingness to bend with the prevailing political wind, so that the potential for an importation of the various

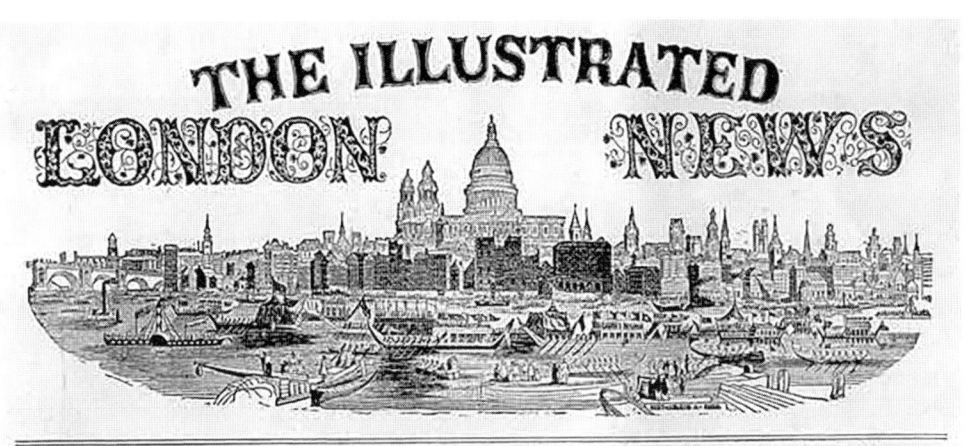

THE ILLUSTRATED LONDON NEWS

No. 1.]   FOR THE WEEK ENDING SATURDAY, MAY 14, 1842.   [SIXPENCE.

OUR ADDRESS.

In presenting the first number of the ILLUSTRATED LONDON NEWS to the British Public, we would fain make a graceful entrée into the wide and grand arena, which will henceforth contain so many actors for our benefit, and so many spectators of our career. In plain language, we do not produce this illustrated newspaper without some vanity, much ambition, and a fond belief that we shall be pardoned the presumption of the first quality by realizing the aspirations of the last. For the past ten years we have watched with admiration and enthusiasm the progress of illustrative art, and the vast revolution which it has wrought in the world of publication, through all the length and breadth of this mighty empire. To the wonderful march of periodical literature it has given an impetus and rapidity almost coequal with the gigantic power of steam. It has converted blocks into wisdom, and given wings and spirit to ponderous and senseless wood. It has in its turn adorned, gilded, reflected, and interpreted nearly every form of thought. It has given to fancy a new dwelling-place—to imagination a more permanent throne. It has set up fresh land-marks of poetry, given sterner pungency to satire, and mapped out the geography of mind with clearer boundaries and more distinct and familiar intelligence than it ever bore alone. Art—as now fostered, and redundant in the peculiar and facile department of wood engraving—has, in fact, become the bride of literature; genius has taken her as its handmaid; and popularity has crowned her with laurels that only seem to grow the greener the longer she is worn.

And there is now no staying the advance of this art into all the departments of our social system. It began in a few isolated volumes—stretched itself next over fields of natural history and science—penetrated the arcana of our own general literature—and made companionship with our household books. At one plunge it was in the depth of the stream of poetry—working with its every current—partaking of the glow, and adding to the sparkles of the glorious waters—and so refreshing the very soul of genius, that even Shakspere came to us clothed with a new beauty, while other kindred poets of our language seemed as it were to have put on festive garments to crown the marriage of their muses to the arts. Then it walked abroad among the people, went into the poorer cottages, and visited the humblest homes in cheap guises, and perhaps, in roughish forms; but still with the illustrative and the instructive principle strongly worked upon, and admirably developed for the general improvement of the human race. Lastly, it took the merry aspect of fun, frolic, satire, and *badinage*; and the school of *Charivari* began to blend itself with the graver pabulum of Penny Cyclopædias and Saturday Magazines.

And now, when we find the art accepted in all its elements, and welcomed by every branch of reading into which it has diverged; now, when we see the spirit of the times everywhere associating with it, and heralding or recording its success; we do hold it as of somewhat triumphant omens, that we are, by the publication of this very newspaper, launching the giant vessel of illustration into a channel the broadest and the widest that it has ever dared to stem. We bound at once over the billows of new ocean—we sail into the very heart and focus of public life—we take the world of newspapers by storm, and flaunt a banner on which the words "ILLUSTRATED NEWS" become symbols of a fresher purpose, and a more enlarged design, than was ever measured in that hemisphere till now.

The public will have benceforth under their glance, and within their grasp, the very form and presence of events as they transpire, in all their substantial reality, and with evidence visible as well as circumstantial. And whatever the broad and palpable delineations of wood engraving can be taught to achieve, will now be brought to bear upon every subject which attracts the attention of mankind, with a spirit in unison with the character of such subject, whether it be serious or satirical, trivial or of purpose grave.

And, reader, let us open something of the detail of this great intention to your view. Begin, *par exemple*, with the highest region of newspaper literature—The Political. Why, what a field! If we are strong in the creed that we adopt—if we are honest, as we pledge ourselves to be, in the purpose that we maintain—how may we lend muscle, bone, and sinew to the tone taken and the cause espoused, by bringing to bear upon our opinions, a whole battery of vigorous illustration. What "H B" does amid the vacillations of parties, without any prominent opinions of his own, we can do with double regularity and consistency, and therefore with more valuable effect. Moreover, regard the homely illustration which nearly every public measure will afford; your Poor-laws—your Corn-laws—your Factory-bills—your Income-taxes! Look at the field of public portraiture presented in your Houses of Legislature alone, and interesting to every constituency in the land. Open your police-offices, your courts of law, your criminal tribunals—all the pith and marrow of the administration of justice—you can have it broadly before you, with points of force, of ridicule, of character, or of crime; and if the pen be ever led into fallacious argument, the pencil must at least be oracular with the spirit of truth.

In the world of diplomacy, in the architecture of foreign policy, we can give you every trick of the great Babel that other empires are seeking to level or to raise. Is there peace? then shall its arts, implements, and manufactures be spread upon our page. The literature—the customs—the dress—nay, the institutions and localities of other lands, shall be brought home to you with spirit, with fidelity, and, we hope, with discretion and taste. Is there war? then shall its seat and actions be laid naked before the eye. No estafette—no telegraph—no steam-winged vessel—no overland mail, shall bring intelligence to our shores that shall not be sifted with industry, and illustrated with skill in the columns of this journal; and whether the cowardice of China or the treachery of Afghanistan be the theme of our abhorrence or resentment, you shall at least have as much historical detail of both as, while it gratifies general curiosity, shall minister to the natural anxieties at home of those who have friends and relations amid the scenes delineated and the events described.

Take another fruitful branch of illustration, the pleasures of the people!—their theatres, their concerts, their galas, their races, and their fairs! Again, the pleasures of the aristocracy—their court festivals, their *fête masques*, their levees, their drawing-rooms—the complection of their grandeur and the circumstance of all their pomp!

In literature, a truly beautiful arena will be entered upon; for we shall not only, in most instances, have the opportunity of illustrating our own reviews, but of borrowing selections from the illustrations of the numerous works which the press is daily pouring forth, so elaborately embellished with woodcuts in the highest style of art.

In the field of fine arts——but let the future speak, and let us clip promise in the wing. We have perhaps said enough, without condescending to the littleness of too much detail, to mark the general outline of our design; and we trust to the kindness and intelligence of our readers to imagine for us a great deal more than we have been able to crowd into the compass of an introductory leader. Moreover, we would strongly premise an expression of gratitude for all suggestions that may hereafter reach us, and assure our volunteers of these, that wherever there seems a possibility of acting upon them creditably, that course shall be taken with promptitude, vigour, and effect.

Here we make our bow, determined to pursue our great experiment with boldness; to associate its principle with a purity of tone that may secure and hold fast for our journal the fearless patronage of families; to seek in all things to uphold the great cause of public morality; to keep continually before the eye of the world a living and moving panorama of all its actions and influences; and to withhold from society no point that its literature can furnish or its art adorn, so long as the genius of that literature, and the spirit of that art, can be brought within the reach and compass of the Editors of the ILLUSTRATED LONDON NEWS!

DESTRUCTION OF THE CITY OF HAMBURGH BY FIRE.

By the arrival of the General Steam Navigation Company's boat Saledonia, off the Tower, on Tuesday evening, news has been brought of an immense conflagration which took place on Thursday morning, the 5th instant, at one o'clock, in that city. The district in which the fire broke out consists entirely of wood tenements, chiefly of five and six stories high, and covering an area of ground of about thirty to forty acres. The whole of the buildings on this large space have been totally consumed to the number of more than 1000. The fire was by some thought to have originated in the street known by the name of the Stein Twite, in the warehouse of a Jew, named Cohen, a cigar manufacturer, and who, upon good grounds, has been taken up on suspicion as the incendiary. The wind at the time blew a stout north-wester, causing the flames rapidly to spread; and proceeding in the direction of Roding's-market, and from thence to Deich-street, entirely consuming the whole of the following streets, among which is the Hoppen-market, and St. Nicholas Church, a fine stone fabric, and the handsomest in Hamburgh, Gratz Twite, Cressonen (back and end), Grosser Burstah, Muhlen Brucke, Alte Börse, Behacka Strasse, Monke-

View of the Conflagration of the City of Hamburg.

revolutions that swept mainland Europe in the 1830s and 1840s never materialised. Following the reduction in stamp tax from 4*d* to 1*d* in 1836, newspaper circulation rose from 39 million to 122 million by 1854.

Most newspapers reserved their front page for classified advertisements, a practice that continued in Dundee-based *The Courier* until 1992. In 1814, a Welsh language periodical was founded and in 1869, *The Western Mail*, describing itself as 'the national newspaper of Wales', was launched. A group of Nonconformist businessmen founded the *Manchester Guardian* in 1821; *The Scotsman* began in 1817 as an outlet for liberal Scottish opinion; and the Chartist *Northern Star*, first published in 1836, briefly shone until it went out of business in 1852 following the decline of the movement. Introduced in 1855, *The Daily Telegraph* appealed to middle-class England; it attained the largest circulation in the world by 1890. Originally sympathetic to the Liberal Party, in 1878 it switched to the Conservative and Unionist outlook, which was its hallmark for the next century or more.

Between 1860 and 1910, newspaper publication experienced a golden age. Journalism became a sought-after profession. The typesetting machine, invented by Ottmar Mergenthaler in 1880, and the monotype machine, invented by Tolbert Lanston in 1887, improved printing efficiency. Mass education, resulting from the extension of elementary school provision and the rise of mechanics' institutes and public libraries, created an increasingly literate working and lower-middle class. The *Daily Mail* first came out in 1896, aimed at the newly literate lower-middle classes. It combined a low selling price with competitions, prizes, features and promotions sitting alongside the news. Newspapers became increasingly partisan and, launched in 1912, the *Daily Herald* became the mouthpiece of the trade union and labour movement.

The invention of the telegraph meant that news from abroad, particularly reports of Britain's imperial wars, could reach home quickly. Business advertising revenues grew, promoting products as varied as health remedies, soap, beer and chocolate, so the ability to reach a massive audience with a repeated message helped the spread of recognisable brand names such as Cadbury's and Pears'.

Consequently, the daily newspaper became a staple purchase in houses of all classes, the length and breadth of the country, during Britain's Industrial Revolution.

Places to visit

- The British Library in Euston Road, London, holds over 34,000 newspaper titles from the UK and overseas, with 60 million individual issues. This includes a comprehensive collection of British newspapers from the 1820s onwards.

Further reading

Alexander Andrews, *A History of British Journalism* (2011).
George Boyce & James Curran, *Newspaper History from the Seventeenth Century to the Present* (1978).
Keith Williams, *The English Newspaper: An Illustrated History to 1900* (1977).
Kevin Williams, *Read All About it: a History of the British Newspaper* (2010).

80: Charles Dickens's Writing Desk

Considered one of the most important artefacts of the Industrial Revolution, this desk is the place where Britain's most famous nineteenth-century novelist created his later works, including *Great Expectations*. This famous desk has featured in several works of art. Made from mahogany, it has an in-built writing slope. Still evident are faint impressions of oily fingerprint marks from the opening of the drawers. Previously in the possession of the Dickens family, the Dickens Museum acquired it in 2015.

Of all the novelists of the Victorian era, perhaps Charles Dickens is the best known for shining a light into the darkest recesses of Industrial Revolution Britain. It affected his early life and certainly affected his work. Being the son of a man imprisoned for debt and his own early working life in a factory shaped Dickens's attitude to a wide range of social issues. His critique of Victorian industrial Britain runs throughout his work. In *Oliver Twist* and *A Christmas Carol*, for instance, he lambasts the assumption that poverty resulted from individual moral deficiency and reflected values such as indolence. The workhouses (*see* chapter 61) reflected Victorian attitudes towards poverty and Dickens is highly critical of the system through Oliver's experiences and Scrooge's reference to their usefulness when asked to donate to the poor.

Also criticised in Dickens's work is the avarice associated with capitalism, such as in *A Christmas Carol*, when Scrooge sees what will happen to him if his greed is not changed. In *Martin Chuzzelwit*, Dickens uses the example of a fraudulent bank and lending scheme to criticise the way capitalism exploits for the sake of profit. In *Hard Times*, Dickens lambasts the Gradgrind approach to education, which sought

Benjamin Disraeli as a young man.

to instil facts into children rather than educating them to think and question.

Many novelists of the era recorded the enormous social and cultural changes brought about by Britain's Industrial Revolution. Writers sought to capture the spirit of the age and its people living through unprecedented upheavals. Stories often first appeared in serial form in popular magazines. Some novels focused on emerging social and ethical dilemmas; others satirised aspects of Victorian society. Vast inequalities of opportunity, wealth and outcomes, set alongside thrilling technological and scientific innovation, offered a rich canvas on which writers could paint their works. The best of the novels shine a light into the inner world of people from all classes of society.

In 1845, Benjamin Disraeli, then a young Tory MP, wrote of the terrible conditions endured by Britain's working classes in his novel *Sybil, or The Two Nations*. Disraeli would eventually lead a reforming Conservative government in the years 1874 to 1880. Some critics claim that Disraeli invented the English political novel, knowns as the 'Condition of England' genre. He contrasts the lives of people in a northern industrial town with society figures enjoying such events as the Derby. The novel's title still resonates today, with 'One Nation' Conservatism a distinct philosophical approach within that party.

Jane Eyre is the most renowned book penned by the prodigious Brontë sisters of Haworth Parsonage. In the novel, Charlotte Brontë weaved in themes of education, women's employment and marriage. The book's heroine receives a rudimentary education in an institution that taught basic skills to children who would then leave to work on a farm or factory. Jane, however, rose to the position of governess for the

Plate from the first edition of *A Study in Scarlet*, by Arthur Conan Doyle.

Rochester household, enabling her to compare the contrasting educational opportunities offered to the rich and poor.

Elizabeth Gaskell's *North and South* (1854) sees heroine Margaret Hale uprooted from an idyllic southern childhood to live in a smoky northern industrial city. She is shocked by the noise, dirt, poverty and inhumane working conditions endured by the working classes and horrified by the violence of the strike action undertaken by those workers. Eventually, her relationship with mill owner John Thornton gives her a more nuanced perspective on the challenges the Industrial Revolution presented to people of all positions.

Wilkie Collins's *The Woman in White* (1859) explored the unequal financial position of married women, whose property solely belonged to their husbands prior to 1882. Arthur Conan Doyle's *A Study in Scarlet* (1887), which introduced Sherlock Holmes to the world, was the first novel in which the detective used a magnifying glass. Thomas Hardy's *Tess of the d'Urbervilles* (1891) served as an indictment of the limited social rights of women and the labouring classes compared with men from a supposedly higher social milieu. *The Jungle Book* by Rudyard Kipling (1894) reflected overtones of British imperialism – class, race and nationalism – and Darwinian views on evolution and the survival of the fittest. *Diary of a Nobody* by George and Weedon Grossmith (1892) satirised the minor woes of the leisured middle classes of the late Victorian era.

Places to visit

- Max Gate in Dorchester is a home personally designed by Thomas Hardy. Now in the care of the National Trust, it was in this house that Hardy wrote *Tess of the d'Urbervilles*.
- The Brontë Parsonage Museum in Haworth, Yorkshire, was the home of the Brontë sisters and is a museum of international reputation and importance.
- The Charles Dickens Museum is located at 48 Doughty Street, London. It was here that he wrote *Oliver Twist*.

Further reading

Claire Tomalin, *Charles Dickens: A Life* (2012).
Claire Tomalin, *Thomas Hardy: The Time-Torn Man* (2012).
Deirdre David, *The Cambridge Companion to the Victorian Novel* (2012).

81: Saltaire Congregational Church

This fine Victorian church was the first public building to be commissioned by Bradford industrialist Titus Salt, a devoted member of the Congregational Church, when he built his model workers' village on the outskirts of Bradford in the 1850s. The place of worship cost him over £1.5 million in today's money and stands as testament to the Christian imperative which saw him strive to better the living conditions of his 3,000-strong workforce.

In contrast to the hastily built, overcrowded and insanitary conditions experienced by many working families who had moved to the cities during Britain's Industrial Revolution, some employers sought to move their enterprises to rural or semi-rural areas. In doing so, they created purpose-built villages to house their workforce. Sometimes referred to as 'model villages', these new settlements provided a better quality of housing and usually included civic amenities such as schools, churches and mental and physical recreational facilities.

Bradford wool industrialist Titus Salt is generally credited with building the first significant model village on the banks of the river Aire upstream from Bradford. During Salt's early years as an industrialist, in the 1830s, infant mortality in the town was high and life expectancy remained low. Pollution from the mills shrouded Bradford with choking smog and sanitation was appalling. In 1848, Salt became Mayor of Bradford and made moves to eliminate smoke pollution. He also took his workers to Malham, a Yorkshire beauty spot, on a works outing, which was a significant gesture and a sign of his developing paternalism.

Relocating his five mills from the smoky Bradford to take advantage of the power of the Aire and the transport links of the Leeds–Liverpool canal and the trans-Pennine railway, Salt set about building Saltaire, a village of neat terraced houses. He put in place an infrastructure of a bathhouse, hospital, Nonconformist church, school, allotments, park and boathouse. In line with the prevailing ethos of 'self-help' (*see* chapter 77), Salt also ensured there was an institute containing a library, concert hall, laboratory, gymnasium and billiard room. Built in the Italianate style, Saltaire had an enduring beauty and charm. Each house had a supply of gas as well as fresh water and sanitation. Titus Salt's paternalism forbade unions and public houses but, in general, workers' lives had improved immeasurably. He was the first employer in Bradford to institute the ten-hour working day. For his efforts, he was bestowed a baronetcy in 1869.

In 1879, chocolatiers Richard and George Cadbury decided to move their expanding business from Birmingham's city centre into a greenfield site 4½ miles south of the city. Aiming

(Sumit Surai/Creative Commons)

Arts and Crafts houses in Kingsley Road, Bournville. (*Steve Cadman/Creative Commons*)

to create a 'factory in a garden', the Quaker brothers named the new settlement Bournville – 'Bourn' was the name of the local stream, and 'ville' because of the French rivalry in chocolate making at the time. The area already possessed a railway station and canal. Cadbury became known as an employer that paid good wages and provided good working conditions.

In 1893, George Cadbury bought 120 acres of land close to the factory and planned a model village that would 'alleviate the evils of modern, more cramped living conditions'. By 1900, the estate included 313 cottages and houses with large gardens and modern interiors. The designs became a blueprint for many other model village estates around Britain. The Cadburys built sports fields, bowling greens, fishing lakes, a lido and the Rowheath Pavilion (also used for balls and dinners).

Many of the house exteriors were in the Arts and Crafts style. Bournville was one of the first settlements to integrate open spaces into its planning, rather than relying on parks added as an afterthought (*see* chapter 96). Workers could thus access green space to maintain their physical and mental well-being.

Located on the Wirral Peninsula, Port Sunlight is a model village built by Lever Brothers to accommodate workers from their famous soap factory. Building commenced in 1888 and the name Port Sunlight derived from the famous brand of cleaning agent produced at the factory. Like Saltaire and Bournville, Port Sunlight was located next to a railway line and navigable waterway.

The factory's owner, William Hesketh Lever, personally supervised planning the village, and employed nearly thirty different architects, with each block varied in style and each house unique. Built between 1899 and 1914, 800 houses were to accommodate a population of 3,500. Facilities included allotments, a hospital, a school,

Hulme Hall, Port Sunlight. (*Rodhullandemu/Creative Commons*)

Hulme Hall concert hall, a temperance house, a swimming pool, a church and later, an art gallery.

Lever's aim was to 'socialise and Christianise business relations and get back to that close family brotherhood that existed in the good old days of hand labour'. He took the paternalist view that he could spend the company's profits more wisely than his workforce, saying:

It would not do you much good if you send it down your throats in the form of bottles of whisky, bags of sweets, or fat geese at Christmas. On the other hand, if you leave the money with me, I shall use it to provide for you everything that makes life pleasant – nice houses, comfortable homes, and healthy recreation.

Saltaire, Port Sunlight and Bournville spawned many imitations across Britain, as some decent employers took it upon themselves to provide a higher standard of living for the workers of Britain's Industrial Revolution.

Places to visit

- Saltaire is located 3 miles north-west of Bradford. It was designated a World Heritage Site by UNESCO in 2001. Salts Mill houses the artwork of David Hockney and contains a bookshop, homeware shop and art store. Virtually all the buildings in the village erected by Titus Salt are still intact.
- Port Sunlight contains 900 Grade II listed buildings, and was designated a conservation area in 1978. The Lady Lever Art Gallery opened in 1922 to enhance the appeal of the model village to its inhabitants.
- Bournville is recognised as one of the most desirable areas to live in the UK and affords a pleasant day strolling its picturesque streets. The sound of the carillon bells in the village green is a delight.

Further reading

Gary Frith & Malcolm Hitt, *Saltaire Through Time* (2010).
Edward Hubbard & Michael Shippobottom, *A Guide to Port Sunlight* (2019).
Michael Harrison, *Bournville: Model Village to Garden Suburb* (1999).

82: Music Hall Pass

This complementary pass, entitling a 'Gentleman and Friend' to attend Canterbury Hall Music Hall in Lambeth, reminds us of a time when the music hall was the favoured venue of popular entertainment for many of the workers, foremen and managers of Britain's Industrial Revolution. Patrons had to arrive 'suitably attired', with no 'children in arms' admitted.

Music halls hark back to the taverns and coffee houses of eighteenth-century London, where performers sang songs while the audience ate, drank and joined in the singing. By the 1830s, taverns had rooms devoted to musical clubs where they presented Saturday evening singsongs and 'free-and-easies'. These grew in popularity to become twice or thrice-weekly affairs. For more middle-class clientele, song and supper rooms opened in the 1830s, which served hot food and provided entertainment until the early hours of the morning.

Often audiences would not sit in silence, but talk through the acts and sometimes throw bottles, boots and even dead cats at the performers. The orchestra was protected from missiles by steel grilles stretched over the pit where they performed. Whilst women were not allowed in the middle-class song and supper rooms, working-class women visited the taverns. In the early days of music hall, they would often accompany their husbands and bring along their children and even babies.

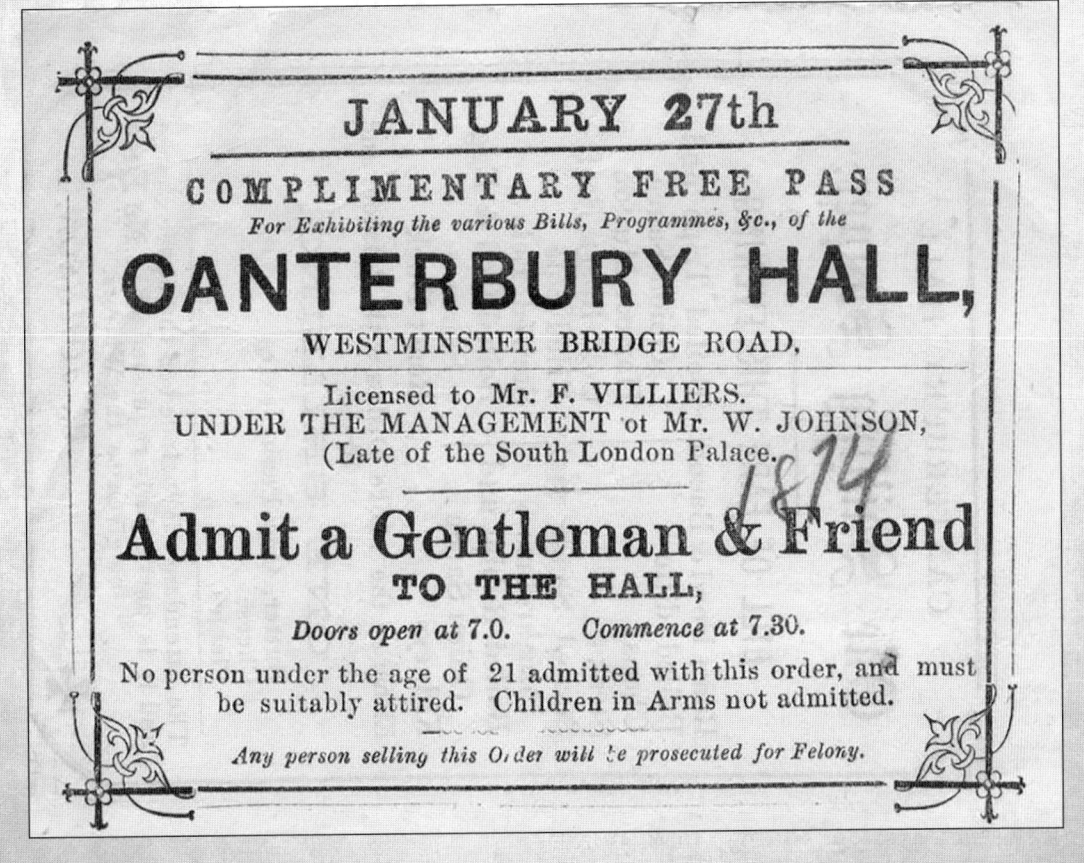

JANUARY 27th

COMPLIMENTARY FREE PASS

For Exhibiting the various Bills, Programmes, &c., of the

CANTERBURY HALL,

WESTMINSTER BRIDGE ROAD,

Licensed to Mr. F. VILLIERS.
UNDER THE MANAGEMENT of Mr. W. JOHNSON,
(Late of the South London Palace.)

1874

Admit a Gentleman & Friend
TO THE HALL,

Doors open at 7.0.   Commence at 7.30.

No person under the age of 21 admitted with this order, and must be suitably attired. Children in Arms not admitted.

Any person selling this Order will be prosecuted for Felony.

Canterbury Hall Music Hall, 1856.

The Eagle, situated at the junction of City Road and Shepherdess Walk in the East End of London, was one of the most prominent music halls from the 1850s onwards. Marie Lloyd first appeared there in 1885 aged 14. Canterbury Hall in Lambeth, opened in 1852, was the first purpose-built music hall. There was a food and drink table service for up to 700 patrons, who paid 6*d* each for entrance and refreshments. The leading star was Stan Cowell, who acted and performed comedy songs. So successful was the business that a new, more ornate hall was built in 1856 on the same site, with over double the capacity. It was decorated with chandeliers and featured a balcony and art exhibitions.

The attendance of women was encouraged, with 'Ladies' Thursdays' introduced, the idea being that gentlemen would take their wives for an evening out. This was not always the case and often prostitutes would walk up and down the aisles of the auditorium touting for customers, giving the halls a vulgar reputation.

By 1875, there were 375 music halls in London. Many women became prominent artistes, finding a means of escape from a life of servile drudgery in a workplace. At the Alhambra and Empire, both in Leicester Square, the seating had been arranged like a theatre, with rows of seats facing a stage and the bar and refreshment rooms separated from the auditorium.

Well-known music hall stars were so successful that they would perform in numerous halls each night, crossing London in their carriages and earning good money. Many died young due to the hectic and frantic lifestyle. Shows could last up to four hours, with about twenty different acts. Eventually, major stars were put on regular contracts rather than rushing around performing separate gigs on the same night.

A show might include the singing of ballads and comic songs, which included social

Marie Lloyd, pictured in the 1890s.

commentary on everyday working-class life – lodgers, mothers-in-law, bailiffs, overdue rent, drink, debt, adversity, unfaithful spouses ... One of the most famous hits, Marie Lloyd's *My Old Man Said Follow the Van*, was about doing a moonlight flit to avoid paying the rent.

Towards the end of the Industrial Revolution era, lavishly designed and decorated music halls sprang up across Britain. They branched out to include variety acts such as magicians, jugglers, actors and impersonators. The largest variety theatre was the London Coliseum, which was owned by impresario Oswald Stoll. It had lifts, a marble staircase and a tea room on every floor. Seats could be booked in advance and the variety show performed four times daily. The variety performance received a royal seal of approval on 1 July 1912, when King George V and Queen Mary attended the Palace Theatre in London's West End for the first Royal Variety Performance. Although most famous performers were present such as Dan Leno and the Russian ballerina Anna Pavlova, Marie Lloyd, whose act was considered too risqué for the Royal party, was omitted. In defiance, she booked a performance for the same night at a nearby theatre. The posters for the event proclaimed: 'Every performance by Marie Lloyd is a Command Performance by Order of the British Public.' Her show sold out.

The Great War marked the high-water mark of the music hall and variety theatre. Cinemas, and eventually the television, became the popular entertainments of choice.

Places to visit

- The replacement Eagle pub in London has a display of old music hall prints.
- Wilton Music Hall was opened in 1859 in London by John Wilton. His ambition was to provide West End glamour, comfort and first-rate entertainment for East End working people. Today, the venue continues to show a variety of entertainment.
- Leeds City Varieties.

Further reading

Midge Gillies, *Marie Lloyd: The One and Only* (1999).
Richard Anthony Baker, *British Music Hall: An Illustrated History* (2014).
Oliver Double, *Britain Had Talent: A History of Variety Theatre* (2012).

83: Methodist Hymn Book

This frontispiece is from *A Collection of Hymns for the Use of the People Called Methodists* (1780) – the most influential hymn book in the history of Methodism. It drew on the extensive output of brothers John and Charles Wesley. It emphasised the Christian experience and provided hymns to accompany and interpret various aspects of Christian life. Intended for use in societal meetings, as well as the smaller groups such as classes and bands, the hymn book was used in chapels that were springing up across the land as Methodists and other Nonconformist denominations sought a spiritual revival to run alongside the dynamically changing society of Britain's Industrial Revolution.

The term Nonconformist to describe Protestant Christians who rejected the authority of the established churches in Britain and Ireland originated in 1662. The Act of Uniformity required all English and Welsh clergy to consent to the entire contents of the Book of Common Prayer. Two thousand ministers and their followers who refused to do so were known as Dissenters and were driven from the established church. The Act of Toleration – passed in 1689 after Britain had been delivered from the fear of the re-establishment of Roman Catholicism as the religion of choice – allowed freedom of worship for Protestant dissenters, as long as their meeting houses, or chapels, were officially registered.

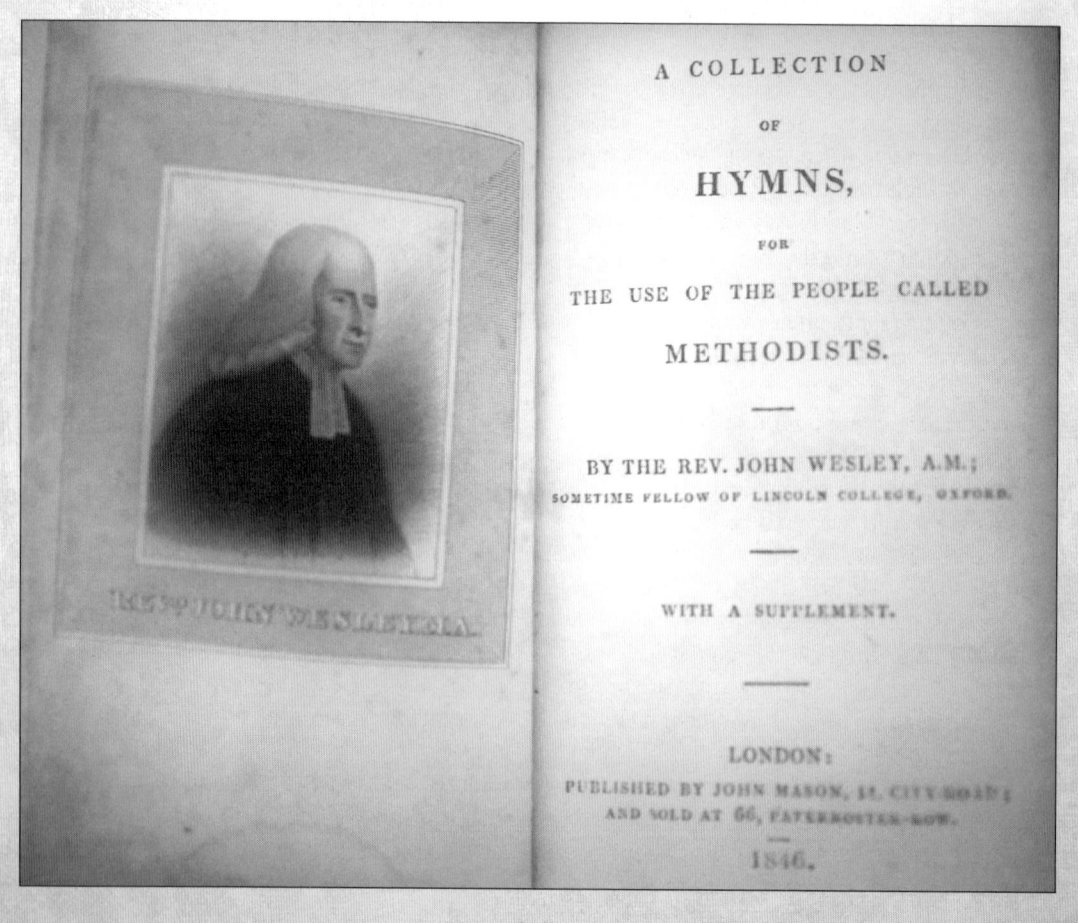

83: METHODIST HYMN BOOK

Old Heath Congregational Tin Tabernacle, Colchester. (*Peter South/Creative Commons*)

Groups classed as Nonconformists included the Methodists, Baptists, Congregationalists, Quakers and the Salvation Army.

Early chapels were designed as plain, rectangular structures but as wealthier Nonconformist patrons poured money into chapel design and construction, two-storey places of worship with classical façades were erected in which to worship God. Some chapels were built in the Gothic Revival style favoured by the Church of England during the 1800s. At the other end of the spectrum were modest chapels built from prefabricated corrugated iron, known as 'Tin Tabernacles'. One such was the Old Heath Congregational Church in Colchester, at which the author's father served as a pastor in the 1960s.

Whilst Baptist, Quaker and Congregational places of worship had existed since the late seventeenth century, the era of mass chapel building largely began in the mid-eighteenth century with the emergence of Methodism.

Initially an evangelical movement inside the Church of England, the new movement was viewed with suspicion by the Anglian hierarchy, who denied John Wesley, George Whitfield and their followers access to their pulpits.

Thus, Wesley established a network of preaching houses and eventually Methodism became a separate Protestant denomination from Anglicanism. The first purpose-built Methodist chapel was John Wesley's 'New Room' in Bristol, begun in 1739. The chapel contained rooms in which Wesley and other itinerant preachers would stay. The Methodists' aim of a spiritual renewal and reawakening in a Britain in the early throes of its Industrial Revolution saw a surge in chapel construction. More than 1,300 new chapels opened between 1750 and 1800.

The Methodist Church reached into areas where the Church of England held least sway – the new industrial districts and among the rural poor. Even as the Methodist Church split into various factions such as the Primitive Methodists, the chapel building continued apace. So too did places of worship built by the older Nonconformist denominations. The years between 1800 and 1850 saw an average of 250 new chapels built per year.

In 1836, Nonconformist places of worship were granted the opportunity to conduct marriage ceremonies, and from 1880, Nonconformist ministers could conduct burial services in parish churchyards. As the nineteenth century drew to a close, Nonconformists redoubled their efforts to reach the urban poor. The Salvation Army built citadels and the Methodists their central halls to dispense welfare and Christian charity to those in need. Many included schoolrooms and social facilities.

By the mid-nineteenth century, the number of Nonconformist buildings – called variously chapels, meeting houses, tabernacles, gospel halls, citadels and missions – in England exceeded that of Anglican parish churches. As well as springing up in the towns and cities of Britain's Industrial Revolution, chapels were frequently found in quiet rural villages the length and breadth of the land.

Grander Methodist churches, such as 2,500-seat Westminster Chapel built in 1863–5, might contain tiers of galleries and ground-floor pews set in a curve. The objective was to provide all members of the congregation with a clear view of the pulpit. Baptist churches would frequently include a pool beneath the floor for total immersion of believers coming forward for baptism. Quakers, with their lack of a preacher or communion service, were of plainer design. Sometimes there was a separate space for female members of the congregation to conduct their services.

As well as providing a space for frequent worship – both on the Sabbath and during weekdays, chapels were often a centre of educational, social, cultural and sporting

Godshill Wesleyan Chapel, Isle of Wight, opened in 1828. (*Hassocks5489/Creative Commons*)

activities. Attendance at Sunday school was a rite of passage for millions of children during the period of Britain's Industrial Revolution.

Many former chapels are no longer used for Christian worship due to the twentieth-century secularisation of British society. The buildings that remain, often converted into dwellings or businesses, remind us of a past of religious observance and faith.

Places to visit

- John Wesley's New Room in Bristol is open to the public and includes a chapel, museum, café and meeting rooms.
- The Engelsea Brook Chapel and Museum near Crewe, Cheshire, resides in a Primitive Methodist building opened in 1828.
- The Quaker Tapestry Museum in Kendal, Cumbria, tells the story of Quaker influence on the Industrial Revolution, developments in science and medicine, the abolition of slavery, social reform, astronomy and ecology. It is set in a former Quaker Georgian meeting house built in 1816.
- The Museum of Methodism & John Wesley's House in London has a wide range of objects relating to the history of the denomination.

Further reading

- David A. Barton, *Discovering Chapels and Meeting Houses* (1975).
- Christopher Wakeling, *Chapels of England: Buildings of Protestant Nonconformity* (2017).

84: Pawnbroker Sign

This distinctive three golden ball shop sign indicated the incumbent was engaged in the trade of pawnbroking. The triumvirate of balls was the symbol of St Nicholas who, according to legend, saved three young girls from destitution by loaning each of them a bag of gold so they could marry. This example is above the premises of an Edinburgh pawnbroker, where the trade stretches back to 1830.

During Britain's Industrial Revolution, the number of pawnbrokers increased greatly and by 1900, the pawnshop was almost as ubiquitous as the public house. Colloquially known as 'Uncle', the pawnbroker offered a vital service for people living close to the breadline who were in regular, yet poorly paid work. In times of need, the pawnbroker would provide loans secured on domestic items such as Sunday best clothing, shoes, jewellery and work tools.

During the early part of Britain's Industrial Revolution, the Pawnbroker's Licence Law of 1785 licensed pawnbrokers for £10 in London and £5 in the country, with an interest rate set at a ½ per cent per month and the length of loans confined to one year. The Pawnbrokers Act of 1800 increased the interest to 1⅔ per cent per month and licence fees were raised to £15 in London and £7.50 elsewhere. From 1860 onwards, pawnbrokers could generate extra revenue by charging a halfpenny for a pawn ticket. The trade grew rapidly. In Ireland, the number of pawnbrokers grew from fifty-two in 1833 to 312 by 1865.

By 1869, pawnbrokers across Britain were processing nearly 208 million pledges, the average value of each being about four shillings. Fourteen thousand articles were known to have been pawned dishonestly. An 1872 Pawnbrokers Act further regulated the amount of interest

(Kim Traynor/Creative Commons)

that could be charged, and pawnbrokers were forbidden from receiving articles from those under 12 years of age or suffering from intoxication. They also needed to show they were of good character to obtain a licence to trade from a magistrate. Sales of unclaimed goods had to take place by auction on the first Monday of January, April, July and October.

A National Pawnbrokers Association was formed in 1892, by which time the trade was a regular feature in the lives of many families. Sunday best clothes were often pawned on a Monday and redeemed on a Saturday after the breadwinner of the family had been paid on a Friday. They were worn to chapel or church on a Sunday, and pledged again the next day. This cycle of pledging and redeeming, week in, week out, might continue for years, and pawnbrokers made their profits on the interest charged. *Living London* magazine described a redemption Saturday in 1901:

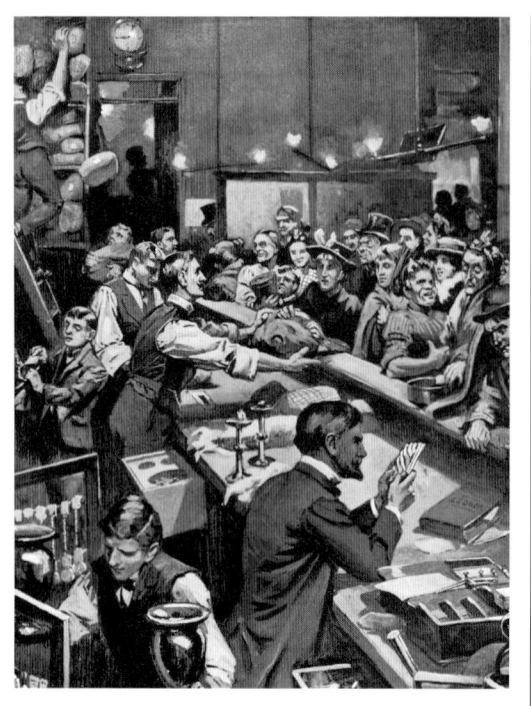

Saturday Night at a Pawnbroker's, from Living London, 1901.

> It is a strangely animated scene, with nearly all the characters played by women. It is a rarity to see a man among them … They betray no sense of shame if they feel it. They talk and gossip while waiting for their bundles, and are wonderfully polite to the perspiring assistants behind the counter.

Charles Dickens, in *Sketches by Boz* (1836), described a pawnshop near Drury Lane in the corner of a court:

> which affords a side entrance for the accommodation of such customers as may be desirous of avoiding the observation of the passers-by, or the chance of recognition in the public street. [The door], half inviting, half repelling the hesitating visitor, who, if he be as yet uninitiated, examines one of the old garnet brooches in the window for a minute or two with affected eagerness, as if he contemplated making a purchase; and then cautiously looking round to ascertain that no one watches him, hastily slinks in.

The entrance to a pawnbroker's shop was usually up a side street. Pledging could be done at an open counter or in separate compartments known as 'boxes', which offered some privacy to those ashamed of their predicament. These could include members of the middle or upper classes who had suddenly fallen on hard times. The pawnbroker would carefully examine the item to be pledged, offer a sum and, if accepted, give the pledger a pawn ticket.

The pawnshops' window displays were made up of unredeemed items pledged for less than ten shillings. After a redemption period of one year and seven days, the pawnbroker was entitled to retain and sell any unclaimed items. This made for an eclectic but sorrowful admixture of items that had once brought joy or comfort to their owners, as noted by Dickens:

Several sets of chessmen, two or three flutes, a few fiddles … some gaudily-bound prayer books and testaments, two rows of silver watches … numerous old-fashioned table and tea spoons … cards of rings and brooches … cheap silver penholders and snuff-boxes … silk and cotton handkerchiefs, and wearing apparel of every description …

Items valued at more than ten shillings were sold at auction with a reserve price to avoid the pawnbroker being out of pocket.

Despite the high interest rates, pawnbrokers provided a vital service to the poorer classes. They provided money for food when cupboards were bare and pockets were empty, and gave people the means to access temporary shelter and warmth. Although a symptom of a grossly unjust and dysfunctional system of welfare that left many below the breadline, without the pawnbroker, many families and individuals would have faced immediate crisis, rather than the hope that one day, finances might improve.

Places to visit

- The Black Country Living Museum at Dudley, West Midlands, includes a recreation of a Victorian pawnbroker's shop. It takes its name from a well-known Black Country pawnbroker, Joseph Wiltshire.
- The Ulster American Folk Park in Omagh, Northern Ireland, includes a recreated pawnbroker's shop, J. Devlin's. The shopfront come from Toberwine Street, Glenarm, County Antrim.

Further reading

- John A. Wilkinson, *Pawnbroking in the Black Country* (1991).
- Kenneth Hudson, *Pawnbroking: An Aspect of British Social History* (1982).
- Melanie Tebbutt, *Making Ends Meet: Pawnbroking and Working-class Credit* (1983).

85: Public House Sign

This late Victorian pub sign, signalling to passers-by that the establishment sold alcoholic drinks, is representative of the wide variety of artwork that adorns Britain's public houses to this day. Pub signs provide an insight into the nation's history and the people who shaped it, depicting kings, battles, inventions, religion, pastimes and landscape.

Inn signs stretch back to the Roman tabernae, outside which owners would hang vine leaves to indicate the availability of wine. Evergreen bushes were often used instead of vines. Thus, pub names such as 'The Grapes' and 'The Bush' originated. In 1393, when most British people were illiterate, King Richard II made it compulsory for pubs and inns to have a sign and the practice has continued down the centuries.

Tabernae, later corrupted to 'taverns', had been built at the sides of the Roman network of roads. When the Anglo-Saxons assumed power over much of modern-day England, they established alehouses based in domestic dwellings. People would gather for social meetings. With the medieval growth of pilgrimages and travel for other reasons, hostelries were established, which came under the guildship of the Worshipful Company of Innholders in 1514. Throughout history, ale and beer have always formed a part of the staple British diet, the brewing process itself making it a much safer option than drinking the polluted water of the times.

Until the advent of Britain's Industrial Revolution, aside from the larger towns, most drinking establishments were little more than a room in a private house, where the beer brewed on site by the publican might be of indeterminate standard. With the rapid population growth of the eighteenth and nineteenth centuries, the demand for venues where customers could both drink beer and socially interact escalated.

The stagecoach age (see Introduction) saw a new era of drinking, eating and sleeping establishments as coaching inns were built along strategic routes across the country. Such inns provided food, drink and accommodation for passengers and crew, as well as changes of

Beer Street, etching by William Hogarth, 1751.

fresh horses for their continued journey. Like the stagecoach with their class distinctions between inside and outside passengers, and the later railways with their First, Second and Third Class carriages, pubs evolved separate areas for different types of customer – the saloon, bar room and snug.

The Beerhouse Act of 1830 resulted in an expansion of beerhouses. The preceding period had seen a return of the gin house. The late seventeenth century had seen a gin craze, with its cheapness leading to a period of drunkenness and lawlessness among the poor. A reduction in duties threatened a return to that period so execrated by William Hogarth in his famous satirical engraving, *Gin Lane*. The Beerhouse Act aimed to encourage the consumption of the more wholesome beverage of beer, the social effects of which were extoled in Hogarth's accompanying print. A beerhouse was a deregulated premise. Any householder, upon payment of two guineas (just under £200 today), could brew and sell beer or cider from their own home. A beerhouse could not open on the Sabbath, or sell spirits, liqueurs or fortified wines.

By 1838, 46,000 new beerhouses had opened. One of those taking advantage of the new legislation was the author's great-great-great-grandfather, Stephen Broom, who became licensee of the Half Moon in East Dereham in 1830. Owners of brewhouses would often combine this trade with other sources of income, as did he with the continuation of his chimney-sweeping business (*see* chapter 15). Similarly, the author's great-great-grandfather combined his licenseeship of the Norfolk town's Grapes Inn between 1851 and 1854 and the Kings Arms at nearby Garvestone between 1858 and 1871, with work as a journeyman tailor.

By the mid-nineteenth century, considered a golden age of pub building, pubs were being purpose-built, with features that distinguished them from private houses. Many of these drew on the inspiration of existing gin houses and

Gin Lane, etching by William Hogarth, 1751.

gin palaces. They included a bar counter, ornate mirrors, etched glass, polished brass fittings and tiled surfaces. Handpumps meant customers could be served quicker. Improvements in the railway network allowed major breweries to deliver their branded products across a wider area.

Attempts to check the growth of public houses were made from 1869 onwards, as new licensing laws and the granting of greater power to magistrates made it harder to obtain a licence, and placed more onus on pub landlords to control drunkenness, prostitution and other undesirable behaviours on licensed premises. The temperance movement sought further curbs on what it saw as the evils of drink, accusing industrial workers of frequently passing a large part of their wages over the pub bar on a Friday night. The 1904 Licensing Act gave magistrates the power to revoke a licence if they believed a pub was not contributing positively to the life of its local community.

The latter half of the nineteenth century saw breweries buying up many local pubs in order to ensure that their drinks were the exclusive products sold there. Publicans were employed

Interior of the Philharmonic, Liverpool. (*Alan Bull/Creative Commons*)

directly by the breweries to run them. These tied houses represented a fundamental shift in the way that many pubs operated. By 1900, more than 90 per cent of public houses in England were owned by breweries.

In order to attract a wider clientele and shake off an insalubrious image, many pubs included separate areas for women. Charles Booth, in his *Life and Labour of the People in London* (1903), found many females congregating in ladies' saloon bars.

As the era of Britain's Industrial Revolution drew to a close, the public house remained very much at the centre of social life in villages, towns and cities across the land. Sadly, many British pubs have closed over the past two decades as social habits change. Many have been converted into restaurants, convenience stores or flats, with historic fixtures and fittings lost in the process. Others have been demolished to make way for car parks or residential buildings. We should cherish those that remain as reminders of a more socially cohesive past.

Places to visit

- UK Brewery Tours, which began in Bermondsey, South London, in 2014, offer a range of historically themed tours of breweries and old public houses in cities across the UK. York, Bristol, Leeds, Birmingham, Manchester and London are cities included.
- The Philharmonic Pub, Liverpool, was the first purpose-built pub in Victorian Britain and has a Grade I listing from Historic England.

Further reading

Paul Jennings, *The Local: A History of the English Pub* (2011).
Pete Brown, *The Pub: A Cultural Institution – from Country Inns to Craft Beer Bars and Corner Locals* (2016).
Richard Tames, *The Victorian Public House* (2003).

86: Shop Doorbell

This nineteenth-century shop doorbell would have signalled to a shopkeeper that a customer had entered the premises and was ready to do business. However, the shopping experience during most of the period of Britain's Industrial Revolution was very different to the 'serve yourself' arrangements of more recent decades.

The majority of shops were owned by men, although some were owned by women or perhaps the widow of a shop owner. In the early part of the period, women were forbidden from owning property or signing contracts. It was believed that buying and selling was an inappropriate role for a female as they lacked the intellectual capacity, stamina and competitive drive to make a success of the trade.

Later, women were often to be found running millinery, sewing and dressmaking shops. Others were street-sellers, trading goods they had made themselves or purchased wholesale, as did the fictional Eliza Doolittle in George Bernard Shaw's *Pygmalion*.

Early shops did not display prices. This information had to be asked of the shopkeeper – thus, haggling was a common feature of shopping. A shopkeeper might charge a higher price to a wealthy looking customer. Many shops had a clerk, of whom a customer would have to ask permission to touch the goods on sale. There were few shop displays as most items were kept in drawers or cases, or behind the counter.

As the influx of people from the countryside and small towns gathered pace in the first half of the nineteenth century, so the personal relationship that often existed between shopkeeper and client was lost. Merchants began to place items on counters, with prices clearly indicated. Greater availability of cheaper glass meant several shops could install large windows in which to display their merchandise during opening hours.

(Vincent de Groot/Creative Commons)

Towards the end of the nineteenth century, shopping became a leisure activity for the moneyed classes, particularly women seeking to keep up to date with the latest fashions. Some larger stores, with different departments selling various types of goods, employed shopwalkers to both deter shoplifters and act as personal shopping assistants to customers. They featured marble-decorated restrooms and a restaurant. Women's clothes were usually located on an upper floor to spare the embarrassment of the male shopper. Stores also featured on-site tailors for customising newly purchased clothing. The author's grandfather held such a post in a Colchester department store.

Smaller shops would generally be family run, with perhaps an apprentice to assist during opening hours. Typically, they would open Monday to Saturday, with a half-day closure on a Wednesday afternoon in many areas. With the extension of leisure shopping, so came an increase in pickpocketing and shoplifting. Sometimes shoplifters were well-dressed middle-class women tempted by consumer goods.

Bon Marché, Brixton Road, Lambeth. Built in 1877 for James Smith of Tooting's department store, it was the first purpose-built department store in the country. (*Reading Tom/ Creative Commons*)

Shopkeepers were not averse to using wiles to increase the attractiveness of goods. In his 1851 book *London Labour and the London Poor*, Henry Mayhew (*see* chapter 66) published details of a number of frauds and scams. In one scheme, goods were marketed as 'smuggled and stolen' as it was thought it would add to their appeal. Other scams included counterfeit money and adulterated foods.

The emergence of nationally recognised brands and pre-packaged products reduced the risk of product adulteration. Royal warrants were created, which permitted the tradesman to have a coat of arms applied to their stationery as a sign of quality of their products. Queen Victoria and her family granted over 2,000 such warrants during her reign.

Three of the earliest department stores were Harrods of London, Bainbridge in Newcastle upon Tyne and Kendal Milne & Co. of Manchester. Stores typically had space for mourning skirts, ball dresses, a silk room, ribbons, parasols, embroideries, lace, and a shawl room as well as furnishing and household departments. In the 1880s, Harvey Nichols, originally formed in the 1820s as an amalgam of Elizabeth Harvey's linen shop and Colonel Nichols' luxury goods business, moved to Knightsbridge in the 1880s. The many layers of clothing worn by fashionable middle and upper-class women helped to transform them into major consumers. Indeed, the size and success of the department store was fuelled by the number of outfits required during a day of morning visits, evening entertaining and formal occasions.

Working-class women could find employment making and selling the goods. The working day for shop assistants was long. Females working for William Whiteley of London in 1875 typically started at 7 am and finished at 11 pm, six days a week. With echoes of the factory discipline system endured by their female forebears (*see* chapter 8), fines were imposed for breaking a myriad of rules. Most assistants had to stand all day, and Whiteley's workers had to live in at the shop, paying for the poor-quality food they were served. A Shop Assistants' Union was formed, leading some retailers to improve conditions for their workers. In 1877, Brixton's Bon Marché opened – the first purpose-built department store in Britain, with fifty staff bedrooms. The philanthropist and social campaigner Mary

A grocer in Sheringham, Norfolk, and his assistants proudly displaying their wares.

Jeune wrote an essay in 1895 on 'The Ethics of Shopping', condemning the conditions that ruined the health of young female shop assistants.

Workers making the goods were exploited, even by an organisation such as the Co-op. The 1895 Co-operative Women's Guild enquiry found that apprentice milliners and dressmakers aged under 18 were receiving no wages as part of their training. Female outworkers were also subjugated, much like the matchgirls (*see* chapter 59). Those making fancy blouses were making only five shillings per week in the early 1900s. As is often the case with modern-day ethical shopping, there were boycotts of certain emporiums where cheap bargains often went hand in hand with exploitative working practices.

Places to visit

- The Castle Museum in York contains a recreated Victorian street containing a range of shops and wares from the era. Meticulous research has ensured that both the façades and their interiors are as authentic as possible.
- The Milestones Museum in Basingstoke contains a range of Victorian shop fronts and interiors.

Further reading

Philip Wilkinson, *Turn Back Time: The High Street – 100 Years of British Life Through the Shop Window* (2010).
Claire Masset, *Department Stores* (2010).
Jon Stobart, *Spend: A History of Shopping* (2008).

87: Colman's Mustard Poster

This iconic poster, which is now to be frequently found in shops and websites specialising in nostalgic images, depicts Victorian Britain's most eminent sporting personality, cricketer W.G. Grace, stepping out to bat in his MCC cap. The portrait carried the message 'Colman's Mustard: Like Grace, Heads the Field'. Issued in 1890, Colman's use of celebrity endorsement was the latest in a series of marketing techniques that resulted from the ability of Britain's Industrial Revolution to mass-produce consumer items.

Technological advances meant that factories were increasingly able to make a wider variety of goods in greater volumes, and manufacturers realised that they could capitalise on this technology to expand both the range, diversity and cost-effectiveness of their products. Advertising methods began to spread information about these products, aiming to reach the emergent middle classes and respectable working class with disposable incomes. With the railway network able to move manufactured goods rapidly around the country for the first time, logos were used to both indicate the manufacturer and act as a symbol of consistency and quality.

Advertising agencies began to appear in Britain in the 1800s, using new and innovative ways to engage customers. As many people had low levels of literacy and did not frequently read newspapers, they employed other advertising tactics, including banners on hand-held poles, people wearing placards, and umbrellas with signs on them.

Leading companies began to promote their brand names through attractive packaging and eye-catching slogans. As mass-production spread, many manufacturers started burning, or branding, their marks on the cases and crates of goods that they distributed in order to distinguish their products from the competition. As time went on, these marks began to stand for quality and brand recognition. A good quality brand could enable a company to raise their prices.

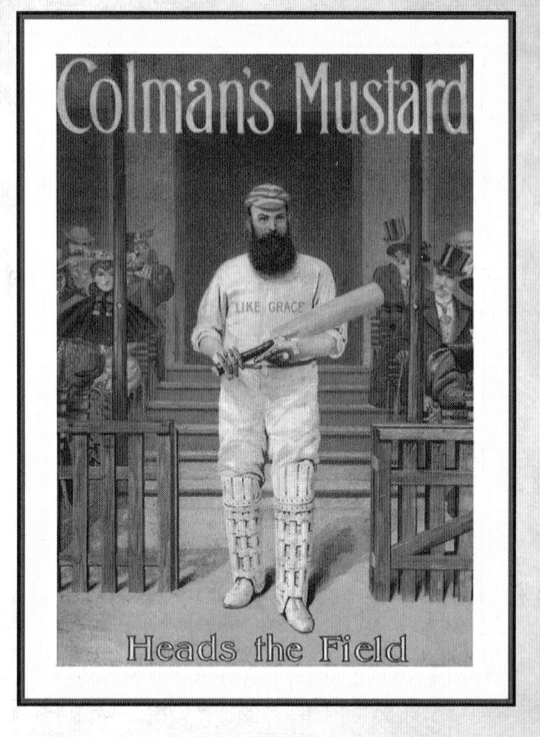

Initially, the manufacturer's name was used, such as Mr Cadbury's cocoa, Mr Colman's mustard, W.D. and H.O. Wills's tobacco, Lipton's tea, Pears' soap or Fry's chocolate. By the 1880s, as the variety of goods increased, there was an increasing need to differentiate between the goods on offer. Names not directly linked to the manufacturer became de rigueur. Identifiable names were developed to enhance the appeal of a product. William Hesketh Lever realised that a brand name like Sunlight soap could give his product greater vitality and allure. Wills's cigarettes came up with Wild Woodbine and Cinderella, whilst Cadbury's used the name of the village they had built for their workers – Bournville – as a name for their cocoa and chocolate bar.

87: COLMAN'S MUSTARD POSTER

An advertisement for Cadbury's Cocoa from 1885, displaying the product's wholesome and athletic properties.

When brothers George and Richard Cadbury took over the family business in 1861, they began to innovate, working on an improved method of extracting butter so that they no longer needed additives. They started using marketing slogans, advertising the new Cadbury's chocolate as 'Absolutely Pure: Therefore Best'. In 1868, they began selling chocolates in boxes. The design of the boxes became more and more elaborate as the company continued to develop a distinctive brand. Other businesses moved away from naming products after the company's owner or founder. Bisto came about as an abbreviation of the Messrs Roberts and Paterson product which 'Browns, Seasons and Thickens in One'. Oxo added an 'o' to their beef-flavoured stock cube.

Jeremiah James Colman, who took over the family mustard manufacturing business in Norwich, was decades ahead of his time as an employer and advertiser. He set up a subsidised school for his workers' children and hired an industrial nurse to help sick employees. J.J. Colman's genius also extended to market his products. He arranged for Royal Doulton to supply cafés with mustard pots bearing the company's trademark. Colman's railway wagons carried the logo with a painted mustard-coloured background. The bull's head Colman logo first appeared on their mustard jars in 1855.

Andrew Pears' method of boiling the impurities out of his soap and adding a delicate perfume smelling of English garden flowers created a product that became popular among wealthy Londoners. To extend sales to the prosperous middle classes around Britain, Pears issued several posters placing his soap within the context of blissful domesticity. A family member, Thomas Barratt, joined the firm and began to take out newspaper advertisements and issue testimonials from scientists and celebrities.

Pears' *Bubbles* advertisement, using the painting bought from John Millais.

Barratt also purchased 500,000 French coins and had the Pears' name stamped on them. The coins were then circulated as British currency, resulting in both a lot of publicity, but also in a law being passed to make use of foreign currency in England illegal. Barratt purchased original artwork from artists for his advertisements, including the well-known *Bubbles* by John Everett Millais, which he had modified to include a bar of Pears' soap. In this, and other Pears' advertisements, sentimentality was heavily emphasised by featuring children and animals.

The relentless marketing that reaches the modern consumer every time they switch on their television or reach for social media on their smartphone can trace its emergence to Britain's Industrial Revolution.

Places to visit

- The Museum of Brands at Notting Hill, London, claims to take 'visitors on a nostalgic journey through 200 years of social change, culture and lifestyle … an exciting new way of looking at history through the things that generations of families have thrown away'.
- Cadbury World in Birmingham features fourteen zones that tell the story of chocolate and the Cadbury business through time.

Further reading

Diane Wordsworth, *A History of Cadbury* (2018).
Robert Opie, *Victorian Scrapbook* (1999).

88: Vimto Monument

This somewhat unusual monument consists of a giant Vimto bottle surrounded at its base by outsized versions of some of the fruits and herbs used in the drink's production. Carved from sustainable wood and refurbished in 2011, it stands on the spot near the centre of Manchester where the beverage was invented.

Vimto, which is a shortening of 'Vim Tonic', was concocted in 1908 by Noel Nichols, a wholesaler of herbs, spices and medicines who was looking to gain a foothold in the soft drink market that he predicted would result from the temperance movement and the passing of the 1908 Licensing Act. The drink was made of a mix of fruits and herbs that gave it the air of a medicine. In 1913, Vimto was reclassified as a soft drink.

The British temperance movement, which began in the 1830s, campaigned against the recreational sale and use of alcohol, promoting total abstinence, or teetotalism. Many of its prominent members were Christians who saw alcohol as corroding the social fabric of society, leading to poverty, child neglect, immorality and economic decline.

The middle classes had become concerned about excessive alcohol consumption during the gin craze of the eighteenth century. John Wesley, the founder of Methodism, stated that 'buying, selling, and drinking of liquor, unless absolutely necessary, were evils to be avoided'. In 1829, the Irish Presbyterian minister John Edgar poured his whiskey collection out of his window, and wrote a letter to the *Belfast Telegraph* advocating temperance. The same year, social activists John Dunlop and Lilias Graham founded the Glasgow and West of Scotland Temperance Society.

The first temperance hotel, where people could socialise while imbibing soft drinks, was opened in 1833 by Joseph Livesey in Preston, Lancashire. The following year he founded the *Preston Temperance Advocate*, a monthly magazine priced at 1*d*.

Whilst many temperance supporters were comfortable with enjoying moderate amounts

(Mike Peel/Creative Commons)

Temperance Fountain, Clapham Common. (*Tristan Forward/Creative Commons*)

of alcohol, others argued for teetotalism, the complete abstinence from beer, wine and spirits. One current within the broad-based Chartist movement (*see* chapter 54) was Temperance Chartism. Their philosophy was that a campaign against alcohol would prove that working people could be trusted with the right to vote.

Founded in Leeds in 1847, the Band of Hope aimed to save working-class children from the evils of alcohol. Education on the effects of drink was provided and Band of Hope members had to sign a pledge promising to abstain from 'all liquors of an intoxicating quality, whether ale, porter, wine or ardent spirits, except as medicine',

The first organisation that sought prohibition was the United Kingdom Alliance, established in 1853. However, they were very much a marginal group within the temperance movement, with most advocating moral persuasion above legal enforcement. The British Women's Temperance Alliance, founded in 1876, aimed to use female persuasion to stop men drinking, framing alcohol consumption in terms of the damage it could wreak on family dynamics and prosperity.

The 1854 Sale of Beer Act restricted the Sunday opening hours of pubs, but widespread opposition, some of it violent, led to repeal.

Scottish physician Dr Norman Kerr founded the Total Abstinence Society and the Society for the Study and Cure of Inebriety (1884). Kerr's view was that drunkenness was a disease, not a vice. In florid Victorian language, he wrote that alcohol addiction was an 'abnormal condition, in which morbid cravings and impulses to intoxication are apt to be developed in such force as to overpower the moral resistance and control'. Kerr wrote a book, *Inebriety or Narcomania*, in 1888.

In addition to the religious aspect, the temperance movement took on a political slant when the National Temperance Federation, which had ties with the Liberal Party, brought together various disparate anti-alcohol groups. The Conservative Party mainly aligned with the interests of the brewing and distilling industries.

Picking up from the message propagated by John Wesley, the Nonconformist churches advocated abstinence to their congregations and lobbied Parliament for the restriction of alcohol. They argued that the economic benefits of employment and taxation that the alcohol industry brought were far outweighed by the overlaps of drinking with gambling, prostitution and corruption. The Wesleyan Methodists built nearly 100 Central Halls, which hosted cheap concerts and comedy shows, as a counterpoint to

Band of Hope banner, Constantine, Cornwall.

the music halls and variety theatres where drink flowed freely. The Salvation Army, founded in 1864, had a heavy emphasis on abstinence. Lady Llanover, a Calvinist Methodist, closed all the public houses on her Monmouthshire estate to show her opposition to alcohol.

The Quakers, too, encouraged alternatives to alcohol by producing drinking chocolate. The well-known firms of Cadbury (*see* chapter 87), Fry and Terry were all run by Quaker families. Even the Church of England had its own Temperance Society, whose volunteers would attend court to befriend people who had fallen into crime through drink, and the Roman Catholic Church had the League of the Cross, founded in 1873 by Cardinal Manning.

Practical measures to turn people away from drink included the instillation of temperance fountains in some cities, where people could be assured of clean drinking water rather than relying on the brewing process in order to produce a safe drink. Temperance bars appeared in many northern towns, including Rawtenstall and Barnsley, which only served soft drinks.

Between 1880 and 1882, the Gospel Temperance movement organised mass meetings across Britain, inviting American abstinence advocate Richard Booth to tour the country. Ultimately, the temperance movement failed in its aim to impose prohibition of alcohol in Britain. However, it did meet with some success, as by the end of the nineteenth century about 10 per cent of Britain's adult population were abstainers. One unusual offshoot of the temperance movement was the naming of Maine Road, Manchester, famous as the home of Manchester City FC for several decades. The American state of Maine had prohibited alcohol in 1851, and prominent British abstainers owned land in that area of Manchester.

Places to visit

- Fitzpatrick's in Rawtenstall, Lancashire, which opened in 1890, is Britain's last surviving temperance bar.
- The Vimto Monument stands in the grounds of Vimto Park at the University of Manchester.
- Temperance Fountain on Clapham Common, first erected near London Bridge by the Temperance Society in 1884, depicts a woman giving water to a beggar. It was moved to Clapham Common in 1895.

Further reading

Brian Harrison, *Drink and the Victorians: The Temperance Question in England, 1815–1872* (1971).

89: Penny Black Stamp

This unused postage stamp, illustrated with a profile of the young Queen Victoria, was popularly known as the Penny Black. It was first issued in May 1840 in order to bring more logic and consistency into the British postal service, as befitted a nation at the forefront of industrial, communication and cultural development.

The stamp indicated that the postage cost had been prepaid by the sender, instead of needing the recipient to pay a fee. Before the arrival of the Penny Black, the amount a person had to pay in order to receive a letter had depended on the number of sheets sent and on the distance it had travelled. The genius of the postal system introduced by Rowland Hill was to standardise the cost of sending a normal letter anywhere in the United Kingdom.

The Royal Mail began in 1516 when Henry VIII appointed a 'Master of the Posts', a position now known as Postmaster General. James I set up a royal postal service between London and Edinburgh when he ascended the English throne in 1603. His son, Charles I, made the Royal Mail service available to the public in 1635, with the postage being paid by the recipient. The General Post Office was established in 1660 by Charles II.

The first mail coach service began in 1784, operating between Bristol and London, and the first mail train was introduced in 1830 on the Liverpool and Manchester Railway. Despite this growth, Rowland Hill, a former teacher and advocate of educational reform, remained convinced that a fairer and more efficient system was needed in order to keep the wheels of Britain's Industrial Revolution turning.

In 1837, Hill had published a booklet titled *Post Office Reform: Its Importance and Practicability*. This was his response to a parliamentary enquiry into the future trajectory of Britain's postal system. Hill challenged the complex and anomalous existing system and his straightforward suggestion caught the public imagination and eventually forced Viscount Melbourne's government to act.

A group of businessmen who were feeling the negative effects of high postage costs formed a committee, with a propaganda newspaper, the *Post Circular*, being published by one of their number, Henry Cole. This Select Committee was chaired by Robert Wallace MP – a long-time campaigner for postal reform. They recommended a low, uniform, prepaid postage rate and a law was passed in August 1839 to prepare for its introduction. Rowland Hill was appointed to expedite the new system. He organised a competition to design the best method of prepayment of postage, bringing forth 2,600 entries. The idea of being able to cancel the labels once they had been used in order to prevent fraud was emphasised by James Chalmers of Dundee. Some suggested that

Rowland Hill, founder of the modern postal system.

the entire envelope should be prepaid; others proposed prepaid labels.

On 5 December 1839, postage rates were reduced to 4*d* and charged by weight. A surge in usage meant that, on 10 January 1840, the rate was reduced to 1*d* for a letter of up to half an ounce. Any existing privileges held by some individuals or institutions to free use of the postal system was abolished. This meant even Queen Victoria could no longer send her post for free.

Three methods of prepayment were introduced, including a lettersheet and envelope containing a design by William Mulready printed on security silk-thread paper. It depicted images of the Empire with a central Britannia and lion at her feet. Despite this noble aspiration, the design was subject to much ridicule and was quickly withdrawn from issue.

For the adhesive labels, Henry Corbould sketched an image of Queen Victoria's head from a sculpture by William Wyon made to commemorate her visit to the City of London in November 1837. Charles and Frederick Heath then transferred the design onto a die for printing by secure white-line machine engraving. For additional security, there was variable lettering on each stamp. A black stamp would cost 1*d*, with a blue stamp for bulkier letters costing 2*d*. This sketch of the young Victoria would remain on British stamps until her death, aged 81, in 1901.

The prepaid stamps proved an immediate hit. To prevent their reuse, a cancellation mark of a red ink Maltese Cross was stamped across them during transit. This proved possible to remove, so after a year, the Penny Black became the Penny Red, so it could be cancelled with black ink. Over 68 million Penny Blacks were issued.

To this day, a silhouette of the head of the reigning monarch features on all British postal stamps. Britain remains the only country that does not state the stamp's country of origin, due to it being the first country to use such a system.

In 1840 – the same year that the Penny Black was issued – Stanley Gibbons was born. The son of a chemist, at the age of 16, he opened a stamp counter in his father's Plymouth shop and in 1863 was fortunate enough to purchase from two sailors a sackful of rare Cape of Good Hope triangular stamps. Realising the collectability of these and other used stamps, in 1865 he published the first Stanley Gibbons stamp catalogue. This cost 1*d* and ran monthly until 1879. In 1890, he brought out a magazine to feed the rapidly expanding hobby of philately – the collection of postage stamps. The Stanley Gibbons Auction House was opened in 1901 and in 1914 the Stanley Gibbons company received a royal warrant from that most eminent of philatelists, King George V.

Rowland Hill's vision had transformed the sending of letters in Britain and spawned a hobby loved by millions for the past 180 years.

A Mulready prepaid lettersheet.

Places to visit

- The Postal Museum in Phoenix Place, London, tells the story of the British postal system and has many stamps, including the Penny Black, on display.
- Rowland Hill's residence at the time of his introduction of the Penny Black in Orme Square, London, features a blue plaque in his honour.

Further reading

Alan Holyoake, *The World's First Postage Stamp* (2013).
Douglas N. Muir, *Postal Reform and the Penny Black: A New Appreciation* (1990).
Christopher West, *First Class: A History of Britain in 36 Postage Stamps* (2013).

90: The Pillar Box

The British letter box has become an iconic symbol of the nation, frequently featuring in tourist brochures, postcards and greetings cards. Decommissioned boxes are sought throughout the world to adorn gardens, office premises and even ships.

The oldest British post box dates from 1809, installed in the wall of Wakefield Post Office. It is now on display at Wakefield Museum.

As a result of a boom in the use of Britain's postal service, brought about by Rowland Hill's introduction of the Penny Post in 1840 (*see* chapter 89), existing systems for collecting, sorting and delivering letters proved inadequate. Previously, senders would have to either take their letter in person to a Receiving House, a de facto early post office, or await the arrival of a bellman, or town crier, in his distinctive uniform. He would walk the streets ringing a bell to alert people that he was ready to collect their letters.

Pillar boxes, or post boxes, had been installed across France by the late 1820s. Anthony Trollope, the future author of the *Barchester Chronicles*, worked as a surveyor's clerk for the Post Office. While in Europe on business, he saw roadside letter boxes in use in France and Belgium. Trollope brought the idea back to Britain and it was agreed that a trial be set up in the Channel Islands.

Four cast-iron pillar boxes were installed in Jersey and came into use on 23 November 1852. In 1853, the trial was extended to Guernsey. Later that year, the city of Carlisle became the first place in the British mainland to receive one. As the use of pillar boxes spread throughout Britain, their commissioning became the responsibility of the local surveyor, so had no uniform design. Beyond having to be pillar-shaped and include a small slit through which letters could be posted, they could be of any colour and height.

Green Guernsey pillar box, 1853. (*Kitmaster/Creative Commons*)

By 1857, horizontal, rather than vertical, apertures had become the norm. Flaps were trialled over the apertures to prevent rain damaging the post. To improve weather

Liverpool Special pillar box, Albert Dock. (*Rodhullandemu/ Creative Commons*)

Penfold post box. (*Rodhullandemu/Creative Commons*)

damage prevention, a small cap was included in new designs. Richard Redgrave's ornate 1856 design, improved on in 1859, became the commonplace standard in Britain's cities. It was to be available in two sizes, a larger, wider version for areas of dense population, and a smaller, narrower one for elsewhere. It failed to prove popular in all districts; in 1862, the district surveyor for Liverpool commissioned his own, non-standard box, known today as the Liverpool Special.

Between 1866 and 1879, the Penfold box became the standard design. Available in three sizes and hexagonal in shape, the original colour chosen was green. This was a deliberate decision in order for the boxes to blend in as naturally as possible to the landscape. However, there were complaints from people who were having difficulty finding them, so from 1874 onwards, they were painted red. It took ten years to complete the programme of repainting. Red remained the standard colour for boxes from then on, with few exceptions.

The Penfold design was not to survive. In 1879, a further standard box was produced. It resembled the letter box that is today an iconic image of Britain – cylindrical with round cap and horizontal aperture under a protruding cap with front opening door and black painted base.

In 1857, as a means of providing cheaper, smaller capacity boxes for smaller towns and more rural areas, wall-mounted boxes were introduced. These were small rectangular boxes mounted either into existing walls or into purpose-built brick pillars. Larger varieties were cast once these began to prove successful, eventually with three basic sizes in production.

In 1896, to answer the demand for more convenient posting facilities for the wealthy and influential inhabitants of London's salubrious squares, small boxes were designed and trialled. Made to attach to existing lamp posts, and big enough only to hold small letters, the boxes soon began appearing in low volume areas around the country.

Today, the red pillar box is a familiar feature across Britain. The era in which they were erected can be gleaned from the monarch's initials on the front: VR, ER, GR or ER. They remind us of a time when an increase in literacy and the importance of a quick and reliable communication system gave rise to their birth. They were vital nodes in the information superhighway of Britain's Industrial Revolution.

Places to visit

- The oldest working pillar box in the UK is at Barnes Cross, near Sherborne in Dorset. The octagonal box was manufactured by John M. Butt & Company of Gloucester, in 1853.
- The British Postal Museum in London has a range of antique pillar boxes on display.
- The Isle of Wight Postal Museum in Newport is a private collection of over 200 pillar boxes. Viewing is by prior arrangement.

Further reading

Jean Young Farrugia, *The Letter Box: a history of Post Office pillar and wall boxes* (1969).
Martin Robinson, *Old Letter Boxes* (2000).

91: Metropolitan Police Helmet

The familiar police force that serves Britain today is yet another product of the Industrial Revolution. This police officer, resplendent in his blue tunic, topped off with a stovepipe helmet, is wearing the uniform of the Metropolitan Police as constituted in 1829. The tunic and helmet distinguished the police from the military red tunic and cylindrical hat and were important signifiers of the nature of Victorian law enforcement.

In 1750, in response to the high level of crime in London, magistrates Henry and John Fielding created a salaried constabulary – the Bow Street Runners. The runners patrolled the highways and lanes within the parish of Bow Street. Several more parishes followed suit. At this point, however, there was little popular or governmental support for the creation of a salaried, professional police force throughout Britain. These salaried, professional watchmen and constables were often former soldiers under the age of 40 who had some training in the laws of the land. Sometimes they wore numbers painted on the back of their overcoats so they were easily identifiable.

In June 1780, a week's worth of rioting occurred when the Protestant Association objected to a slight easing of laws against Roman Catholics. Known as the Gordon Riots after their instigator, General George Gordon, they had to be put down by soldiers. However, the Lord Mayor, Sir Watkin Lewes, who valued the independence of the City of London Corporation's institutions, rebuffed suggestions of establishing a professional police force across the whole of London. The prevailing laissez-faire philosophy of the time (*see* chapter 39) stipulated that the less that central government raised taxes and involved itself in public life, the better. Thus was resisted the idea of a centralised mainland police force.

Early Victorian police officer with stovepipe hat.

The Dublin Police Act (1786) created a professional, uniformed and armed centralised police force in Dublin – the second largest British city – consisting of forty horse police and 400 constables. Raised at a time of intense political unrest, by 1812 Dublin was considered relatively free of crime.

The Scottish economist Patrick Colquhoun wrote *A Treatise on the Police of the Metropolis* (1796), in which he applied business principles to police administration. According to Colquhoun, a constable needed to be efficient and zealous in his work, possess integrity and be of high moral character. In 1798, he formed the Marine Police to tackle theft and looting from ships anchored in the Pool of London and in the lower reaches and docks of the Thames. It became the Thames River Police force in 1800. The force was financed by merchants and had eighty permanent staff and more than 1,000 on call. It used visible, preventive

91: METROPOLITAN POLICE HELMET

A group of police officers in blue tunics and stovepipe helmets.

patrols and ensured officers received a full-time salary to avoid bribery.

Following incidents of unrest that ensued after the end of the Napoleonic Wars, Parliament grew increasingly sympathetic to the idea of a politically independent and non-militarised police force. Appointed Home Secretary in Lord Liverpool's administration in 1822, Robert Peel worked towards the setting up of the first disciplined police force with the Metropolitan Police Act of 1829. Peel's aim was uniformity in the prevention and detection of crime across London, although the City of London was permitted to make its own arrangements – a system still in place today.

Peel's reforms were unpopular with the more affluent London parishes, who had been able to afford more constables and watchmen. Ratepayers resented paying for a force over which they had no direct control. Peel's 'New Police' was organised in a ranking hierarchy, with a system of internal promotion based on merit. It was designed to draw support from those it served – the principle of policing by consent. Crime prevention was the main focus of the force, with regular and visible patrols in operation. There would be no additional monetary reward for solving crimes or recovering stolen property.

The Metropolitan Police were nicknamed 'bobbies', or 'Peelers', after their creator. Initially jeered at, they gradually gained a reputation for excellence. Charles Rowan and Richard Mayne, the first commissioners, instilled 'Peel's Principles' into their men: impartiality, focus on crime prevention, duties to be carried out within the limits of the law, co-operation with the public and the minimal and necessary use of force.

The Metropolitan Police managed to quell the Chartist risings, not only in London, but also in Birmingham, to where a contingent of officers was sent. The Municipal Corporations Act of 1835 ordered all boroughs to set up police forces, and in 1856, Parliament passed the County and Borough Police Act, which extended the principles of police authority deriving from the Crown and policing by consent to forces across the country. Like many developments during Britain's Industrial Revolution, these principles would inform policing in many other countries across the world. Once again, Britain's ruling class had decided to provide an element of consent alongside coercion, so the fruits of Britain's Industrial Revolution were not swallowed up in revolution as with so many of its European neighbours.

Places to visit

- The Bradford Police Museum includes a collection of Victorian police truncheons, uniforms and a photographic archive.
- The Bow Street Police Museum tells the story of the Bow Street Runners and the Metropolitan Police officers who patrolled the streets of Covent Garden in their footsteps.
- The Museum of Policing in Cheshire, located in Warrington, preserves and researches the heritage of policing in the county.

Further reading

Clive Emsley, *The Great British Bobby: A History of British Policing from the 18th Century to the Present* (2009).
Clive Emsley, *A Short History of Police and Policing* (2021).
Simon Patrick Dell, *The Victorian Policeman* (2004).

92: 1861 Census Return

This census return, which shows the author's great-great-great-grandfather and his household in 1861, was the sixth such enumeration of the population undertaken during Britain's Industrial Revolution. Recorded as the second household on this particular sheet in the enumerator's record book, it tells us that Stephen Broom was 74 years old, working as a Master Sweep employing one man and one boy. His wife, Susan Broom, aged 58, had no stated occupation whilst the remainder of the household consisted of Robert Head, recorded as having a servant relationship to Stephen and working as a journeyman sweep, and John Wilson, a 12-year-old apprentice chimney sweep. Also recorded were their places of birth.

Census returns provide invaluable information for today's family historians about the jobs and family relationships of their ancestors but the origins of the census are shrouded in controversy. In his book *An Essay on the Principles of Population* (1798), political economist Thomas Malthus argued that population growth was occurring hand in hand with Britain's industrial growth and would soon outstrip the supply of food and other resources. The country would then descend into famine, disease and disaster. Malthus failed to foresee the tremendous growth in wealth that Britain's Industrial Revolution would generate and that, far from descending into disaster, the succeeding century would be one of prosperity for many. However, convinced by his arguments, and seeing the need to have an accurate record of population numbers and distribution, Parliament passed the Census Act in 1800, the first official census of England and Wales taking place on 10 March 1801.

Overseers of the Poor and a range of other public officials were commissioned to collect data from every household in England and Wales, and in Scotland, the task was given to schoolmasters. However, Ireland had to wait until 1821 for its first census. The 1801 census calculated a population of 9 million across Great Britain.

Sadly, most of the census returns from 1801, 1811, 1821 and 1831 were destroyed once the data on populations of different localities had been created. A major change in census enumeration came in 1841. John Lister was appointed the first Registrar General of England and Wales and local officers of a newly created registration service collected the data. This formed the basis of the system still in use in the twenty-first century. Each householder was required to complete a census schedule, giving the address of the household, the names, ages, sex, occupations and county of birth of each individual residing in the accommodation. From 1851, householders were asked to give more precise details of the places of birth of each resident, to state their relationship to him or her, marital status and the

The 1861 census return for the household of Stephen Broom, East Dereham, Norfolk.

Thomas Malthus, whose alarming predictions led to the first census in 1801.

nature of any disabilities from which they may be suffering. The enumerator then collected the census schedules, which were copied into census enumerators' books.

The 1861 and 1871 censuses elicited the same information. Sometimes anomalies arose as heads of households were confused as to whom to include. The 1861 census records the author's great-grandfather, 16-year-old William Broom, as residing both at the family residence – the King's Arms in Garvestone, Norfolk – and at the Grapes Inn in East Dereham, his family's previous residence. It is likely that he frequently stayed at both residences and was at the latter during the night of the census but his father included him along with the rest of the family at the primary residence. By the time of the 1881 census, officials noted a marked rise in the number of individuals recorded as 'deaf and dumb' – found to be a result of enumerators including babies who could not yet speak in this category.

The 1891 census introduced the innovation of recording each adult or older child's employment status – e.g. employed, self-employed or living by own means. The Welsh census of the same year included a question on the primary language spoken by each person. The 1901 census was the same in scope as that of a decade earlier, although it required collective returns for institutions where several people were residing on census night – such as docked ships, hospitals, prisons, workhouses and military barracks.

The final census date of Britain's Industrial Revolution period was 2 April 1911. In addition to the information requested on the previous census, the head of household was asked to supply each person's nationality, length of current marriage and the number of children born, died and living. By this time, medical conditions were couched in terms that might give offence to twenty-first-century sensibilities: 'Deaf and Dumb, Blind, Lunatic, Imbecile, Feeble-minded'.

Conceived in an era of anxiety about excessive population growth, as Britain's Industrial Revolution progressed, the census became a valuable means of organising the nation's resources and framing public policy.

Places to visit

- The original census enumeration books are at the Public Record Office at Kew, although most people access the information digitally.

Further reading

Roger Hutchinson, *The Butcher, the Baker, the Candlestick-Maker: The story of Britain through its census, since 1801* (2017).

Boris Starling & David Bradbury, *The Official History of Britain: Our Story in Numbers as Told by the Office for National Statistics* (2020).

Alan Macfarlane, *Thomas Malthus and the Making of the Modern World* (2018).

93: Michael Faraday's Electrical Generator

This ingenious device, an electrical generator built by Michael Faraday in 1831, revolutionised domestic and industrial power supplies throughout Britain and the world.

Whilst improvements in the application of steam power had gone a long way to meeting industrial demand, smaller-scale business could not afford access to it. In the 1820s, Michael Faraday, a scientist working at the Royal Society in London, realised a more useful form of power was needed. He began conducting experiments building on the work of Alessandro Volta and Hans Christian Oersted on early batteries, magnetism and motion.

In 1831, Faraday made a revolutionary discovery. By wrapping a tube in copper wire and insulating it with cloth and hooking the wire up to a galvanometer, he realised that when passing a magnet backwards and forwards through the middle of the tube, the needle on the galvanometer moved. He had created the first-ever generator of electricity. His generator converted mechanical energy – the motion of the moving magnet – into electricity. This was the foundation of modern dynamos. Today, almost all electrical power is generated using Faraday's principles – be it from water, steam, wind, oil, coal or nuclear reaction.

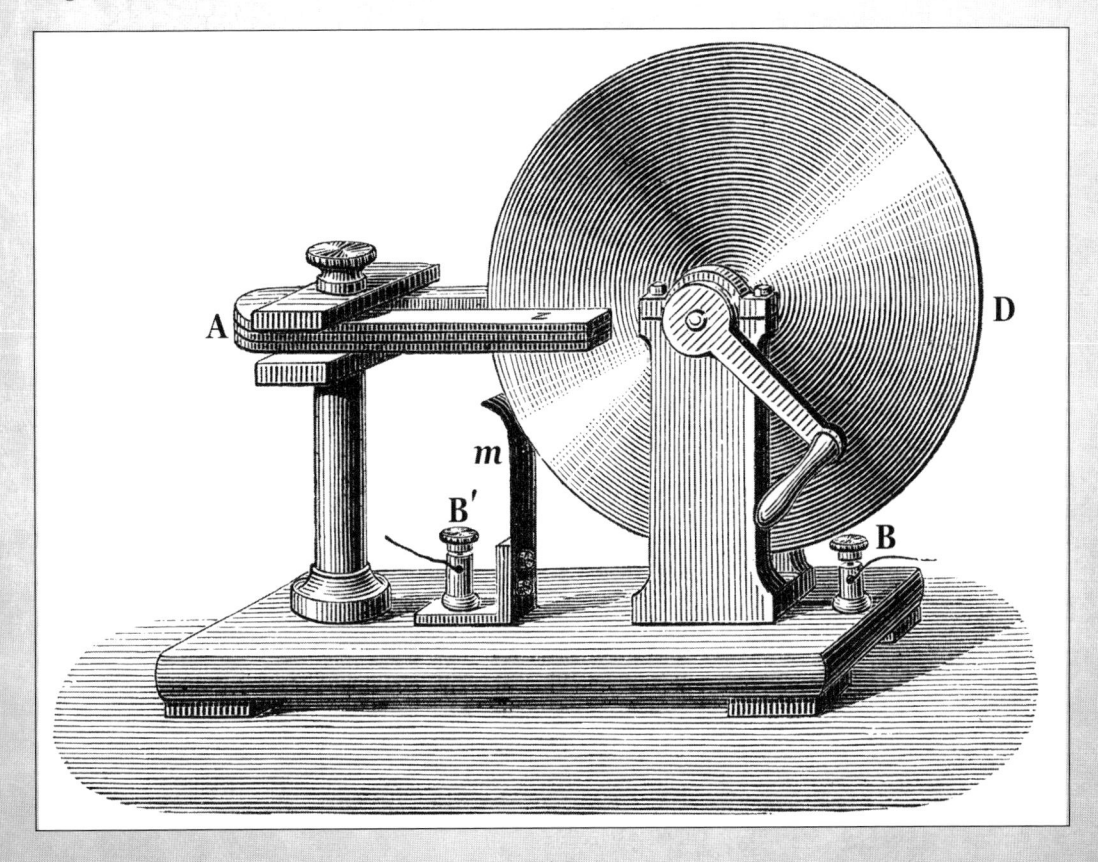

Faraday delivering one of his Christmas lectures.

Michael Faraday also pioneered the Christmas Lectures, talks designed specifically for young people to help them understand scientific principles and discoveries. Begun in 1826 as the Royal Institution's Friday Evening Discourses and Christmas Lectures, Faraday himself gave many talks, establishing a reputation as the outstanding scientific lecturer of his time. The Royal Institution as well as universities and organisations around the country continue to deliver these engaging and interactive talks and shows for young people every year.

Faraday was born on 22 September 1791 in South London. His family was of modest means and he received little formal education. He was apprenticed aged 14 to a local bookbinder and, for the next seven years, educated himself by reading books on a wide range of scientific subjects. In 1812, he attended four lectures given by the chemist Humphry Davy at the Royal Institution. Faraday subsequently wrote to Davy asking for a job as his assistant, and in 1813 was appointed as chemical assistant at the Royal Institution.

A year later, Davy invited Faraday to accompany him and his wife on an eighteen-month European tour, meeting many influential scientists. On his return in 1815, Faraday continued to work at the Royal Institution, assisting Davy and others with their experiments. In 1821, he published his work on electromagnetic rotation – the principle behind the electric motor – and in 1831, he discovered electromagnetic induction, the principle behind the electric transformer and generator.

This discovery transformed electricity from an academic curiosity into a powerful new technology. During the remainder of the 1830s, Faraday worked on developing his ideas about electricity. His scientific knowledge was harnessed for practical use through various official appointments, including scientific adviser to Trinity House (1836–65) and Professor of Chemistry at the Royal Military Academy in Woolwich (1830–51). However, when, during the Crimean War, he was asked to advise the British government on the production of chemical weapons, the staunchly Christian Faraday refused on religious and ethical grounds. Upon Davy's retirement, Faraday was appointed Professor of Chemistry at the Royal Institution.

From the early 1840s, Faraday did less research as his health began to deteriorate. He died on 25 August 1867 at Hampton Court, where he had

Faraday working in his laboratory at the Royal Institution, London.

been given official lodgings in recognition of his contribution to science.

Faraday's work revolutionised the way domestic and business apparatus were powered. He invented the electric motor, transformer and generator, advancing the capabilities of both manufacture and communication. As someone who had had to rely on self-teaching as a young man, his passion for popularising and communicating science widened its appeal. His discoveries paved the way for many of the innovations of the latter part of Britain's Industrial Revolution.

Places to visit

- The Michael Faraday Memorial, situated at the Elephant and Castle, London, is a stainless steel box-shaped structure. Appropriately, the interior contains a London Underground electrical substation.
- The Faraday Museum, housed within the Royal Institution, contains Faraday's magnetic laboratory displayed as it was in the 1850s.

Further reading

Charles Ludwig, *Michael Faraday: Father of Electronics* (1988).
Iwan Rhys Morus, *Michael Faraday and the Electrical Century* (2017).
James Hamilton, *Faraday: The Life* (2005).

94: Public Lavatory

One less celebrated, but persistently convenient, invention of Britain's Industrial Revolution was the flushing public toilet. Until the 1800s, chamber pots and cesspits were the main repositories for human waste, although the first English patent for a flushing loo was granted to Alexander Cumming in 1775. This included the first example of an S-pipe, designed to reduce odours by trapping returning water in the pipe. A further patent was granted to Joseph Bramah in 1778, but until the 1850s, waste disposal in most of Britain's towns and cities consisted of night soil men emptying cesspits (*see* chapter 67).

The 1848 Public Health Act moved responsibility for waste disposal to local health boards, stipulating that new houses be built with drainage facilities. To link into Joseph Bazalgette's immense London sewage system, George Jennings popularised the use of the flushing public toilet.

Jennings had grown up at the edge of the New Forest and left school at 14. After serving an apprenticeship at his grandfather's glass and lead merchandising business, his uncle, John Jennings, employed him in his Southampton plumbing business. At 21, he joined the London firm of Messrs Lancelot Burton, for whom his late father had previously worked. In 1838, Jennings set up his own business in Paris Street, Lambeth, having received a family inheritance. His speciality was a toilet that was 'as perfect a sanitary closet as can be made'. Jennings also branched out from the domestic to the public sphere, designing underground public conveniences. Surrounded by elaborate metal railings and lamplit arches, these testaments to Victorian engineering genius would initially have an interior of slate tiles, with ceramic ones being in later use.

In 1851, Jennings was invited to install a Retiring Room at the Crystal Palace for the

Lord Bute's Victorian Bathroom at Cardiff Castle. (*Alan Jones*)

Great Exhibition (*see* chapter 71). He had already won plaudits from Prince Albert, being awarded the Medal of the Society of Arts for an India rubber tube for water supply. He had also branched out into manufacturing pottery water closets, sanitary pipes and drainage systems. The Retiring Rooms caused great excitement, with 827,280 visitors each paying a penny for their clean seat, towel, comb and shoeshine. Jennings stated that the 'civilisation of a people can be measured by their domestic and sanitary appliances'.

In 1854, the first underground convenience, designed by Jennings, opened at the Royal Exchange. A year later, Jennings turned his attention from the domestic to the international sphere, acting as part of a sanitary commission sent out to improve the condition of a

94: PUBLIC LAVATORY

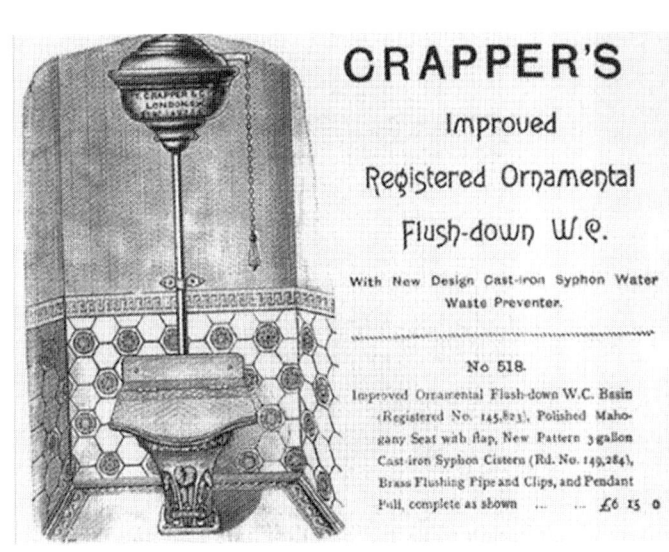

An 1880s advertisement for the products of Thomas Crapper & Co.

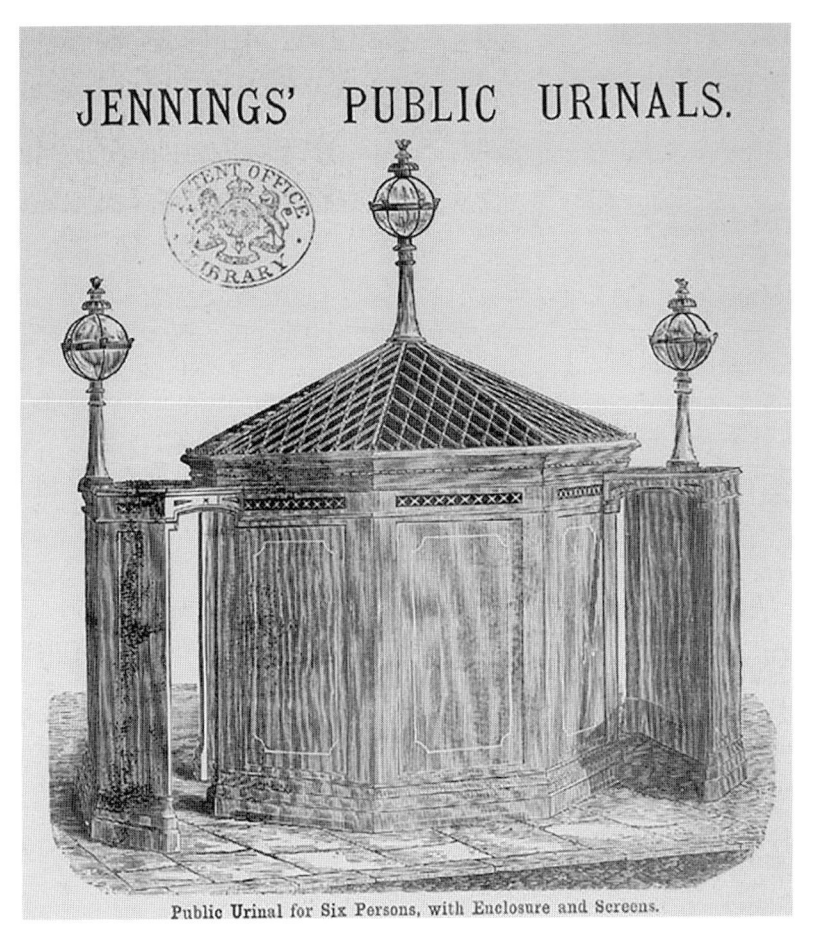

A George Jennings design for gentlemen's public urinals.

military hospital at Scutari at which Florence Nightingale and her team were caring for victims of the Crimean War. Jennings also installed a mahogany shower cabinet for the Khedive of Egypt and suppled the Empress of France with a copper bath.

Jennings patented a flushing mechanism for a water closet, an example of which he installed in Bute Tower at Cardiff Castle. In 1872, a thanksgiving service was organised by the Prince of Wales at St Paul's Cathedral to celebrate his recovery from typhoid. For the occasion, Jennings was invited to supervise the public lavatory facilities. He went on to install lavatories across London that were freely accessible to the public apart from a small charge given to the attendants who furnished towels for visitors to use.

Jennings died aged 72 in 1882, leaving a fortune of over £76,000 (nearly £10 million in 2023 value). His Pedestal Vase won a posthumous Gold Medal award at the International Health Exhibition in London in 1884 for its flushing capacity. In a test, its 2-gallon flush washed down ten apples, a flat sponge, a plumber's smudge coated over the pan and four pieces of paper adhering closely to the soiled surface.

Thomas Twyford made further improvements in 1883 with the first one-piece porcelain toilet, the Unitas. This meant the unit could be kept entirely clean and include a hinged seat, thus doubling up as a male urinal. Thomas Crapper obtained a royal warrant and was the first person to establish a showroom for his mass-produced toilet wares in 1870. He developed the S-pipe into the modern U-bend and was granted nine patents, including one for the ballcock.

That most of us pay no second thought to a visit to a public lavatory is testament to those whose ingenuity paved the way to healthy and sanitary homes and public spaces.

Places to visit

- Cardiff Castle houses Lord Bute's Victorian Bathroom.
- The Gladstone Pottery Museum in Stoke-on-Trent contains the Flushed with Pride gallery, which is dedicated to the history of the toilet and lifts the lid on the role that potters played in its development.

Further reading

Julie L. Horan & Deborah Frazier, *The Porcelain God: A Social History of the Toilet* (1996).
Judith Flanders, *The Victorian House: Domestic Life from Childbirth to Deathbed* (2004).
Adam Hart-Davies, *Thunder, Flush and Thomas Crapper: An Encyclopedia* (1997).

95: Swimming Bath Tile

This ornate tile, which once formed part of the Mayfield Public Baths in Manchester, was uncovered in 2021 during excavation work for a new public park. Archaeologists from the University of Salford discovered several such tiles depicting images of blue cotton flowers, a clear homage to where the wealth had been earned by the world's 'Cottonopolis' to build such facilities.

The Manchester and Salford Baths and Laundry Company built and managed the Mayfield Baths. Private subscriptions ensured that they were financially viable. Over £41,000 was raised to build three baths across Manchester and Salford. Shareholders, who invested in increments of £5, were rewarded with profits of nearly £14,000 between 1856 and 1878, during which time 3,733,293 visitors had paid to either swim or take a hot or cold bath, with over 600,000 taking their laundry down to wash.

With the unhygienic slums that were thrown up to accommodate the workers of Britain's Industrial Revolution came many social problems. Those seeking cleansing relief by swimming in rivers and lakes might often come to grief in strong currents. Victorians also developed an aversion to the thought of dirt, associating it with ignorance and immorality. Furthermore, it acted against the development of an efficient workforce.

The first bath and wash house for use by the general public opened in Liverpool in 1828 – the St George's Pier Head saltwater baths. The Victorians, keen to emulate the Romans in so many ways, sought to recreate the idea of thermae – the public bathing space. Meanwhile, private initiatives encouraged the growth of hygiene, During the 1832 cholera epidemic, Liverpudlian Kitty Wilkinson, known as the 'Saint of the Slums', offered the use of her domestic water supply to about eighty families so that they could wash their clothes at the cost of a penny per week. She also demonstrated the use of bleach as a cleaning agent.

(John Schofield)

Woolwich Public Baths. (*Kleon3/Creative Commons*)

For some, pools could also be a sporting facility. By 1837, there were six indoor pools with diving boards in London, but it was not until the advent of the first modern Olympic Games in 1896, which featured swimming, that the popularity of swimming pools really took off.

The Baths and Wash-Houses Act of 1846 granted local authorities powers to establish these facilities, and enabled them to take out loans to build them. In Sunderland, the corporation quickly took advantage of the new powers to begin the process of building the greatly needed baths and washhouses. In some areas, many ratepayers considered the public health reforms a step too far, revealing deeply rooted social prejudice. Improved productivity through advances in the physical and moral condition of the labouring classes was a concept often rejected by the new entrepreneurial middle classes. There was a tension between the concepts of self-reliance and the helping hand needed to enable people to reach that situation.

The 1846 Act fixed the maximum fees bathers could be charged – the lowest-class warm bath was 2*d*, whilst the cold was 1*d*. Open-air baths were also 1*d*. For this price, customers received clean water and the use of a towel. There were higher fees for the more superior facilities, which in a first-class private bath enclosed in a compartment might include a carpet, chair, mirror, brush and comb. In many cases, there were no taps inside so the attendant controlled the temperature of the water from outside. In other baths, particularly first and second-class ones, the bathers had taps inside the rooms.

Prince Albert laid the foundation stone of the first public baths in London, opened in Whitechapel in 1847. Subsequently, baths opened across the capital and elsewhere. By the late nineteenth century, Manchester had thirty bath houses, built using both private and public funding. Following the success of early private ventures, the second half of the nineteenth century saw an expansion in public provision, with more prevalent notions of the health, comfort and well-being of industrial workers. However, public provision was far from uniform.

Most bath houses employed rigid enforcement of social stratification, with first and second-class baths catering for their respective clients. This echoed the system in place for railway tickets (*see* chapter 32). Generally relegated to laundry duties, women rarely had the opportunity to learn to swim. The sinking of the pleasure cruiser *Princess Alice* in the Thames in 1878 highlighted this inequality of proficiency. More than 600 people drowned, most of them female passengers who were unable to swim, dragged under by their heavy clothing.

The Tooting Bec Lido, opened in 1906, was one of Britain's first open-air pools. The Reverend John Anderson, Rector of Tooting, had proposed the digging out of the pool as a project to provide work for unemployed local men. However, it would not be until the 1930s

Victoria Baths, Manchester. (*Matt Verrill/Creative Commons*)

that open-air swimming reached a zenith of popularity.

The need for improved public health and hygiene resulting from the effects of urban development caused an expansion of public bathing facilities in Victorian and Edwardian Britain. A handful of examples of these temples of cleanliness and recreation are still in use today.

Places to visit

- Bathway Quarter, Woolwich, London. The building that houses the Woolwich Public Baths, built by H.H. Church in 1894, still stands. It had five entrances for various social class and gender designations, two large swimming pools and fifty-two slipper, or private, baths.
- Victoria Baths is a Grade II* listed building in the Chorlton-on-Medlock area of Manchester. The Baths opened to the public in 1906 and cost £59,144 to build.
- Bramley Baths in Yorkshire opened in 1904 and visitors can still enjoy a swim in its Edwardian splendour.

Further reading

Christopher Love, *A Social History of Swimming in England, 1800–1918: Splashing in the Serpentine* (2008).
Christopher Beanland, *Lido: A dip into outdoor swimming pools: the history, design and people behind them* (2020).

96: Postcard of West Park, Hull

In this pastoral scene, a man holds a small child by the hand while two older girls look on and a passing youth turns his head to gaze across the lake. In the middle distance, a pagoda rises through the foliage. The place is West Park, Hull – the year, 1905. Just a mile from this tranquil place beats the heart of the third-largest port in Britain. Tightly packed terraced houses crammed the streets surrounding West Park yet the five individuals on this postcard, and tens of thousands of their neighbours, work colleagues and classmates, were able to enjoy this oasis of calm amidst the noise and bustle of an Edwardian city.

In 1894, amended legislation permitted picture postcards to be sent via the Royal Mail and from 1902, the backs of postcards had space allotted on which to write a message. Thus, the Edwardian age offered an opportunity for the exchange of everyday messages with pictures at very low cost. Major cities enjoyed up to six deliveries a day and during the period, 6 billion cards were sent. Many of them depicted picturesque scenes of public parks laid out across Britain over the previous six decades.

Before the 1840s, there were no public parks in Britain. Pleasure gardens, narrow 'walks' and private estate parks were the preserve of the well-to-do, but the nation lacked large urban green spaces that were open to all. Until the Victorian era, such parks were deemed unnecessary, as most towns had not yet grown to the extent where the rural hinterland was outside of walking distance. However, by 1851, the number of urban dwellers finally exceeded those living in the countryside. Towns encroached on surrounding fields and urban populations found themselves increasingly cut off from the natural world and the physical and psychological recreation that access to open spaces allowed. Campaigners such as Edwin

(Author's collection)

96: POSTCARD OF WEST PARK, HULL

(Author's collection)

Chadwick and Robert Peel began to champion the creation of green spaces for the benefit of all.

A concept known as 'rational recreation', which would provide social, educational and moral improvement for urban populations, became common currency. An 1833 Select Committee, chaired by Robert Slaney MP, demonstrated the links between rational recreation and social reform and progress. The Select Committee on Public Walks was formed to promote the 'Health and Comfort of the Inhabitants' of populous towns by securing open spaces to be used as 'Public Walks and Places of Exercise'. The committee concluded that such spaces would augment the 'comfort, health and content' of the 'middle and humble' classes. Highlighted were towns in Lancashire, Yorkshire and the Midlands for being in dire need of open spaces. These would also serve as an alternative to spending time in pubs and drinking dens.

In London, free access to the Royal Parks was granted in the 1830s and early 1840s. Derby claims to have had Britain's first public park, the Derby Arboretum, opened in 1840 and commissioned by local textile manufacturer Joseph Strutt. It had free entry for two days per week. After unsuccessful attempts to establish partially private parks, the principle of free access for all underpinned the laying out of vast public spaces in industrial towns and cities across Britain. Birkenhead Park on the Wirral peninsula opened in 1847, the People's Park in Halifax in 1857, and the vast Cannon Hill Park in Birmingham in 1873.

The Town Improvement Act of 1847 made it easier for local authorities to purchase land for parks. Article 74 of the 1848 Public Health Act gave local authorities the power to 'provide, maintain, lay out, plant, and improve Premises for the Purpose of being used as public Walks or Pleasure Grounds'. Designed by noted landscape architect Joseph Paxton, the money for the construction of Birkenhead Park had been offset against the rates. Over the next two decades, numerous parks opened in British cities, embodying Victorian ideals of health, order, scientific enquiry, civility and personal enlightenment. They were often bereft of spaces for sport so that rowdy pastimes were kept to a minimum. Until 1884, music was not permitted in Alexandra Park, Manchester, and many organised entertainments were prohibited on the Sabbath.

Some parks were created as massive public works programmes. Alexandra Park in Oldham was built by the townsfolk during the cotton famine sparked by the American Civil War, which prevented the export of raw cotton from America to the town. Roundhay Park to the north of Leeds, opened in 1872, had an open-air swimming pool, a 'lido' added by unemployed citizens in 1907 at a cost of £1,600.

Vast areas of greensward were common in Victorian and Edwardian parks. As the decades passed, they were commonly used for sporting activities, military drilling, fun fairs and dog walking. A well-appointed park might possess an ornamental lake, miniature woodland, flower beds, fountains and statues. Frequently added over time were children's play areas, cycle paths and glasshouses. More recently, the parkrun movement has seen Britain's antique parks hum with the buzz of runners each Saturday morning at 9 am. People who today might enjoy outdoor circuit classes, yoga, painting, snoozing, reading, appreciating flowers and trees, Frisbee throwing or the freedom and inventiveness of childhood games, might pause awhile to think of the generations of pleasure-seekers who have enjoyed special moments before them on that collective ground.

Places to visit

- Roundhay Park in Leeds is one of the largest in Europe. It covers more than 700 acres of parkland, lakes, woodland and gardens, and includes a cricket ground. It attracts nearly a million visitors annually.
- Queen's Park in Crewe opened in 1888. The London & North Western Railway bought the land and donated it to the town. It includes a lake, Victorian clock tower, Boer War memorial, fountains and a man-made waterfall.
- Lister Park in Bradford is a formal park with well laid out walks past the Mughal Gardens, art gallery, boating lake, café and bandstand. The Cartwright Art Gallery is a permanent memorial to Edmund Cartwright – the inventor of the power loom upon which much of Bradford's prosperity was founded.

Further reading

Hazel Conway, *Public Parks* (1996).
Katy Layton-Jones & Robert Lee, *Places of Health and Amusement: Liverpool's historic parks and gardens* (2008).

97: King George III's Bathing Machine

King George III was a frequent visitor to the Dorset seaside resort of Weymouth, believing its waters to have the healing properties to address his various maladies. He first visited the town in 1789, and, in common with every other respectable person of the era, would change into his bathing costume as his bathing machine was pulled by horse into the sea. About thirty such machines were in use in Weymouth by 1785.

Bathing machines were a common sight on British beaches from the latter half of the eighteenth century to the first part of the twentieth. A sign of respectable morals, the roofed, wooden, wheeled carts allowed men and women to change out of their day clothes into swimwear and wade directly into the sea. Members of the opposite sex would not see each other's bathing costumes, thus avoiding any sense of impropriety.

Following King George's lead, 'taking the waters' became a fashionable means of improving one's health amongst the well-to-do of Hanoverian Britain. The Yorkshire town of Scarborough laid claim to having been Britain's first seaside resort and amongst those visiting to drink and bathe in its healing spa waters in the nineteenth century was Anne Brontë. The 29-year-old member of the famous novelist family of Haworth, she had gone seeking relief from the tuberculosis that was to end her life in 1849. She is buried in St Mary's Churchyard, Scarborough.

Replica bathing machine, Weymouth. (*SkymasterUK/Creative Commons*)

Bathing machines at Bognor. (*Library of Congress*)

The development of a railway network made Britain's beaches accessible for many working-class families, with many resorts seeing a mass influx of holidaymakers from certain industrial towns during Wakes Weeks. These were designated holiday periods, when the major factories in a town would cease production. Bridlington earned the nickname 'Sheffield by the Sea' and Blackpool welcomed pleasure-seekers from the cotton towns of Lancashire, whilst workers from Glasgow favoured Morecambe. Inhabitants of Liverpool tended to descend on the North Wales coast, leading to the development of resorts such as Rhyl and Colwyn Bay. For Londoners, Brighton and Margate were popular destinations.

Donkey rides had been available on the beaches as early as the 1790s and grew in popularity, whilst the Punch and Judy show became a seaside staple during the Victorian period. Rock-pooling became a popular children's activity and those with well-heeled parents might be fortunate to have an ornately decorated bucket for the making of sandcastles. Ice cream was consumed in the form of a penny lick, as improvements in refrigeration in the latter half of the nineteenth century meant that it could be served ice-cold in a hollow-top glass.

Piers adorned over 100 resorts across Britain. The first, at Ryde on the Isle of Wight, opened in July 1814. Originally, piers were just landing docks for pleasure steamers but, as the railways reached into every major British resort, piers became more elaborate and multi-purpose. Cafés were added to the entrances and bandstands to the end. The larger piers also contained music halls and swimming pools. Eugenius Birch designed fourteen early piers, bringing the oriental influence to their design that would endure. Towns sought to outstrip their rivals in the length and attractiveness of their designs. Southend Pier, the longest in Britain, stretches out over 7,000 feet into the Thames Estuary. It was extended in 1833 and 1848 as the Essex resort welcomed day-trippers and holidaymakers from London's East End. The Second World War saw the dismantling of several southern piers, as the government was concerned they might become landing points for any German invasion.

Blackpool boasted three piers, but the most iconic attraction in the Lancashire resort is the Blackpool Tower, which when it opened in May 1894 was the tallest man-made structure in the British Empire. Tourists paid 1*s* 6*d* for entry to the Tower complex, a ride on the lift to the top and circus entertainment. Afterwards, holidaymakers might buy a stick of rock; credit for the invention of this iconic part of the British seaside experience goes to Ben Bullock, who began to create the brightly coloured candy sticks in 1887. Blackpool and Morecambe were the first resorts to have their name stamped through sticks of rock and holidaymakers would often buy several as a souvenir gift for friends. Fish and chips became the signature seaside dish from the 1850s onwards. British businessman John Moore patented a seaside deckchair in 1886, easily foldable and made of robust fabric.

Today, several features of the Victorian and Edwardian seaside experience remain all around the British coastline. Visitors can imagine themselves back in the era where a trip to a coastal resort was the height of a summer's pleasures for those to whom the Industrial Revolution had given the financial means and modes of transport to enjoy all the British seaside resort had to offer.

Clevedon pier pagoda, built in 1869. (*Philip Halling/Creative Commons*)

Places to visit

- Cromer Pier in Norfolk retains much of its Victorian charm. Variety shows feature at the Pavilion Theatre on the pier, which has gone through various iterations over the past two centuries as the North Sea destroyed the 1822 and 1843 versions.
- A replica of King George III's Bathing Machine stands at the western end of Weymouth seafront.
- Minehead in Somerset retains much of its Victorian charm. Arriving in the town by the steam train that runs from Bishop's Lydeard on the restored West Somerset Railway evokes the experiences of previous generations.
- Llandudno is one of the prettiest of seaside resorts in Britain. Its Gothic pier is the longest in Wales and its seafront resplendent with Victorian architecture and decoration. An Edwardian cable car transports visitors up the Great Orme for a sense of peeling away the decades.

Further reading

Kathryn Ferry, *The British Seaside Holiday* (2009).
John Hannavy, *The English Seaside in Victorian and Edwardian Times* (2003).
James Walvin, *Beside the Seaside: Social History of the Popular Seaside Holiday* (1978).

98: John Hulley's Wenlock Olympian Society Silver Medal

This 1864 silver medal represents the huge interest in athletic and gymnastic competition that occurred during the high point of Britain's Industrial Revolution. An inscription on the reverse reads:

> Presented to John Hulley Esqre by the Members of the WENLOCK OLYMPIAN SOCIETY at their Fifteenth Annual Festival Octr. XXth 1864 as a mark of their appreciation of his TALENTED & VALUABLE SERVICES in the cause of PHYSICAL EDUCATION.

(Eriboll/Creative Commons)

The Wenlock Olympian Society formally recognised John Hulley's prowess in the field of physical education in October 1864, when they elected him to honorary membership and awarded him this silver medal as a mark of their appreciation of his work.

On 25 February 1850, the Wenlock Agricultural Reading Society resolved to establish a class called The Olympian Class:

> for the promotion of the moral, physical and intellectual improvement of the inhabitants of the town and neighbourhood of Wenlock and especially of the working classes, by the encouragement of outdoor recreation, and by the award of prizes annually at public meetings for skill in athletic exercise and proficiency in intellectual and industrial attainments.

The secretary of the class was Dr William Penny Brookes, who was inspired to create these events through his work as a doctor and surgeon in the sprawling borough of Wenlock, which consisted mainly of Madeley, Broseley and Much Wenlock. The inaugural event was held at Much Wenlock racecourse on 22–23 October the same year. Games included running, hurdles and cycling saw crowds of up to 10,000 gather at Mount Vernon in the city centre to watch athletes and gymnasts compete in organised events.

French gymnast Louis Hugeunin trained Hulley in the 1840s. This inspired Hulley to open a gymnasium in a former billiard hall in Bold Street, Liverpool. He became known as the Gymnasiarch, originally a term used for a coach and sporting official in ancient Greece. He co-founded Liverpool Athletic Club in January 1862 and became its first secretary. It was from this organisation that the Liverpool Olympics sprang.

The day – a 'programme ... of a novel and attractive character', according to one newspaper – began with a guard of honour provided by the bands of the Childwall Rifles and the Liverpool Artillery Volunteers. *The Illustrated London News* carried a report that described a grandstand 'profusely decorated with flowers' filled by 'a large and fashionable body of spectators'. There was no shortage of female interest as, 'The occupants of the stand were principally of the gentler sex, who were present in great numbers and evidently took a deep interest in the day's proceedings.'

Saxon-inspired Edgar Athelstane Browne, who had submitted an essay on physical education, was the first-prize winner. His essay recommended that females spend half an hour in the morning using a trapeze or dumb bells in a fitness routine. He opined, 'Women are not meant for such severe exercise as men, but they are the better for some.'

Members of the Manchester Athenaeum Club claimed eleven prizes in the gymnastics and fencing events. One of their number, Alexander Fairweather, won a special medal as the champion individual performer.

Other events included a steeplechase on foot, with runners dressing in jockey costume. There were also competitions for jumping, boxing, quoit throwing, wrestling and broadsword. The event finished at half past nine in the evening, with 7,000 spectators leaving satisfied. The following

Statute of John Hulley on Liverpool's Waterfront. (*Rodhullandemu/ Creative Commons*)

on penny-farthings as well as traditional country sports such as quoits, football and cricket. The 1851 games had an 'Old Women's Race', with the prize being a pound of tea.

In 1859, a connection was made with the ancient Greek Olympics when the Wenlock Olympian Class sent £10 to Athens as a prize for the winner of the Long Foot Race at the Zappas Olympics. First held in 1861, the Shropshire Olympian Games saw Brookes team up with John Hulley and others to bring about the National Olympian Games in London. Eventually, the International Olympic Committee was formed in the 1890s after Baron Pierre de Coubertin had visited the Wenlock Olympian Society.

On 14 June 1862, John Hulley, recipient of the above Wenlock Olympian medal, inspired by the popularity of athletics and gymnastics in the city of Liverpool, inaugurated the Liverpool Olympic Festival. The multi-sport competition year saw an increase, with 15,000 people keen to pay their shillings and more to enter the grounds. One Liverpool vicar, the Reverend Nevison Lorraine, proclaimed in a sermon: 'I am heartily glad that increased attention is being given to the subject of physical education. I witnessed with considerable satisfaction, the athletic display of Mount Vernon.' What the *Liverpool Mercury* referred to as 'manly exercises' were sweeping the country. The Liverpool Zoological Gardens and Llandudno also hosted events, making six Olympic Games in all.

Hulley made contact with Dr William Penny Brookes of Much Wenlock, and visited the Shropshire town's Olympics. He also watched the German Gymnastic Festival held at Crystal Palace. In 1866, Hulley, Brooks and Ernst Ravenstein organised the National Olympian Games spread across the King's Cross Gymnasium, Teddington Lock and Crystal Palace. Hulley also set up the Liverpool Cycling Club and introduced the velocipede to the city. Ironically, the supremely fit Hulley died after a prolonged bout of chronic chest problems aged just 42 in 1875. His gymnasium's motto – '*Mens sana in corpore sano*' (Healthy mind in a healthy body) – is inscribed on his grave in the Smithdown Road Cemetery, Toxteth.

Hugh Stowell Brown, a well-known Baptist minister, conducted Hulley's funeral. Brown spoke of the value of physical conditioning: 'exercises benefit the pupils in bodily health, but they led to the cultivation of manly habits, of temperance, and of self-denial, and so acted upon the moral character as well as the physical frame.' The cult of physical prowess thus chimed in with the Victorian ideals of temperance and self-discipline. Barely a dozen people attended the funeral of the once-famous Hulley.

Places to visit

- A plaque commemorating John Hulley was unveiled at the Lifestyles Park Road Sports Centre in Liverpool.
- A statue of John Hulley was unveiled at Coburg Wharf, Liverpool, on 14 June 2019 by Princess Anne.
- An annual Wenlock Games still takes place in the Shropshire town.

Further reading

Martin Polley, *The British Olympics: Britain's Olympic Heritage, 1612–2012* (2011).
Chris Cannon & Helen Cromarty, *The Story of the Wenlock Olympian Society and William Penny Brookes* (2016).

99: FA Cup Final Programme, 1882

This FA Cup final programme, dating from 1882 and listing the team formations of Old Etonians and Blackburn Rovers, marks an important pivot in Britain's national game. In winning the match at Kennington Oval 1-0, the Etonians became the last-ever amateur side to lift the famous trophy. For the subsequent 140 years, football in Britain and around the world has been a decidedly professional and commercial affair. Perhaps the most enduring cultural legacy of Britain's Industrial Revolution, the game has embedded itself into virtually every country and culture across the globe.

Football of some description has a tradition in Britain stretching back centuries. A form of mob football was often played between neighbouring villages and towns, with a mass of inhabitants from both settlements striving to deliver an inflated pig's bladder to the other's centre to score the only 'goal'. Kicking and punching of both the bladder and one's opponents was permitted and there were few, if any, rules of conduct.

A similar game was also played in Britain's public schools and in 1848, representatives from those institutions met at the University of Cambridge to standardise a set of rules that could be followed in all their inter-school matches. The Cambridge Rules formed a code, adopted by Eton, Harrow, Rugby, Shrewsbury and Winchester.

Contemporaneously, a set of rules for clubs in northern England, known as the Sheffield Rules, was in use. As the popularity of the game spread, Hull-born solicitor Ebenezer Cobb Morley convened a meeting at the Freemason's Tavern in Great Queen Street, London, to standardise playing conditions across the country. A comprehensive set of rules was thrashed out across six meetings in October and November 1863, and the Football Association was formed.

The removal of a rule that would have allowed players to pick up and run with the ball in their hands was dropped, causing the withdrawal of the Blackheath club, their secretary, F.W. Campbell, claiming, 'hacking is the true football'. Another discarded rule would have allowed players to trip up and hold on to opponents. Further dissenters joined with Blackheath and went on to form the Rugby Football Union.

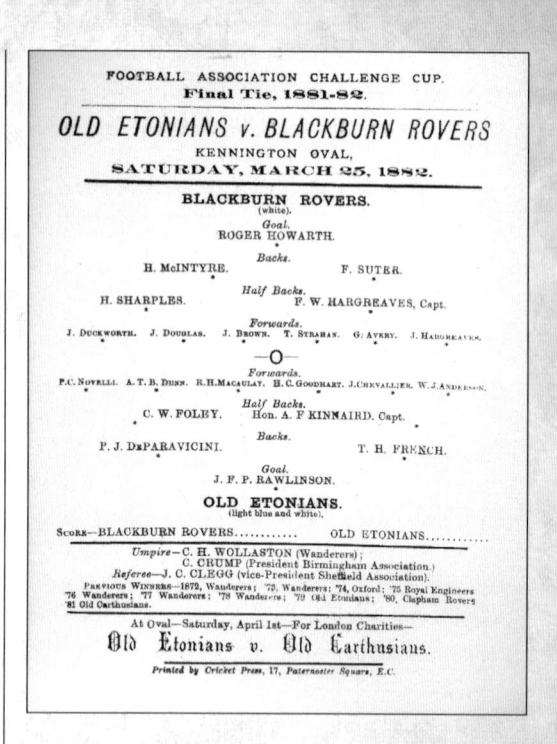

Charterhouse and Westminster schools were influential in forming the less combative set of rules. Their matches were confined to the school cloisters, which were not conducive to the type of rough and tumble favoured at schools like Rugby. Representatives of both schools called for a passing game whilst Eton, Shrewsbury and Harrow preferred a dribbling-based game with an offside rule. By 1867, the Football Association had chosen in favour of the Charterhouse and Westminster game and adopted a looser offside rule that permitted forward passing.

A set of thirteen rules were ratified by eleven clubs, although the Sheffield rules continued in some areas of the north for a further decade.

99: FA CUP FINAL PROGRAMME, 1882

The FA rules stipulated a maximum length and breadth for the pitch, the procedure for kicking off, and the definition of terms such as goal, throw-in and offside. Passing the ball by hand was still permitted, provided the ball was caught 'fairly or on the first bounce'. However, there were no specific rules on number of players, penalties, foul play or the shape of the ball, with captains of the participating teams expected to agree on these things prior to the match.

Clubs started to play matches based on the new FA Code. Sheffield FC played a London team under FA Rules at Battersea Park. The hosts won the game by two goals and four touchdowns to nil. After this match, keenly watched by FA officials, the rule was introduced that allowed only the goalkeeper to handle the ball. Through the 1860s, it became common to have eleven men on each side and to play with round balls. The rule that eliminated the passing of the ball forwards by making all players in front of the ball offside, much like in rugby today, was dropped. A red tape was added between the two goalposts to indicate the top of the goal, and a national competition was proposed. The year 1867 saw the introduction of the Youdan Cup, the oldest continuing trophy in football. Twelve teams contested the cup, Hallam FC emerging victorious.

The first FA Cup competition, in 1872, saw Wanderers beat Royal Engineers 1-0 in front of 2,000 paying spectators. Within a few years all clubs in England, both the southern amateur clubs such as Old Etonians, and northern professional ones such as Darwen and Blackburn, wanted to take part. In order to do so clubs had to accept the FA Code, which then became the standard rules for association football.

The football associations of England, Scotland, Wales and Ireland formed the International Football Association in Manchester 1886. The first international football match had taken place on 30 November 1872 between Scotland and England, the venue being the West of Scotland

The Preston North End team that won the 'double' in 1889.

Cricket Club Ground in Glasgow. It finished in a 0-0 draw in front of 4,000 spectators.

In 1888, twelve Lancashire and Midlands-based professional clubs came together to form the Football League. Their concern was that the existing FA Cup, with its knockout format, could leave a team eliminated early without serious competition for a year, thus suffering financial loss. Fans could now enjoy regular matches and when clubs from the Football Alliance joined in 1892, a two-division system came into operation with promotion and relegation.

During the 1870s and 1880s, association football was a strictly amateur game. Then, teams in the north of England began hiring players known as 'professors of football', often from Scotland. Gradually, clubs with hired professionals overtook the southern amateur ones in terms of playing strength. The first northern club to reach the FA Cup final was Blackburn Rovers in 1882, where they lost to Old Etonians, who were the last amateur team to win the trophy. In 1885, it was agreed that clubs were allowed to pay players that had been born within a 6-mile radius of the ground or had lived for two years within that radius. In 1889, Preston North End became the first club to win the double of the league and FA Cup in the same year.

Old Etonians v Blackburn Rovers, c.1871. Note the oval-shaped ball and the shoulder-barging.

By the end of the period of Britain's Industrial Revolution, association football had become the country's most popular sport. Players became household names, frequently appearing on cards given away in cigarette packets and other products, and there were detailed match reports in the press. A remarkable transformation from a minority-interest public school game to Britain's national sport had occurred within half a century. The clarity and simplicity of a ninety-minute match between two teams of strong town or city-based identities, which occasioned the football 'derby' and keen rivalries, had proved a winning formula.

Places to visit

- The National Football Museum in Manchester tells the story of the game from its earliest days. Exhibits include the first-ever rule book, from 1863, and a shirt from the first-ever international football match between England and Scotland.
- The Scottish Football Museum at Hampden Park, Glasgow, contains over 40,000 football-related objects, which help tell the story of Scottish football from 1867 onwards.
- Wrexham Museum is currently home to the Welsh Football Collection, although plans are afoot to create a separate museum dedicated to Welsh football.

Further reading

Richard Sanders, *Beastly Fury: The Strange Birth of British Football* (2010).
Matthew Taylor, *The Association Game: A History of British Football* (2007).
The English Game is a Netflix television series based on events that led to the eclipsing of the amateur game by the professional one in the 1870s and 1880s.

100: W.G. Grace Bats and Balls

This collection of seven cricket bats and three balls, all belonging to the 'Champion Cricketer', W.G. Grace, are mainly mementoes from his illustrious and unparalleled cricketing career. Alongside W.E. Gladstone, one of the most two easily recognisable men in England in the last quarter of the nineteenth century, Grace was a giant of Britain's national summer sport. His aggregate of runs, centuries and wickets dwarfed those of his contemporaries, as did his physical presence. Grace played first-class cricket across an amazing forty-four English summers, and when he died in his South London home in the autumn of 1915, his demise symbolised the end of an era of British sporting and cultural pre-eminence that had sprung from the confidence of the thrusting nature of Britain's Industrial Revolution. The transformation of cricket from a localised pastime to a cultural phenomenon was a remarkable one.

As Britain went into its Industrial Revolution, cricket was a sport mainly played in London and the South East, but was slowly gaining popularity in other parts of the country. As it spread, it became necessary to establish a set of laws, so that there was some consistency in match arrangements. This occurred in 1744 by members of the Star and Garter Club, which subsequently became the Marylebone Cricket Club (MCC) in 1787. Matches were frequently of variable length and team size, and usually involved substantial gambling.

The village of Hambledon in Hampshire became the epicentre of cricketing excellence for three decades from the 1750s onwards. The Hambledon club revised the laws of cricket, including the addition of a middle stump and regulation of the width of a cricket bat.

It was during those 'glory years' of Hambledon Cricket Club, throughout the latter half of the eighteenth century, that the club played an England XI on fifty-one occasions and managed to defeat them twenty-nine times. Perhaps only Australia can similarly claim to have had the better of England over the years! The development of the game then passed to the MCC in 1787, with Hambledon reverting to a village club.

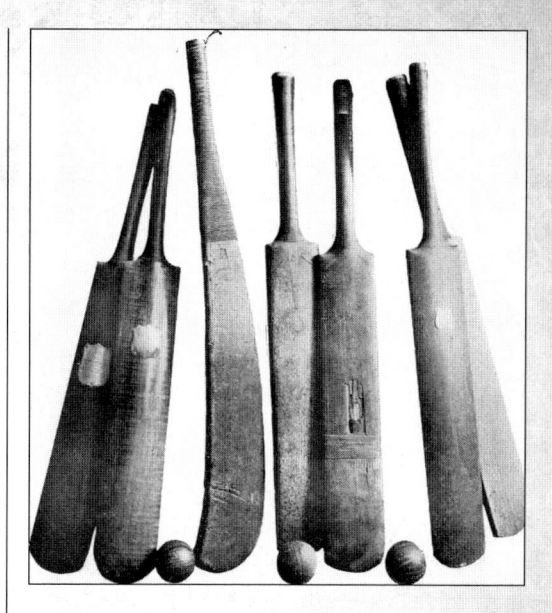

Thomas Lord opened his first cricket ground in London the same year, as bowlers started to pitch rather than roll the ball and the straight bat replaced the old hockey-style curved one. The game spread throughout Britain's colonies during this period, taking root in North America, India, the West Indies, New Zealand and Australia.

Cricket suffered a period of stagnation in the early nineteenth century as the wars with France drew attention and investment. However, on the eve of the Battle of Waterloo, British soldiers played a cricket match in the Bois de la Cambre in Brussels.

For the first half of the century, clubs formed variously at village, town and county level, as there was no unified organisational structure. In 1846, William Clarke formed his All-England XI, a

A scene from a match played at the Lord's Ground, Mary-le-bone, on 20–21 June 1793 between teams raised by the Earls of Winchelsea & Darnley for 1,000 guineas.

commercial venture that saw some of the best players in the land taking advantage of the new railway network to play matches for money the length and breadth of Britain. Large crowds were also able to attend due to improvements in railway transport. Other all-star XIs followed suit and for three decades, this model became the template for most competitive cricket in Britain.

Meanwhile, British Army units stationed across the Empire would play the game, often against teams of locals, an important staging post in the transformation of cricket from a south-eastern pastime to a world game. Women also played cricket extensively, often with large crowds in attendance, the first women's county match taking place in 1811.

As the technological innovation of the railways allowed for the rapid spread of cricket, so, in turn, did cricket innovate from within. In 1864, overarm bowling was legalised. The same year also saw the first edition of *Wisden Cricketers' Almanack*, widely regarded as the cricketers' Bible.

The increasing efficiency of ocean crossings occasioned by the development of steamships saw a team of English professional players tour Canada and the USA in 1859. In 1862, the first English team toured Australia and six years later, a team of Aborigines became the first Antipodeans to visit these shores for cricketing purposes. Inter-continental tours occurred with increasing frequency, and by the end of our period, frequent representative Test matches were taking place between England, Australia and South Africa.

The formalisation of cricketing competition received a further boost with the constitution of the County Championship in 1890. This marked the beginning of a period cricket historians term the 'Golden Age', when playing standards were high and cricket became a metaphor for standards of upper and middle-class notions of the right behaviour. 'It's not cricket' became a phrase that sought to enshrine characteristics of fair-mindedness, honesty and playing by the spirit as well as the letter of the rules.

Cricket became a pillar of a broadly Christianised culture which sought to impose British values across the globe. Grace's collection of bats and balls symbolised the triumph of a set of values that Britain had exported across its Empire, utilising the technology of Britain's Industrial Revolution.

100: W.G. GRACE BATS AND BALLS

The first English cricket team to tour overseas, on board ship to North America.

Places to visit

- The MCC Museum at Lord's lays claim to being the world's oldest sporting museum. A vast array of cricketing treasures are on display, including the Ashes, the little urn contested in England v Australia Test matches for nearly 140 years.
- The Bat and Ball inn at Hambledon sits next to the ancient cricket ground, which was the most prominent in English cricket in the eighteenth century. Many of today's cricketing conventions were drawn up within its walls.
- Several leading county and Test cricket grounds, including Chelmsford, Headingley, The Oval, Trent Bridge and Taunton, house fascinating museums dedicated to the game's history and culture.

Further reading

David Frith, *Pageant of Cricket* (1989).
Simon Rae, *W.G. Grace: A Life* (1988).
Derek Birley, *A Social History of English Cricket* (2003).

Index

Aberdeen, 215
Act for the Abolition of the Slave Trade (1807), 115
Africa, 58, 113–15, 132, 134, 190, 296
Albert, Prince Consort, 53, 158, 209–11, 230, 276, 280
Aldersey, Mary Ann, 134
Allport, James, 90–1
Anderson, John, 221
Andover, Hampshire, 179
Anti-Corn Law League, 152–6, 225
Arkwright, Richard, 21, 22
Arts and Crafts Movement, 206–208, 239
Ashley-Cooper, Anthony, 35, 152, 216
Ashton-under-Lyne, 123
Association Football, 292–4
Attercliffe, Sheffield, 6–7
Australia, 58, 67, 84, 93, 124, 127, 149, 169, 190–3, 202, 295, 296, 297

Bakewell, Robert, 57–8
Band of Hope, 260–1
Baptist Church, 14, 15, 245–6, 291
Barnardo, Thomas, 214, 217
Barnes, Edward & Son, 10
Barnsley, S. Yorkshire, 13, 15, 33, 39, 106, 261
Barratt, Thomas, 257–8
Baths and Wash-Houses Act (1846), 280
Bazalgette, Joseph, 198–9, 276
Beerhouse Act (1830), 251
Beeton, Isabella, 231
Beeton, Samuel, 231
Belfast, 84, 105, 175, 232, 259
Bell, Henry, 93
Bell, John William, 39
Bell, Richard, 175
Bell, Robin, 6
Benthall, Shropshire, 3
Bentham, Jeremy, 187–8, 231
Berkshire, 60–1, 147
Bermuda, 193
Besant, Annie, 172

Besant, Walter, 196
Bessemer, Henry, 8–9
Betjeman, John, 82
Birch, Eugenius, 286–7
Birkbeck, Dr George, 221
Birkenhead Park, Wirral, 99, 283
Birmingham, 12, 16, 18, 52, 73, 87–8, 105–106, 144, 156, 157, 208, 209, 238, 252, 258, 270, 283
Birmingham and Gloucester Railway, 87
Blackburn, Lancashire, 27, 124, 292–4
Blackpool, Lancashire, 101, 286, 287
Blaenau Ffestiniog, Gwynedd, 47–9
Blatchford, Robert, 106
Blincoe, Robert, 31
Boot, John, 186
Booth, Catherine, 200–202
Booth, Charles, 252
Booth, Richard, 261
Booth, William, 200–202
Boulsover, Thomas, 10
Boulton, Matthew, 16–18
Boulton & Watt Company, 14, 16–18, 93
Bournville, Birmingham, 239–40, 256
Boxer Rebellion, 134
Bradford, W. Yorkshire, 106, 151, 175, 205, 238–40, 270, 284
Bradlaugh, Charles, 172
Bradshaw, Charles, 84–6
Bramah, Joseph, 276
Brewster, George, 44
Bridgewater, Duke of, 70, 78
Bridgewater Canal, 70, 78–9
Bridlington, E. Yorkshire, 286
Bright, John, 152, 153, 155, 156
Brighton, Sussex, 100, 102–103, 160, 286
Brindley, James, 70, 71, 72, 78–80
Brine, James, 149–50
Bristol, 18, 30, 84, 87–8, 93, 94, 97, 114, 116, 145, 245, 246, 252, 262
Brixham, Devon, 53–4
Broadhead, William, 164–5
Brontë, Anne, 236–7, 285

INDEX

Brontë, Charlotte, 209, 236–7
Brookes, William Penny, 289–91
Broom, Alfred, 180
Broom, Margaret, 180
Broom, Stephen, 42, 251, 271
Broom, Susan, 271
Broom, William, 272
Broom, William George, 106
Brotherton, Joseph, 219
Brown, Hugh Stowell, 291
Brown, John, 8
Browne, Edgar Athelstane, 290
Brunel, Isambard Kingdom, 79, 87–8, 92–4
Bryant & May, 169, 171–3
Buckingham Palace, 42
Buckinghamshire, 75, 100, 147
Burkinshaw, Joseph, 33
Burrows, Herbert, 172
Burslem, Staffordshire, 50–1
Bury, Lancashire, 25–6

Cadbury, George, 238–9, 256–7, 261
Cadbury, Richard, 238–9, 256–7, 261
Caernarfonshire, Wales, 21, 47, 48
Calico Acts (1700 & 1701), 120–1
Calley, John, 14
Camber Sands, Sussex, 98
Cambridge, University of, 292
Cammell, George, 8
Campbell, F.W., 292
Canada, 58, 84, 150, 210, 296
Cannock Chase, Staffordshire, 36
Canterbury, Kent, 147, 219
Cape Town, 190
Cappe, Catherine, 225
Cardiff, 67, 84, 276, 278
Carlisle, Cumbria, 75, 82, 265
Carnegie, Andrew, 219, 220
Carroll, Lewis, 209
Carron Ironworks, Falkirk, 15, 21
Cassell, John, 85, 230
Castleford, W. Yorkshire, 20
Census Act (1800), 271–2
Chadwick, Edwin, 282–3
Chalmers, James, 262
Chambers, Robert, 230

Chambers, William, 230
Chartism, viii, 145, 155, 157–9, 166, 167, 168, 191, 219, 225, 227, 234, 260, 269–70
Cheltenham, Gloucestershire, 8
Cheshire, 21, 24, 28, 31, 74, 78, 106, 121, 122, 140, 152, 180, 246, 270
Chesterton, G.K., 86
Chimney Sweeper and Chimneys Regulation Act (1840), 43
Chimney Sweepers Act (1834), 43
Chimney Sweepers Regulation Act (1864), 44
China, 58, 125–7, 128–30, 132–4
Cholera, 75, 86, 194–6, 197–9, 217, 227, 279
Christie, Agatha, 86
Church Missionary Society, 132
Churches, 18, 52, 116–17, 123, 132, 189, 200–201, 213, 216, 238, 240, 244–6, 248, 260–1
  see also Religion
Clanny, William, 36
Clarion Cycling Club, 105–106
Clarke, William, 295–6
Clarkson, Thomas, 113, 115
Cleckheaton, Huddersfield, 138
Clevedon, Somerset, 288
Coal Mines Regulation Act (1842), 35
Coal Mines Regulation Act (1887), 39
Coal Mining, 32–5, 36–7, 38–41
Coalbrookdale, Shropshire, 2–4
Cobbett, William, 45–6, 140, 150, 221
Cobden, Richard, 153–5, 232
Colchester, Essex, 25, 245, 253
Cole, Henry, 209, 211, 262
Colfer, John, 42
Collins, Wilkie, 237
Colman, Jeremiah James, 256–7
Colquhoun, Patrick, 268
Colwyn Bay, Clwyd, 286
Combination Acts, 168, 225
Communism, 130, 166–7
Commutation Act (1784), 125
Congregationalism, 175, 238, 245
Conservative Party, 102, 175, 229, 234, 236, 260
  see also Tory
Constable, John, 143
Conwy, N. Wales, 47
Cook, James, 190

Co-operative Movement, 24, 150, 160–2, 222, 255
Corbould, Henry, 263
Cork, Ireland, 99
Corn Laws (1815), 46, 140, 152, 153–6, 225
Cornwall, 17, 41, 220, 261
Coubertin, Pierre de, 290
Coventry, 71, 103, 104–106
Cowell, Stan, 242
Cowper, Daisy, 212
Cox, Francis, 39
Craig, John, 18
Cranleigh, Surrey, 182
Crapper, Thomas, 277, 278
Crimean War, 274, 278
Cromer, Norfolk, 288
Cromford, Derbyshire, 22–4
Crompton, Samuel, 28
Crooks, Samuel, 165
Crystal Palace, 209–11, 276, 291
Cubitt, William, 187
Cunard, Samuel, 93–4
Cunninghame, William, 118
Cutlery, 5–6, 8, 10–12, 163
Cutty Sark, 126–7

Darby, Abraham I, 2–4, 114
Darby, Abraham II, 2–3
Darby, Abraham III, 3, 79
Darwin, Charles, 58, 209, 231, 237
Darwin, Erasmus, 52
Davidson, Robert, 100–101
Davis, Mary, 35
Davy, Humphry, 36–7, 274
Denmark, 210
Derby, 144, 283
Derbyshire, 22, 30, 44, 77, 101, 106, 122, 124
Devon, 14, 53, 71, 88
Devonshire, Duke of, 209
Dickens, Charles, 179, 195, 209, 216, 231, 235–7, 248–9
Didcot Railway Centre, 87–8
Disraeli, Benjamin, 169, 236
Dix, William Spicer, 62–3
Doherty, John, 152
Doré, Gustave, 195
Dorset, 145, 147, 148–50, 267, 285

Dover, Kent, 93, 147
Downe, Jonathan, 30
Doyle, Arthur Conan, 86, 230, 236–7
du Cane, Edmund, 189
du Maurier, Daphne, 86
Dublin, 51, 268
Dublin Police Act (1786), 268
Dudley, W. Midlands, 14, 249
Dudley, Dud, 2
Dukinfield, 123
Dundee, 153
Dunlop, John, 259
Dunlop, John Boyd, 105
Durden, James, 131
Durham, 38, 101, 104, 153

East Dereham, Norfolk, 42, 251, 271, 272
East India Company, 96, 120–1, 125, 128–30, 132
Edgar, John, 259
Edinburgh, viii, 15, 100–101, 112, 208, 221, 247, 262
  University of, 227
Edinburgh and Glasgow Railway, 101
Edwards, Edward, 219
Edwards, John Passmore, 220
Elder, John, 94
Elementary Education Act (1870), 213
Eliot, George, 209
Elsecar, S. Yorkshire, 13–15, 39, 145
Engels, Friedrich, 163, 166–7, 222
Epworth, Lincolnshire, 5
Equiano, Olaudah, 115
Etruria Works, Stoke, 50, 51, 52
Euston Station, 81–3
Ewart, William, 219

Fabian Society, 174
Factory Act (1833), 35, 152
Fairbairn, William, 21
Faraday, Michael, 209, 273–5
Fearnehough, Thomas, 164
Fielden, John, 152
Fielding, Henry, 268
Fielding, John, 268
Fitzwilliam, Earl, 145
Fitzwilliam, Maud, 39

INDEX

Forbes, James, 109
Ford, Henry, 13
Fox, Charles, 82
Frampton, James, 149
France, 5–6, 8, 22, 26, 58, 109, 111, 116, 149, 168, 265, 278, 295
Friendly societies, 43, 148–9, 169, 224–6

Garvestone, Norfolk, 251, 272
Gaskell, Elizabeth, 237
General Medical Council, 181
George II, King of England, 25
George III, King of England, 285, 288
George V, King of England, 243, 263
Germany, 5, 104
Gibbons, Stanley, 263
Gibraltar, 190, 193
Gladstone, William, 52, 89–91, 165, 169, 171, 174, 295
Glasgow, 18, 96, 101, 116–18, 121, 208, 221, 259, 286, 294
    University of, 16, 110
Glassford, John, 116, 117
Glossop, Derbyshire, 124
Gloucester, 87, 267
Gordon, George, 268
Gothic Revival, 81, 204, 206, 208, 222, 245, 288
Grace, W.G., 256, 295–7
Graham, Lilias, 259
Grand Union Canal, 74, 80
Grand Western Canal, 70–1
Grantham, Lincolnshire, 218
Gravesend, Kent, 126
Gray, Faith, 225
Great Eastern steamship, 92–3
Great Exhibition (1851), ix, 155, 209–11, 276
Great Northern Railway, 87, 108
Great Western Railway, 84, 87–8, 108
Great Western steamship, 93–4
Great Yarmouth, Norfolk, 53, 93
Greaves, John Whitehead, 48
Greenock, Renfrewshire, 17–18, 116
Greg, Robert Hyde, 153
Grey, Earl, 144–5
Grimsby, Lincolnshire, 53–4
Grossmith, George, 237

Grossmith, Weedon, 237
Guernsey, 265

Hadleigh, Essex, 201–202
Halifax, W. Yorkshire, 283
Hambledon, Hampshire, 295, 297
Hammett, James, 149, 150
Hampshire, 147, 191, 295
Handsworth, Birmingham, 18, 99
Handsworth, Sheffield, 5
Hardie, Keir, 174–6
Hardwick, Philip, 82
Hargreaves, James, 27–8
Harmsworth, Alfred, 230
Harvey, Elizabeth, 254
Hazledine, William, 80
Head, Robert, 271
Heath, Frederick, 263
Hednesford, Staffordshire, 36
Helmshore Mills, Lancashire, 28, 29–30
Herefordshire, 208
Herefordshire and Gloucestershire Canal, 70
Hill, Rowland, 155, 262–4, 265
HMS *Victory*, 178
Hobhouse, John Cam, 152
Hogarth, William, 250, 251
Hong Kong, 126, 129
Honley, W. Yorkshire, 66
Hornung, C.C., 210
Howard, John, 187, 189
Hudson, George, 82
Hugeunin, Louis, 290
Hull, E. Yorkshire, 53, 54, 96, 97, 115, 161, 214, 219, 282, 292
Hulley, John, 289–91
Hunt, Henry, 140–1
Huntsman, Benjamin, 5–7, 9, 10
Huxley, Thomas, 231
Hyde, Cheshire, 123

Independent Labour Party, 106, 169, 174–6
India, 27, 58, 84, 94, 119–21, 125, 128–30, 132, 134, 197, 210, 276, 295
Ingram, Herbert, 230–1, 232
Ironbridge, Shropshire, 3–4
Isle of Dogs, 92, 95

Isle of Man, 19–21, 54, 101
Isle of Wight, 101, 158, 246, 267, 286

James, Thomas, 28
James, William, 80
Jefferson, Thomas, 117
Jennings, George, 209, 276–8
Jerrold, William Blanchard, 195
Jessop, William, 80
Jeune, Mary, 254–5
Jowett, Fred, 175

Kay, John, 25–6, 27–8
Kelham Island, Sheffield, 5, 7, 8, 9, 12, 165
Kennet and Avon Canal, 69–71, 74
Kent, 147
Kerr, Dr Norman, 260
Killingworth Colliery, 36
Kingsley, Charles, 44
Kipling, Rudyard, 237
Knatchbull, Edward, 147
Knell, William Adolphus, 53
Knight, Charles, 230

Labour Party, viii, 150, 169, 174–6
    see also Independent Labour Party
Lancashire, 25–6, 27–8, 29, 46, 54, 84, 99, 121, 122–4, 136, 138, 140, 159, 161, 259, 261, 283, 286, 287, 294
Lansbury, George, 150
Lanston, Tolbert, 234
Lauder, Harry, 39
Lawson, Henry, 102–103
Leech, John, 194
Leeds, 25–6, 93, 100, 101, 151, 161, 183, 227, 229, 243, 252, 260, 284
Leeds and Liverpool Canal, 71, 238
Leicester, 73
Leicestershire, 57–8, 136, 145
Leng, William, 164, 165
Leno, Dan, 243
Lever, William Hesketh, 239–40, 256
Lewes, Watkin, 268
Liberal Party, 49, 123, 156, 165, 169, 174–6, 219–20, 234, 260
Lincoln, Abraham, 124

Lincolnshire, 5, 53, 189, 214, 218
Linley, James, 164–5
Lister, John, 271
Lister, Joseph, 181–3
Liverpool, 51, 70, 78, 81–3, 93, 95–7, 106, 115, 121–4, 196, 212, 221, 238, 252, 266, 279, 284, 286, 290, 291
Liverpool, Lord, 269
Liverpool and Manchester Railway, 81–4, 262
Livesey, Joseph, 259
Livingstone, David, 131–4
Llandudno, Clwyd, 101, 288, 291
Llanover, Lady, 261
Lloyd, Marie, 242, 243
Locomotive Act (1865), 102
Lomas, John, 153
London, viii, ix, 9, 10, 15, 18, 20, 27, 42, 50, 51, 52, 53, 60, 68, 71, 73, 81, 84, 87, 90, 91, 95–7, 98, 99, 100, 102, 103, 105, 107–109, 115, 116, 117, 126, 130, 132, 149–50, 153, 157, 158, 165, 166, 167, 169–70, 171, 172, 174, 175, 183, 186, 187, 188, 189, 195–6, 197–9, 200–202, 205, 207, 208, 209–11, 214, 215–17, 218, 221, 230, 231, 232–4, 237, 241–3, 246, 247–8, 252, 254, 257, 258, 261, 262, 263, 264, 267, 268–9, 273, 274–5, 276–8, 280, 281, 283, 286, 287, 290, 292, 293, 295
London and Birmingham Railway, 81, 88
London and Blackwall Railway, 100
London Working Men's Association, 157
Lord, Thomas, 295
Lorraine, Nevison, 291
Loughborough, Leicestershire, 57, 138
Loveless, George, 148–50
Loveless, James, 149–50
Lovett, William, 157
Luddism, 136–8, 152, 191
Lytham St Annes, Lancashire, 99

MacGregor, Ann, 18
Madeley, Shropshire, 3, 289
Maidstone, Kent, 147
Malthus, Thomas, 63, 271–2
Manchester, 26, 46, 47, 70, 76, 78, 80, 81, 82, 83, 84–5, 99, 120, 121, 123, 124, 139–42, 144, 153, 155, 156, 160, 161, 167, 169, 170, 173, 176, 208,

INDEX

215, 218, 219, 220, 222, 223, 224, 234, 252, 254, 259, 261, 262, 279, 280, 281, 284, 290, 293, 294
Manchester and Birmingham Railway, 88
Manning, Cardinal, 261
Margate, Kent, 286
Marsden, W. Yorkshire, 77, 136, 138, 222, 223
Marx, Karl, 166–7, 175, 209
Maughan, Benjamin Waddy, 205
Mayhew, Henry, 196, 254
Mayne, Richard, 269
McDougal, Colin, 179
Mechanics' Institutes, ix, 219, 221–3, 228, 229
Meikle, Andrew, 62–4
Melbourne, Viscount, 149, 150, 262
Mergenthaler, Ottmar, 234
Merthyr Rising (1831), 46, 191
Merthyr Tydfil, Glamorgan, 35, 46, 174
Methodism, 149, 151, 175, 200, 213, 244–6, 259–61
Metropolitan Law Amendment Act (1867), 182
Metropolitan Railway, 107–109
Midland Railway, 89–90
Mill, John Stuart, 211
Millais, John Everett, 257, 258
Minehead, Somerset, 288
Monitorial System, 213
Monmouth, Wales, 158
Moore, John, 287
Morecambe, Lancashire, 286, 287
Morley, Ebenezer Cobb, 292
Morris, William, 206–208
Morrison, Robert, 132–4
Much Wenlock, Shropshire, 289–91
Municipal Corporations Act (1835), 270
Murdoch, William, 17
Murray, John, 231
Music hall, 241–3, 261, 286

Napoleon III, 8
Napoleonic Wars (1803–15), 63, 136, 140, 147, 269
National Coal Mining Museum, 35, 37, 41
National Society for the Promotion of Education, 213–14
Navvies, 71, 75–7, 82
Neath, W. Glamorgan, 99

New Lanark Mills, S. Lanarkshire, 23, 24, 29, 31, 160, 162
New South Wales, 147, 149, 191–2
New York, 93
New Zealand, 58, 84, 124, 295
Newcastle upon Tyne, 36, 254
Newcomen, Thomas, viii, 3, 13–15, 16
Newnes, George, 230
Newport, Isle of Wight, 267
Newport, Gwent, 97, 157, 159
   Newport Rising, 157–8
Nichols, Colonel, 254
Nichols, Noel, 259
Nightingale, Florence, 179–80, 278
Nonconformism, 7, 15, 49, 50, 175, 234, 238, 244–6, 260
Norfolk, 42, 55–6, 180, 251, 255, 271–2, 288
   Duke of, 144
North Eastern Railway, 82
Norway, 86
Norwich, 42, 218, 257
Nottingham, 27–8, 73, 98, 144, 186, 202, 226, 230
Nottinghamshire, 31, 56, 136, 145, 180, 205
Nuneaton, Warwickshire, 14

Oastler, Richard, 151–2
Old Sarum, Wiltshire, 143–4
Oldham, Lancashire, 124, 152, 284
Olympic Games, 280, 289–91
Opium Wars, 125–6, 128–30, 132, 134
Oswaldtwistle, Lancashire, 27
Owen, Robert, 23–4, 29–31, 160–2, 168
Oxford, 103, 218
   University of, 60
Oxford and Rugby Railway, 88
Oystermouth Line, 81, 98

Packham, Henry, 147
Packham, William, 147
Palmerston, Lord, 102, 123
Pavlova, Anna, 243
Pawnbrokers, 247–9
Paxton, Joseph, 209, 283
Pears, Andrew, 234, 256, 257–8
Pearson, Charles, 107–108
Peel, Robert, 35, 155–6, 269, 283

Pendleton, Lancashire, 84
Peninsular Steam Navigation Co., 93–4
Penitentiary Act (1799), 188
Peterloo Massacre, 139–42, 144, 153
Phillip, Arthur, 191
Pitt, William (the Elder), 144
Pitt, William (the Younger), 144, 168
Plymouth, 187, 190, 263
Police Force, 123, 141, 157, 189, 195, 268–70
Pontypool, Gwent, 41
Pontypridd, Mid Glamorgan, 41, 92
Pontcysyllte Aqueduct, 79–80
Poor Laws, 122–3, 147, 152, 168, 178–9, 181, 182
Pope, Alexander, 56
Port Sunlight, Wirral, 239–40
Porthmadog, Gwynedd, 47, 49
Portillo, Michael, 86
Portsmouth, 187, 190, 215
Pounds, John, 215
Presbyterianism, 17, 117, 227, 259
Preston, Lancashire, 259, 293–4
Prevention of Crime Act (1908), 189
Prisons, ix, 31, 44, 144–5, 147, 149, 152, 157–8, 168, 178, 187–89, 190–3, 215, 272
Prisons Act (1865), 189
Public Health Act (1848), 276, 283
Public Houses, 222, 238, 247, 250–2, 261
Public Parks, 124, 174–5, 238, 239, 282–4
Public Works (Manufacturing Districts) Act (1864), 123–4
Punch magazine, 86, 194, 196, 197, 198, 230

Quakerism, 5–7, 86, 114, 153, 171, 189, 239, 245–6, 261
Quarry Bank Mill, Cheshire, 21, 24, 28, 31, 121, 152, 153

Ragged Schools, 212–14, 215–17
Railway Regulation Act (1844), 89–90
Railways, viii, 3, 8–9, 16, 47–8, 49, 67, 71, 72, 73, 75–7, 79, 80–3, 84–6, 87–8, 89–91, 98–101, 102, 107–109, 121, 123, 155, 169, 195, 204, 209, 217, 227, 228, 232, 238, 239, 251, 256, 257, 262, 280, 284, 286, 288, 296
Ravenstein, Ernst, 291
Redgrave, Richard, 266

Religion, 132, 217, 244–6, 250
see also Churches
Rennie, John, 69, 70, 79
Representation of the People Act (1832), 145
Rhyl, Clwyd, 286
Richards, Morgan, 48
Rio de Janeiro, 190
Roads, viii, 66–8, 70, 99–100, 101, 102–103, 108, 111, 192, 250
Robertson, J.C., 221
Rochdale, Lancashire, 153, 156, 161–2
Roebuck, John, 16, 18
Rolls, Charles, 102
Roman Catholicism, 213, 230, 244, 261, 268
Roundhay Park, Leeds, 101, 284
Rowan, Charles, 269
Royal Automobile Club (RAC), 103
Royal Institution, 274–5
Royal Institution of British Architects, 82
Royal Navy, 75, 115, 178, 190–1, 193
Royal Society, 9, 17, 20–1, 36, 209, 273
Rugby Football, 292–3
Russell, Lord John, 150, 156

Sadler, Michael, 30, 152
Sale of Beer Act (1854), 260
Salford, Greater Manchester, 40, 141, 219, 279
University of, 279
Salt, Titus, 221–2, 238–40
Saltaire, W. Yorkshire, 221–2, 238–40
Salvation Army, 172, 200–202, 245, 261
Sankey Canal, 70
Scarborough, N. Yorkshire, 53, 54, 285
Senghenydd Colliery Disaster (1913), 38
Sergeant, Joshua, 3
Shaw, George Bernard, 253
Sheffield, S. Yorkshire, 5–7, 8–9, 10–12, 76, 153, 163–5
Shrewsbury, Shropshire, 30, 45, 222, 292
Shropshire, 2–4, 74, 79, 290–1
Silkstone Disaster (1838), 33–5, 38
Six Acts (1819), 142
Slaney, Robert, 283
Slavery, 3, 12, 52, 95–6, 113–15, 116, 124, 132, 151, 231, 246
Smeaton, John, 20–1

INDEX

Smiles, Samuel, ix, 77, 111, 227–9
Smith, Adam, 18, 110–12
Smith, Francis Pettit, 94
Smollett, Tobias, 116
Snow, John, 181, 197–9
Soho Works, Birmingham, 16–17
South Africa, 58, 132, 296
Southend, Essex, 287
Spain, 58
Staffordshire, 17, 36, 93
Staffordshire and Worcestershire Canal, 72
Standfield, John, 149–50
Standfield, Thomas, 149–50
Stanley, H.M., 131
Starey, S.R., 216
Starley, James, 104
Starley, John Kemp, 104–106
Stell, Joseph, 25
Stephenson, George, 36–7, 79, 87
Stephenson, Robert, 82
Stockport, Cheshire, 124, 153
Stoker, Bram, 86
Stoll, Oswald, 243
Strutt, Joseph, 283
Studd, C.T., 134
Suez Canal, 94, 127
Sunderland, 36, 280
Surrey Iron Railway, 98
Sussex, 98
Swansea, Glamorganshire, 81, 98–9
Swing Riots, 62, 146–7, 149, 168, 191
Sydney, Viscount, 191
Symington, William, 93, 94

Taff Vale Case, 169, 175
Tasmania, 158, 192
Tate, Henry, 220
Tay Bridge Disaster, 9
Taylor, Enoch, 136
Taylor, J. Hudson, 134
Telford, Thomas, 79–80
Temperance, 125, 189, 225, 240, 251, 259–61, 291
Tennyson, Alfred, 209
Thackeray, W.M., 209, 231
Thornhill, Thomas, 151, 152

Tolpuddle Martyrs, 148–50, 158, 168, 170, 191, 192
Tory, 49, 140, 144, 151, 155, 156, 169, 231, 236
Town Improvement Act (1847), 283
Townsend, Charles, 55–6
Trade Unions, viii, 149–50, 151, 163–5, 168–70, 174–6, 225, 234
Trades Disputes Act (1913), 176
Train, George Francis, 99
Tramways Acts (1870 & 1879), 99–100
Transportation (penal), 138, 149, 158, 188, 190–3
Trent and Mersey Canal, 50, 72
Trigge, Francis, 218
Trollope, Anthony, 265
Tull, Jethro, 59–61
Turnpikes, viii, 66–8
Tyneside, 3

University of Manchester Institute of Science and Technology (UMIST), 222
Unlawful Oaths Act (1797), 149
USA/America, 10, 11–12, 13, 21, 47, 58, 70, 75, 84, 93, 99, 103, 110, 113, 115, 116, 117, 121, 122, 124, 128, 131, 134, 136, 165, 190, 202, 220, 231, 249, 261, 284, 295, 296, 297

Victoria, Queen of England, 53, 107, 109, 186, 209, 219, 222, 254, 262–3
von Drais, Karl, 104

Wakefield, W. Yorkshire, 35, 37, 41, 265
Wales, 21, 35, 46, 47–9, 67, 68, 81, 84, 143, 145, 157, 178, 180, 189, 192, 212, 234, 271, 286, 288, 293
Walker, Benjamin, 138
Walker, James Scott, 84
Walker, Ralph, 95
Wallin, Edward, 15
Walthamstow, Essex, 104
Warrington, Cheshire, 106, 219, 270
Warwickshire, 80, 103
Washington, George, 117
Watkin, Edward, 109
Watson, William, 215
Watt, James, viii, 14, 16–18, 93, 96
Webb, Philip, 208

Wedgwood, Josiah, 50–2, 114–15
Wellington, Duke of, 144, 145
Wesley, Charles, 244
Wesley, John, 244–6, 259, 260
West India Dock Company, 95, 96, 97
West Indies, 95, 113–15, 295
Wexford, Ireland, 42
Weymouth, Dorset, 285, 288
Whigs, 144–5, 147, 153, 156, 231
Whiteley, William, 254
Whitfield, George, 245
Whitmore, William, 80
Wilberforce, William, 114–15
Wilkinson, John, 16
Wilkinson, Kitty, 279
Williams, John, 149
Wilson, John, 271
Wiltshire, 71, 74, 143, 147
Wraight, William, 147
Wright, Richard, 93
Wyer, William, 44
Wyon, William, 263

York, 82–3, 86, 138, 225, 252, 255
York and North Midland Railway, 82
Yorkshire, 5, 20, 35, 37, 53, 54, 66, 77, 82–3, 115, 124, 136, 143, 145, 151–2, 159, 221, 237, 238, 281, 283, 285